The origins of democratic thinking

The origins of democratic thinking

The invention of politics in classical Athens

CYNTHIA FARRAR

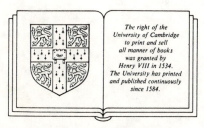

The right of the
University of Cambridge
to print and sell
all manner of books
was granted by
Henry VIII in 1534.
The University has printed
and published continuously
since 1584.

Cambridge University Press

Cambridge
New York   New Rochelle   Melbourne   Sydney

JC
75
D36
F37
1988

Published by the Press Syndicate of the University of Cambridge
The Pitt Building, Trumpington Street, Cambridge CB2 1RP
32 East 57th Street, New York, NY 10022, USA
10 Stamford Road, Oakleigh, Melbourne 3166, Australia

First published 1988

Printed in Great Britain by
Redwood Burn Limited, Trowbridge, Wiltshire

British Library cataloguing in publication data
Farrar, Cynthia
The origins of democratic thinking: the
invention of politics in classical Athens.
1. Democracy   2. Athens (Greece) – Politics
and government
I. Title
321.8′0938′5   JC75.D36

Library of Congress cataloguing in publication data
Farrar, Cynthia.
The origins of democratic thinking.
Bibliography.
Includes index.
1. Democracy – History.   2. Political science – Greece –
History.   3. Political science – History.   I. Title
JC75.D36F37   1987   321.8′09   87–26787

ISBN 0 521 34054 3

RB

Contents

To Jonathan Lear

ὑπερβολὴ γάρ τις εἶναι βούλεται φιλίας ...

Aristotle, *Nicomachean Ethics* 1171a11

Preface

In May 1985, I gave a talk based on chapter 5 of this book to a seminar at the Institute of Classical Studies in London. My host introduced me as someone who was about to do the opposite of what Thucydides did, by leaving history for politics. I replied that I hoped to show that for Thucydides, as for me, to do history was to do politics, and vice versa.

The tale of how I came to see Thucydides' task – and my own – in this way is a long one, peopled with many remarkable friends and teachers. As a student at Yale, I was interested in politics but had little understanding of what politics was about or what it was for. A course on the origins of war, ancient and modern, taught with singular energy and vision by Donald Kagan, persuaded me that the study of ancient politics and political ideas would help me to understand how people think and behave politically. Don Kagan guided me in my first encounter with Thucydides, and he has been mentor and valued friend ever since.

The Paul Mellon Foundation made it possible for me to spend two years at Clare College, Cambridge studying the classics. When I returned there to write a Ph.D. on Greek political ideas, I was welcomed back by Clare College. The Mistress and Fellows of Girton College rescued me from impending financial difficulties by awarding me a studentship for two years, for which I am most grateful.

During the time that I was writing the first version of this book, I was blessed with two demanding and compassionate supervisors, Peter Garnsey and Malcolm Schofield. They were invaluable critics and allies. I had the great good fortune to be befriended by Gregory Vlastos during his time in Cambridge. He inspired and prodded and supported me, and watched over the fate of my manuscript. He is this book's godfather.

Louise Mills loyally and carefully typed draft after draft on to the Cambridge University Computer. In the later stages, ever cheerful, she deciphered obscure instructions sent from abroad. She made it possible for me to finish the thesis and the book on schedule.

In my last three years in Cambridge, as I finished the Ph.D. and transformed it into a less specialized book, I was privileged and happy to be the Rouse Research Fellow at Christ's College. I thank the Master and Fellows of that venerable institution for their generosity. They made me feel fully a member of the College at once.

Cambridge became my home. There, I found companionship and intellectual rigor. My friends challenged me to think differently and harder; my intellectual mentors became my friends. There, I learned to think about politics historically, and history politically. There, I had the time and the incentive to come to understand the character of Thucydides' achievement, and to understand what I myself wished to achieve.

It is an irony, and a source of personal sadness, that what I learned in Cambridge confirmed my desire to move on, after finishing this book, to active (and reflective) participation in political life. I felt compelled to return to the U.S. and leave behind a community which, self-contained as it was, offered abiding friendships and a rare sense of belonging. To all my Cambridge *philoi*, I am deeply grateful.

Among the friends I made in Cambridge, I wish to mention three by name who contributed directly and significantly to the shape of this book: Simon Price, who read and reread successive drafts with a keen eye for problems and an equally keen desire to be helpful; John Dunn, who kept reminding me, affectionately and firmly, that I was writing a book; and Jonathan Lear, who by personal example and direct intervention challenged me to reflect.

I   Ancient reflections: a force for us

Democracy was cobbled together, thousands of years ago, by the Athenians. It was at Athens, too, that political theory first appeared. The citizens of fifth-century B.C. Athens lived democracy, for the first time in the history of the world, and they thought about it. Democratic politics enabled all citizens, rich and poor, to express and pursue their own aims. Democratic politics also prompted citizens to construe their aims politically, and to reflect on their actions in terms of general, relatively abstract considerations. Political theory was part of democratic politics; self-understanding was political. This dynamic synthesis of the concrete and the reflective was a striking achievement – so striking, indeed, as to be practically unintelligible from a modern perspective. Modern thinkers have tended to see the Athenians as mired in the concreteness of a communal, stratified, and in some sense primitive existence, immune to the claims of political reflection that exalt and afflict us. On the assumption that political theory must be abstract, scholars have denied or ignored the existence of a democratic political theory in fifth-century Athens, reserving the title of 'first theorists' to those undemocratic and politically alienated thinkers, Plato and Aristotle. And in the belief that democracy is fundamentally a matter of rules and procedures designed to safeguard human rights and express the will of the people through its elected representatives, theorists have characterized the triumphant practice of direct, participatory democracy at Athens as mob rule, or as the hollow creation of a slave-owning elite or, at best, as admirable but outmoded.

The purpose of this book is to retrieve a distinctive and neglected form of democratic thought from behind the shadows cast by Plato, by Aristotle, and by our own preconceptions. This version of democratic theory is to be found in the ideas espoused by Protagoras, Thucydides and Democritus. All were fifth-century thinkers; Thucydides and Democritus probably lived to see the fourth century. Protagoras was an itinerant teacher of the art of persuasion, a sophist; Thucydides was the historian of the greatest war of his day, between his native Athens and the mighty Spartans; Democritus was a cosmologist, one of the creators of the theory of atomism. For all their differences, these three thinkers are importantly alike. In this book I attempt to show, first, that the similarities reveal a coherent analysis and critique of democratic man, i.e. of the possibility of achieving order and freedom when all citizens, rich and poor, exercise autonomy. Secondly, I argue that the differences reveal the difficulty of maintaining a stable and integrated understanding of democratic man and avoiding extremes of order or freedom.

To accomplish this dual task, I place the three thinkers in the context of contemporary political and intellectual developments and present the ideas of each in their full range and complexity. In each case, various scholarly obstacles to understanding, such as fragmentary or problematic source material, make detailed exegesis necessary. A detailed and comprehensive study of the ideas of each thinker is also essential to display the character and power of their approach as distinct from our own. Precisely because Protagoras, Thucydides, Democritus and their contemporaries did not divide up human life in the way that we do, their understanding of politics is more closely tied to an account of human psychology, of man's desires, interests and powers, and of cosmology, the forces of order in the universe. However, it is not merely because they participated in ancient Greek culture that these thinkers provide an integrated account of man's political existence. Their attempt to weave together the many strands in man's experience of the world sets them apart from contemporaries who wished to undermine or transcend democracy. Democratic order and freedom depend upon the dynamic reconciliation of man's particularity and autonomy with the requirements of communal life. To exhibit the nature and extent of this integration of ethics, politics and cosmology is to reveal a distinctive democratic theory. To exhibit the process of disintegration is to demonstrate the weaknesses and instabilities of such a theory and the virtues of its strongest, most stable version, the historical politics of Thucydides.

If this book is essentially a historical reconstruction of a form of political theory overshadowed by its successors, it also has a further aim, articulated explicitly only here and in the concluding chapter, but implicit throughout. Precisely because the ideas of Protagoras, Thucydides and Democritus do not look to us like democratic political theories, we would do well to attend to them. The very characteristics of the modern perspective which have kept us from appreciating the achievement of the Athenians have also left us in need of their example. The origins of democratic thinking have been neglected. As a prelude to the exploration of those origins, this introductory chapter will suggest, briefly and schematically, why they have been neglected and that they are both instructive and accessible. The Athenians were reflective about democracy; like us, they struggled with the difficulties of reconciling autonomy and order. To recognize this struggle for what it was, and to appreciate that the ideas of Protagoras, Thucydides and Democritus were contributions to it, is to acknowledge some deficiencies in our own self-understanding.

From where we stand, in a modern, western, liberal, capitalist culture, it is difficult to apprehend the possibility of uniting reflective social understanding and rootedness in concrete social practices in a political life. We understand both democracy and political theory in abstract terms, and both are remote from the lives we lead. Modern conceptions of political as well as economic and natural order envision an impersonal system constituted by the unguided interaction of undifferentiated elements or agents.[1] The uprooting of men from their places in local, traditional, stable hierarchies has led to greater egalitarianism and homogeneity. The world is seen as ordered in terms of unmediated individual relationships. Men approach their god as individual believers. Education is centralized and purveys information in a shared, deracinated idiom. In such a world, principles of justice, construed as treating all men equally and impartially, are of primary importance. Equality takes precedence over community, and liberty over fraternity. Differences among individuals are to be ignored, and so far as possible flattened out: loyalty to and identification with kin or cultural sub-groups is deplored, as is the discrimination associated with such attachments. When the political order ceases to be a stratified ethical community, relations among men assume the shape most suited to industrial society: unhampered by stable personal relationships and responsibilities and the long-term calculations characteristic of life in a closely-knit society, man can readily engage in reliable, standard, impersonal transactions. The forces that shape human life are seen to operate at a level remote from the concrete aims and interests of particular individuals.

Modern democratic institutions and liberal theory embody the formal and abstract reconciliation of individual aims with a general, objective order. Via democratic procedures (periodic voting, majority

---

[1] For a discussion of some of the developments mentioned in this paragraph, see Gellner (1983), Taylor (1985) 248–88, Bellah et al. (1985), esp. 39–51, 117–63, 204–11 and, at the level of ideas, Aron (1965) and (1967).

rule, representation) our views and interests are rendered commensurable and aggregated; conflicts are formally dissolved in a decisive procedural resolution. Liberal visions of freedom and democracy emphasize either the unmediated exercise of personal freedom by individuals in the world as they find it or the conditions which render that freedom compatible with the exercise of a similar liberty by others in society.[2] Liberty and democracy are construed negatively as the absence of coercion or the least coercive way of securing social order. This negative construal of individual liberty and social order leaves us to choose between the primacy of present circumstance and motivation and the primacy of pure rationality and procedural justice. Liberal theorists, deprived of a natural teleology, and confronted instead with a mechanical universe, were unable to construe man, capable as he is of reason and the deliberate pursuit of ends, fully as part of the order of nature. Man's 'nature' was therefore divided. His needy, instinctual, crudely self-interested aspect was sharply distinguished from his capacity for rational self-control, autonomy and freedom. It is this second, 'rational' aspect that figures in the liberal vision of democratic order. In different ways, liberal theorists drain the idea of a person, and of a community, in order to construct an order out of identical, interchangeable, unconditioned units neutrally disposed. Thus the liberal theorist seeks to avoid confronting fundamental questions about how human beings should live or what kinds of creatures they are. But a political theory based on an abstract understanding of rationality and motivation, a negative conception of freedom, and a view of politics as neutral is inadequate to the task of characterizing a determinate, viable social order.[3] Man is condemned either to adopt an abstract, rational, conception of order, at the cost of distancing himself from his concrete concerns, or to reject the possibility of an order capable of expressing his concerns and resign himself to addressing those concerns through self-interested struggle. The self of a rational ethical and political order, like the self of procedural democracy, is too abstract and remote to be genuinely continuous with the self who participates, even reflectively, in concrete social interaction. There must be more to politics, more to the experience of

[2] See, e.g., Nozick (1974), Rawls (1971), Habermas (1971), Dworkin (1978a and 1978b).
[3] A number of contemporary thinkers have criticized the abstract, universalist approach and have sought to formulate, or at least point to, an alternative. See, e.g., Walzer (1983), Williams (1985), MacIntyre (1981), Lear (1984), Hampshire (1978), Taylor (1985), Galston (1980), Beiner (1983), Sandel (1982). Williams, MacIntyre, Lear, Galston and Beiner explicitly invoke the ancient Greeks in so doing.

political community, than is contained in liberal theory or liberal institutions.

The failure to observe the existence of democratic theory in ancient Athens rests on a misunderstanding of the nature of democracy and theory, and on a related misperception of Athenian society. It has been argued that there was no room for democratic political thought in Athens. In the first place, it is said, the standard-bearers of democracy, the politicians and the politically-active citizens, were too busy, too engaged in political life, to indulge in philosophical reflection about democratic principles.[4] If such men were to have fashioned a theory of democracy, it would have been the mirror-image of criticism of democratic practices.[5] There was no such direct justification of democracy, *ergo* no democratic theory whatever. A second, related strand of this argument holds that the Athenian democratic consciousness was a clear reflection of the institutions of the democracy: (1) politics was a way of securing material advantage and (2) brazen exploitation – of slaves and subject allies – left little scope for ideology.[6]

To construe the political consciousness of the Athenians in these terms is to miss the distinctiveness of their self-understanding. Each of the facets of the portrait reflects something true: democratic political reflection was not disengaged; the political system did enable the Athenians to be arbiters of their own well-being; ideology was not structured so as to convince the downtrodden that they were meant to be walked on. However, these truths are seriously incomplete. The democratic political community (*polis*) was ideological and it was reflective. The world of Achilles and Pericles was not Eden. The ancient citizen did not live contentedly inside his skin, part of a world wholly unified and integrated, protected by his innocence. The citizen of the *polis* experienced the pull of the outer, reflective perspective against that of the inner self. This oscillation of perspective was contained within, and shaped by, a type of political society which in its de-

[4] See Finley (1973) 28, where he excluded Protagoras from this judgment. Cf. Finley (1962), Jones (1953) 41–2, Loraux (1981) 180, 219–22. It is worth noting that there was, so far as we know, no theory of oligarchy either, in the sense of a specific justification of oligarchic practices. Aristotle comes closest to offering such a theory, though he takes himself to be praising aristocracy, in teleological terms.

[5] As Jones's attempt to infer such a theory from extant criticism assumes (Jones (1953) 41–72). Finley (1973) rejects this view.

[6] Finley (1973) 65–6, 50–1. Cf. the discussion of ideology in the sense of *Weltanschauung* in Finley (1982) 17: at Athens 'the links between ideology and behavior were indirect and invisible,' and in Finley (1983) 122–41.

veloped form (most notably at Athens, though some of these features were evident elsewhere) exhibited certain resemblances to the modern democratic polity, though in an importantly different context. The *polis* encompassed a group of men deemed to be equal (though never regarded as identical). In contrast to tribal or feudal societies, ancient Athens boasted no priestly class, no secretive keepers of the high culture. The social and political space of the *polis* was not divided into stable enclosed portions; the relation of the individual to the political unit was relatively unobstructed by local power and/or kinship structures,[7] though it was mediated by personal and familial relationships. Friendship was experienced not simply as a source of private satisfaction, but as constitutive of one's social identity.[8] Thus the males who made up the citizen body participated in the face-to-face, directly democratic politics of the city, not merely by voting but by speaking in the assembly and by serving on the council, on juries, and in administrative positions, and thus shaped themselves through active and intimate interaction with others.

However, the character of political life in a *polis* like Athens, with approximately 40,000 full citizens at its height, based as it was on discussion and debate, also fostered a countervailing tendency, a tendency toward abstraction and the formulation of general principles.[9] It is no accident that the Greeks invented both self-government and philosophy.[10] These competing elements in the life and consciousness of the *polis* – the one context-bound, imbedded, and many-stranded, the other abstract, rational, and distancing – shaped reflection on the individual's relation to society, indeed constituted this reflection. The experience of being a member of a self-governing citizen body was a process of individuation, of reflection on the connection between social order and social demands and the aims of individuals. The growing awareness of an unmediated relationship between the individual and the social order prompted concern about conflict between private interests and the public good. It also prompted reflection about means of reconciling these conflicts. Yet the character of the *polis* kept these reflections from leaving behind the claims of intimate communal life and the constitutive force of social interaction.

[7] In Athens this was in part due to the effects of the tyranny of the Pisistratids and the reforms of Cleisthenes. See below, ch. 2.

[8] The *locus classicus* is Aristotle, *EN* 1155a10–1172a15 (cf. Plato, *Phaedrus* 231a–257b); see Cooper (1980), Nussbaum (1985) 343–72, MacIntyre (1981) 146–9, Beiner (1983) 79–82.

[9] See Williams (1978) on public vs. private reliance on reasons.

[10] See Lloyd (1979) 240–67.

Democratic ideology and democratic political thought – the one implicitly, the other explicitly – sought to reconcile freedom and the pursuit of one's own good with public order. The Athenians invented democracy. They were the first to confront its implications, including a gradual and partial separation of political from social or economic order. The Athenians did not construe the good to be secured politically solely in terms of direct material advantage. Political life expressed a shared, ordered self-understanding, not a mere struggle for power; political status, the status of citizen, both marked and shaped man's identification with those aspects of human nature that made possible a reconciliation of personal aims with social order. At the level of ideology, the self-image of the citizen was shaped by the implications of two sorts of power: the power of aristocrats within the democracy and the subjection of slaves by free men. And democratic political reflection was not limited to the attempts at political analysis prompted by the public debates of the day.[11] Some analyses were systematic interpretations of the *polis* that took the form they did – philosophical but not detached – because they were interpretations of a democratic *polis*. These interpretations were attempts to understand and to define the condition of political man in relation both to the natural world, the cosmos, and to the best and worst in human experience, the aristocrat and the slave. They offer a striking vision of man and politics which, as the product of a genuinely democratic and reflective society, poses a challenge to our own self-understanding.

The Athenians, like other Greeks, defined their own freedom by way of contrast with enslavement. Political liberation meant, psychologically and historically, distancing oneself from the status of slave. The beginnings of Athenian self-rule coincided with Solon's liberation in the sixth century B.C. of those who had been 'enslaved' to the rich. The enfranchisement of the local laboring classes was succeeded by the development of chattel slavery, the enslavement of, in large part, foreigners. Many foreigners were regarded as naturally slavish; tyrant and master were linked in the Greek perception of Persian despotism.[12] Athens' successful resistance to enslavement by the Persians in the early fifth century was, says Herodotus (5.66), a consequence of Athenian liberation from tyranny.[13] According to the Hippocratic

---

[11] See Finley (1983) 125. Note that Finley does not allow the example of Protagoras to affect his overall assessment, but see his comments on Plato and Aristotle, p. 20.

[12] See, e.g., Aesch. *Supplices*, discussed below, ch. 2.

[13] See also Aesch. *Persae* 241f. and Hdt. 5.78; and note the establishment of the cult of Zeus Eleutherios at Plataea, Thuc. 2.17.2.

author of the medical treatise *Airs, Waters, Places*, independent men
(*autonomoi*), unlike those enslaved to kings, are brave because they
run risks 'on their own behalf and not on behalf of others' (23). Freedom means not being subject to another, not toiling for the sake of
another, being able to realize one's own purposes – in sum, not being
like a slave. Yet if the free man is untrammeled in the pursuit of his
own good, is not his aim tyranny? The free man seeks to avoid being
ruled by someone who rules in his own interest and yet the free man
himself seeks to order the world in accordance with his own
interests.[14] This tension is contained within the *polis*: freedom is compatible with being ruled under circumstances of self-rule, when the
citizens govern on their own behalf and self-interest is the collective interest.

The Athenians created a society in which all free (and male) members not only enjoyed the benefits of political life but also, with varying degrees of intensity, practiced politics. Politics enabled those who
practiced it to escape exploitation;[15] as free possessors of power in a
successful conquest-state, the Athenian people (*demos*) did not see fit
to challenge the continued existence of a social, economic and even a
loose political hierarchy within the *polis*.[16] Participation in politics,
which depended materially upon the domination of others (slaves and
subject allies), was the expression both of freedom and of identification with aristocratic values.[17] Where the group of those who
govern spans both rich and poor, the urge to regard oneself as free, to
distance oneself from slaves, promotes the continued influence of
aristocratic values. The freedom the Athenian citizen aspired to was
defined in aristocratic terms: leisure, freedom from the necessity of
labor, self-sufficiency. To work for a wage, as artisan or hired laborer,
to satisfy the needs and serve the purposes of another was considered
degrading, and this contempt extended to all manual labor.[18] Even the
peasant, who labored to meet his own needs, was diminished: he
lacked leisure. The democracy at once palliated this stigma and confirmed it: the *polis* enabled everyone to participate by paying magis-

---

[14] See Connor (1977b), who argues that the Greeks believed tyranny was bad for the city,
good for the tyrant.
[15] See Finley (1983) *passim*, with Murray (1983) 895, col. 3.
[16] See Finley (1983) 27–8, 97–121, with Murray (1983) 895.
[17] This formulation is not intended as an alternative to the instrumental view of politics (see
Finley (1983), 97f.) but its complement.
[18] See Mossé (1969) 28, Aymard (1948), Finley (1965) 194.

trates and jurors, and later the assembly, a wage. This payment was a bulwark of the radical democracy (the oligarchs of 411 were quick to end it), yet it also seems to have discomfited the Athenians. It is striking that this feature of the democracy, the wage for political participation which was both sign and mitigation of the poorer Athenians' lack of leisure, is not mentioned in any of the fifth-century texts that praise democratic Athens – but it appears in an oligarchic exposé.[19]

Participation in the politics of democratic Athens was an extenuation of the menial status of the *demos*, and it was such in part because the *polis* expressed not merely the material interests of those who ruled and were ruled, but also their freedom and nobility. The Athenians were unwilling to regard themselves as men who simply pursued their own advantage, externally or internally. The funeral oration, the traditional eulogy to those who fell in battle and the quintessential *polis* discourse, masks the realities of power both internal and external.[20] The orator chosen by the people celebrates an Athens unified, homogeneous, harmonious, a city of free and cultivated men. It is not merely the critics of democracy who believe that the *polis* must 'stand outside class or other factional interests.'[21] Nor is criticism of Athenian leaders for pursuing their own interests rather than those of the *polis* simply a moral judgment by hostile sources.[22] Certainly it was a charge leveled by Plato and Thucydides against the demagogues of the late fifth century. But the demagogue Cleon, in a debate reported by Thucydides, is made to accuse another speaker of misleading the public 'for his own gain' (3.38.2).[23] Moreover, the same criticism seems to underlie the comments and actions of a much earlier opponent of faction, namely Solon. According to Solon it was the rich whose greediness was destroying the community.[24] In both Plato and Aristotle, good rulers are distinguished from bad ones according to

[19] [Xen.] *Ath. Pol.*; it does not appear in the funeral orations: see Loraux (1981) 223. Nor is there any reference in these texts to the maritime character of the democracy, Loraux (1981) 213. Contrast the reference to the use of the lot in Hdt. 3.80.

[20] Loraux (1981) e.g. 336–9. Note the contrast between *to sumpheron* and *eleutheria* in Thuc. 2.40.5.

[21] Finley (1962) 6, with Loraux (1981) 200. Note that Finley himself cites Aeschylus' *Eumenides* on p. 7.

[22] Finley (1962) 4f.

[23] Cf. Thuc. 3.40.3, 3.42.3. Thus I do not fully agree with Humphreys (1977/8) 103 that a criticism first used against aristocrats was then turned by them against the demagogues.

[24] Arist. *Ath. Pol.* 5.3. See Humphreys (1977/8) 99f. on the role of personal ties in public life and on Pericles' efforts to harden the boundary between public and private.

whether they rule on behalf of themselves or the ruled.[25] The exercise of power for one's own advantage is characteristic of the tyrant and, as Aristotle indicates, of the master.[26] The pursuit of personal gain or one's own exclusive needs can be regarded as base,[27] alternatively as menial or tyrannical. Yet all free men are expected to pursue their own good, not abstract duty or obligation. The democratic *polis* enables each citizen to do as he likes and this free interaction somehow both yields the collective good (so that to be ruled is not to be exploited or tyrannized) and constitutes an order which displays those virtues associated with the aristocracy.

How is this possible? Each of the three fifth-century thinkers I shall be considering, Protagoras, a sophist, Thucydides, a historian, and Democritus, a scientist, explored this question in his own way: how or in what sense does the *polis* express and secure the aims of each individual and the common good? This is in part a question about legitimacy and obligation: neither the legitimacy of particular authorities within the *polis*, nor the legitimacy of the *polis* as opposed to other forms of life, but simply the legitimacy of the *polis* as articulator of the interests of its citizens.[28] It may be asked in what sense an attempt to answer this question can be regarded as a peculiarly democratic account, or an account of a democratic *polis*. Is it not a theory about the *polis* in general, or indeed about man in general, in the abstract? Theories always bear birthmarks, impressions of the social/historical/ intellectual world from which they emerge.[29] For the fifth-century thinkers, as for modern neo-Kantian theorists, it is the democratic experience and the concerns peculiar to democracies which inform their reflections on politics. Their theories, again like the modern ones, are not, however, intended to be limited in application to the experience of a democratic community. The difference between the ancient and the modern theorists is that the modern ones aspire to provide a universally applicable theory, a theory about the rational agent as such; the theory, although it has the virtue of treating all men, whatever their political status, as worthy of respect, is much too thin to be a

---

[25] Plato, *Rep.* 342e, 346e–347e, Arist. *Pol.*, e.g., 1279a.

[26] Tyrant: see, e.g., Hdt. 3.80–1; Soph. *Antigone* 506, with Connor (1977) 101–4. Master: Arist. *Pol.* 1278b32–7. Note that Aristotle concedes this in spite of his view that the natural slave and the master actually have the same real interests.

[27] See, e.g., Hom. *Il.* 2.149, Eur. *Hecuba* 864.

[28] Cf. Finley (1982).

[29] See, for example, Sandel (1982) on Rawls (1971), *re* the influence of liberal democratic assumptions on the vision of the moral subject and the construction of the social world in modern neo-Kantian political theory.

theory grounded in a concrete society, and too much shaped by liberal democratic assumptions to fulfill the aspiration to universality. The ancient theories, though responsive to the democratic experience, are sufficiently general to suit any *polis*, that is any relatively small self-governing community, whether or not the assembly of citizens includes the poor and is sovereign. These theories do not aim to characterize all individuals or social entities, but only those for whom and in which politics is possible.

In both content and form, the fifth-century theories are democratic interpretations grounded in concrete practices. The questions addressed by these thinkers are questions posed by democratic self-government and by the corresponding difficulty of explaining the orderliness of a cosmos whose elements are neither ruled by gods nor intrinsically ordered. The issues of aristocracy and autonomy, order and freedom, figured in these construals. If a civic value and a prerequisite for realizing the collective good is the order, *dikē*, traditionally associated with the rule of the religious-cum-political elite, how is this to be achieved through the interaction of autonomous and vulgar citizens? And if those who have or seek power are pursuing their own good, how can this fail to be tyranny? How is it that my interests are involved, my autonomy expressed? The greater the sense of individual agency and autonomy, of liberation from a traditional order, the greater the difficulties of construing the *polis* as the ordered expression of the good of each man *qua* individual and of all men *qua* citizens. The solution to these difficulties lay in an interpretation of man's freedom and of the forces for order operating in society, and of the interdependence of the two.

The Athenians were concerned to identify man's freedom and his essence – what is genuinely internal – against the background of cosmic, social and psychological forces. Freedom was defined as both the absence of constraint and the exercise of self-government.[30] The realization of one's purposes demanded that one be an active citizen of a self-governing *polis*. In the first place, it made no sense to think of leading a genuinely human life outside a political community. Membership of such a community was not merely essential for survival, but also greatly extended the range of ends which it was possible to pursue. A self-governing community enabled men to act to secure the ends they desired, to express their autonomy, and by its very operation ensured that the social order was such as to preserve the liberty of its

---

[30] For a discussion of 'negative' vs. 'positive' theories of liberty, see Taylor (1985) 211–29 and Skinner (1984).

members. The political and social interaction characteristic of a self-governing community fostered those capacities and dispositions essential to the preservation of the autonomy of all citizens, their security against tyranny and exploitation.

In form as well, the interpretations offered by Protagoras, Thucydides and Democritus, unlike those of their successors, Plato and Aristotle, are democratic and imbedded in a particular kind of political society. They do not seek to construct an ideal city, but rather to reveal the sources of human well-being by interpreting the city of ordinary experience. The interpreter invites his audience to investigate the structure of the world as they experience it; he seeks to guide collective interpretation, not to impose an absolute truth. The theory is, therefore, itself part of the process it interprets, part of the dynamic (democratic) process of preserving order, unity and continuity, as well as autonomy and diversity, in the course of change. The theory both exemplifies and promotes reflection within political society – not a society constructed abstractly so as to generate certain social principles, but society as perceived, experienced, and assessed by real agents in real and changing contexts.

To recover the political thought of Protagoras, Thucydides and Democritus is, I suggest, to reveal the existence of a distinctive approach to the characterization of what men have good reason to do. Unlike either the Platonic/Aristotelian or modern liberal theories, this approach is suited both to democratic politics and to the reflections of men in a concrete social context. All three thinkers – Protagoras, Thucydides and Democritus – offer theories of the self as it is and as it experiences itself in the world. For them, reflection does not mean detachment, but rather the refinement of practical understanding. The source of political order and collective well-being is neither an institutional structure and system of rules nor the capacity for theoretical comprehension, but rather the virtue of political judgment, developed by means of experience guided by interpretation, interpretation both of particular real circumstances and of imaginative constructions of possible situations. Reflection and judgment are fostered by and imbedded in a constant process of social and political interaction. However, as I shall try to show, Protagoras' theory proved to be vulnerable to the pull of an external, asocial view of the self and, once challenged, lacked the resources to appeal to a concept of man's real or objective interests. Democritus mounted such an appeal, an appeal addressed to each individual *qua* man, but at the cost of moving away from a political ethics grounded in experience and interaction. By tracing the development of political ideas in the fifth century, it is possible not just to recapture an alternative vision, but also to observe how and why it gave way to more abstract and revisionary theories.

The continuing dialectical process of identifying what was genuinely internal to man in relation to the universe, society and the soul, eventually led, in the philosophy of Plato and Aristotle, to a 'disempowering of the self.' This process was conceived as the liberation of man's true nature. In their abstractness, these theories resemble modern moral theories. Kant attempted to preserve man's essential dignity, his free will, by defining him as independent of material causality, of fortune and of desire. The neo-Kantian argument for the arbitrariness of all attributes that distinguish one man from another can also be seen as the end result of such an attempt to free man's essential self by externalizing those elements previously regarded as constitutive.[31] Ironically, most discussions of ethical theory invoke Aristotle as a pointed contrast to the Kantian approach in this respect. Yet when Aristotle is compared with pre-Platonic theorists, one can see that a great deal of abstraction has already taken place. Aristotle constructed an abstract theory of the concrete. The attempt to contrive an ethical/political theory which provides a reason to each man, whatever his circumstances, to live a certain kind of life leads in Aristotle, as in modern Kantian theories, to an appeal to a vision of man more or less remote from the characteristic and concrete lives of men. This process of abstraction and 'dis-empowerment' is instructive: it provides perspective on our own motivations for adopting theories designed to apply categorically to each person, and it also reveals the sources of stability and instability for a theory that seeks to remain within the world of concrete experience and is founded on an account of what sort of life is good and rational for men in general.

The weaknesses of Protagorean and Democritean theory and the abandonment of democracy by Plato and Aristotle point to the strengths of a historical understanding of man's condition and his well-being, the approach embodied in the writings of Thucydides. Thucydides is able to appeal to what is the case, to reality, without resorting to a metaphysical standard beyond experience, and without abandoning the democratic insight that order must emerge through interaction. Historical experience and historical analysis give content and force to the claim that collective prudence and well-being are cultivated, as Protagorean theory alleged, by means of political interac-

---

[31] See especially Rawls (1971), and see Sandel (1982) 93–4 on the modern process of 'dis-empowering the self.'

tion. Thucydides' historical theory is not designed to bind each individual regardless of his circumstances; indeed the theory leaves room for the possibility that a person may in fact be so placed as to have good reason to contravene social or political conventions. However, most men do not understand the implications of particular circumstances for their own well-being or appreciate the danger to prudence inherent, as history demonstrates, in the ignorant indulgence of desire. Historical interpretation is a political activity; the capacity to interpret and to act on an assessment of the prudent course of action is fostered by political interaction of a certain kind, which leads citizens to consider the basic motivations and reactions evinced by men through time and the requirements for well-being in the world as it genuinely is at present, a reality to be understood historically.

In imitation of Thucydides' *History*, this selective history of fifth-century reflections on the self and the community aspires to be at once history, metahistory and politics. It seeks to make visible, through historical reconstruction, a possible way of living reflectively and politically. This possibility has *force* for us because it poses a genuine and challenging alternative to current modes of life and thought. And it has force for *us* because it can be seen to have been the response to conditions importantly analogous to those that have fostered our own unease. The possibility of concrete reflection revealed by this history is that embodied in Thucydides' demonstration of the value of his own history and of Athenian politics under Pericles as modes of prudent self-understanding. Thucydides showed that Pericles' appeal to men to understand their real, historically-shaped condition made possible both autonomy and order, and in so doing he vindicated his own historical approach to the question of what men have good reason to do. My aim is at one and the same time to illuminate and to argue, by implication, for a certain kind of democratic politics and a certain approach to political reflectiveness. Unlike Thucydides, I do not do this by telling a tale of contemporary times. It is significant that we have no Pericles, and (or?) no Thucydides to make such a leader's qualities manifest. By recovering the Thucydidean project, I merely allude to our need for statesmen and analysts capable of playing comparable parts in our very different drama. By placing Thucydides in the context of other fifth-century attempts to construe politics and thus revealing the virtues of his approach and of the reflective democracy he valued, I seek to do for Thucydides, in some small measure, what he did for Pericles.

2   Order in autonomy: the ungoverned
      cosmos and the democratic community

Man's awareness and understanding of himself as an agent is shaped through interaction with the world. The self-conception peculiar to the citizen of a political community (*polis*) in ancient Greece, therefore, has a history. By following the outlines of this history one can trace the development of a highly intense and reflective form of political self-understanding, the self-consciousness of democratic Athens. In a context established in large measure by local experience, but also by general developments in man's understanding of his relationship to the cosmos, the Athenians posed and explored the question of reconciling autonomy, or self-determination, with political order. A self-conscious sense of agency arose in conjunction with social change, which sparked a growing awareness of the sources of order in the natural and social world. Men experienced themselves and their relation to others differently. These changes were reflected in and enhanced by altered forms of self-expression: oral poetry gave way to written poetry and prose, epic to tragedy and unwritten convention to written law.[1] In this chapter I shall attempt to bring into focus this very general formulation of the way in which the Athenians came to think reflectively about themselves as autonomous agents in a political community. Here and in the next chapter, I indicate how they sought to resolve the issues raised by such reflection. These attempted resolutions, mooted in the writings of the tragedians and pursued analytically by the sophist Protagoras, themselves contributed, along with heightened social and international tension, to a more skeptical, even cynical, and distanced perspective on social order. As I shall seek to show in ch. 4, an increasingly reflective sense of human agency and the human good threatened to burst the bonds of the political community.

---

[1] For detailed accounts of various aspects of this process, see Havelock (1978), Segal (1961), Simon (1978).

The emergence of political autonomy

A brief consideration of certain aspects of the epic and archaic conception of agency and order will help locate later developments. The Homeric epics portray man as submerged in and infiltrated by the world.[2] Mental states and the actions associated with them are often depicted as contrived by the gods or by some part of man as opposed to an integrated self. Man is composed of parts which are not structured, not consistently differentiated in terms of body and soul, or reason and emotion. Mental life is conceived not as internal and bounded by a strong notion of the self, but as public, a process of intervention by individual gods or interaction between personified parts of men. This view of man as open to and interpenetrated by forces construed as external is appropriate to a world in which man is deeply imbedded in a social unit, and does not experience himself as isolated or autonomous. Yet the individual man does not dissolve; when he is moved by a god or some part of himself, it is the whole man who is moved. He possesses functional integrity. The forces that move him are those that move *him*. If even the most ordinary mental processes can be externalized, this may reflect the strong identification and blurred sense of self characteristic of highly organic social units (cf. the child within the family) and expressed and confirmed in the dynamic relationship among the epic bard, the traditional poetic material, and the audience.[3] The externalization of the extraordinary, strong passions implies a basic sense of self, for it is the self which is endangered by these impulses and seeks to alienate them. Such impulses are those that threaten the social or cosmic order and thus place the hero himself, or his status, in jeopardy.

By alienating these threatening desires, the hero not only preserves his own integrity, but restores the sense that his actions are part of a larger order, an order beyond his understanding or control. Thus, famously, in the *Iliad* Agamemnon asserts that he is 'not responsible for' or 'not a cause of' (*ouk aitios*) his wrath against Achilles, because Zeus and Fate and the avenging Furies 'put into (his) wits a savage delusion (*atē*)' (*Il.* 19.86; cf. 2.375, 9.17f.). When Agamemnon denies that he is responsible for his anger, he neither claims that he acted unwillingly nor invokes any other subjective consideration, but asserts that 'deity will always have its way' (*Il.* 19.89). The gods literally took away his wits, deluded him: in illustration of his claim, Agamem-

---

[2] See especially the classic works by Snell (1960) and Dodds (1960), and more recent assessments by Simon (1978) and Irwin (1983a).

[3] See Simon (1978) 85–7.

non offers a tale about the power of the goddess Delusion (*Atē*) (*Il.* 19.91f.). The participation of the agent is minimal: ruled by 'savage delusion,' Agamemnon stripped Achilles of his prize (*Il.* 19.89). It is because he was not himself the cause of his own anger and its dreadful consequences, because all knowledge and power was in the hands of the gods, that Agamemnon professes his willingness to 'make all good and give back gifts in abundance' (*Il.* 19.137; cf. 9.119). That is, neither his offense nor his peace-offering is any reflection on him or his honor; both are elements of a divine, and divinely-motivated, design.[4] The entire action of the *Iliad* is from one perspective the work of the gods, who intervene directly to guide the intercourse of mortals. In general, this intervention takes the form of rousing or calming men in ways explicable in human terms or of dealing with them directly, as one man-like being to another. The phenomenon of *atē*, the infatuation caused by god-sent blindness, is invoked when man is compelled to do something rash, ignorant, imprudent, ultimately disastrous; not something he would not otherwise have done,[5] but something man could not rationally *wish* to do. Such actions are alienated, and explained and excused as the work of a divinity or spirit.[6] (Compare the modern jury's tendency to believe that a woman who killed her child *must* be or have been insane and therefore innocent.)

Yet the act of a man deluded by the gods remains in some sense his act;[7] before offering his excuse, Agamemnon acknowledges that the Greeks have faulted him for his anger (19.85–6),[8] and even while excusing himself he does not deny that he himself (in some sense) performed what the gods wished accomplished.[9] To restore the order which the gods themselves, for their own obscure reasons, have made him disrupt, Agamemnon must offer restitution. The fact that he was deluded is relevant to the assessment of blame and responsibility, but whatever the cause, an objective order has been threatened and must be reconstituted. In early Greece, whatever the circumstances of (for example) a murderer's act, the consequence was pollution. This objective aspect of crime, namely the liability implicit in the bare occurrence

[4] *Contra* Mackenzie (1981) 70–87.

[5] As Vlastos (1975) 14 thinks. See Dodds (1951) 38f.

[6] Note that even Zeus suffers from the blindness and imprudence caused by Delusion (*Il.* 19.95f.).

[7] See Vlastos (1975) 13f.

[8] And see the alternative descriptions of Achilles' anger by Ajax (*Il.* 9.628f.), discussed by Vlastos (1975) 17.

[9] After Agamemnon has made restitution, he is chided by Odysseus to 'be more righteous to another man' (*Il.* 19.181); Odysseus is not referring to Agamemnon's initial anger, but to his behavior thereafter, which is apparently thought to be under his control.

of an act offensive to the order sanctioned by the gods, persisted alongside the development of a more subjective approach to blame-worthiness and responsibility.[10] In the realm of cosmic or divine caus-ality, as in the case of Agamemnon, the question of subjective responsibility need not arise. Agamemnon's consciousness was literally hijacked. With the emergence of civic institutions and law, the causal role of the agent is interpreted in more subjective terms. The conditions assumed to affect man's responsibility remain those con-nected in the Homeric world-view, namely ignorance and compul-sion: the Homeric hero cannot comprehend the forces that move him. In the later period, man's consciousness is not ordinarily considered to have been invaded. But the mode of thought is structurally similar, and this continuity involved a paradox: from one perspective, a mis-deed was essentially an error, a mistake, the product of ignorance. It was, that is, ignorance that caused, or rather constituted, the misdeed; and yet it was also ignorance that excused it, that marked the absence of conscious participation.[11] The former perspective presents man, like javelins and animals, as part of the cosmic, divinely orchestrated order. The agent's conscious participation is itself controlled by the gods, and his ignorance is the mark of his status as instrument. Not surprisingly, therefore, it is also his ignorance which marks the realm beyond his control.

The paradox of ignorance, the consequence of man's growing awareness of himself as a cause, appears already in Homer. But the conflict is not yet fully joined; the double causation implicit in the paradox is as yet only intimated. In the *Iliad* and the *Odyssey*, the plea that one has acted involuntarily, in ignorance or under compulsion, is intended to absolve the agent of responsibility.[12] To say, as Tele-machus does of the bard who claims he sang for the suitors under com-pulsion, that an agent is not responsible (*Od.* 22.351f.), is to say at once that he is not to blame and that he is not the *cause*.[13] The subjec-

---

[10] On the objective character of responsibility, see Vernant (1981) 40, drawing on Gernet (1917). This objective aspect of crime persisted at Athens in, for example, the legal pro-vision that objects and animals involved in causing injury were to be prosecuted and banished. See Plato, *Laws* 873e, Plut. *Per.* 36 and Antiphon, *Tetralogia* B, esp. iii.7, where the object is not convicted, but the question of pollution arises along with issues of intent.

[11] Vernant (1981) 41–2.

[12] *Il.* 23.514ff. and *Od.* 22.351, discussed by Vlastos (1975) 15–16, 98, against Dodds (1951) and Adkins (1960), cf. Mackenzie (1981) 84–5. On the term for acting volun-tarily, *hekōn*, see Vernant (1981) 37–8 and Irwin (1980) 119–20.

[13] The term used, *aitia*, means both a legal 'charge' or 'blame' and 'cause.' See Allan (1965) 2.

tive conditions of responsibility for one's actions are not investigated; the law does not discern degrees of willfulness.[14] What matters for the assessment of responsibility is simply the source of the act: does it lie within the agent, as evidenced by consciousness and deliberation? If exculpation depends upon ignorance or compulsion and is concerned not with divine control but with accidental as opposed to intentional acts, and the coercion of one man by another, then the scope of human responsibility is very great. Man's awareness of the constraints imposed on him by tradition and the demands of social order and his social role has its own weight. If he acts deliberately, and in accordance with his own character, then he acts knowingly and responsibly. The preservation of social order, and even of divine order so far as it is intelligible, is the responsibility of man, however it may fit into, or even be prompted by, the obscure workings of divinity.

For Aeschylus' Agamemnon, the conflict implicit in double causation is stark. Even imprudent and disastrous actions are the product of deliberation *and* divine determination. In deciding to sacrifice his daughter Iphigeneia, Agamemnon 'put on the yoke of necessity' (*Ag.* 218).[15] He *decides* to sacrifice her, knowingly and deliberately, yet also in accordance with the determinations of the gods. A shift in the center of gravity of double causation is marked by the role of delusion, *atē*: in Homer, *atē* is the cause of Agamemnon's anger, and he himself acts accordingly, while in Aeschylus, *atē* enables Agamemnon to act on a decision he himself has made (*Ag.* 219). Although divine *atē* is invoked as an explanation of human foolishness and imprudence in a variety of contexts as late as the fourth century,[16] nevertheless a conceptual change is discernible. The change is not a change in the criteria of responsibility: already in Homer, ignorance and compulsion are considered exculpatory. The difference rests in the extent to which personal responsibility – personal knowledge and agency – is in fact a feature of man's experience of participation in the world order. Man comes to differentiate himself more clearly from the social order, to mark the boundary between internal and external. He experiences himself as a source of order and control, at the expense of the cosmic order embodied in the term for providence or fortune, *tuchē*.[17]

---

[14] See Vernant (1981) 38, Dover (1974) 157–8, J. W. Jones (1956) 261, Sorabji (1980) 264f., Mackenzie (1981) 81f.

[15] Williams (forthcoming) provides an ingenious and illuminating discussion of this passage.

[16] See Vlastos (1975) 13–15, Dodds (1951) 38f.

[17] In addition to the works cited in n. 1 above, see Nussbaum (1986).

The transition from an externally-imposed order in which man figures as an all-but-unwitting agent to conscious participation in or ratification of an order still external and mysterious, and eventually to a self-determination which declares its virtual independence of *tuchē* or external control, is ultimately a political transition. It is the political community, the *polis*, freed from the arbitrary, autocratic rule of nobles or tyrants and ordered by customary law (*nomos*) that expresses at once man's autonomy and his participation in a divine pattern. Divinely-sanctioned *nomos* is construed by the aristocrats and approved by the people. Political order is the image of intelligible (not obscure or arbitrary) divine order, mediated by the traditional rulers, the nobles, whose authority was both religious and political. Double causation operated at the level of the *polis* as well as the agent, for *nomos* was divine, and good order (*eunomia*) a goddess.[18] Within this ordered realm, men pursued their own ends in accordance with social determinations. As the Spartan King Demaratus, according to Herodotus, said in describing the Spartans to the Persian king, 'they are free yet not wholly so; for *nomos* is their master whom they fear much more than your men fear you' (Hdt. 7.104). Herodotus associates Athenian freedom with the city's escape from the archaic tyranny of Pisistratus and his sons (546–510 B.C.). He argues that freedom is the source of bravery:

So long as they were held down by authority they deliberately shirked their duty in the field, as slaves shirk working for their masters; but when freedom was won, then every man amongst them was interested in his own cause. (Hdt. 5.78)

Here, as elsewhere in Herodotus' *Histories*, the significant contrast is not between democracy and oligarchy or tyranny, but between freedom on the one hand, and irresponsible, despotic (and narrowly self-interested) rule on the other.[19] Athens and Sparta fall on the same side of this divide: they both count as free and responsible political orders.[20] The medical treatise *Airs, Waters, Places*, cited earlier, echoes Herodotus' view that to be a member of a community ordered by law is to be free and, therefore, courageous.[21]

[18] See the discussion of *eunomia* in Meier (1970) 17–24.
[19] See Hdt. 5.92. Cf. Loraux (1981) 209f., Will (1972) 507ff. on Hdt. 3.82, Raaflaub (1983) 522–3, 527.
[20] See Hdt. 5.91.
[21] *Contra* Ostwald (1982) 11, the despotism envisaged is not the domination of Greek city states by Asiatic powers, though *autonomia* can be used to denote self-determination in this sense; the contrast in this passage is between Europeans and Asiatics and refers primarily to despotic civic institutions. On the connection between internal and external self-determination, see Raaflaub (1983) 521–2.

If the Greek political community was at first conceived, by Spartans as much as Athenians, in contrast to the despotism represented by local tyrants and the Persian king, as the order created through communal interaction in subservience to law, it was the Athenians who went on explicitly to explore and revise this conception of man's freedom and autonomy. Political developments at Athens loosened and eventually broke the grip of the traditional hierarchy which had mediated the relationship between social interaction and the order sanctioned by the gods. These developments prompted the Athenians to conceive of themselves in specifically political terms, rather than in terms of the social and economic relations constitutive of traditional order.[22] In the early sixth century B.C., as the result of economic changes which had reduced many of the poorest residents of Attica to a condition of virtual or real servitude and elevated others to a position from which they were minded to challenge the aristocratic monopoly on political power, social homogeneity and harmony came to an end. The ensuing conflict was resolved through the forging of a genuinely political solidarity. Solon, the mediator appointed by the Athenians to end the crisis, gave shape to the idea of the *polis* by absorbing the traditional aristocracy in a definition of citizenship which allotted a political function to every free resident of Attica.[23] Athenians were not slaves but citizens, with the right, at the very least, to participate in the meetings of the assembly. Solon's reforms did not, however, succeed in preventing further social turmoil and the eventual triumph of a tyrant, Pisistratus, in 546 B.C. The rule of the Pisistratids, anxious as they were to stifle their fellow aristocrats, hastened the dissolution of the traditional hierarchy and promoted the self-conscious sense of unity and solidarity of the Athenians as a whole. After the expulsion of the son of Pisistratus in 510, aristocratic strife of the kind which had led to tyranny was ended by the appeal by one contender, Cleisthenes, for the support of the populace. He embarked on reforms designed to undermine the local domination of aristocratic families and to connect every Athenian politically to the wider community. In the course of his reforms, Cleisthenes fixed the boundaries of the *polis* as a political rather than a geographical entity – boundaries which Solon had left permeable – by formally identifying the free inhabitants of Attica at that time as Athenian citizens. Therefore, citizenship con-

---

[22] See Meier (1970) 17–21, (1980) 86–90, 149–50 and *passim* on the development of self-conscious political identity at Athens.

[23] For this and what follows on Cleisthenes see Davies (1977/8). Cf. Aristotle's discussion, *Pol.* 1275a1–1276b15.

sisted not just in residence at Athens or membership of the assembly, but in these two plus eligibility for the Cleisthenic Council through membership of a local township (*deme*) and descent from the group of families identified as citizens by Cleisthenes. Thus the Athenians came to regard the political realm as the preserve of a restricted subset of the free population of Attica – a kind of aristocracy of birth – and to regard citizenship as an opportunity for more than acquiescence: for real participation.[24] The significant political distinction no longer corresponded to the social divide between noble and commoner, nor even between free man and slave, but was defined in purely political terms: citizen versus non-citizen.[25] This conception of a political identity and a political order was fully realized only in the fifth century, when the institutional dominance of the elite came to an end, and political status was firmly distinguished from personal, social or economic attributes, and freedom and order were construed politically, as the product of the interaction of political equals.

In the 460s and 450s, Athenian political life bordered on revolution. As Aristotle recounts in his study of the Athenian constitution, Ephialtes 'launched an attack on the Areopagus,' the body of aristocrats who had long dominated Athenian political life, and distributed its powers among the council, the assembly and jury courts (*Ath. Pol.* 25. 1–2). This shift in the center of gravity of the Athenian political system was completed and consolidated in subsequent years, and meant an effective transfer of power from the few to the many. To recapture the flavor of the period, it is important to remind oneself that there was nothing inevitable about the triumph of democracy at Athens. During and after the Ephialtic Reforms, questions of leadership and active political participation were unsettled and contentious. Shortly after his successful attack on the Areopagus and the vote to impose political banishment (ostracism) on his chief rival, Cimon (461), Ephialtes was murdered.[26] In 458/7, a Spartan force returning from a campaign against the Phocians dallied in the territory of Athens' neighbor, Boeotia: 'To this course they were partly influenced by some Athenians, who were secretly inviting them into the *polis*, in

---

[24] Compare Boeotia where, according to the Oxyrhynchus historian (11.2), only the wealthier citizens were eligible for the council. And see Arist. *Pol.* 1274b3–1275b21 and 1276a6–1276b15.

[25] See Meier (1980) and Raaflaub (1983) 534–5.

[26] Antiphon 5.68 asserts that the assassins were not identified; Arist. *Ath. Pol.* 25.4 identifies the murderer as Aristodicus of Tanagra, about whom we know nothing.

the hope of putting an end to the rule of the people (the *demos*) and to the building of the long walls' (Thuc. 1.107.4).[27] The assertion of political control by the populace of imperial Athens – over foreign affairs, religious matters and the administration of justice throughout Attica – provoked fierce, even violent opposition.

The existing equilibrium in relations between the populace and an active political elite was being challenged and upset. As various inscriptions from this period indicate, the power to administer the affairs of the *polis* had devolved upon the people (*demos*) in assembly; the democratic council and committees executed and formulated policy, but the assembly was sovereign.[28] Moreover, there are indications that the assembly exercised its sovereignty at the expense of both sacred and local authorities. *The Suppliants* of Aeschylus and the Praxiergidai decree (*SEG* XIV 3) suggest that in the 460s and 450s religious claims were explicitly absorbed into the sphere of secular authority.[29] In the play, the plea of the suppliants – acceptance or rejection of which would endanger the *polis* as a whole – is referred to the *demos* (*Suppl.* 365–9, 397–401); in the decree, the sacral prerogatives of an aristocratic family are set forth in detail, and are thus implicitly *limited* to the areas specified by the *demos*. The evidence for the centralization of democratic authority is less direct, but equally suggestive. Whatever the intentions of those who introduced and supported it, Pericles' citizenship law of 451 enabled the people as a whole, instead of the individual townships, to decide who was to share in the privileges of citizenship.[30] A somewhat earlier measure – two years earlier, according to Aristotle – has similar implications: 'The

---

[27] See Gomme (1945) 314, who suggests that the oligarchs realized that the walls, designed to protect the territory of Attica from invasion by land, would increase Athenian dependence on the sea, and thus mean 'the permanent domination of the democracy,' because the poorest citizens, unable to afford armor and therefore excluded from the hoplite phalanx, would become the bulwark of the state as rowers. This last ascribes too much foresight to the oligarchs, though the likelihood of increased dependence on the sea would have been obvious. He cites Plut. *Them.* 19.4, [Xen.] 1.2, 2.15–16, Arist. *Ath. Pol.* 24.1, cf. *Pol.* 1302b2–4, 1303b10.

[28] See, e.g., *SEG* X 24, discussed by Davies (1978) 66–7.

[29] Ostwald (forthcoming). Professor Ostwald kindly allowed me to see portions of an early draft of a book on Athens. Cf. Davies (1978) 69f., who also discusses these two texts. Note also, as evidence of this trend, Meiggs and Lewis 44, a decree concerning the appointment of a priestess (by lot, with all Athenian women eligible) and the building of a temple of Athena *Nikē*.

[30] This is the conclusion reached by C. Patterson in a recent study of the law, Patterson (1981) 129f.

thirty justices were reestablished[31] who were known as the magistrates of the townships' (*Ath. Pol.* 26.3). The revival of this institution, which originated under the Pisistratid tyranny in 453/2, would
have facilitated settlement of local disputes in rural Attica, and may
also have served to ease the burdens on the jury courts.[32] Thereby it
also ensured that even if he could not afford (or his case was too minor
to warrant) a trip to Athens, no Athenian citizen need abandon his
claim or resort to a local, probably private, and perhaps aristocratic
arbitrator: he could seek justice from officials of the *polis*.

The jurisdiction of the popular courts was extended to meet the
demands of democratic (and imperial) administration. In this period
the jury-courts acquired the privilege of sitting in judgment on the
character and performance of all those who served the state. Pericles,
we are told (*Ath. Pol.* 27.3), 'introduced pay for those serving in the
lawcourts,' probably not long after the death of Ephialtes.[33] Compensation for the exercise of this privilege enabled many (and a range of)
Athenian citizens to participate.[34] The citizens also confronted directly the issue of access to high office. In 458/7 members of the
second property class were officially declared eligible for the chief
magistracy, the archonship,[35] and an archon from this class was duly
selected. It is also possible that the principle of compensation for
public service was at this time extended to the magistrates – some of
whom would now be men of modest means – and, before long, to the
members of the council.[36] Inscriptional evidence reveals that members
of the assembly who are not known to have been officials or ex-
officials were initiating substantive motions or proposing radical
amendments to measures submitted by the council.[37] This kind of evi-

---

[31] See Arist. *Ath. Pol.* 16.5, Hignett (1952) 218–19, Finley (1983) 46–7.

[32] For a speculative discussion of the likely functions of the traveling judges, see Bonner and
Smith (1930) 351–2. See also Hignett (1952) 219, cf. 152 n. 4.

[33] See the discussion of the evidence by Hignett (1952) Appendix IX, 342–3, Rhodes (1981)
338f.

[34] See Arist. *Ath. Pol.* 27.4.

[35] Arist. *Ath. Pol.* 26.2; the first archon from the second property class was selected in 457/
6, which must mean the reform was instituted earlier.

[36] There is no direct evidence of the date of institution of pay for magistrates, though Arist.
Ath. Pol. 27.3–4 does imply that pay for juries was the first instance of pay for office. See
Hignett (1952) 219f., Griffith (1966) 124f. Magistrates and councilors were being paid
by 411 (Thuc. 8.69.4, Arist. *Ath. Pol.* 29.5). The existence of such pay at an earlier date is
implied in Arist. *Ath. Pol.* 24.3, and [Xen.] *Ath. Pol.* 1.3. See Hignett (1952) 220, Hansen
(1979) 13, with n. 27.

[37] See *SEG* X 24, *c.* 450, discussed by Davies (1978) 66–9, Tod I.42, *c.* 446/5, the motion of
Anticles and the amendment by Archestratus, with Jones (1953) 113; note also an amendment to the provisions for an alliance with Egesta, 454/3, Tod I.31.

dence is difficult to assess: there are no comparable sources for the period before 460,[38] and, moreover, we have no way of knowing that the proposers of these measures were *not* officeholders or members of the council. However, the very fact of this unprecedented flood of public documentation of the actions of council and assembly is itself significant.

The evidence of growing initiative on the part of the assembly raises the issue of freedom of speech in the assembly, *isegoria*. The changes instituted by Cleisthenes at the end of the sixth century, after the expulsion of the tyrants – particularly the establishment of a council of 500 drawn from throughout Attica – were a necessary condition for the diffusion of political experience and self-confidence that must have preceded the emergence of *isegoria*, but they were by no means sufficient.[39] It seems likely that those who spoke in the assembly were simply those who were regarded as men of substance and/or experience; these tended, even after the Cleisthenic reforms, to be wealthy and distinguished men, many of whom were also office-holders.[40] The most significant change occurred when office and traditional status ceased to coincide, that is after Ephialtes' assault on and redistribution of the powers of the Areopagus. The admission of men from the second property class to the archonship and the provision of pay to the members of the council (probably a year or two earlier) both signal a shift in the character of the governing class: pay is a sign that some non-wealthy citizens are already members of the council, and access to the archonship is an indication that men of the third class, that is men of foot-soldier status, have already secured lesser offices.[41] The vertical redistribution of power gave men with no previous experience of public responsibility the opportunity to consider and discuss matters

[38] Except Tod I.11 – a decree relating to Salamis, tentatively assigned to the late sixth century; one mutilated decree does not a comparison make. But the difference of scale is not likely to be due to accidents of survival.

[39] See Woodhead (1967) 134. Cf. Griffith (1966) 125.

[40] The replacement in 487/6 of election of magistrates by the people with the casting of lots among men elected (still from the top two property classes) by the townships (Arist. *Ath. Pol.* 22.5, *contra* 8.1; see Moore (1975) 220–1, 245, Rhodes (1981) 272–4) and the first use of ostracism in 487 to expel a relative of the tyrants (Arist. *Ath. Pol.* 22.3–4) look like attempts to change the character of the governing elite only in the direction of a horizontal, not a vertical, redistribution of power. In the years immediately following the Athenian victory over the Persians at Marathon in 490, the Areopagus retained its grip on the administration of the city. On the 'aristocratic' character of these years see Griffith (1966) 125–6.

[41] On the dates of the introduction of these measures, see Rhodes (1981) 13, 330, Griffith (1966) 125; see above, n. 27.

of state in a large body (500 members) and increased the number of knowledgeable experienced men in the assembly.[42] We do not know how many – or what kinds of – citizens took advantage of this opportunity once the barriers of convention had been breached. However, the range of persons who expressed their opinions about proposals in the assembly must have broadened, and certainly came to include men who were not sitting magistrates or members of the council.[43] The practice of *isegoria* may have helped to bring about the independence and control characteristic of the assembly of democratic Athens.[44] The assembly's willingness to ignore the advice of 'the authorities' if better or more congenial advice was available on the hill called the Pnyx, where the assembly met, was in part a function of the diffusion of political responsibilities (which weakened the very notion of 'an authority'), and is likely to have proceeded in tandem with the development of *isegoria*. Political power came to rest in the capacity to persuade the assembly.[45]

The period in which radical, direct democracy was created, and political power gradually devolved to the people in assembly and absorbed local and sacral authorities, raised deep questions about the sources of political order and harmony. In a struggle whose outlines we can barely decipher, the populace won control over magistrates, access to political office, and the right to participate actively in the determination of policy. Radical democracy had not yet triumphed; disgruntled aristocrats would not have regarded that triumph as inevitable, nor would they have yet perceived the extent to which they could continue to wield power in the *polis*. On the other hand, the ambitions of the *demos*, once kindled (and stoked by the achievement of naval supremacy), could not simply be snuffed out. Thoughtful citizens would have pondered the implications of entrusting the management of the *polis* to a large and heterogeneous group of citizens, each of whom could, if he wished, actively attempt to persuade his fellows of the wisdom or folly of a particular decision. The prayer which opened meetings of the assembly included the invocation 'that who-

---

[42] A process well described by Woodhead (1967) 132–4.

[43] The number of amendments to council proposals suggests that at least some of them were made by non-councilors who disagreed with what had been done in the council. Cf. Griffith (1966) 129.

[44] Griffith (1966) 129–30 and 136 n. 44. Cf. Hignett (1952) 155f., 243; not only could the assembly amend a preliminary proposal of the council, it could also instruct the council to submit one.

[45] See Finley (1962), Griffith (1966) 128ff.

ever acts and speaks in the best interests of Athens may prevail.'[46] Three bits of evidence suggest that the Athenians in the period down to the death of Pericles may have been concerned about ensuring that those who spoke in the assembly, and the assembly as a whole, would indeed act in the best interests of Athens. The first is the institution of the indictment for introducing an illegal proposal,[47] a provision designed to hold proposers of measures in the assembly responsible for the compatibility of those measures with existing laws. It may have been designed as a check on the potential recklessness of assembly decisions or of particular proposers. The second is the fact that the Athenians did not go beyond the reform of eligibility for the archonship and alter the requirement that magistrates be drawn from the three upper classes:[48] in theory and, in the early period at least, probably in practice, the lowest class were excluded from acquiring the experience which would secure them a hearing or indeed prompt them to speak in the assembly. And the third is Pericles' assertion, as reported by Thucydides (2.44) that 'they cannot possibly offer fair and impartial counsel, who, having no children to hazard, do not have an equal part in the risk.'[49] The last two considerations point to a belief that those who have the power to determine what is in the interests of the city as a whole should themselves have a stake in the city's future well-being. They must have something to lose by giving their fellow citizens bad advice. The *demos* itself was concerned about the implications of the revolution it had wrought.

Here the significance of the shift to democracy for political self-understanding and reflection becomes apparent. The social and personal qualities traditionally associated with power and order are no longer politically decisive. Political power has come to rest with an assembly of men who are not themselves, as individuals, powerful;[50] unity is no longer to be secured by traditional authority or respect for a social hierarchy; the assembly is to direct Athenian policy, yet individual members may be inexperienced, uneducated, unused to responsibility. Men were prompted by these developments to reflect on the sources of political order, unity and prudence. If order, unity and prudence were not a function of personal qualities or social distinctions, what might secure them? Or if they were a function of personal

[46] Reconstruction by Rhodes (1972) 37, based on Ar. *Thesm.* 295–311.
[47] On the date of introduction, see Hansen (1978).
[48] Arist. *Ath. Pol.* 7.4. See Hignett (1952) 225 with n. 3, Rhodes (1972) 2.
[49] Cf. Dinarchus 1.71, with Griffith (1966) 136–7 with n. 54; Hignett (1952) 224.
[50] Meier (1970) 38.

attributes, how might such attributes be fostered in the people as a whole? Political relations had long been a matter of personal relations; in a sense they remained so,[51] but they had ceased, in large part and at least formally, to be mediated by the social structure. The problem now was to reconcile genuine autonomy with order and collective determination of policy with unity and harmony. The advent of democracy put pressure on the question of how a community acts as an entity and on the relationship of personal qualities and aims to political ones. A reflective observer of the events of the 460s and 450s would have noted the real possibility of social disintegration and would have wondered about the status of political authority. Why should those who had traditionally administered the affairs of the *polis* accede to the active participation of the populace? Why should they bow to the *demos*' assertion of authority in matters of sacred ritual or local justice? What – if anything – ensured that the populace would administer the *polis* responsibly and prudently? These questions suggested others. In what sense did a propertyless member of the assembly or a dissatisfied member of the highest property class – or indeed any citizen – have a stake in promoting or a reason to promote communal solidarity? And how were unity and purposefulness possible in a society governed by the interaction of a large, diverse citizen body, each member of which had his own ideas and perceived interests?

The shaping of autonomy

The new, explicitly political conception of the social order did provoke doubts and questions; it also embodied a way of answering them. By emphasizing the political at the expense of the social, the Athenians were able to construe themselves as an elite, the elite of the free as opposed to the slave, of the citizen as opposed to the noncitizen. Within the civic realm all men were politically equal, despite persisting social and economic inequalities, and all men were capable of pursuing the leisured, genteel activities of warfare, politics and public service, despite the fact that they had to work for a living. All personal qualities and aims were politicized and converted into properties of – or seen in relation to – the community as a whole. Aristocratic influence and values were expressed in democratic terms. The Periclean Funeral Oration recorded by Thucydides, one of a genre which bears the marks of having acquired its definitive form in the

[51] See Rist (1982) 97–8, Laslett (1956).

460s, when the Athenians turned toward greater democracy, both expresses the influence of aristocratic values and transposes them into a democratic context.[52] The constraints associated with the old aristocratic order are now conceived as self-imposed and compatible with autonomy. Pericles appeals to fear as the force that restrains the citizens from lawlessness. The oration emphasizes the unity of the *polis* guided by traditional values: 'For we render obedience to those in authority and to the laws, especially ... to those which, though unwritten, bring upon the transgressor an acknowledged disgrace' (2.37.3).[53] Willing obedience to unwritten laws epitomizes a form of political double causation, but one which operates via collective convention and fits the growing power of the people themselves to make and fix written law. Pericles stresses the continued weight of aristocratic influence and values in democratic Athens (see 2.37.1), and he ennobles the democracy. Herodotus had made Demaratus refer to lordly *nomos*, law, as the power which constrained the Spartans to stand and fight (7.104). In the Funeral Oration, Pericles argues that Spartan courage is the product of externally-imposed discipline and that this discipline is degrading and servile; it is toilsome (2.39.1) while Athenian bravery is a free and spontaneous excellence (2.39.4). This depiction of the Spartans is paradoxical: they are the citizenry who, because of the existence of a huge population of subjugated laborers, the helots, do not have to 'labor'. By contrast, the Athenians, many of whom are preoccupied with work (see Thuc. 2.40.2), can only aspire to the leisure associated with the aristocracy, which democratic payment for office makes possible to a limited extent. Pericles has made the aristocratic pursuits of the Spartans seem servile, while glorifying the form of personal excellence (*aretē*) cultivated in all citizens by the Athenian way of life. Moreover, honor is to be allocated and excellence assessed in terms of the capacity to contribute – not, through wealth or gentility, to a narrow social order, but politically, to the community as a whole (Thuc. 2.37.1). The Funeral Oration portrays the power and unity of the *polis* as the product of aristocratic values in a democratic context.

Pericles' portrayal of the Spartans as unfree captures the essence of a significant change in political self-understanding which accompanied the transition to democracy. Political interaction in obedience to law is no longer to be construed as freedom, as opposed to subjection to a

[52] See Loraux (1981) 56–64.
[53] See Loraux (1981) 187. Significantly, the clause I have left out refers to private rather than public law.

tyrant; rather, traditional law is itself conceived as external, despotic and antithetical to true freedom. Freedom is to be secured through democratic politics. In a democracy the laws are self-imposed, and men enjoy *autonomia*,[54] self-rule. Only if the people rule themselves will they be able to avoid the servile dependence to which lack of social status had long consigned them. Moreover, only in this way and not, as Herodotus and the Hippocratic writer mistakenly believed, simply by escaping tyranny, will the citizens be genuinely brave in the defense of their liberty. Freedom is collective, a property of the community as a whole. In so far as the citizens rule themselves by actively participating in political decision-making, the city will remain free, both internally and externally, and the freedom of every individual citizen will be secure.[55] Qualities once associated with the individual excellence characteristic of members of the aristocracy – nobility, courage, honor, glory – are now cultivated and expressed in the exercise of political freedom, which secures to each citizen the liberty to pursue his own aims.

Tragic drama, whose emergence coincided with the period of political upheaval that gave birth to Athenian democracy, both instantiated and promoted exploration of the questions raised by, and the answers embodied in, democratic politics: what is political freedom, and what underlies a purely political claim to authority? How does democracy in fact transform claims grounded in personal or social considerations into political claims, and political claims into ones grounded in personal or social considerations? As this formulation suggests, concern about democracy, and about order and freedom, arises from two adjacent angles: doubts about whether the consequence of assembling the views of individuals freed from a traditional hierarchy and traditional values will in fact be order, and about whether such an order is in fact compatible with the expression of personal aims, particularly when these appeal to conflicting values. The plays of Aeschylus offer interpretations of both freedom and order and suggest that only democratic politics can reconcile them. Both *The Suppliants* (pro-

[54] *Contra* Ostwald (1982) *autonomia* was not restricted to the realm of relations between states. The connotation he identifies, namely a condition at odds with arbitrary external coercion, was relevant to the attainment of self-rule within the city as well as in relation to other cities: his interpretations of various passages are therefore too restrictive and occasionally misleading (e.g. *Airs, Waters, Places* 23; Hdt. 1.96, cf. 1.95; Thuc. 2.63). Ostwald (1982) 10–11 dismisses the use of the term to describe a personal quality of Sophocles' Antigone as 'metaphorical' and does not mention Democritus' use of the term.

[55] See Raaflaub (1983) 521–2; cf. Skinner (1984) 206–7 on Machiavelli's use of the idea that personal liberty is possible only in self-governing communities.

duced *c.*465–459 B.C.) and the *Oresteia* (produced in 458) raise the question of the relationship between personal and political claims. In each of them, but in different ways, Aeschylus suggests that democratic institutions may be able to resolve these claims at the pragmatic and perhaps even at the theoretical level by absorbing the personal into the political, that is by expressing and affirming personal claims through political means. In *The Suppliants*, Aeschylus anachronistically portrays an archaic city state as a democracy. The king of Argos, Pelasgus, is a central figure. Contrasts between democracy and despotism, Greeks and barbarians, women and men shape this portrayal of the Danaids who flee from marriage to their Egyptian cousins and attempt to secure Argive protection.[56] The claim which conflicts with the political one is in some sense a religious claim, yet it is posed in terms of a self-willed act motivated by personal feelings. The conflict is stark in *The Suppliants*, because the wishes of the Danaids do not coincide with the claims of kinship. And the conflict is the deepest theme of the play, binding together the other basic contrasts.

From the very beginning of the drama, the Danaids invoke Zeus the savior, god of suppliants. They bolster their plea for protection by claiming kinship with the Argives through their ancestor, Io. They also appeal to Zeus's 'virgin daughter' to protect their own virginity, to spare them 'the bed of man' (lines 444ff.). They refer to themselves as 'exiles' (e.g. line 74) and to the proposed marriage as impious (line 9) and forbidden by law (line 37). Yet it is clear from the start that the status of these claims and invocations is parasitic upon the actions and feelings of the Danaids themselves, their 'self-will.' They are suppliants, exiles, virgins solely because of their 'hatred of the marriage bed' (line 332). In their first song, the Danaids explain that they fled into exile not because they were expelled for murder by the decree of the people but 'escaping impious marriage by self-imposed banishment' (lines 4–10).[57] Not only have they deliberately sought exile, but they are also prepared to kill themselves, that is to do whatever is necessary – without the sanction of the community or even, if it comes

---

[56] See North (1966) 35–47 on Aeschylus' political use of the term *sophrosunē* (roughly 'moderation') to mean respect for limitations. She observes that for Aeschylus *sophrosunē* is associated with freedom, justice, defense against aggression, masculinity and Hellenism as opposed to tyranny, injustice, aggression, femininity, barbarism and *hubris*. She identifies the following offenses against *sophrosunē* in *The Suppliants*: the violence of the suitors and the excessive emotionalism, distorted view of life and fierce chastity of the Danaids.

[57] *Contra* LSJ, the item I have translated as 'self-imposed' (*autogenē*) here does not modify marriage (*gamon*) and mean 'kindred.' It sharpens the contrast with 'expelled by people.' In any case, the meaning is clear: they escaped by their own action.

to it, of the gods (lines 159–60 – see 465f.) – to avoid the marriage they abhor. Pelasgus' questioning reveals the personal character of their claims:

'Why do you hold the fresh white olive branch?' 'To be no household slaves to Aegyptus' sons.' 'By hatred or by law?' 'Who would buy a master from kin?' [Note the evasion.] 'By such practices is the strength of mortals increased.' (lines 334–8)

The Danaids attempt no further justification of their revulsion; instead they appeal to the king to help them in their present distress (line 339). In response to their assertion that reverence for the gods requires him to resist Aegyptus' sons and wage a 'new war,' and that the goddess Justice (*Dikē*)[58] protects her allies, Pelasgus expresses doubt that *dikē* underlies the plea of the Danaids: 'If only she (*Dikē*) had been a partner in these matters from the start!' (line 344). The Danaids insist upon their independence. They refuse to adapt their personal desires to the demands of political authority in the form of the law of their land or symbolically in the form of male domination in marriage. Moreover, they reject the real claims of kinship, though they exploit a diluted form of this tie to persuade the Argives to protect them. For Pelasgus, political authority is the primary consideration, superior to the claims of kinship, although the two may happen to coincide. 'If Aegyptus' sons rule you by the laws of the community, claiming to be nearest of kin, who would wish to resist them in this?' (lines 307–9). The Danaid appeal to Argive kinship, to their own sensibilities, to their status as suppliants, is, the king implies, inadequate: 'You must plead according to the laws of your homeland that these men lack authority over you' (lines 390–1). The Danaids reject this view, and declare their desire, in their view a just desire, to be free of male or political control: 'I wish never to be subject to the rule of men. Under the stars I plot a course: escape from a grievous marriage' (lines 392–5).

The conflict between Pelasgus' political perspective and the self-assertion of the Danaids encompasses the contrast between Greek and barbarian, democracy and despotism. The Danaids invoke Zeus the omnipotent, Zeus 'of endless sovereignty' (line 574), who is ruled by no one and respects no one (lines 595f.). Their experience of politics is of arbitrary rule, despotic personal power. Thus they do not understand when Pelasgus insists that he cannot respond to their appeal as if

[58] Note that for the Greeks the concept of justice was linked to notions of order, appropriateness and custom.

they were suppliants at his own hearth (line 365). They maintain that he *is* the *polis* and the people, sole ruler of Argos: 'A prince is not judged' (line 371). Indeed they threaten him formally with the vengeance of Zeus: *his* house and children will pay the price of impiety (line 434). Pelasgus appreciates the seriousness of the situation he confronts; yet in his mind there is no question but that the risk and the responsibility of taking action rest not with him alone, but with the people as a whole. The Danaids seek political protection, and by doing so they threaten every member of the *polis*. The only 'cure' is for the citizens themselves to unite in responding to the threat: 'If the *polis* incurs defilement of what is common, in common let the people work a cure' (lines 366–7; see 397f.). The decision is not an easy one to make (line 397), and 'justice' is not, in the king's view, the relevant criterion, for it is unclear on which side justice stands. What is needed is careful thought (lines 407f.). Goaded by the Danaid threat to hang themselves from the statues of the gods, Pelasgus himself decides that it would be preferable to risk Egyptian rather than divine wrath (lines 471f.; cf. 615f.). Yet the ultimate decision rests with the *demos*.

The Argives vote to protect the Danaids: under no circumstances are the suppliants to be surrendered to force (lines 607f., 941). Indeed the citizens decree that anyone[59] who fails to help the women resist abduction will suffer loss of civic rights and honor and banishment (lines 611f.). These decrees of the democratic *polis* rest on principles antithetical to those of the Danaids, who are exponents of self-will and barbarian despotism. The Danaids refer to the *hubris* and violence of their pursuers. They represent themselves as resisting an unjust attempt to force them into marriage against their wills. As the actions of both the Danaids and the Egyptians reveal, barbarian society, unlike the Argive city state, provides no means for the reconciliation of personal freedom with political authority. The sons of Aegyptus attempt to rule by force. The Argive *polis* is ruled by persuasion and consent. Thus Pelasgus chastises the Egyptian herald: 'If these [the Danaids] were willing, being well-disposed, you could lead them away, if pious speech persuaded them' (lines 940–1). The Danaids refuse to bow to political authority. The Argives, by their own deliberate act, bind themselves to uphold the policies they have decreed (even to the extent of punishing those citizens who fail to do so).

[59] The text refers to *geomoroi*: in Argos, the wealthy landowners, in Athens, the bulk of the citizens. There may be an implication here that even those with the most to lose in a war must respect the will of the *polis*.

In his portrayal of Pelasgus' encounter with the Egyptian herald near the end of *The Suppliants*, Aeschylus weaves together the references to being female (emblematic of the non-political) and to the behavior of barbarians and despots, to underscore the themes of the play. The herald exercises his authority by dragging the Danaids toward the sea. He refers to subduing the women as an end to anarchy (line 907). Man, in his view, embodies power, and it is the Egyptians who are the 'men' (line 950). Pelasgus declares that the Egyptian claim to power and manhood is in fact insolence: the Argives, who govern by political authority, are the true men (line 951). Yet the Egyptians, he maintains, are acting as if the Argives and their political claims need not be respected: 'By what insolence dare you insult this land of Pelasgian men? Do you think you have come to a woman's land? You are barbarians, and you trifle insolently with Greeks, and, off the mark in everything, you do nothing right' (lines 911f.). When the herald asks in what way he has acted contrary to *dikē* (line 916), Pelasgus replies: 'You know not how to be a stranger' (line 917). The Egyptians do not respect the wishes, institutions (note line 919) or beliefs of others: 'I do not fear these gods before me: they did not nourish me ... ' (lines 893–4). As Pelasgus points out, the herald refers to particular gods, yet he lacks reverence (line 921). The herald retorts that he reveres his *own* gods, the spirits of the Nile (line 922). Pelasgus is incredulous: 'Do I understand you? These gods are *nothing*?' (line 923). Earlier in the play, Pelasgus had argued that the Danaids must justify their behavior in terms of the laws (*nomoi*) to which they were subject. Pelasgus respects the political authority of others in their own sphere and expects this respect to be reciprocated. As the later encounter reveals, the king respects the authority of others only in so far as they do reciprocate, and thereby act politically. Just as 'reverence' is not restricted to respect for particular gods, so, too, authority is not defined solely by particular *nomoi*, but also in terms of a more general standard: the rejection of coercion. And it is adherence to this standard which underlies the Athenian democracy's claim, as it is represented in this play, to express personal aims in political actions.

It may be that this vision of democratic interaction as in principle reconcilable with – indeed, essential to – personal autonomy was inspired by the contrast between Athens and Sparta. Awareness of the extent and character of this contrast was undoubtedly heightened when Athenian soldiers were sent in 465 to help the Spartans vanquish the helots, and were then summarily dismissed by the Spartans for fear that they might radicalize the rebels or prove sympathetic to them. In any case, a few years later, after Ephialtes the Reformer had been murdered, and not long before some Athenians plotted to betray the city to Sparta, Aeschylus analyzed political events in rather different terms. In the three plays of the *Oresteia*, he still relied on the institutions of the Athenian *polis* – though in this case the most aristocratic and archaic element in the political system – to resolve an apparently unresolvable conflict. The trilogy may reflect Aeschylus' concern that the thrust toward full democracy at the expense of traditional authority would result in anarchy. This concern is articulated not in terms of a conflict between democracy and aristocracy, but rather of the clash between political and familial claims. As in *The Suppliants*, the 'female' element – Queen Clytemnestra, her lover Aegisthus (see *Ag.* 1625), the Furies – represents disorder, rebellion against authority (*Eum.* 354) and personal grievance, as well as the commitment to ties of blood (the murdered Iphigeneia, daughter of Clytemnestra, and Thyestes, father of Aegisthus) above the claims of political order or authority.[60] The Furies also represent the claims of the 'traditional,' the 'elder' gods (*Eum.* 150f., 778f.). Apollo, on the other hand, speaks for the male principle. The murder of a great man, 'lord of the host of ships' (*Eum.* 637) by a woman is a greater crime than matricide. Apollo's argument that a woman is not in fact 'related' to the child she bears (*Eum.* 657f.) is sophistical and one-sided,[61] as is the Furies' claim that the killing of a man by his wife is not 'the shedding of kindred blood' (*Eum.* 212). Both crimes – the one against kin, the other in violation of the covenant of marriage – are outrages (*Eum.* 213–24).

Athena is confronted with this dilemma. As a woman and a motherless goddess, she is the ideal arbiter. Yet, like King Pelasgus in *The Suppliants*, she herself cannot determine what is 'just' and 'true' in such a case: 'Even I have not the *themis* to judge cases of murder where wrath's edge is sharp' (*Eum.* 471). Since the outcome of the case will affect Athens, Athenians must judge (*Eum.* 473ff.). In *The Suppliants*, the conflict is irreconcilable because neither the Danaids nor the sons of Aegyptus are capable of subduing arrogant self-will in the interests of collective harmony: they have no framework, no genuinely political

---

[60] Note *Ag.* 672f., where Clytemnestra asserts that 'we shall bring good order to our household at least.'

[61] Though not as bizarre in the context of ancient beliefs as it would be today. See Aristotle's discussion of sexual generation, *GA*: 'The male contributes the principle of movement and the female the material' (730a27).

context, for doing so. Political deliberation at Argos, by contrast, succeeds in forging a collective response to the danger posed by this conflict among non-political barbarians. In the Athens of the *Oresteia*,
however, irreconcilable conflict has come home to roost inside the
political community. Each side appeals to a powerful, divinely-
sanctioned set of values, both of which have force for political order
within Athens. Thus, while the decision of the Argives was unani-
mous, the Athenians who constitute the Areopagus are divided.[62] This
division highlights a number of significant features in Aeschylus' treatment of the issues. The implications of a purely political basis for
order are exposed to view. Political validity is founded on a decision-
making procedure, not on a divinely-ordained truth or order. This is
part of the point of politics since, as the *Oresteia* itself illustrates, the
gods may well demand conflicting things. Yet political deliberation
cannot in itself *dissolve* a deep and tragic conflict between legitimate
claims, as the divided role of the Areopagites confirms. The political
community must therefore absorb and domesticate conflict, and
express the various demands to which men take themselves to be subject. The conflict at issue in the *Oresteia* poses this challenge in
extreme terms, for the rival claims are in fact claims about the proper
basis of communal order. The choice of the Areopagus, the traditional
aristocratic body, as political arbiter is emblematic of both claims, the
claims of traditional authority and of the explicitly political structure
of power. Before judgment is rendered, Athena speaks for the values
of both the Furies and Apollo. She has established the Areopagus as a
court for all time. Although the court (like the real Areopagus once
stripped by Ephialtes of its political powers) is to judge in cases of
homicide, Athena also speaks of it as 'a sentry on the land' (*Eum.*
705). Athena refers to the role of the Areopagus in preserving
reverence and fear, and warns the citizens against 'muddying their
own customary laws with foul infusions' (*Eum.* 690f.). She values the
role of traditional authorities in ordering the *polis*. She echoes the
Furies: 'no anarchy, no rule of a single master ... do not cast fear
utterly from the city' (*Eum.* 696f.). However, she also echoes Apollo.
She declares herself an advocate of the male principle (*Eum.* 735f.).
The political bond triumphs. But the divided vote of the Areopagites,
which vindicated the male, political principle, is ultimately no solution.

The Furies, despite their earlier willingness to let Athena and the
Areopagus judge the validity of their claim, threaten Athens with

[62] See Meier (1980) 190–1, 194–5.

deadly revenge: they will abandon their traditional role. Institutions alone, though they ground the validity of decisions, cannot serve as the foundation of political authority powerful enough to prevent factional strife and *hubris*. Even the Areopagus, guardian of the *polis*, cannot prevent fear from leaving the city, for its power is in the end political. However, the political community has other resources to draw upon. It can incorporate the values represented by tradition and nobility, the ties of blood and attachments of family, by at one and the same time disseminating and domesticating these constraints. The demands of political order are turned into personal and traditionally-sanctioned demands. The point of installing the Furies at Athens is to ensure that each citizen is constrained by fear of inevitable punishment. The order implicit in *dikē* is still sanctioned by the gods, and grounded in a universal and conscious human motivation, as men 'learn through suffering.' Conscious fear, man's spontaneous observance of the laws laid down by the gods,[63] is (here as in the Funeral Oration) expressed in civic institutions and the civil law. The Areopagus is to be the 'human guarantor' of justice, while the Furies, incorporated in the city, are to serve as its divine counterpart.[64] As the integration of the Furies and their transformation into *Eumenides* (i.e. beneficent ones) suggest, social and personal demands are also turned into political demands. Having been persuaded by Athena, who deployed her political skills, the Furies are willing to accommodate themselves to the new order.[65] Their influence is not restricted to the household or to blood relationships: they are to sanction even the ties of marriage and to watch over the whole range of relations within the community.

Aeschylus' explorations of political questions and possible answers are figurative, indirect and allusive; they constitute neither an analysis nor an argument. But they are guided by the question which haunted the creation of democracy at Athens: in what sense does the democratically-determined policy and the political character of the community express the values of all its citizens? As Aeschylus' plays indicate, this concern had two related aspects: (1) how do political determinations correspond to the individual citizen's sense of what he ought to do *qua* man rather than *qua* citizen and (2) if all it is to act *qua* citizen is to contribute one's own, unmediated, untutored beliefs and desires to a collective determination of policy, then why think that

---

[63] Macleod (1982) 136, cf. 144. See Dodds (1951) 40 on the alleged 'primitivism' of the Aeschylean portrayal of the gods.

[64] Macleod (1982) 136.   [65] See Meier (1980) 195–9.

the result will be orderly, prudent or just? *The Suppliants* and the *Oresteia* evoke, respectively, (1) a conception of the democratic *polis* as enabling the free expression and determination of common aims and values, thereby combining unity with respect for the autonomy of the citizens and (2) the belief that if the exercise of autonomy is indeed to produce unity and harmony, then it must be tempered by respect for socially-imbedded, traditional, behavioral norms. In these plays the realm of the political is portrayed as, on the one hand, the exercise of power through collective self-expression and, on the other, as the achievement of order through collective self-restraint.

Cosmic autonomy

As the conception of order and autonomy shifted from acquiescence in divine determinations to active participation in an order mediated even in its divine aspect by civic institutions, tyrants and irresponsible aristocracies were replaced by the communal law-governed interaction of elite and *demos* characteristic of the developed *polis*, particularly in its democratic form.[66] These two transformations were matched by a third, in the realm of cosmology, which gradually leached divinity from the cosmos. In all three realms, order ceased to be construed as something imposed on the world or as something built up from ordered or qualified constituents: in the *polis*, for example, the political order was no longer interpreted as the consequence of the character of individual aristocrats or a social hierarchy, nor even straightforwardly as the sum of individual perceptions of the good. The conceptual difficulty raised in its most extreme form by democracy – namely, that the political order is abstract, founded on a formal construal of the citizen, and yet organized as a collective expression of the character, aims and perceptions of individuals (e.g. the assembly as a whole is powerful though its members, as individuals, are not) – has a parallel at the level of the cosmos. Viewed from the perspective of the philosophers, the gods were alien and remote from human experience. Divinity existed, but it was 'not at all like mortals in body or in mind' (Xenophanes, DK 21 B 23). Philosophical scrutiny of the

---

[66] Many of the pre-Socratic philosophers who mused about the universe were not citizens of advanced democracies. They were, however, exposed to the emergence of law-governed political communities; the most challenging questions about reconciling autonomy and order, however, were raised by the democratic experience and for the most part addressed by citizens or residents of Athens (e.g. Anaxagoras, who was a friend and adviser to Pericles).

cosmos transformed 'deity conceived as the supreme patriarch of a quasi-human family' into 'the ruling principle of an orderly universe,'[67] and thereby opened a chasm between man's experience of the social and physical world and his ability to understand the character and sources of order, unity and stability. In a world created and ruled by man-like gods, such order as existed came about through humanly intelligible motivations and actions. In a cosmos ruled by a systematic divine principle, order and unity were either read into the experience of change and conflict – by characterizing the principle itself in terms analogous to those which defined man's actual perceptions of the world around him, as in Heraclitus' formulations – or they simply *were* the cosmos, the stable and ordered reality underlying apparent multiplicity, as in the cosmologies of Parmenides and Empedocles.

Heraclitus, writing at the end of the sixth century B.C., 'naturalized' justice by moralizing nature, which was itself divine:[68] 'This ordered universe (*kosmos*) which is the same for all, was not created by any one of the gods or of mankind, but it was ever and is and shall be ever-living Fire, kindled in measure and quenched in measure' (DK 22 B 30). Although divinity no longer resembled man, the divine principle in Heraclitus' system remained the principle of human existence. Heraclitus' cosmos was 'the same for all' (B 2) and at least in theory, knowledge of the ruling principle of order was available to all men.[69] The extant fragments, difficult as they are to interpret, do reveal that, unlike Anaximander before him and Parmenides and Empedocles after him, all of whom merely used political concepts to describe the structure of the world, Heraclitus attempted a genuine synthesis, a truly universal basis for cosmic and political order.[70] Heraclitus adopted from the Milesians the idea of a single world structure and a single ruling principle which unifies the world physically and governs it.[71] However, the 'principle' of Heraclitus' thoroughgoing monism is not 'matter,' but a 'process of transition from one state to another ... the very element of paradox': fire, associated with both life and death.[72] No doubt part of the reason Heraclitus chose fire, transition, paradox, conflict, as the essence of universal order is because they are characteristic of the world men actually experience. In any case, it is relatively clear that Heraclitus hoped to combine a characterization of the uni-

[67] Kahn (1979) 11; cf. Vlastos (1970).
[68] For this way of describing his project, see Vlastos (1970).
[69] But see B 1–7, B 19 and Kahn (1979) 99.
[70] See, e.g., B 114; cf. Kahn (1979) 14–15, 181ff.
[71] See Vlastos (1970) and (1975) 6f.   [72] Kahn (1979) 138.

verse as a cosmos[73] – ordered, divine, and intelligent – with the claim
that appearances are reliable evidence for the cosmic pattern[74] *and*
that this pattern underlies, and unifies, the psychic, social and cosmic
aspects of existence.

Precisely because he is so committed to all three aims his account is
incoherent. The realms which Heraclitus attempts, by the use of
analogy and the resonant repetition of key words, to weld together,
are in fact radically separated by his own assumptions. Heraclitus
observed that contrast, opposition and conflict are the salient and
defining features of human experience. Conflict is also (therefore?) the
basis of cosmic order. The cosmos is, by definition, ordered; some
sense must be made out of strife if it is to serve as the stable, divine, ordering principle of the universe. This can be achieved by a shift in perspective, literally, by coming to *see* conflict with an informed (not a
barbaric, *barbaros*) mind (B 107). The wise man, who listens to (and
understands) the defining reason (*logos*) 'agrees that all things are one'
(B 50). Only the cosmic view can transform conflict into unity. The
cosmic view is, therefore, wisdom. But wisdom has nothing to offer
the *polis* except perspective. At the political level, conflict is a problem
for unity, a problem which is in no way resolved by the recognition (or
re-vision) that variance is also agreement.

Parmenides of Elea (whose school of thought was therefore dubbed
'Eleatic') adopted a different approach to the understanding of cosmic
order and unity. According to Parmenides, who lived in the first half
of the fifth century, man inhabited a world of illusion (DK 28 B 8).
Greek musings about how to reconcile being, becoming and ceasing to
be led to the Eleatic extreme:[75] truth had a 'motionless heart' (B 8, 26–
8). The choice, it seemed, was between a cosmos which resembled the
world men experience but whose unity and stability existed only at the
cosmic level, and one which was stable and unified but in every respect
alien to human life, a world without change. Parmenides' theory
reflects both (1) arrogant faith in the power of reason[76] and (2) rejection of the world men actually experience. Parmenides did not believe
that 'nothing existed except thought.' He seems to have had a conception of language and thought as 'having a content only because they

---

[73] See Kahn (1979) 219f.   [74] See B 55.

[75] For a general account of Parmenides and Zeno and the implications of their ideas, see
Hussey (1972) chs. 5–7.

[76] See Williams (1981a) 219, a subtle account of Parmenides' ideas and their implications,
to which I am indebted. Parmenides sets out 'to determine the basic nature of reality entirely by argument from premises self-evident to reflection.'

touch or are in contact with what is.'[77] Language guides our inferences about what is or is not. Yet men in general are radically confused in their use of language and in their perceptions of reality. What men perceive through their senses are delusions. Men perceive change, and coming-to-be out of not-being; their opinions, too, differ and change, and are, therefore, as unreal as the perceptions they describe.[78]

After Parmenides, various thinkers attempted to save the phenomena while preserving reasoned access to the character of the cosmos. They tried to establish a causal, not merely an analogical, connection between cosmic categories and human ones.[79] They struggled to explain continuity and change, unity and multiplicity, the original emergence of the cosmos and its apparently ordered stability. Anaxagoras, a fifth-century natural philosopher and friend of Pericles, invoked a cosmic mind (*nous*) to initiate motion and impose order (DK 59 A 45, 58 B 12). *nous* exhibited the characteristics of divinity: omniscience, omnipotence and infinity, but divinity cleansed of non-rational impurities (B 12). This (material?)[80] creator and choreographer of the stuff of the universe was evidently (witness its name) conceived as a force in which intelligent beings participate. But just *how* minds participate in *nous* is obscure.[81] All-powerful *nous*, source of motion and (presumably) order in inert matter and animate nature alike, coexists with an explanation of cosmic behavior in terms of mechanical causation (B 12; cf. B 13, A 58, A 47). Anaxagorean explanations tend to be mechanical and naturalistic: men are clever because they have hands, not (as Aristotle protested) the other way round (A 102).[82] *nous* determines everything; this cosmic determination is analyzed in terms of natural causes. Thus *nous* is responsible for the initial movement and ultimate order of the cosmos, but that order is

[77] Williams (1981a) 220, 223ff.

[78] Parmenides does not account for his own capacity to see things as they really are except as a mysterious revelation from the goddess *Dikē*. See Hussey (1972) 79–81. Note that Parmenides (through the mouth of the goddess) also offers a 'plausible' cosmology, thereby acknowledging that even the delusory world accessible to the senses is in some way (but not rationally) ordered. See Hussey (1972) 97–9. Thus even the order that men purport to find in experience is utterly meaningless. Appearance and reality, reason and the senses, are mutually exclusive.

[79] See, e.g., Empedocles DK 31 B 9, 23, 26, 35; Anaxagoras DK 59 B 4; Archelaus DK 60 A 1, 4. Cf. Hussey (1972) ch. 7. For uses of political language in Greek cosmology see Vlastos (1970).

[80] See Barnes (1979) 104.   [81] See Barnes (1979) 104ff., Hussey (1972) 138ff.

[82] See also Plutarch's anecdote about Anaxagoras' explanation of the single-horned ram = DK A 16. Cf. Barnes (1979) 114.

caused by natural interaction. The behavior of the minds which share in *nous*, and whose power and autonomy the connection is meant to suggest is also, presumably, to be described in terms of natural causation.

While most phenomena are merely ordered by *nous*, it exercises direct control over all animate beings:[83] '*nous* controls all the things that have soul' (B 12, cf. B 11). The cosmogonical *nous* is conceived as an enlarged version of a human mind: it 'wants' to separate out the kinds (A 45).[84] The control of *nous* over beings with souls is not regarded as an infringement of the autonomy of ensouled beings, but rather accounts for this autonomy.[85] This is so because *nous* exercises its control through minds; an external cause is also an internal one. Anaxagoras' cosmology is a rationalized version of the doubleness of divine causation and/or a cosmic replica of the doubleness of political causation.[86] Just as the substitution of mind for man-like deities in cosmology enables Anaxagoras to explain the patterned, orderly world as humanly intelligible[87] and as founded on regular interaction undisturbed by irruptions of irrationality,[88] so, too, in the realm of human behavior it enables him to portray actions as simultaneously part of a pattern and genuinely controlled from within. To echo the last line of Sophocles' *Trachiniae* about the pervasiveness of divine order, with the appropriate substitution, 'there is nothing here which is not *nous*.' Anaxagoras' universalization of mind reflects the contemporary desire, in banishing man-like deities and an irrational universe, to affirm natural causality,[89] cosmic order and man's status as a cause.

Yet Anaxagoras' attempt to unite the universe as *nous* relies on an ambiguous portrayal of the human mind's participation in the transcendent order of the cosmos. Man's mind is evidently meant to share

---

[83] See Barnes (1979) 116 on the distinction between ordering (*diakosmein*) and ruling (*kratein*).

[84] See Barnes (1979) 115.

[85] See Sedley (1983) 14, comparing Anaxagoras with Epicurus, who admired Anaxagorean theory. See DK 59 A 58.

[86] The gods often abstain from personal intervention and manipulate man's fate from within. See Vlastos (1975) 12ff., Vernant (1981). *Atē* is often mentioned in this connection; the gods, as Athenian tragedy suggests, often work through the ordinary desires of men, without causing *madness*. See, e.g., Soph. *Trachiniae*, e.g., 860f. with Winnington-Ingram (1980) 86f., *Antigone*, 62–4.

[87] See Hussey (1972) 134; cf. Heraclitus' account of the universe as 'fire.'

[88] See Vlastos (1975) 19f.

[89] On natural necessity as the replacement for Zeus, see Ar. *Clouds* 377, 405, 1075 and Eur. *Trojan Women* 886f.

in *nous*, and this connection is intended to make order immanent while ensuring that it is in fact order. Yet *nous* remains in a sense external; it initiates cosmic motion and imposes cosmic order. Its capacity to do these things rests on qualities which set it apart from mind in man (B 12). Unlike *nous*, the human mind is not omniscient or unerring,[90] nor is it 'by itself' but is 'obstructed' by embodiment. Thus a theory which aimed to make room for natural necessity and the human mind in a moving and ordered cosmos must, because of its reliance on a primordial mover and shaper, remove the source of order and control from the world as men experience it. The participation of mind in *nous* means indifference to the world of action and sensation.[91] Aristotle reports that Anaxagoras 'said that he would not be surprised if the happy man were to seem to most people a strange person; for they judge by externals, since these are all they perceive' (A 30). Aristotle elsewhere adds that according to Anaxagoras it was the possibility of contemplating the cosmos that made life worthwhile (A 30).

It was under the influence both of the philosophical issues raised by speculation about the cosmos, and of the conceptual and practical issues posed by the structure of the democratic *polis*, that Protagoras, Thucydides and Democritus formulated their political theories. They offered mankind access to reality, order and stability through the medium of experience of a changing and heterogeneous world. The inquiries pursued by these three thinkers were prompted and marked by the belief that such order as there is in the world is not transcendent, but immanent. Knowledge is knowledge of the order implicit in interaction or of the elements making for constancy and stability in change. All three theories locate the meaning and the evaluative standards of human experience in a relationship, a constant interaction between man and his world. Man is simultaneously the source of change and of order. The analyses of man and the *polis* and the interaction between the two are interpretations of the world which at once appeal to and focus man's experience. Different as they are in significant respects, all three theories are construals of man's nature and the nature of the world he inhabits which attempt to show that and how political order is achieved through democratic interaction, and that this order is genuinely an expression of what man himself takes to be his autonomy and his interests.

---

[90] See Hussey (1972) 140.   [91] See Hussey (1972) 140.

3   Protagoras: measuring man

From the perspective of a modern scholar, the sophist Protagoras resembles the world postulated by his infamous doctrine that man is the measure of all things: he himself is a collocation of appearances.[1] The problem is not merely that Protagoras' appearances are mediated by observers whose perceptions are indirect or, as it seems to us, sharply angled, but also that these appearances are disjointed. Should we link the Platonic bits of Protagoras in the way that Plato has done? Do we have any choice? Despite his fragmentary persona, Protagoras has long been identified as a political thinker. The fragments from sources other than Plato hint at the existence of intellectual projects rather different from those of Plato – and indeed from those implicitly attributed to the Sophist in the Platonic dialogues. There is good reason to believe that although Protagoras is made to answer Platonic questions, nevertheless the answers (especially the Great Speech in the *Protagoras*, probably written in the 390s or 380s, and the Defense of Protagoras in the *Theaetetus*, a dialogue written in the same period as the *Republic*, in the 360s or so) contain material which does not correspond to the issue under discussion, but rather to earlier and differently-conceived political concerns. To reassemble the historical Protagoras it is necessary to restore him to the proper context, namely Athens during the years when radical democracy developed and was consolidated. Whether his date of birth is fixed at 490 or closer to 480,[2] Protagoras is unmistakably part of the 'older generation' of

[1] Protagoras and his doctrines appear in the following texts: Diogenes Laertius 9.50; Sextus Empiricus, *Adv. math.* 9.55–6, 7.389, 7.60; *Pyrr.* 1.216; Arist. *Met.* 3, 1046b29, 997b32, 1007b18, 1062b13, *Rhet.* 1402a23, 1407b6, *SE* 173b17, *Poet.* 1456b15; Plato, *Protagoras, passim,* and *Theaetetus* 152–83, but also *Meno* 91d–e, *H. Maj.* 282d–e, *Cratylus* 266d–267c, *Euthydemus* 286b–c, *Phaedrus* 266dff.; *Sophist* 23d–e. See the more extensive collection compiled by DK.

[2] According to Apollodorus (DK A 1), Protagoras' *acme* occurred in the 84th Olympiad. It seems likely that he has simply identified the most significant event of Protagoras' mature years (his role as lawgiver for Thurii, 444/3) as his *acme*. Protagoras may have been in his late 40s when he served as lawgiver: in Plato's *Protagoras*, Protagoras asserts that he is old enough to be the father of any person there (317c); the assemblage included Hippias, Pro-

fifth-century thinkers, a contemporary of Herodotus, Aeschylus and Sophocles. Certain features of the dialogue *Protagoras* suggest that the Sophist was resident and professionally active in Athens – though not necessarily continuously – in the 460s and 450s.[3] His ethical and political teachings – whether or not published as independent works[4] – were evidently influential enough to secure him the commission to draft laws for the Panhellenic colony of Thurii in 443.[5] It is primarily to the two previous decades that we should look in specifying the relevant political context for his ideas.

The claim that a community's standards and decisions are legitimate because they are the standards believed in and the decisions made by the community was characteristic of Protagoras' time.[6] Herodotus, apparently provoked only to reflection, not defensiveness

dicus and Socrates, who was born in 469. An approximate *terminus a quo* is established by the evidence of Eupolis that Protagoras was alive and in Athens in 421 (*Kolakes*, cited in DK A 11) combined with the tradition that he died when he was about seventy (Plato, *Meno* 91d–e). Thus Protagoras was born at Abdera not before 490 or so, though probably not long thereafter, and in any case not later than 484 (15 years before Socrates). See the discussions of Protagoras' life by von Fritz (1957), Davison (1949) and (1953), and Morrison (1941).

3 Already in antiquity doubts were raised about the historical accuracy of the setting of Plato's *Protagoras* (DK A 11). Modern discussions have led to the conclusion that, despite an anachronistic reference to the *Agrioi* of Pherecrates, the dramatic date of the dialogue is *c.* 433 B.C. See Davison (1953) 34–5. Hippocrates' comment that he was 'still a child when Protagoras was here before' (*Prot.* 319c5) suggests that Protagoras ended his previous sojourn in Athens at least five years before the dramatic date of the *Protagoras*; the establishment of the colony at Thurii in 444/3 provides a reason for his departure. See Morrison (1941) 4–5; cf. Davison (1953) 27, Kerferd (1981) 42–3. We have no reason to think that Protagoras' previous visit to Athens was brief (*pace* Davison (1953) 37), and some reason to believe that he had spent a considerable amount of time in the city. (Note that the word Hippocrates uses in referring to the last time Protagoras was in Athens is *epidemeo*, which means 'to come to stay, to reside.') In the *Meno* (91e) Socrates remarks that 'for more than forty years *all Greece* failed to notice that Protagoras was corrupting his associates...' However, since Protagoras was in 443 known to and respected by Athenian leaders, and imperial Athens was the most powerful magnetic Greek *polis*, it is reasonable to assume that Protagoras was in Athens for much of the 450s. *Re* the hypothesis (Davison (1949)) that Protagoras was twice forced to leave Athens, see Plato, *Meno* 89e; and on the general issue of his alleged 'trial,' see Dover (1975) esp. 31–2, 34–7, 47, Derenne (1930) 48f.

4 See von Fritz (1957) 919–20, Guthrie (1969) 264. We are told (DK A 1) that his treatise *On the Gods* was the first of his works that he read publicly at Athens. Among the titles preserved by Diogenes Laertius are *Concerning the Ancient Condition (peri tēs en archēi katastaseōs)* and *Concerning the Political Order (peri politeias)* (D.L. 9.55); note also a fragment about education (DK 83) and the allegation that Plato's *Republic* was largely copied from Protagoras' opposing arguments (*Antilogikoi*) (D.L. 3.37). See Winton (1974) 1–3.

5 See the recent discussion by Muir (1982). However, as has been pointed out to me by K. J. Dover, the testimony of Heraclides Ponticus cannot be regarded as firm evidence.

6 See Heinimann (1945) 61f., Cole (1972) 42, Kahn (1981) 106, Dihle (1981) 59f.

or doubt, by the subversive implications of Parmenidean reasoning or indeed of his own researches into the diversity of human customs, cites Pindar's dictum that '*Nomos* is king' (3.38): 'Everyone without exception believes his own customs . . . to be the best.' Herodotus also expresses the view, though he does not always observe it in practice,[7] that only personal experience is a secure basis for knowledge. Having recounted the various extant stories about how East and West first came into conflict, he remarks:

So much for what Persians and Phoenicians say; and I have no intention of saying about these matters that they happened in this or some other way. I prefer to rely on my own knowledge, and to point out who it was in actual fact who first injured the Greeks. (Hdt. 1.5)[8]

For Protagoras, the weakness of Parmenides' theory was its dismissal of human beliefs. His own ideas are a response to Parmenides, and he is therefore less innocent than Herodotus in his assessment of the status of *nomoi*, but he nevertheless shares the historian's belief in the power and tenacity of communal standards (indeed, as I shall suggest, such considerations, particularly in their political aspect, may in part account for his having recoiled from Parmenides' logic). Moreover, while later thinkers were impressed by the relativistic implications of cultural development and divergence, Protagoras, like Herodotus and Aeschylus, stressed the fact that men share certain fundamental qualities. This assumption underlies Herodotus' tales of bizarre and improbable behavior: not only do all men value their own customs above all others, but all worship gods (indeed, Herodotus often interprets foreign gods as 'versions' of Greek ones). In Aeschylus' plays, this emphasis is more explicit: in *The Suppliants*, reverence and respect for others are portrayed as basic standards which transcend differences between cultures. And in *The Eumenides*, Apollo bases the need for obedience to political authority on the fact that men, unlike the gods, are mortal, and acts of violence cannot be made good (1644f.).

Both the variety of belief and the existence of basic human qualities and needs find their place in Protagorean theory. In the face of both philosophical and political contempt for what men think they know, Protagoras attempted to rehabilitate practical reason founded on experience, to give legitimacy to human beliefs (*ta nomizomena*). This first aspect of Protagorean theory is expressive of man's autonomy

---

[7] Fornara (1983) 7.
[8] Translation adapted from Fornara (1983) and Sélincourt.

and his pursuit of what he himself takes to be his interests, and of the possibility of achieving order through interaction. A second aspect confirms this possibility: the Protagoras lurking in the *Theaetetus* suggests that wisdom (*sophia*) plays an important role in guiding the operation of practical reason, and in the *Protagoras* the sophist's analysis of the *polis* both explains and instantiates this. Construed together, and in context, the two Platonic portrayals and the independently-attested fragments provide a coherent picture of Protagorean theory which brings together two realms, cosmos and community. Order in these realms is to be understood not as transcendent, but as built up through interaction, and stability and regularity are to be seen as implicit in the world of change, the world of experience. Protagoras formulated a view of human knowledge which located the development of beliefs in the interaction of persons as they experience themselves in the world – and a view of human needs which suggested that all men must and can display civic qualities.

Man is the measure

Measuring Protagorean reflections

In the shadow of Parmenides' radical theory, Protagoras fashioned a set of beliefs which would allow what the Eleatic Parmenides, against all the urgings of common sense, had rejected: the validity of appearance, opinions and change.[9] That Protagoras' doctrines were a deliberate response to the rigors of Eleatic logic, and not merely influenced by Eleatic method, is suggested by the titles of two Protagorean works: *On Being* and *Truth*. The latter began with the assertion that 'man is the measure of all things . . .'[10] Some scholars have interpreted man–measure as 'a seriously intended contribution to a serious philosophical problem,' even 'the keystone of a systematic and sophisticated epistemology.'[11] Others have regarded it as a largely negative response to the outrageous conclusions reached by Parmenides, perhaps even a response shaped by political and rhetorical rather than metaphysical concerns.[12] I shall suggest that the first in-

---

[9] See von Fritz (1946) 22, Vlastos (1956) xii, Williams (1981a) 225.

[10] DK 80 B 2: Porphyry reports that in his work *On Being*, Protagoras criticized the notion that being is one. DK B 1: Plato, *Theaetetus* 151e–152a; Sextus (*Adv. math.* 7.60) refers to the work containing the man–measure doctrine as *The Downthrowers*, probably a later title based on the character of the arguments.

[11] The former is Kerferd (1981) 93, the latter Barnes (1979) 243.

[12] E.g. Maguire (1973) 127, who cites H. Maier, *Sokrates*, 207–19; see Hussey (1972) 109, 116, and Winton (1974).

terpretation may well be true (though I shall not argue this in detail
here), but that the considerations which have led to the second interpretation are compatible with and should be incorporated into this
view. Protagoras did not conceive of himself as a contributor to natural philosophy.[13] His claim that man is the measure of all things was
not designed to counter Parmenidean logic about the true character of
the cosmos. Rather, Protagoras rebelled against Parmenides' conclusions, but in a way that acknowledged the power which Parmenides' reasoning exerted over contemporary philosophers. Protagoras
did not assert that what is real is changing. He did not maintain that
what people actually think constitutes reality. Protagoras did not seek
to provide a cosmology, an alternative to the Eleatic view of the world
as it is in itself. However, his views are not merely negative. He did, it
seems, wish to argue that a theory of knowledge must at least begin
from what we ourselves can know. Protagoras' response to Parmenides' radical dissociation of truth and reality from appearances
was to repudiate his vision of man's access to knowledge. The fragmentary remains of Protagorean theory suggest that Protagoras did
not challenge Parmenides' dichotomy between what is unified, stable
and unchanging and what men experience, but rejected the Eleatic's
belief in privileged insight. According to Parmenides, man (or at least
Parmenides) was capable of deep and accurate insight into the nature
of being, but in general exhibited seriously defective judgment about
such matters. Protagoras challenged both claims; no man has privileged insight into such matters, and what someone is capable of judging is the only insight available.[14] We may never know what the
cosmos is like; the reality to which we do have access is our personal
experience. This is suggested by the emphasis of Protagoras' formulation: *man* is the measure and the measure of *all* things. In his treatise
On what is, Protagoras reportedly argued against those who depict
being as one (DK 80 B 2). His main target is likely to have been Parmenides, his main aim to show that what there is cannot be divorced
from what there seems to be, as in Parmenides' postulation of a unitary, unchanging world of true being as opposed to the realm of il-
lusory appearance. The point was not to argue for a different account
of the world as it is in itself, e.g., that what is real is a plurality,[15] but to
claim that truth and knowledge are grounded in human experience,
and relative to human concerns.

[13] See *Prot.* 318e, where Protagoras distinguishes himself from other Sophists.
[14] See Maguire (1973) 136–7, with n. 41 and refs.
[15] As Kerferd (1981) 92 infers.

It is not possible, on available evidence, to establish with certainty the meaning or orientation of Protagorean theory. However, I shall seek to indicate that the man–measure theory is unlikely to have postulated subjectivism (all appearances exist) as later commentators supposed,[16] or a relativism (what appears to you is true for you) which posits the existence of private worlds of incorrigible experience, as the Platonic construal presumes.[17] Before I proceed to defend this interpretation, I shall simply set out what I take Protagoras to have meant. According to Protagoras, 'Man is the measure (*metron*) of all things: of those which are, that they are, and of those which are not, that they are not' (Plato, *Tht.* 152a3–8). What man measures is not, as the literal translation inevitably implies, merely existence or nonexistence, but rather the *way* things are: of the things that are *f*, he measures *that* they are *f*.[18] 'Things' are not limited to objects in the world but also include what happens or is the case. Relatedly, measuring is not limited to perceiving an object or feature of the world but includes the rendering of judgments. For Protagoras, man the measurer is both what we would call a 'sensing' and a 'judging' being, and his standard is his own – but not merely his immediate – experience.[19] The man–measure doctrine makes a claim about all men; but it does not claim that the measure is the species man, except in so far as such a unified view could emerge from the experience of individual men. Yet simply summing together each man's private sensations will not exhaust or indeed capture the character of the world men experience. The reality to which we do have access must be conceived in terms which explain what appears to every man and to all men. It does not follow from this that reality is flux, or that the world possesses contradictory qualities in itself. Man's interaction with the world defines the only reality we can know, and this interaction is broadly stable as well as locally variable.[20] All the scraps of Protagorean

---

[16] See Burnyeat (1976a) and Kerferd (1981) 107, who terms this view objectivism.

[17] On the character of the Platonic construal, I follow Burnyeat (1976b); *contra* see Kerferd (1981) 106–8.

[18] So Kerferd (1981) 86, Barnes (1979) 242, McDowell (1973) 118. For the interpretation of other terms, e.g. *anthropos, hōs, chremata*, I agree with, e.g., McDowell (1973) 118–19, cf. Mansfeld (1981) 43.

[19] McDowell (1973) 118–20, Mansfeld (1981) 43–4; cf. Kerferd (1981) 108f.

[20] An account of Protagoras' theory in the writings of Sextus Empiricus is formulated – under the influence of Plato and Aristotle – in subjectivist terms which Protagoras himself did not exploit (*contra* Kerferd (1981) 107–8), yet it may preserve some characteristic features of his argument: 'He says that the *logoi* of all the appearances subsist in matter, so that matter, so far as it depends on itself, is able to be all those things which appear to all. And men, he says, apprehend different things at different times owing to their differing

theory that remain to us suggest that the Sophist opposed theories or approaches to understanding not grounded in personal experience. His own theory, although it includes reflective statements about the grounds of belief, did not fall foul of this stricture. For man–measure is open to confirmation by personal experience, and as a statement about the necessity of appealing to personal experience, it would be regarded as self-validating. For experience of the world leads, at any rate readily and naturally, to the conclusion that the only way of resolving questions about what is the case, if indeed they are resolvable at all, is through analysis and comparison of the experiences of individuals. If the title of the work in which Protagoras sets out his doctrine, i.e. *aletheia, Truth*, indicates a desire to respond directly to the teachings of the Eleatics, and to offer his own theory of truth, the name later given to it, *The Downthrowers*, suggests that his response (which included the man–measure theory) was to cast the truth down to earth, down to *man*.

Three Protagorean fragments confirm his agnosticism about the nature of the world as it is in itself and his attempt to ground knowledge in human experience. The agnostic fragment *par excellence* is, of course, Protagoras' comment on the possibility of knowledge about the gods (DK B 4), a fragment said (by Eusebius) to derive from a treatise *On the Gods*. However, it seems likely that this 'title' has been culled from the first words of the statement and that the treatise was not about divinity, but about knowledge. In Plato's *Theaetetus*, 'Protagoras' (or, as I shall call him, Platagoras) is made to protest Socrates' references to the gods, 'whom I exclude from my speaking and writing, not discussing whether there are any or not . . .' (162e1–3).[21] The reasons Protagoras gives for his inability to speak knowledgeably about the gods are the obscurity of the subject and the brevity of human existence.[22] This peculiar argument can readily be seen as

dispositions; for he who is in a natural state apprehends those things subsisting in matter which are able to appear to those in a natural state, and those who are in a non-natural state apprehend the things which can appear to those in a non-natural state . . . Thus, according to him, man becomes the criterion of things that are; for all things that appear to man also are, and things that appear to no man, also are without being' (DK 80 A 14). Translation by Kerferd (1981) 107–8. Note the conflict between the last sentence and the late, subjectivist characterization of *logoi* as 'subsisting in matter.' See Vlastos (1956) xiii n. 26a. Man is the measure in two complementary senses: ontology is answerable to the experience of individual men, and human experience is sufficiently stable and regular to provide an objective standard.

[21] The statement as reported is the first half of a *men/de* sequence: *peri men theōn . . . peri de . . . anthropōn?* Barnes (1979) 148. Cf. Mansfeld (1981) 43.

[22] See Mansfeld (1981) 39ff. The Greek term for obscurity is *adelotēs*; cf. the 'new' Protagorean fragment, discussed below, and Anaxagoras' statement that the phenomena provide a glimpse of what is *adelōn*, DK B 21a.

exemplifying a general claim about the possibility of knowledge: 'The only criterion which would enable (Protagoras) to accept that there are gods would consist in a clear and distinct *personal experience*.'[23] Gods (if they exist) are such – and men are such – that Protagoras has not and does not expect to experience the gods. Protagoras does not conclude from this that the gods do not exist (even 'for himself'). There is no 'insight' which could enable him to infer anything about their existence or nature (except their obscurity) in the absence of personal experience. Unlike Xenophanes, the sixth-century poet and critic of the vision of the gods offered in Homer and Hesiod (DK 21 B 34), Protagoras did not believe that there was any point in speaking of the *truth* about things which man could not know for himself.[24] The contrast between Protagoras and his Parmenidean contemporary, Empedocles, brings out the peculiarities of the Protagorean view even more clearly.[25] What men in general think they know, according to Empedocles, is entirely the product of 'that upon which as individuals they chance to hit as they wander in all directions . . .' (DK 31 B 2). By this means they can never attain knowledge of 'the whole.' But such knowledge is attainable through *nous*, which is capable of understanding a revelation from the gods (DK B 17, 21–6). Protagoras, by contrast, believes that precisely because individuals cannot 'hit upon' the 'whole,' there is nothing to be said about such cosmic 'truths.'[26] Man is the measure, and the gods are silent.

Protagoras' statement about his own ability to know the gods reflects a critical attitude to belief within the framework of the man–measure doctrine. That is, if he were to believe (or disbelieve) in the gods in the absence of any personal experience of them, his belief would be defective. Similarly, he can argue that the beliefs of others are defective; he appeals to what they can and do know, what they have experienced or are capable of experiencing, and invites them to

---

[23] Mansfeld (1981) 42, cf. 40. Note his references to Socrates' comments which allude to this argument: Xen. *Mem.* 4.3.13, Plato, *Crat.* 384b.

[24] Mansfeld (1981) 39–40. Cf. Williams (1981a) 235–6, Fränkel (1974). Xenophanes is probably drawing on the traditional distinction between what one can establish first hand and by inference.

[25] Mansfeld (1981) 41. Note also his discussion of Heraclitus, who believed that individual experience can be transcended.

[26] See Williams (1981a) 235ff. on the ancient treatment of the problem of certainty. If Williams is right that 'to Greek thought the distinction between appearance and reality was so basic, and knowledge so associated with reality, that knowledge which was merely of subjective appearances perhaps did not count as genuine knowledge at all,' then it is understandable that Protagoras' attempt to restrict knowledge to what individuals can themselves be certain of was interpreted as skepticism or (as by Plato – see below, pp. 56–71) assimilated to a theory about the nature of 'the world as it is in itself.'

criticize their own beliefs.[27] Thus he is said to have contradicted those
skilled in arts and crafts (DK B 8),[28] and Aristotle has preserved a
glimpse of a Protagorean attack on the mathematicians (DK B 7). This
is the second relevant fragment: 'For no perceptible thing is straight or
curved in the way in which (the geometer) defines "straight" or
"curved"; for a hoop touches a straight edge not at a point, but as Protagoras said it did, in his refutation of the geometers.' Protagoras
bases his argument against the geometers on what he (and others?)
have gleaned from personal experience.[29] In contrast to the issue of
the existence of gods, questions of geometry are susceptible of consideration in terms of personal experience. Protagoras' criticism is
based not on an impossibility for him, and perhaps for others as well,
of mathematical claims, but rather on the fact that these non-
empirical claims conflict with what, on the basis of personal experience, he thinks he does know. Protagoras might have said about this,
as he was unable to say about the gods, '*that* view is not true,' or
better, '*this* view is the stronger argument (*logos*), because it is consistent with what I can know.'[30] If, however, he were persuaded by
another argument to interpret his experience differently or were to
add to his experience in significant ways, he could come to regard his
previous belief as defective.

The third fragment which provides a glimpse of Protagoras'
attempt to ground justified belief in, and restrict it to, personal experience is the so-called 'new' fragment, preserved by the first-century B.C.
scholar, Didymus the Blind.[31] According to Didymus, Protagoras
said: 'To you who are present I seem to be sitting. To someone not
present I do not seem to be sitting. It is unclear whether I am sitting or
not sitting.'[32] Didymus' rendering of this fragment is a distortion,
because it is influenced by skepticism and relies on a distinction between sense-impressions and the 'real world': different people in different circumstances may take different views of whether or not I am

[27] Cf. Mansfeld (1981) 46ff.

[28] This may have been an attack on the non-empirical, theoretical arts, including medicine.
See Mansfeld (1981) 49.

[29] Mansfeld (1981) 49–50.

[30] See Mansfeld (1981) 50. According to Mansfeld, 'Personal experience is at variance with
mathematical theory, but it cannot thereby disprove this theory; the existence of gods
cannot be disproved either.' Equating these two spheres of inquiry is misleading.

[31] Psalmenkomm. T.III (Pap. T.U. Abh. 8, Bonn 1969) 380–1; for the present passage, see
Gronewald (1968) 1f. and Mejer (1972).

[32] The Greek reads: *phainomai soi tōi paronti kathemenos. tōi de aponti ou phainomai
kathemenos. adelon ei kathemai ē ou kathemai.*

sitting.[33] However, there is some fact of the matter which sense-impressions cannot establish.[34] The fragment is far more straightforwardly and appropriately read as an illustration of the significance of 'personal experience as a condition of knowledge.'[35] Ignoring the stop after the second 'sitting,' and restoring three letters likely to have been dropped mistakenly by the transcriber of *adelon* (ΑΛΛ')[36] (so that the second sentence reads: 'To someone not present I do not seem to be sitting but it is unclear whether I am sitting or not sitting') we can see that whether Protagoras is or is not sitting is only unclear or obscure – like the existence of the gods – to the person who has no direct perception or knowledge of, in this case, the fact that Protagoras is sitting. There is no good reason to deny the authenticity of the fragment;[37] indeed it makes good sense as a response to statements like that of Parmenides (DK 28 B 4 and 1) that the mind can 'behold what is not present equally with what is firmly present.'[38] A fragment from a (no doubt fictitious) dialogue between Zeno and Protagoras[39] offers a similar construal of Protagorean doctrine. Asked by Zeno whether a grain or part of a grain of wheat makes any noise when it falls, Protagoras asserts that although the fall of a measure of wheat is audible, the fall of a single grain is not. The implication is that for Protagoras there is simply nothing to be said about inaudible sounds.[40]

Platonic appearances

Protagoras' theory of truth, and its implications, are discussed at length in Plato's dialogue *Theaetetus*. Does the Protagoras of this dialogue, hereafter to be called Platagoras, bear any resemblance to the thinker whose doctrines I have sketched on the basis of the man–measure statement, independently-attested fragments, and considerations of context? The real Protagoras is, I suggest, barely visible in his Platonic counterpart. Protagoras does not appear in the dialogue; he is impersonated by Socrates in the course of a discussion of his views.

---

[33] Mansfeld (1981) 51–2. Cf. Barnes (1979) 315 n. 16.

[34] See Mejer (1972).

[35] Mansfeld (1981) 52.

[36] ΑΛΛ could easily have been absorbed into the first letters of ΑΔΗΛΟΝ. This was suggested to me by K. J. Dover. The solution offered by Mansfeld (1981) 52, namely reading the period as a comma, results in asyndeton.

[37] Cf. Kerferd (1981), Barnes (1979) 315 n. 16 with Mansfeld (1981) 51 n. 45.

[38] Mansfeld (1981) 52, with other references.

[39] Preserved by Simplicius (DK 29 A 29).

[40] Kerferd (1981) 109 interprets the passage in these terms.

Although in some instances Plato does explicitly distinguish between ideas he is foisting upon Protagoras and genuinely Protagorean claims, the dialogue as a whole is not designed to do justice to, or even capture, the original point and orientation of Protagoreanism. Plato is writing some fifty to eighty years after the appearance of Protagoras' *Truth*. Consciously or not, he manipulates the man–measure doctrine to fit his own interests. If it be objected that to say this is to impugn the integrity of a great and conscientious thinker, one need only point to the way in which Plato eventually portrayed the views of his own beloved teacher, Socrates. He is concerned to draw out implications of Socratic doctrine and pursue them in ways of which Socrates never dreamed, to conclusions he would have rejected.[41] In a similar way, Plato in the *Theaetetus* draws out what he takes to be the implications of Protagorean theory, but his concerns are no longer those which motivated Protagoras and gave his theory cogency. Protagoras was concerned to counter the Parmenidean vision of human experience as a delusion, whereas Plato was anxious to counter the view of the world derived from the Protagorean and post-Protagorean attempt to save the phenomena.

In the *Theaetetus*, Plato investigates the nature of knowledge. More specifically, he is interested in establishing the difference between knowledge and perception. To sum up rather schematically a discussion with numerous subtle twists and turns, Plato wants in the end to restrict perception to directly perceiving the objects of experience, thus excluding from the category of perception what one might be tempted to call 'perceiving' that something is the case.[42] According to Plato, perception cannot achieve truth; it is non-propositional. He wishes to show that knowledge is to be attained by the mind, independently of experience, through the knowledge of what a thing is, namely a thought about being, which perception cannot attain.[43] By contrast, Protagoras' man–measure doctrine, conceived as a challenge to Parmenides, did not distinguish the various aspects of human un-

[41] This has been well brought out by Vlastos in a number of contexts. See, e.g., his articles on Socrates' elenchus (1983a), his view of democracy (1983b) and the disavowal of knowledge (1985), and in greater detail his unpublished papers. My claim is not that Plato is dishonestly *fudging* the argument (which, as Burnyeat (1976) warns, is unlikely) but that he is construing, interpreting, and elaborating it.

[42] McDowell (1973) 118–20, with refs.

[43] See 179c with McDowell (1973) *ad loc.* See also McDowell (1973) *ad* 147b4–5, 186c7–e12. Note, however, that Plato himself is not very clear or careful about the distinction between knowing a thing, i.e. being familiar with an object, and knowing what it is; but for him the object of knowledge is different from the object of perception, e.g. a form, or the type of familiarity involved is qualitatively different. See McDowell (1973) 189, 193.

derstanding, namely perceptions and judgments, but tied them equally to experience. What man measures (like what, according to Plato, man knows) could be an object (in Protagoras' case, strictly an object of experience) and/or its character. For Protagoras it makes no sense to speak of the objects of experience as existing independently: all we can know about what is, or what is the case, is what we measure. Plato, anxious to show that knowledge has a grip on a stable reality, argues in the *Theaetetus* that a theory of truth of the Protagorean sort is incoherent because it makes claims about what exists absolutely, which make a nonsense of all interpersonal or diachronic understanding, even of the form posited by the man–measure doctrine itself and other Protagorean beliefs. However, in his attempt to show that Protagoras' theory is incoherent as a theory of truth or knowledge, i.e. as an account of the way the world is in itself, Plato reveals that genuine Protagorean doctrine, though intended as a theory of truth, was not a theory of this kind. Those facets of the doctrine which Plato identifies as incompatible with other features, namely questions of advantage, the future, and wisdom, and an undifferentiated appeal to perception and judgment, are indeed so incompatible with Protagorean doctrine as Plato construes it as to suggest that Plato has at once revealed genuine features of the Protagorean view and distorted the orientation of the theory as a whole. Protagoras was not concerned to distinguish knowledge from perception or the understanding achieved by the mind from that derived from experience.[44] Indeed, in the face of the challenge posed by Parmenides, he was concerned *not* to distinguish them. But Plato believed that any theory that aspired to be a theory of truth *must* be a theory about the world as it is in itself, apart from experience, and construed Protagorean doctrines accordingly.

Plato's attempt to pin Protagoras down to a view of what exists absolutely and to show that this view obviates the claim of the man–measure doctrine to be a valid theory of knowledge or truth takes three related forms in the *Theaetetus*: the identification of man–measure with the theory that knowledge is perception, which obscures Protagoras' emphasis on man and his capacity for judgment; the triumphant demonstration that the man–measure doctrine is self-refuting, which seems odd, given Protagoras' own habit of turning doctrines (including, evidence suggests, his own) against themselves in opposing arguments; and the distinction between judgments about advantage or the future and those about justice or the present, which attributes an account of wisdom to Protagoras while depriving him of

[44] Cf. Kerferd (1981) 109–10.

any basis for formulating one. Taken together, and particularly in view of Plato's move from one to the next in order to wrestle Protagorean theory to the ground, the three arguments reveal that Protagoras' real doctrine could not be reduced to or judged as a theory of truth and the world as Plato thought these had to be understood. It encompassed both what Plato would call strict or direct perception and the formulation of judgments. It embodied a coherent understanding of wisdom, which emerges in disguised form in the action of the *Theaetetus* which offers a defense of (in fact a subtle attack on) Protagoras. Protagoras' integrated account of knowledge as founded in personal experience is obscured but lurking in Plato's complicated efforts to prove Protagorean theory incoherent.

Measurement as perception of what is

In response to Socrates' inquiry about what knowledge is, his young interlocutor Theaetetus offers the suggestion that knowledge is perception (151e). In reply, Socrates invokes Protagoras:

> Well, it looks as though what you've said about knowledge is no ordinary theory, but the one that Protagoras, too, used to state. But he put that same point in a different way. Because he says, you remember, that man is the measure of all things: of those which are, that they are, and of those which are not, that they are not. You've read that, I take it?' 'Yes, often.' 'And he means something on these lines: everything is, for me, the way it appears to me, and is, for you, the way it appears to you.' (*Theaet.* 152a3–8)[45]

Plato assimilates Protagoras' view to Theaetetus' even though, as Plato has made Socrates acknowledge, Protagoras' view was at any rate formulated rather differently. The term translated as 'appears' can refer both to what someone perceives and to what he thinks, and Plato indicates later that the man–measure doctrine encompassed both.[46] But in his attempt to show that the doctrine, like the equation of knowledge and perception, secretes a vision of absolute reality, Plato in practice restricts 'appears' to 'is directly perceived': he discusses perceptions of temperature, and other cases of the same type (152c1–3).[47] Thus he slips easily from questions of knowledge to questions of existence. He equates Protagoras' 'appears' (*phainetai*)

---

[45] Translation of the *Theaetetus* here and in what follows from McDowell (1973). Plato's gloss on man–measure in terms of what appears to individuals is probably an accurate paraphrase of the Protagorean view, but perhaps simply a Platonic elaboration of the doctrine. Cf. *Crat.* 386a, Mansfeld (1981) 43, McDowell (1973) 119.

[46] See, e.g., 161e8–10, 167a8–b4.

[47] See McDowell (1973) 119–20.

with Theaetetus' 'perceive': 'So it looks as though things are, for each person, the way he perceives them . . . So perception is always of what is' (152c1–5). Plato is then able to move on to the views of Heraclitus about the nature of the world as it is in itself, namely that it is flux, and to associate this with both Theaetetus' claim and the man–measure theory (152d1–160e2).[48] Here as elsewhere in the dialogue's portrayal, interrogation, defense and refutation of Platagoras, Plato signals his own awareness that he is distorting the theory put forward by Protagoras in order to expose what he takes to be its true nature and consequences. Occasionally, as here, Plato indicates that he is straying from the actual teachings of Protagoras by drawing out implications which Protagoras himself did not consider and assimilating them to quite different doctrines. When he moves from knowledge = perception through man–measure to an analysis of being, not-being and becoming, Plato makes Socrates refer to Protagoras' 'secret doctrine' (152c8–10), a doctrine shared, he says, by any number of different thinkers (152e), including Homer. What follows is a Platonic argument.[49]

Plato is concerned to pave the way for what I shall call his 'absolutist' theory, which limits knowledge to knowledge of a reality totally independent of human experience. By construing man–measure as a theory about the character of objects of perception, and indicating the way the world in itself would have to be in order to account for such a theory, Plato undermines Protagoreanism *qua* theory of knowledge in the *Platonic* sense.[50] In his final sally against the definition of knowledge as perception, *after* he has refuted the claim that 'every judgment of every person is true' (179c), Socrates argues that to ascribe authoritativeness to present sensory experience is to postulate a world in which all knowledge and understanding is impossible. For if everything changes, reality will be impossible to grasp in language, since nothing will be one way or one thing rather than another (182d–183b). Moreover, if present sensory perception is all there is to knowledge, then men must forgo such notions as 'difference' and 'similarity' and all other concepts which are the result not of bumping up against objects, but of reflectively assessing, with the mind not the

---

[48] See McDowell's discussion of Plato's interest in the Parmenidean question of predication and reality in McDowell (1973) 12–8. On 'Heracliteanism' in the dialogue see 129–30. Note Heinimann (1945) 166 on the Platonic language in the characterization of Protagoras' views.

[49] For other hints of this, see 155d6–7, 10, 163a9. See McDowell (1973) 121ff., 130. Cf. 154b9.

[50] See *Theaet.* 181c–183c.

senses, what is the case (185a–186c). As he indicates by separate treatment of the claim that every individual judgment is true, and the use both of 'perceive' and 'judge' in paraphrases of man–measure, Plato was well aware that Protagoras' doctrine was not restricted to immediate sensory experience. Interpreting the doctrine in this fashion enables him to suggest that Protagoras *should* have distinguished between perception and judgment, since it is impossible for knowledge to be based on the personal experience of change, of which direct sensory perception is the purest example. There is no content to the quintessentially human capacity for understanding, no basis for interpersonal communication or criticism, unless there is something stable and independent for the mind to apprehend.

Yet Plato's distortion of Protagorean doctrine preserves the outlines of the original theory. If man–measure is assimilated to the claim that knowledge is perception, then, according to Plato, there is no basis for criticism of belief, nor even for distinctively human knowledge.[51] So Protagoras was mistaken to insist, as he did, that *man* is the measure, and to set himself up, as he did, as a teacher of others. Socrates' treatment of these difficulties is at once an argument and a parody. Socrates insists that he is not a 'bag of arguments,' and that in order to assess the Protagorean case he must 'try to get an argument from Theaetetus, not to say anything [himself]' (161b). Yet in fact he immediately proceeds to deliver an attack on Protagoras' doctrines (161c1–e4). Plato's tacit point is that if Protagoras is right, and all men are measures, then it makes no difference how one proceeds, as Socrates himself is made to say about his own 'art of midwifery,' and 'the whole business of dialectic': 'It must be (mustn't it?) a long and protracted bit of foolery to set about inspecting and testing one another's appearings and judgments, if everyone's are correct, as they are if Protagoras' *Truth* is true' (161e5–10). Thus it *also* does not matter whether Protagoras himself answers objections or someone does it on his behalf (162d3).[52] Socrates' attack on Protagoras asserts that the Sophist had no right to claim that it is *man* who is the

---

[51] See McDowell (1973) *ad* 161c, 162d.

[52] It is ironic but true that the Platonic Socrates' strictures would apply to the historical Socrates, who engaged in elenctic questioning, not dialectic, and believed the search for the truth about ethics (and he did not pursue any other truth) was a matter of investigating and analyzing men's beliefs and rendering them consistent. See the brilliant analysis of the elenchus by Vlastos (1983a); for this very reason it mattered that one person should answer, and answer according to his own real beliefs (compare Socrates' behavior toward the Sophist in the *Protagoras*). In its emphasis on the integrity of a person's set of beliefs, Protagoras' theory was far closer to Socratic practice than to the parody offered by Plato.

measure, or that he himself is wise. It thereby confirms the place of these claims in the original theory and indicates that the theory's character and orientation must have been rather different from the Platonic version.

Socrates expresses surprise that Protagoras did not begin his treatise

by saying that the measure of all things is a pig or a baboon or some other creature that has perception, still more out of the way than those. That would have been to begin what he said to us with something haughty and utterly contemptuous, proving that while we admired him like a god for his wisdom, he was actually no better in point of intelligence than a tadpole, let alone another human being. (161c3–d1)[53]

Socrates' language suggests that Protagoras, by beginning his treatise in the way Socrates says he expected, would not only have explicitly acknowledged that all perception, human, divine and reptilian, is equally veridical, but by doing so would have demonstrated that he *was* no smarter than a tadpole, for such a claim would have been a blatant (haughty, contemptuous) admission of the theory's implausibility. As it was, Protagoras began his treatise with the claim that *man* is the measure, which was not, or at least not blatantly, implausible. In doing so, he was appealing to distinctively human capacities, and certainly not assimilating human judgment to that of beasts or gods. When Socrates asks Theaetetus if he had realized he was every bit as wise as the gods, he adds 'or do you think the Protagorean measure isn't meant to be applied to gods as much as to man?' (162c5). Protagoras is not interested in what gods think; indeed, as Socrates had Platagoras say, he was not even prepared to say whether there are such beings or not (162e1). He defined knowledge in terms of what man, not any perceiver whatever, thought over time, as a person who both perceived and judged. Again, Platonic parody is revealing. Platagoras accuses Socrates of 'making debating-points' by referring to the gods and animals (162d5–e4). But Socrates has just explained to Theaetetus that it is because he is convinced by debating-points that he is confused about what he thinks. Platagoras' admonition is, therefore, both Socrates' reproach to himself for arguing in this manner (i.e. for having briefly abandoned dialectic) and a portrayal of the kind of procedure to which Protagoras himself must resort: 'You say things that the masses would accept if they heard them . . . But there's absolutely no proof or necessity in what you say; on the contrary, you're relying on plausibility' (162e2–6). Socrates and his interlocutors are not satis-

[53] Other references to the 'measure' as an animal include: 154a, 162e, 166d, 167b5, 171c, 171e5.

fied with mere 'persuasiveness and plausibility' (162e8). For Protagoras, they are important criteria of truth.

Self-refutation: some judgments are false

Platagoras' retort is thus itself meant to suggest the incoherence of Protagorean theory: man–measure sanctions what the masses believe, yet (according to Plato) it is not itself sanctioned by them and must lay claim to some firmer grounding. Plato exploits this alleged consequence to mount the argument that the man–measure doctrine is self-refuting. Both the self-refutation argument and the argument about the future mark a tacit retreat from the ascription to Protagoras of the belief that knowledge is equivalent to perception in the restricted sense[54] and an attack on the implications of the more plausibly Protagorean view that knowledge is founded on personal experience, including both perceptions and judgments. Plato's strategy is to show that even on this view of man–measure Protagoras is committed to making claims about what exists absolutely, and thus undermines his own doctrine. In the so-called 'Defense' of Protagoras (166a–168c), Socrates once again places admonitions about procedure in the mouth of the Sophist. Platagoras warns Socrates not to spend his time 'logic-chopping' (167e4, 168c1–3, 188c1, cf. 164c7–d1) and to do justice to Protagoras' claim that it is men, not pigs or children (166a, 166c8, cf. 168e, 169c–d1) who are the measures and indeed that each measure has integrity and persists over time. Platagoras protests: 'When it's something of mine that you're investigating by putting questions, I'm refuted if the person who had the question put to him trips up because of giving the sort of answer I'd give; if he has given a different sort of answer, he's the one who's refuted' (166a7–166b2). Platagoras insists, and by resorting to a self-refutation argument Plato acknowledges, that with respect to assessing a particular human judgment it matters whom one questions. Platagoras' language is ambiguous: by intimating both that the individual is the arbiter of the validity of his own beliefs *and* that some individuals will do a better job of defending a particular belief than others, Platagoras' comment points to an internal conflict which Plato is anxious to see in Protagorean doctrine (see 179b). When it comes to refuting man–measure, it is essential to discover what Protagoras himself would say, because Protagoras will

---

[54] Plato attacks the theory that knowledge is perception from two separate angles: by invoking judgments about the future he seeks to show that not all instances of knowledge are cases of perception, and by invoking (1) the unintelligibility of a world in perpetual flux and (2) the independent necessity of mind (184b–186e) that not every instance of perception counts as knowledge.

provide a better defense of the doctrine than, for example, Theaetetus, who was frightened and unable 'to see ahead' (166a4). Platagoras evidently believes that it is possible to refute someone's beliefs (so interpersonal criticism, over time, *is* possible) and that some men are better at argument than others, *and* that individual judgments are authoritative. Later in the 'Defense,' Platagoras spells out an account of wisdom compatible, he says, with man–measure, and concludes: 'Thus it's true, both that some people are wiser than others, and that no-one judges what's false; and you have to put up with being a measure whether you like it or not, because that doctrine of mine is saved on these grounds' (167d). The self-refutation argument and the argument about the future are designed to show that Protagoras cannot have it both ways; the fact that Protagoras thought he could, on some construal of the two claims, suggests that his own construals differed from Plato's.

Socrates denies that he has to 'put up with being a measure' whether he likes it or not (see 179b). For the question of whether he likes it is crucial to the success of the theory. Socrates applies the man–measure theory to the judgment embodied in man–measure itself (170e–171d). Most if not all men, including Socrates, believe that some judgments are false. They therefore believe that the man–measure doctrine, which asserts that no judgments are false, is itself false. The self-refutation argument is effective because, as Socrates points out, the measure doctrine is false for many individuals, and therefore 'Protagoras' *Truth* does not, as it is purported [by Plato] to do, give a valid theory of truth for their judgments and beliefs.'[55] Moreover, as Socrates goes on to show, the theory is not merely false for Protagoras' opponents, but because Protagoras is forced by the argument to concede that this is so, it is false for Protagoras as well, for what he admits is that 'not everyone is a Protagorean measure.'[56] Man–measure is not true for *anyone* (171c5–7).[57] In the 'ontological setting' which Plato provides for man–measure, in which truth must latch on to some fact of the matter about what the world is like in itself, 'each of us lives in a private world constituted by a succession of momentary appearances, all of which are true in that world quite independently of what happens next in a given world,' and man–measure makes claims about what is true, or what is the case, in each such private world.[58] An individual's disbelief in man–measure automatically alters what is the

[55] Burnyeat (1976) 183–4, cf. 181, 190. Burnyeat provides a superb analysis of the 'complex structure of reasoning formed by the sequence of three linked refutations' (p. 185).
[56] Burnyeat (1976) 188.   [57] Burnyeat (1976) 186.   [58] Burnyeat (1976) 182.

case for him in his world, thereby rendering the theory false. The self-refutation works against man–measure construed in Platonic fashion, and confirms the misleading impression that this is the way in which it must be construed.

Socrates claims that all men reject man–measure because they believe in wisdom: 'In the greatest of dangers . . . they treat the leading men in each sphere like gods, expecting them to be their saviours, because they're superior precisely in respect of knowledge' (170a). The language is revealing. When it comes to knowledge, on the view Plato attributes to men, some men are like gods, while others contribute nothing. There is some truth, some fact of the matter, to which most men have no access. It is to a view with this implication, not Platonic but Parmenidean, that Protagoras' theory was addressed. His theory would not countenance the existence of one real world to which only a few men with knowledge have access. In the context of a theory which detached what is true from what seems, the claim that what seems to individuals is what is true for them was significant; it pointed to a theory of knowledge founded on personal experience. There is no need to read into it, as Plato does, in line with his own views about truth, the claim that what appears is real in some private world. Protagoras was saying that men have to rely on what seems to them to be the case,[59] and that this fact of experience itself vindicated man–measure as an account of knowledge. Contrast Plato's account: to what do the men who believe that some judgments are false and that man–measure is therefore false appeal? If, as Plato implies, to

[59] The fact that Socrates, at 171d, echoes such a claim, is not (*contra* Burnyeat (1976b) 181) evidence that Protagoras meant to do more, i.e. to link judgments to the world as it actually is. After the self-refutation, in response to Theodorus' protest that they are running Protagoras too hard, Socrates says: 'But it isn't clear that we're running past where we ought. Of course he's older than we are, so it's likely that he's wiser. If he suddenly popped up out of the ground here, from the neck up, he'd very probably convict me of talking a great deal of nonsense, and you of agreeing to it, and then he'd duck down again and rush off. But we have to make do with ourselves as we are, I think, and always say what seems to us to be the case. Let's do that now. Shouldn't we say that anyone whatever will admit at least this: some people are wiser than others, some more ignorant?' (171c9–d7). One of the subtle points being made in these ironic remarks is that Protagoras asserted both that there was such a thing as wisdom and nonsense and that man is the measure, and he could do so only by failing to take either concept seriously. Wisdom is not simply a matter of assertion or argument-bashing (see 154e) or of interpreting the wisdom of the poets (see *Prot.* 347b–348a), which for Protagoras would count as useful, constructive forms of socialization; if Protagoras seriously explored (with integrity, not just briefly and from the neck up) what men make of the world, it would become clear that men think there must be more to knowledge and wisdom than the sifting of ordinary beliefs (see 154c). This is a critique of a theory that aimed to integrate wisdom with ordinary human judgment, not one which maintained that the latter was incorrigible.

some fact of the matter beyond experience, what warrants this move? If to experience itself, then this confirms man–measure in what I take to have been its original form. Sextus (*Adv. math.* 7.61) preserves such an approach to the defense of man–measure: anyone who denies that man is the judge of all things actually confirms it, for he is rendering a judgment which can only be based on what he himself claims to know.[60]

There is no evidence that Protagoras himself used such an argument to turn the tables on opponents of man–measure. He was not, after all, writing in response to Plato and his self-refutation argument, but to Parmenides and his claim that appearances were no guide to reality. It is, however, likely that Protagoras applied the man–measure doctrine to itself. His theory was designed to counter non-empirical characterizations of the world, and could itself appeal to experience for confirmation: men do in fact reason on the basis of experience. The idea that Protagoras thought man–measure, like all other claims, had to be assessed in terms of human experience, possesses more than mere prima-facie plausibility. Protagoras, according to Diogenes Laertius and others, was 'the first to say that there are two arguments (*logoi*) concerning everything, these being opposed to each other' (DK 80 A 1, 6a; cf. A 20, B 6). Protagoras himself composed opposing arguments (DK 80 B 5).[61] According to Seneca, the two-opposed-arguments doctrine meant that any question could be argued equally well from either side – including the question of whether this was so (DK 80 A 20). Protagoras was infamous in antiquity for his ability to argue both sides of any question (DK 80 A 20), and to 'make the weaker argument (*logos*) the stronger' (DK 80 A 21). The two techniques are linked by Eudoxus (DK 80 A 2) who reports the latter and comments that Protagoras set his students to censure and praise a single argument. These were not, I suggest, mere rhetorical tricks. Aristotle condemned Protagoras for promising to train students to 'make the worse appear the better argument' (*Rhet.* 1402a24).[62] Protagoras sought to make (and teach others to make) the less persuasive, the apparently less plausible, argument into the more persuasive. By strengthening both sides of a question, the sophist could make clear to

---

[60] Cf. Burnyeat (1976) 180–1.

[61] See Rankin (1981) 25–6; Mansfeld (1981) 48; Kerferd (1981) 84–5. And note Protagoras' own contradictions of others, e.g. DK B 7 and 8.

[62] According to Aristotle, this involved representing a particular probability as a universal one, Arist. *Rhet.* 1402a7–26. *Contra* Kerferd (1981) 101, following Freese, the promise of Protagoras is not *itself* a merely apparent probability, but rather concerns the manipulation of such probabilities.

himself, and to others, what was at stake in the controversy, with respect to his own doctrines as well as to issues of more general concern.[63] In arguments about knowledge, as in political discussions in the assembly, all claims could be questioned, and no one disputant could trump the others by appealing to some privileged access to things as they really are. The point of exploring opposing claims was to discover the best argument, to be assessed in terms of persuasiveness and plausibility or, in modern parlance, reflective acceptability.[64] There is room in such a theory for wisdom, and for contradicting or correcting others, but not for a level of understanding or reality removed from experience. Thus men can believe and show one another to be mistaken, but nothing that a man believes is in an absolute sense false, and all 'measurings' must be taken into account.

The dramatic nuances of the dialogue indicate that Protagoras did not present his theory in the terms which enable Socrates to execute the table-turning argument.[65] When Socrates sums up the argument, which depends for its force on the assumption that Protagoras was offering a theory that postulated private worlds of incorrigible experience, Theodorus objects: 'We're running my friend too hard' (171c8). This comment is not, I would argue, intended to suggest that Plato is dissatisfied with the argument he has just presented,[66] but rather that the argument is not true to Protagoras' own interpretation of his doctrine. Socrates retorts: 'But it is not clear that we're running past where we ought' (171c9–10).[67] Although Protagoras has been convicted 'out of his own mouth,' yet the real Protagoras, Socrates acknowl-

---

[63] *Contra* Kerferd (1981) 108, who argues that with respect to characteristics such as good/advantageous/wise, there was only one truth, not the two *logoi* which apply to perceived qualities. This rests on an implausible divorce between the 'two-opposed-arguments' and the 'weaker/stronger' doctrines. The twofold arguments were unlikely to have been restricted to hot/cold, beautiful/ugly, etc.

[64] Note Plutarch's story about a day-long debate between Protagoras and Pericles, *Per.* 36. See Kerferd's discussion (1981) 102–4 of the conception of the best or right argument (*orthos logos*). I cannot, however, agree with him that the 'substitution of one experience for another' illustrated by the example of the doctor in the Defense is an instance of making the weaker argument the stronger. It is man's *condition* that is being changed.

[65] When, in the long run-up to the self-refutation, Socrates asks Theodorus whether he or any of Protagoras' followers would be willing to maintain that 'no person ever believes of another that he is stupid and makes false judgments,' Theodorus is incredulous. He has to be told in detail why man–measure entails this result. Thus while some 'followers of Protagoras' allegedly made use of the sophisticated doctrine (*Euth.* 286c3), it was not at any rate an obvious corollary of man–measure.

[66] As McDowell (1973) 91, suggests. McDowell regards the argument as unsuccessful because of the inconsistent use of the relativizing qualifier; but see Burnyeat (1976).

[67] Socrates is here ironically echoing Protagoras: note *adelon* and *orthos* (*logos*). See n. 56, above.

edges, would protest this interpretation of his doctrine: 'He'd very probably convict me of talking a great deal of nonsense, and you of agreeing to it' (177d1–3).[68]

In his attempt to show that the Protagorean theory could not coherently be applied to itself, that it failed as a theory of *truth*, that to proceed by opposing *logoi* based on experience is to seek in vain to grasp flux when what is required is intellectual apprehension of reality, Plato reveals his own distortion of the doctrine's original orientation. Plato asserts that the man–measure doctrine inevitably leads to the conclusion that genuine disagreement is impossible.[69] If every man is a measure of what the world is for him, then he cannot be contradicted, nor can he contradict himself. In the *Theaetetus* Platagoras is made to say that 'no one judges what's false' (167d2) and that 'it isn't possible to have in one's judgments the things which are not, or anything other than what one's experiencing, which is always true' (167a8). In this indirect manner, Plato connects Protagoreanism, interpreted in Platonic terms, with the argument sometimes encapsulated in the phrase 'it is impossible to contradict.' The argument that it is impossible to contradict or to say what is false is explained roughly as follows: either one of two people who disagree is saying something untrue, in which case he fails to refer to anything at all; or both are saying what is true, in which case (since they disagree) they must be referring to different things. In neither case does disagreement rest on genuine contradiction.[70] There is no good reason, apart from the im-

[68] See Vlastos' recent discussion of the Socratic elenchus (Vlastos 1983) in which he contrasts the method of the real Socrates (in the early dialogues), which relied completely on the extraction of concessions from real persons, with the procedure of Plato. But the present instance, though part of a highly Platonic dialogue, in a sense analyzes the Socratic method: if Protagoras were present, he could perhaps have been bullied by Socrates into grudging acceptance of a version of his doctrine which he never intended; since he is absent, Socrates indicates both that Protagoras would *have* to make such admissions and that he would refuse to do so. Note 171d4–6: 'We have to make do with ourselves as we are, and always say what seems to us to be the case.' Cf. 169e, 166a–b: note 'it makes a great deal of difference' whether or not the concessions are legitimate. See Lee (1973) and Burnyeat (1976) 191f. for discussion of the meaning of the image Socrates uses.

[69] Cf. Aristotle, *Met.* 1007b18, 1062b13. This is a view shared by modern interpreters. See Burnyeat (1976) 181–2, Kerferd (1981) 87f. But cf. Rankin (1981) 25–6 and 31, and Mansfeld (1981) 48.

[70] See Kerferd (1981) 88–9 for this account of the *Euthydemus* argument. Socrates notes that he has heard this argument frequently: 'The followers of Protagoras made great use of it, as did others even before his time' (*Euthyd.* 286c). The form of attribution does not clearly rule out Protagoras (*hoi amphi X* can mean *X and* his followers) but it also does not unequivocally include him (see LSJ *ad amphi* C.3). I have not been able to consult M. Dubuisson, *Hoi amphi tina, hoi peri tina*, diss. Liège (1980) drawn to my attention by an anonymous reader. The dialogue seems to be the basis for Diogenes Laertius' attribution

plications of the Platonic construal of man–measure, to attribute the argument to Protagoras himself.[71] And there is good reason not to do so for, as I have already noted, Protagoras was famous for formulating opposing arguments. It has been suggested that Protagoras' two-opposing-arguments doctrine can be reconciled with both the argument that it is impossible to contradict and the interpretation of man–measure as postulating private worlds of incorrigible experience by supposing that Protagoras meant that contradiction was possible at the verbal level, but not at the level of the things to which words refer.[72] This stratagem rescues all three attributions at the cost of reducing the best-attested of them to a mere cipher. If anything whatever is genuinely contradictory, it is 'it is not possible to contradict' and 'there are contradictory arguments.'[73] According to Protagoras, shared experience made disagreement possible and fruitful.

At various points in the *Theaetetus*, Plato represents Protagoras as willing, even eager, to acknowledge that some men are wiser than others, and refers to Protagoras' practice of teaching for a fee as evidence of this belief. Plato seems to regard this concession and this behavior as damaging to Protagorean doctrine (see, e.g., 161d9–e3, 169d5–e2, 179b), and yet he is also clearly uncomfortable with this interpretation. He keeps returning to the point and trying in one way or another to show that acknowledging the existence of wisdom commits Protagoras to recognition of a form of knowledge independent of personal experience. In the Defense of Protagoras (166a–168c), Plato makes Platagoras defend an account (in fact, as we shall see, two subtly different accounts) of wisdom with respect to the harmful and the beneficial. As Socrates remarks afterwards, he has 'had Protagoras concede that some people are superior to others on the question of what's better or worse, and it's those people who are wise' (169d7–9,

of the claim to Protagoras (DK A 1 and 53). Cf. Philoponus, *Cat.* 81.6–8, cited by Kerferd (1981) 89. It is not clear exactly whom Plato has in mind; see Rankin (1981). There is now evidence that Prodicus, said to have been taught by Protagoras (DK 84 A 1), expounded this view. See Binder and Liesenborghs (1976). Cf. Plato, *Cratylus* 429b–431e, *Sophist* 251c; Isocrates, *Hel.* 1; Antisthenes *apud* Aristotle, *Met.* 1024b32, *Top.* 104b21.

[71] *Contra* Kerferd (1981) 89–90.
[72] Kerferd (1981) 90–2.
[73] *ouk estin antilegein* and *eisi antilogiai*. Isocrates, *Hel. (ab init.)*, groups together three doctrines: the impossibility of (1) saying what is false, (2) contradicting and (3) opposing two *logoi* concerning the same things; he ascribes such doctrines to Protagoras, among others. He has apparently adopted the Platonic characterization of Protagoras, and associated his teachings, so described, with a doctrine that runs directly counter to the teachings of the historical Sophist.

cf. 166d5–e1). Does this 'concession' point to something genuinely Protagorean?[74] There is no good reason to regard the Defense as containing genuinely Protagorean doctrines. Indeed, Socrates admits as much, saying that the concession must be 'put on a firm footing' (169e2), and proceeds to get Protagoras' agreement that men are *not* self-sufficient in wisdom 'not through others but from Protagoras' own words' (169–8), via the self-refutation argument. Plato is uneasy about whether he has in fact shown the concession to be damaging on all construals. The self-refutation begins with a reference to superior wisdom about what is beneficial (170a10–b1), i.e. precisely the realm in which Platagoras in the Defense has been made to acknowledge the role of wisdom, yet it does not show that some people are superior on the question of what is better or worse, but rather that some judgments are false. Moreover the self-refutation, even though it allegedly forces even Protagoras himself to accept that man is not the measure, and, on Platonic assumptions, succeeds in so doing, is not treated as a fatal blow to the theory. Plato's argument about advantage and the future marks a different strategy, designed to cope with Protagoras even if his theory were not regarded as having postulated private worlds of incorrigible experience. Wisdom cannot be based on personal experience in any sense, for it could not then account for judgments about advantage, benefit, and other future states of affairs, since such judgments make claims about the way the world will or will not be, i.e. about what exists absolutely. Thus Plato describes the (or rather, one) version of man–measure adumbrated in the Defense as a form of the doctrine which distinguishes between present perceptions, which are assumed for the sake of argument to be authoritative and incorrigible, and judgments about the future, between questions of (for example) justice and questions of advantage. This 'strengthened' version, apparently intended to give Protagoras grounds for claiming both that no one judges what's false and that some men are wiser than others, and framed so as in fact to undermine the doctrine's original coherence, is not attributed to Protagoras, but to Protagoreans, and it corresponds only to one of the subtly differentiated accounts of the wisdom which man–measure can afford to acknowledge. Moreover, with respect to the later argument about knowledge of the future, which reiterates one version of the account given in the Defense, Socrates comments that 'at any rate those who don't altogether assert Protagoras' theory carry on their philosophy on some such lines as

[74] McDowell (1973) 169, 172–3.

these' (172b7–9).[75] Both the self-refutation and the argument about the future, which seek to show that Protagoras' recognition of wisdom is damaging, leave one of the Defense versions of this recognition untouched.

In his recapitulation of the account of wisdom given in the Defense, Plato frames the issue in ways amenable to the absolutist – and thus damaging – construction he wishes to place on Platagoras' concession. At 171e, summing up the doctrine he has attributed to Protagoras, Socrates refers to the standard of health, which appears in the Defense, and indicates that although perceptions are incorrigible, there is wisdom about what is healthful. He goes on to suggest (172a–b) that in the political realm, the theory holds that the state is never mistaken in its judgments about what is just or lawful, yet must recognize the superiority of some advisors with respect to what is advantageous. Plato reveals the point of ascribing such a distinction to Protagoras when he says that in the case of justice, legality and the like, 'Protagoreans' 'insist that none of them has by nature a being of its own' (172b4–5). Plato is trying to force Platagoras to acknowledge that there are some realms in which man is *not* the measure, i.e. where there is a truth and reality independent of human experience.

Plato's distorted account of wisdom at 171c–172b corresponds to the second set of examples provided in the Defense;[76] just as (in the first set of examples) doctors are wise where bodies are concerned, so gardeners are wise about plants: 'They too, whenever any of their plants are sick, instill perceptions that are beneficial and healthy, and true too, into them instead of harmful ones. My claim is, too, that wise and good politicians make beneficial things, instead of harmful ones, seem to their states to be just' (167b6–c4). Both the gardener and the politician are wise because they know what is good for their respective 'patients.' The inclusion of 'plants' among the examples cited by Platagoras, though apparently justified on the assumption that basic sensory responses count as 'appearances' (note the sophist's strictly irrelevant, perhaps defiant 'and true, too'),[77] subtly sabotages the Protagorean doctrine. Plato strips Protagoras' theory of its emphasis on

---

[75] See McDowell (1973) 172–3. Note the Platonic character of the concerns mentioned at 168b4–8, with Maguire (1973) 123f.

[76] See McDowell (1973) 172, Cole (1966) 116. Maguire (1973) takes a somewhat different view of the Defense, but agrees with Cole that Plato has (later in the dialogue) altered Protagoras' account for his own purposes. The following analysis owes much to the articles by Cole and Maguire.

[77] See McDowell (1973) 168.

'man.'[78] Although Platagoras begins the Defense by accusing Socrates of 'acting like a pig himself' for talking about pigs and baboons (166c7–d1), he goes on to cite as an example of a 'measure' a 'creature still more out of the way': a plant.[79] Also, by making the 'measure' a merely sentient, not a *judging* being, Plato suggests that wisdom as to what is better or worse is defined independently of experience. Certain objects of perception simply are healthful or beneficial (167c). In the same way, as Platagoras points out in the sentence which follows the passage cited above, what *seems* just and admirable to the state *is* just and admirable for it, but the wise man changes 'appearances' so that what 'seems' just to the state coincides with what is genuinely beneficial for it.[80] By incorporating a distinction between judgments about what seems admirable and those about what is beneficial, this account preserves the Protagorean claim that 'what seems is' and presents a picture of the operation of wisdom in terms of this principle, thus enabling Platagoras to assert that he has shown that 'some people are wiser than others, and that no one judges what's false' (167d1–2). By means of his formulation of these examples, Plato introduces an inconsistency into Protagoras' conception, an inconsistency which he later exploits.

In his final sally against the man–measure doctrine, Plato draws on the distinction used to 'strengthen' it, namely a distinction between judgments about what is beneficial and other assessments of experience. Plato acknowledges, for the sake of argument, that if present perceptions are veridical, then whatever a state determines to be just *is* just for that state so long as the *polis* continues to regard it as such. However, the judgments involved in political decision-making, Socrates argues, are judgments about utility or advantage, and therefore judgments about what will actually occur in the *future* (177c5–179a8). Whatever may be the case with respect to present perceptions (179c)[81] the judgments about the future which *men* as ongoing 'measures' must make turn out to be right or wrong: *wise* persons are the only measurers of the future (179b). If, as Plato suggested in the Defense, Protagoras is willing to acknowledge that some men are

---

[78] See n. 53 above. The point, for Plato, is to reduce Protagoras' doctrine to one about sense-perceptions, in contrast to the human capacity to calculate 'with respect to being and usefulness' (186b–c). Cf. 174b. See Burnyeat (1976) 188 n. 18.

[79] Cf. Lee (1973) 260.

[80] See Guthrie (1969) 172f., Cole (1966) 110f., (1972) 26f., McDowell (1973) 167. Cf. Maguire (1973) 127–8, Kerferd (1981) 104.

[81] See McDowell (1973) 179; cf. 118 on Plato's restricted view of perception, which he holds back.

better judges than others of what is beneficial, then he must also acknowledge that wisdom is *not* founded on personal experience, for judgments of advantage are judgments about the future, of which no man can now claim to have experience. Plato is again attempting to commit Protagoras to a distinction between a realm in which personal experience is decisive and one in which it is irrelevant, between a realm of seeming and one of being. The doctor, who was depicted in the Defense as responsive to the perception of the patient, is here distinguished from the ordinary individual by his ability to predict the future. If a patient thinks he is going to have a fever, and the doctor disagrees, 'which one's judgment should we say the future will turn out to accord with?' *Mutatis mutandis*, the same is true of other wise men – they, and no one else, can predict the future (178d–e). Yet the distinction between judgments about present and future is never explicitly attributed to Protagoras himself, and Plato confirms that Protagoras never adopted the 'strengthened' version of man–measure by arguing that Protagoras' own activities and expertise suggest a commitment to judgments about the future incompatible with his own doctrine's alleged reliance on present experience. He will be 'a better judge than any ordinary person . . . in anticipating what's going to be convincing . . . in lawcourt speeches' (178e).

Plato's portrait of the sophist in the *Protagoras* confirms what the implicit portrait of Protagoras' ideas and activities in the *Theaetetus* suggests, namely that Protagoras did not distinguish between justice and advantage (both are tied to the good for man), nor did he distinguish categorically wise judgments about the present from prudent assessments of the likely course of the future. The future cannot, on Protagoras' account, be predicted, as Socrates' reference to a prophet intimates; it cannot be known.[82] The future has no static, absolute content. Its character can only be estimated, and wide, deep experience of people and events can help. Moreover, the attitude of citizens to the future, or to their own advantage, in part determines what they will experience when the future arrives. The sophist or politician is therefore not a seer, but a constant guide, goad and interpreter. All human experience, including present perceptions and judgments about the future, admits of discriminations according to a standard, a human standard: some ways of perceiving the world are characteristic

[82] 179a: *mantis*. On this point, I perhaps diverge from the conclusion reached by Mansfeld (1981) 40, who excludes the question 'if tomorrow there will be a seabattle' from the category of things too obscure to be known. It is true that tomorrow the answer to the question we asked today will be knowable by all observers; but *today* the answer is obscure and undeterminable-responsive to what we do today.

of men as they naturally and regularly are. All forms of wisdom are answerable to human experience, but they also interpret and sharpen it. As a claim about the *human* basis of knowledge rather than thoroughgoing epistemological relativism ('no one judges what's false'), Protagorean theory can readily accommodate the existence of men who are 'wise' because they are experienced, and perceptive about the experience of others. They know the truth, but not a truth independent of human experience.

The Protagoras hiding in Platagoras

A genuinely Protagorean conception seems to be lurking in the other – the first – set of examples cited in the Defense. These examples offer a glimpse of man–measure as part of a world-view which embraced political as well as epistemological concerns. In the world postulated by man–measure the sophist does have a role to play, and one which does *not* depend, as Plato implies, on distinguishing between present and future or justice and advantage in the way that a Platonic theory of being and truth demands and that destroys the man–measure doctrine's claims to coherence. Platagoras describes the proper function of doctors and sophists:

To a sick man what he eats appears, and is, bitter, whereas to a healthy man it is and appears the opposite. Now what must be done isn't to make either of them wiser, because that isn't even possible, nor is it to accuse the sick one of being ignorant because he makes the sort of judgments he does, and call the healthy one wise because he makes judgments of a different sort. What must be done is to effect a change in one direction; because one of the two conditions is better. In education, too, in the same way, a change must be effected from one of two conditions to the better one; but whereas a doctor makes the change with drugs, a sophist does it by what he says. (166e–167a)

It is important to note that this description is not strictly parallel to the second set of examples. In this case, the subject is not so much the wise as the men who need their help, namely men 'to whom bad things appear and are' (166d7). Platagoras refers to conditions of sickness and health and their effect on what men perceive. Health, it seems, is regularly associated with experiencing food as sweet, and this condition is better than its opposite. By his application of 'wise' and 'false' and 'true' to what may well be a genuinely Protagorean account of the stability of human nature and human 'measurement,' Plato renders the whole passage obscure as an extrapolation from man–measure.[83] For his own purposes, he conflates a conception of the stability of

[83] See McDowell (1973) 167.

human perceptions with a conception of the status of human judgments about truth and falsity. Why isn't it possible to make a sick or
healthy man wiser? The sick man's perceptions are not, it is true,
skewed because he is ignorant, but rather because he is ill. Yet could
he not be taught the doctor's art, the knowledge required to cure himself? Plato's language indicates that 'the change from sickness to
health is not *eo ipso* a change in the direction of being wiser.'[84] As his
condition changes, an individual's perceptions become more representative of the experience of man *qua* man; they become 'better' perceptions (his food appears sweet), but not 'truer' or more 'real' (167b34).
However, Plato's language also suggests that there is no question of
the perceiving subject becoming wiser; for Plato, becoming wise
means moving from absolutely false judgments to absolutely true
ones.[85] Protagoras' vision of wisdom, by contrast, is continuous with
(though not identical to) the process of becoming a measure (becoming 'healthy'), referred to by Plato in this passage. The doctor or the
sophist (note the sophist's account of human nature in the *Protagoras*,
discussed below) restores men to the condition of proper measures;
they are then capable of exercising their own capacity to gauge and
interpret experience, guided by the informed experience of others.
Plato has insinuated into Protagorean doctrine an alien element,
namely his own conception of wisdom,[86] but he seems to have preserved fragments of an anomalous idea[87] – a conception of 'better' and
'worse' human conditions which does not rest on a standard of absol-

[84] McDowell (1973) 167.

[85] See McDowell (1973) 167. I attribute the obscurity of the passage not to an attempt by
Plato to make Protagoras express himself ineptly, as McDowell speculates, but to his
attempt to assimilate an indigestible doctrine. Compare Plato, *Laws* 719e8–720e5 and
857c5–e5, on the importance of encouragement and persuasion, not blank injunction, on
the part of doctors as of legislators. The *slave* doctor prescribes 'with the brusque confidence of a dictator' while the doctor who treats free men 'burns something from the sick
and at the same time gives the individual patient all the instruction he can' (720). The
Laws' vision of political society is correspondingly different from that of the *Republic*.
Note the role of the 'noble lie' in the latter, and see Morrow (1941).

[86] In Socrates' reference, in his own voice, to the passage cited above, he reports that Protagoras conceded 'that some people are superior to others in the question of what's better or
worse, and that it's those people who are wise' (169d7–9). Yet the sick and healthy men
who are, in this first example, the measures of what is 'better' or 'worse,' are precisely not
wise in Plato's sense, as Plato himself has just made Protagoras point out. See Cole (1966)
116. Cole does not note that the 'Protagorean' comment, as well as Socrates' identification of the distinctions between healthy/sick and wiseman/layman, assumes an absolutist outlook. It is those who treat them who are Platonically wise, and they, as the
example of the plant suggests, require no input from their patients.

[87] See Cole (1966) 116–18, for a possible account of Plato's attitude to the varying interpretations he provides of Protagorean theory.

ute truth – and hints at the existence of a corresponding notion of wisdom.

The critical standard used by the doctor or sophist is a general notion of what is 'normal' which is derived from human experience and answerable to it. This notion has two aspects. The first is the conception of the experiences characteristic of men *qua* men. Health and well-being are associated with experiencing as pleasant/unpleasant what human beings in general tend to experience as pleasant/ unpleasant. Unlike the politician in the later example, the doctor does not make beneficial foods appear pleasant but rather modifies the patient's condition with drugs so that he experiences pleasant sensations instead of unpleasant ones:[88] 'When a man, because of a bad condition supposes related qualities, then by means of a good condition one makes him suppose other and corresponding qualities' (167b2–7).[89] The patient's perception is the doctor's guide to the necessity and efficacy of treatment.[90] The doctor relies on the individual patient's 'measurings' in formulating his own assessment of the problem, and in deciding whether or not the treatment has been successful. Moreover, it is his experience of many such cases which suggests how he should go about altering the patient's condition. This does not mean, as Plato's later comments suggest, that the doctor knows for a fact what the cause of a particular illness will be (see 178c4–6) or that certain kinds of treatment are bound to benefit the patient, as the later example of the politician implies (167c3–d1, cf. 171e5). As the example makes clear, the doctor is operating with an interpersonal standard which helps him to determine how to meet the needs of his patients and enables him to criticize and suggest revisions of the patient's feelings and desires on the basis not only of consistency, but also of a general notion of what humans tend to experience under certain circumstances.

Human experience suggests when individuals will be good 'measures' and why they are unreliable when they are. In general, men who experience their food as bitter are unwell. There is nothing to be said

[88] McDowell (1973) 166, Cole (1966) 109f.

[89] Following Cornford's text (see McDowell (1973) 111); see Cole's (1966) interpretation of *doxasai suggenē* 109: the doctor's task, as revealed by regarding *suggenē* as an external accusative, is to make the patient 'feel better by bringing him to the point where food is enjoyable again.' Cole may well be right, but the same meaning is produced if, with Maguire (1973), one does not interpret *poneros* and *chrestos* as 'unhealthy' and 'healthy' but simply as good and bad, or if one regards *suggenē* as referring not to thoughts which are themselves healthy, but which are associated with feeling well (i.e. in general, people who feel well tend to taste certain foods as pleasant).

[90] Cf. Hippocrates, *Vet. med.* 9, Cole (1972) 28.

about the 'ill health' of a man who (over time) experiences nothing odd or unpleasant. Yet a man who tastes food as bitter (by his own standard, unpleasant) and refuses to admit that he is ill would justifiably be regarded as odd, even mistaken.[91] An attempt could legitimately be made to help him perceive the situation the way others do, though if this is unsuccessful, there is nothing to be said to the individual, though something could be said *about* him. Moreover, the man who tastes his food as bitter and wishes to taste it as sweet yet refuses to adopt the regimen prescribed by the doctor because he experiences it as unpleasant is also open to criticism, this time on the grounds that his desires and actions are inconsistent.[92] The corollary in the *polis* of the radical disorientation which causes unhealthy men to experience all nourishment as unpleasant would be disaffection with political life itself. The doctor is entitled to say that human well-being requires that men desire nourishment; the patient is expected to appreciate that he is not supposed to be repelled by food. (In the *Protagoras* the sophist argues that political life is analogous to food in this respect, namely that it is essential to the well-being of every man *qua* man.)

The second aspect of the critical standard of 'normality' also depends upon considerations which follow from the fact that it is *man* who is the measure, but this second criterion applies not only to the most basic elements of human experience, but also to quotidian interpretations of the world. Each person judges for himself, but he is expected to have consistent beliefs and to be responsive to rational argument. The sophist or politician can only proceed from what the student or assembled *polis* already know, believe and are or from what they can be brought to know, believe or be (as a result of social 'conditioning').[93] The politician may attempt to make the citizens recognize the inconsistency of their beliefs; he may use his wide experience to help them appreciate the implications of their views and actions and to suggest to them other ways of realizing their wishes; he

[91] Cf. Cole (1972) 27–8, who notes that on this reading of the Defense, 'The doctor will be unconcerned with the man who because of illness finds harmful food enjoyable.' But although there is no meaningful content to the notion of food being 'harmful' if it does not negatively affect the (long-term) experience of the person who eats it, this does not mean that the doctor or sophist is prohibited from criticizing a patient's beliefs or experiences, as Cole implies.

[92] Cf. Cole (1972) 25–6, who makes the interaction between patient and sophist too uncomplicated, and defines the authoritativeness of the patient too neatly. It is the doctor's experience, especially its scope, which enables him to criticize a patient's 'measurement.' On the requirement of consistency, see Mansfeld (1981) 56–9.

[93] See Mansfeld (1981) 46–7 on Protagoras' notion of a person.

may try to revise their beliefs and desires on the basis of what he himself knows.[94] Men respond to experience as persons, not as momentary 'sensors,' and as such they appreciate the importance of achieving
coherence and integrity in their beliefs and actions. The sophist or
politician who seeks to advise the citizens does not have access to
knowledge of what is in an absolute sense advantageous; he does not
'make beneficial things be and seem just and admirable to them,
instead of any harmful things which used to be so for them' (167c6–
8). Rather, he tries to persuade the citizens to think about their own
advantage, or what will benefit the *polis*, in the way that he thinks
about it.

In the *Theaetetus*, Plato does not directly attack the man–measure
doctrine as it applies to the city state's determinations of justice, which
are construed by Plato as present 'appearances,' as opposed to assessments of advantage.[95] In a long digression, however, Plato points to
his own radically different view, namely the view that justice as well is
absolute.[96] He does this by means of an extended contrast between
men 'who have been knocking about in lawcourts and such places
since they were young' and those 'who have been brought up in philosophy and other such pursuits' (172c). This sketch provides a general
critique of Protagoras' ideas (note that Socrates explicitly associates
Protagoras with the lawcourts, 178e) and a glimpse of the gulf which
divides the Platonic from the Protagorean world-view. In its indirect
and extreme characterization of the ideas associated with Protagoras,
the digression confirms what has been argued above about the orientation of Protagorean doctrine and what will be argued below about
their political import. Socrates begins the digression by describing the
men of the lawcourts. The point of the description is that these men
have been deformed by the life they lead and the company they keep,
by the 'slavery they have suffered' (172e–173b). Those who practice
philosophy, by contrast, abstain from *all* political and legislative activity (173d–e). The comparison Plato repeatedly draws between the

[94] See Mansfeld (1981) 46.

[95] McDowell (1973) 174, suggests that 'to argue explicitly against it would perhaps take
him too far from the original topic of perception.' But see the related argument concerning the legislator's judgments of utility (177c5–179b6). Since the distinction between
what seems just (*dikaios*) to and what is laid down as law (*nomos*) by the *polis* was not a
clear one, Plato here again implies that decisions about what is 'just' may also be subject
to a purely external standard.

[96] 175c, 176c–d. See McDowell (1973) 174–7. Plato may be referring here to the doctrine of
the Forms. Note that the force of the critique is directed against the Protagorean view of
politics as a whole, i.e. determinations of both justice and advantage, another indication
that this distinction was strategic.

boorish, uneducated man engaged in slavish pursuits and the gentle-
man of leisure (174d6, 175d–e) suggests that he regards democratic
politics as particularly degraded. For Plato, writing in the early fourth
century, the social interaction characteristic of the *polis* he knew,
Athens, is lethal to the sound development of intellectual character.
The philosophical man neither notices nor inquires about the experience of ordinary men. He looks beyond what is 'near' to the 'total
nature of each of the things which are' (173e–174a). Thus 'such a
person really does fail to notice his next-door neighbor':

He's oblivious not only of what he's doing, but almost of whether he's a man or
some other creature. But as for the question what, exactly, a man is, and what it's
distinctively characteristic of such a nature to do or undergo, that's something he
does ask and take pains to inquire into. (174b)

The contrast with the Protagorean outlook is implicit, but evident. For
Protagoras, awareness of being a man is essential to an assessment of
what man is like, and it is precisely social interaction which shapes the
men who are the 'measures.'[97]

As I shall show, the Great Speech in the *Protagoras* expresses the
sophist's belief, reflected in the *Theaetetus*, in the beneficent socializ-
ing effect of *polis* life and democratic political action. The man–
measure doctrine conceives of the experience and understanding
attained by ordinary men as the touchstone of social values. Protagoras' measure is a man who notices his neighbor and who moves
through life and interacts with others as a human being, with all that
that implies about basic needs, responses and capacities. In a democracy, and indeed in response to democracy, epistemology and political
ethics coincide. Man–measure sanctions the judgment of ordinary
men and the collective, critical appraisal of human belief. The form of
Protagoras' doctrine suggests that he is concerned to build social unity
and purpose out of individual beliefs and motivations, so in a sense he
has come to regard the individual as prior to society; and man–
measure itself raises the possibility of a distinction between man *qua*
man, who measures the world, and man *qua* citizen, who measures the
polis. Yet democratic politics, which inspired this elevation of human
judgment, also masks the theory's potential for cleaving man's sense
of himself. Protagoras' vision of the individual is as a part of the social
process characteristic of existing *poleis*. The question of what a man is
is inseparable from the question of what one's neighbor is like. Plato,
by contrast, believes that questions of 'justice' or 'happiness' can only

[97] See Mansfeld (1981) 46.

be pursued in abstraction from the social world as men actually experience it. 'Human nature,' although still conceived in terms of social existence, is investigated as a distinct concept: 'what, exactly, a man is' (174b). Unlike Protagoras, Plato, repelled by the politics of democratic Athens, is anxious to show that people are not as and what they think they are (176d). The socialization characteristic of the *polis* is now seen as a destructive influence, and politics as a struggle for power rather than a realization of order. Plato's language is designed to evoke the teachings of the man who legitimized 'appearances' and thereby, in Plato's view, fortified the subversive, pernicious beliefs of the masses (176b). According to Plato, men glory in being powerfully crafty; behaving unjustly or impiously seems good to them, for it means that they are 'real men, the sort one needs to be to survive in a *polis*' (176d). Compare Protagoras' view (as recorded by Plato in the *Protagoras*) that to be a 'real man' is to exhibit the qualities – justice and respect (*dikē* and *aidōs*) – which enable one to survive, and flourish, by participating in the order and freedom shaped by life in the *polis*.

Measuring man

Protagoras was, so far as we know, the first democratic political theorist in the history of the world. The society he analyzed was a direct participatory democracy which included even the poorest residents of Attica. Protagoras sought to demonstrate what Aeschylus dramatized: that political action is both collective self-expression and collective self-restraint.[98] Again like Aeschylus, and because of the political and intellectual context he inhabited, Protagoras interpreted the process of democratic interaction as itself providing answers to the questions it had raised. He offered an account of human nature and the nature of politics founded on the way in which man actually experienced his life in society. Order was fully immanent: man had unleashed himself from all double causation except in the form im-

---

[98] Two kinds of interpretations of Protagoras as a political thinker are mistaken. The one characterizes him as the spokesman for a particular Athenian 'party' or policy (e.g. 'Periclean': Morrison (1941) 11ff., who divides Athens into three 'parties' each committed to a different 'type' of democracy). The other treats him as the creature of Plato's dialogue, that is either as a defender of particular democratic practices (this is sometimes linked to a version of the first interpretation, as by Morrison (1941) 7) or as a theorist whose ideas are not tied to any particular political context. See the works cited by Nicholson (1980/1) n. 2. Nicholson himself takes the 'detached theorist' view. The one reduces Protagoras' ideas to political propaganda while the other adopts Plato's distortion of historically conditioned ideas.

plicit in the democratic interaction of elite and citizenry. (Thus Protagoras differed from Aeschylus in at least one important respect: he did not rely on fear of the gods – even mediated by the *polis* – as the source of self-restraint, but solely on the force of human reason and its expression in human action.) With respect to the first element of the question raised by democratic practices and reflected in Aeschylean drama, namely how political demands correspond to the individual's sense of what he ought to do, Protagoras sought to make political values primitively personal, to interpret what a person *qua* person has reason to do in terms which coincided with civic requirements. To do so, he formulated an account of the human species which entailed (1) that civil society is a necessary feature of human existence. This in turn entailed both (2) that to survive, man had to exhibit certain social, civic qualities, and (3) that society not only required social harmony, but also fostered it: that, after all, was its *contribution* to human survival. Because of the latter implication, this account also suggested a partial answer to the second aspect of the question: interaction would lead to social order – and perhaps even to prudence and justice – because the citizens were constantly being shaped and tempered by that social interaction even as they controlled it.

To get at Protagoras' account, it is once again necessary to interpret Plato. In the *Protagoras* as in the *Theaetetus*, Plato has manipulated Protagorean ideas in pursuit of the truth about knowledge.[99] Socrates explicitly assumes that Platagoras is claiming to teach human excellence, *aretē* (note Socrates' insertion of this term at 320c1), and that this is a technical skill (*technē*), like painting or flute-playing (318b5–d4, 319a). The question for Plato is, is ethical excellence indeed a skill? Does it depend upon knowledge? Does it aim at a determinate object?[100] To explore these questions, Plato begins by arguing that what Protagoras claims to teach cannot in fact be taught because it is not *knowledge* of how one should act, i.e. ethical virtue. The examples he gives to demonstrate this are apparently independent of Protagoras' own activities, but in fact they suggest indirectly the incoherence of the sophist's position. Socrates cites the behavior of the Athenians in assembly as evidence that (the Athenians believe that) no one has knowledge about *aretē*. This example suggests that each man judges for himself when it comes to political questions (319c7–d8) –

[99] See Ostwald (1977) for a straightforward account of the speech. Both Maguire (1977) and Adkins (1973) have noted that the Great Speech confuses, in Adkins' words, 'cooperative excellences with administrative and political skills.'

[100] For an account of Plato's problems with the craft analogy and his approach to the issue in the *Protagoras*, see Irwin (1977) ch. III, esp. 102f. and Annas (1981) 25.

that is, it refers to the man–measure principle in its political aspect.[101] As in the *Theaetetus*, but here indirectly, Protagoras is being asked to reconcile his teachings with his teaching. And – again as in the *Theaetetus*, where he divided perceptions from judgments of the future or of abstract qualities – Socrates introduces a distinction between two kinds of judgments, one of which evidently does involve knowledge, while the other apparently does not. The Athenians, he asserts, recognize the existence of expertise with respect to 'technical' matters, but with respect to political questions they practice what amounts to free speech (319b–d). In order to respond to Socrates, Platagoras incorporates this distinction into his argument. The second example Socrates provides to show that virtue cannot be taught is the fact that 'in private life the wisest and best citizens are unable to hand on to others the excellence (*aretē*) they possess' (319e).[102] Despite the reference to 'private life,' Socrates is still interested in political excellence: note 'citizens,' and his choice of Pericles as exemplar.[103] Again, the implication is that Protagoras himself is mistaken: how can he claim to teach political excellence when even the best men, including those whom he has trained, do not in consequence possess any *knowledge* which they can transmit to their sons?

Although Platagoras defends at length both the practices of the Athenians and the possibility of transmitting excellence, his argument is condemned to incoherence by Plato's formulation of the issue. The young Athenian aristocrat, Hippocrates, comes to Protagoras because he wishes to be eminent in the city (316c); Protagoras undertakes to make him extremely effective in political affairs (319a1). Socrates proceeds to equate this political excellence with being a good citizen (319a4–5) and affirms this point by citing Pericles as one of the wisest and best of the citizens who, in private life, fails to transmit his excellence (319e). This equation of citizenship and leadership is not only plausible, given Athenian assumptions about political life,[104] but it also eases the transition to Platagoras' argument for the teachability of a political virtue which is merely competence, not excellence. By his emphasis on the authoritativeness of every citizen's political judgments,

---

101 Cf. Winton (1974) 73. Note the implication in Xenophon's *Memorabilia* 3.6 (Socrates' discussion with young Glaucon) that in fact the members of the assembly demand that their leaders be knowledgeable and experienced.

102 On the connection between this example and the *Dissoi Logoi*, see Taylor (1976) 78–9.

103 At 319a Platagoras claims to teach *euboulia* (good judgment) with respect to both private and public matters. See also Plato, *Gorgias* 520e and Aristotle, *EN* 1140b for a similar assimilation of the two realms.

104 See Taylor (1976) 71–2, Adkins (1973).

and on the universal competence which makes these judgments socially valid, Platagoras seems to concede that he does not in fact teach *excellence*, at least not in the conventional sense. And by adopting Socrates' distinction between other skills and a shared and minimal political 'art,' Platagoras makes way for the claim that the proper paradigm for the teaching of *excellence* in politics is precisely the technical skills in which expertise is acknowledged. Plato has made one aspect of Protagoras' pedagogic role, namely his analysis of fundamental features of human existence and man's status as measure, answer for the claims of another, namely his own superior ability to guide man's measurings, and to train others to do so. Plato thereby implies that the two – universal competence and individual excellence (like, in the *Theaetetus*, knowledge founded on personal experience and wisdom) – are incompatible, which they are not.

Before I discuss the various clues in the Speech to the incorporation of authentic but garbled Protagorean doctrine, it is worth asking *why* Plato should have provided Platagoras with a Great Speech which may have included genuinely Protagorean ideas.[105] Plato, I suggest, recognized in Protagoras' doctrines certain features of his own outlook. In the Speech Platagoras asks: 'Is there or is there not one quality which every citizen must have, if there is to be a city at all?' (324d9). For Plato and Socrates, as also for Protagoras, human excellence is the basis of political harmony and intellectual virtues underlie political ones. However, for Protagoras, the responsibility for deciding what is right ultimately belongs to the individual, who judges on the basis of his own experience and what he himself knows. Plato, on the other hand, believes that an art of measurement can achieve knowledge of the absolute truth about what is good for a man (356d–357a). The contrast between the two views, and Plato's concern to overrule Protagoras on this question, is reflected in Plato's discussion of the art of measurement versus the power of appearance (356d), and the very use of the term 'measuring skill,' which conjures up Protagoras' infamous 'measure.' At the end of the dialogue, Socrates notes that Protagoras regards excellence as 'anything other than knowledge,' and unfairly concludes that Protagoras has abandoned his original claim that *aretē*

---

[105] In their differing accounts of what is going on in the Speech neither Adkins (1973) nor Maguire (1977) addresses satisfactorily the question of why Plato should have been interested in what they allege to be his portrayal of Protagorean doctrine. For an account of the whole dialogue in these terms, see Winton (1974) who maintains that the structure of the dialogue as well as its argument is designed to undermine Protagoras' claims about the legitimacy of democracy.

is teachable (361b4–c1).[106] Socrates characterizes his own argument as the claim that 'all things are knowledge'[107] – a formula designed to indicate rejection of Protagoras' claim that man is the measure of all things.[108]

Plato wished to refute the view that something other than knowledge of the absolute truth is the key to human survival (see 356d–357b). He therefore used the notions of Protagoras, which he understood as articulating this view, in such a way as to obscure their original coherence and to emphasize distinctions which pointed to the unique importance of knowledge in the Platonic sense and the (alleged) impossibility of teaching anything which is *not* in this sense knowledge. However, the Great Speech is by no means a seamless web. The crookedness of the seams reveals scraps of Protagorean material and hints at their original character and integrity. To anticipate: what Plato seeks to represent here and in the *Theaetetus* as an incoherent conflation of claims about competence and excellence is in fact a coherent account of the existence and function of both levels of ability and the relationship between them.

Competence and excellence

In response to Socrates' challenge to show both that the Athenians are justified in treating all citizens as competent in political matters *and* that he himself is justified in charging fees for inculcating political excellence,[109] Protagoras begins by telling a story about the gods' attempt to equip newly-created and defenseless man for survival.

The crooked seams are created by the incorporation into Protagoras' story of a particular distinction between technical and political understanding at the level of competence. In the first instance, Prometheus gives man survival skills (321d4), also called technical wisdom (321d1) and the art of fire (*empuron technēn*) (321e1), which enables him to invent speech, to fabricate houses, clothes, shoes and bedding, and to secure nourishment from the land (322a5–8). Since this technical skill as represented in Protagoras' myth includes both material skills and the capacity for discourse, it is difficult to see why it is later described (by Hermes) as having been distributed only to particular

---

[106] See Taylor (1976) 214.

[107] The Greek phrases are, respectively, *panta chremata estin epistemē* and *pantōn chrematōn metron estin anthropos*.

[108] Taylor (1976) 214.

[109] This is analogous to the challenge in the *Theaetetus* to show both that no one judges what's false *and* some men are wiser than others.

individuals (322c5–7).[110] If technical skill is the capacity to survive, then every member of the species must have been endowed with it by Prometheus; if it is specialized knowledge, the product of division of labor (as Hermes' example of the doctor implies, 322c6), then it would seem to presuppose precisely the sort of communal life which Platagoras asserts is impossible without political skill. *politikē technē*, understood as the capacity to live in peace with other human beings, is distributed to all men, just as the original gift of the gods, the capacity to provide food and shelter for oneself, must also have been distributed to all men if the species was to survive. A minimal competence in both skills must be possessed by all. Thus the underlying force of the argument undercuts Platagoras' conclusion, apparently on the basis of the story, that:

When there is a question about carpentry or any other expertise, everyone including the Athenians thinks it right that only a few should give advice ... and quite right too, in my view – but when it comes to consideration of how to do well in running the city, which must proceed entirely through justice and soundness of mind, they are right to accept advice from anyone, since it is incumbent on everyone to share in that sort of excellence if there is to be a city at all. (322d6–323a4)[111]

That Protagoras in fact regarded competence as appropriate to both political and other skills, despite Plato's insertion of a distinction, is also suggested by the example of the flute-player. At first, Plato makes Platagoras contrast flute-playing with the excellence of the citizen. A man who asserts that he is a good flautist, yet is not, will be ridiculed or treated as a madman, whereas every citizen is expected to lay claim to political excellence (*aidōs* and *dikē*) whether or not he actually possesses it (323a7–c1). Again, the effectiveness of the contrast depends upon a conflation of competence and excellence. The competent but uninspired flautist who boasts of his muscial *aretē* is in the same position as the law-abiding citizen who makes false claims about his abilities as a political leader: both risk ridicule.[112] Later in the dialogue, Plato has Platagoras use the flute-playing analogy in a way which reveals this parallelism and thus the illegitimacy of the earlier contrast. In his attempt to respond to Socrates' assertion that 'good men often have worthless sons' (326e6), Platagoras again initially interprets as

---

[110] Winton (1974) 19 argues that Prometheus would have preferred to have given men *politikē technē* from the start, *instead* of this *demiourgikē technē*. This makes sense only if the former *includes* the latter. On the inclusion of language, see Maguire (1977) 115, Winton (1974) 19 n. 49.

[111] Cf. 324c6–d1; here and in what follows, translations are from Taylor (1976).

[112] Note the illustration of this in the Xenophontic portrayal of Socrates mentioned in n. 101 above.

'excellence' what is in fact competence: he does not show that good men produce excellent sons in the ordinary sense of that term, but rather that all sons of citizens are skilled practitioners of justice by comparison with anyone brought up outside a law-governed society (327c5–e1). To clarify this claim, the sophist asks Socrates to imagine a *polis* to whose continued existence flute-playing is essential. In such a *polis*, every citizen would receive constant instruction in flute-playing from every other citizen. As a result every member of the *polis* would be a competent flute-player by comparison with someone completely unskilled and unacquainted with flute-playing (327c3–4).

According to Platagoras, Socrates has failed to perceive that teaching of social – like other – skills occurs at two levels: (1) those who are themselves competent teach the basics (Socrates has failed to notice these teachers because, when it comes to social virtues, and similarly the Greek language, everyone is a teacher (327e–328a)) and (2) the talented few teach those who are already competent but wish to be proficient. Thus Socrates would also not find it easy to locate a teacher if he were 'looking for someone to teach the sons of craftsmen the craft they learn from their father, in so far as he and his friends in the craft can teach them ... though it's perfectly easy to find someone to teach complete novices' (328a2–8).[113] The existence of society both requires and ensures that everyone learns the social virtues and language, so everyone teaches them.[114] Once one has learned these basic virtues, one is in the position of the son of the craftsman, who has been taught what he needs to know but not necessarily everything he wishes to know or is capable of learning. Thus the distinction between the technical and political realms introduced by Plato in the analysis (*logos*) as well as the story (*muthos*) to adapt Protagorean material to Socratic concerns can be seen to be irrelevant to – indeed, implicitly at odds with – the shape of Protagoras' account. Protagoras acknowledges two levels of ability which characterize all forms of human action; the distinction he draws is between those qualities essential to the existence of the *polis* and those which are not, and, corre-

---

[113] As Winton (1974) 9f. has discussed in detail, the reasons why Socrates will fail to find a teacher of Greek and crafts respectively are not, as the text implies, the same or strictly parallel. The former has to do with Socrates' blindness to reality, the second with the real scarcity of men capable of teaching 'those who already possess the essentials of a craft.'

[114] As Taylor (1976) 98–9 points out, Protagoras seems to assume that it is only necessary to show that excellence is taught, not to demonstrate that it is in fact *successfully* communicated in civilized society. I would suggest that the historical Protagoras was not interested in the question of whether *aretē* is something (e.g. knowledge of some determinate thing) that can be taught, but rather was interested in the fact of socialization.

spondingly, between two ways in which excellence and competence
are related.

Universal competence is possible – in crafts, arts, linguistic ability,
justice – and in skills deemed essential it has been achieved. However,
Protagoras also acknowledges that talent, intelligence and virtue are
unevenly distributed. Within a society governed by laws, some men
are less just than others (see 327c5) although all are competent, just as
in the flute-playing *polis* some men turn out to be better musicians
than others (327b5). It is, therefore, hardly surprising that the sons of
accomplished men often do not match their fathers' achievements, for
natural aptitudes differ (327b8).[115] As Platagoras suggests by means of
the flute-playing analogy, the reason why it may appear in the arts and
crafts as if excellence is transmitted from father to son is that under ordinary circumstances the best flute-players teach only their own sons.
In the flute-playing *polis* these men would also teach other people's
sons, so that each person would fulfill his natural potential.[116] In the
existing *polis*, everyone teaches, or transmits, the essential social
virtues and skills like obedience to law and language, so that everyone
achieves competence. Above this basic level, however, the social and
the technical diverge – or rather, they diverge in the democratic *polis*.
In the oligarchic *polis*, the best men teach only their own sons or peers,
just as, in all *poleis* whatever, the best craftsmen tend to transmit their
skills to their sons. There are no flute-playing *poleis*. In all *poleis*,
above the most basic level, the level of linguistic ability, the capacity to
use fire and the like, there is a division of labor in the technical skills.
In the democratic *polis*, however, there is no political division of
labor. The most skilled and virtuous citizens teach everyone, via interaction in the assembly and on the council, and as a result everyone
achieves the competence associated, in the technical realm, with the
son of the craftsman, and *all* those who are naturally gifted, not
merely the sons of the gifted, attain excellence. Thus Protagoras suggests, in defiance of aristocratic tradition, that political excellence is a
social achievement, not a natural legacy, and that the political realm,
unlike the technical or social, is a realm of universal competence and
equal opportunity to achieve excellence. It is this distinction between
the political and the technical, i.e. the difference in their social function,
and not the implied difference between the objects of competence and
the objects of knowledge that Plato insinuates into Protagoras' account,
which enables Protagoras to explain Athenian political behavior.

[115] See Taylor (1976) 99–100, Winton (1974) 6ff.
[116] I owe this point to Winton (1974) 6ff.

Socrates asks Platagoras to defend the alleged Athenian practice of seeking only expert advice on technical matters while allowing all and sundry to speak on issues of public policy. The inappropriateness of Platagoras' account considered as a response to *this* question is evident from two complementary points of view. The first is the incoherence in detail of the distinction between technical and political ability at the level of competence. If the politically competent man is capable of contributing to a political discussion, why is not a technically competent man capable of contributing to a technical one?[117] The second is the corresponding incoherence of the distinction at the level of excellence. If some men, like Platagoras and those he trains, do indeed surpass others in their political understanding and/or ability, as he concedes (328b), why are not they alone consulted on political questions, like experts in shipbuilding on questions about the seaworthiness of the navy? The true character of Athenian behavior is more complicated than the sketch Socrates offers, and the Protagorean account visible in the Great Speech does justice to it.[118] Those who were technically competent but not expert, e.g. men with experience in the rigors of battle, would no doubt have contributed to discussions about equipping an expedition. However, because of the difference revealed by the fact that there is no flute-playing *polis* but there is a democratic one, competence in technical skills is not universal, so most men are not expected to be able to contribute. In the democratic *polis*, since all men profit from the guidance of the noble and good men, including those men trained by sophists, and from their own experience of political decision-making, all men have something to con-

[117] Cf. Taylor (1976) 83.
[118] It has been suggested by Irwin (1985) *contra* Kraut (1984) that Socrates' example concerns only the unteachability of virtue, and is not intended to impugn democracy nor to suggest a connection between the two, because even after listening to experts the entire assembly rendered a decision by majority vote. However, this view assumes that what was essential to democracy as conceived by Plato and Protagoras was a formal mechanism akin to modern voting, when in fact what is at issue is the existence of a civic competence that justified general participation not just via voting but by speaking in the assembly and serving as magistrates and jurors. The question for Socrates, Plato and Protagoras was: is there a general political competence inculcated through socialization? Although Socrates does not here directly attack the idea that the many are qualified to make political decisions (cf. Thuc. 6.38.5–39.1). This was in general a target of Socratic and Platonic criticism (as Irwin himself indicates elsewhere in the review, n. 20). Moreover, Plato's treatment of Protagorean doctrine in the *Protagoras*, conflating as it does the issues of competence and excellence in response to a question about the teachability of virtue, suggests that Plato saw the two as connected to each other and to the question of whether political virtue can be inculcated. Cf. *Theaetetus* 172a–b, discussed above (p. 68).

tribute to a political discussion. Universal competence is, however, both complemented and made possible by the excellence of a few. For Protagoras, universal competence and expertise are not mutually exclusive: expertise is not knowledge of a sort that renders all other beliefs irrelevant, but rather consists of prudence based on experience.

In the first section of the *Protagoras*, Plato sought to undermine an account of political life which assumed that men could be taught both competence and excellence, and that this process did not involve the transmission of 'knowledge' in the Platonic sense. Plato's strategy was to insert his conception of the relationship between knowledge and excellence (on the craft analogy) into an integrated exposition composed of elements from two distinct but related aspects of Protagorean doctrine: socialization and leadership. These two aspects and their interrelation are made to seem incoherent as a unified answer to a Platonic question. However, they are coherent as in part a response to an earlier, differently conceived but (for Plato) usefully similar question about the status of democratic decision-making: had not the Athenians placed control of political affairs in the hands of incompetents?[119] Incompetence did not refer to lack of expertise or of specialized knowledge, but rather to the characteristic ignorance and indiscipline of the *hoi polloi* as compared to the traditional elite. Thus Herodotus makes Megabyzus praise oligarchy by attacking the masses: nothing, he says, is less intelligent and more arrogant than the 'useless' mob (3.81).[120] The coherent, integrated analysis visible within the garbled Great Speech indicates that all the citizens are competent; this competence, combined with experienced leadership, not only makes possible but is constitutive of a well-ordered society. Protagoras' ideas are responsive to the question of democratic legitimacy both positively and negatively: the interaction characteristic of and essential to the *polis* ensures that the decision-making *demos* is *not* uncontrolled and ignorant and that the best possible leadership flourishes; both the *demos* and its traditional leaders[121] must recognize that their interests rest with the active participation of all the citizens.

Protagoras himself is one of the talented few who surpass other men

---

[119] See Winton (1974) 21; cf. O'Brien (1967) 74.

[120] Cf. Hdt. 3.82, Ar. *Knights* 188–93: leadership is not for the learned or *chrestos* man, but for the *amathes* and *bdeluros*; [Xen.] *Ath. Pol.* 1.5, 1.7, where the people are described as exhibiting *amathia, ataxia, poneria*. For other references, see O'Brien (1967) 74, though I disagree with his formulation of the question as one about 'experts'/'laymen' rather than 'traditional elite'/'rabble.'

[121] See Loenen (1941) 19f. for the suggestion that Protagoras was in part responding to the danger of aristocratic self-assertion.

in making people noble and excellent (328b). There are two related aspects to his teaching: the one, his analytical account of social relations, is addressed to all citizens and forms part of the general inculcation of virtue, while the other, the training of successful politicians, enables young men of talent to (1) extend and organize their understanding of human society[122] and (2) bring others around to their own view, based on that understanding, of the interests of the *polis*. Protagoras is not, of course, a citizen; he is a sophist who teaches the wealthy. As Platagoras notes, some members of society – namely the wealthiest – are able to send their sons to school for a longer period (326c); yet such private tutoring is continuous with the broader, public forms of socialization which ensure that, as in the flute-playing *polis*, everyone realizes his potential ability to contribute to the good of the *polis*. Those who have received extensive or specialized training – from, e.g., a sophist – become the city's leaders and 'teach' the citizens in assembly. The democracy does not efface social and economic differences, but it does absorb them into the political realm. Protagorean teaching is not only continuous with socialization in form – i.e. by operating through political leaders – but also in content. What Protagoras teaches is not a skill divorced from a consideration of human needs and ends, but rather a way of analyzing and promoting them. The reflection he provokes is not only compatible with, but even essential to, the vitality of democratic interaction. Protagoras' analysis of society served as an instrument as well as a description of the reconciliation of free interaction and order.

Protagoras' story as argument

To appreciate this, it is important first to understand how and why Protagoras fashioned an argument out of the materials of myth and naturalistic anthropology. If we assume that the myth recounted by Plato is broadly Protagorean, then it seems that the sophist participated in some way in the fifth-century attempts to specify the origins of culture, technology and civilization, to which the fragments of Archelaus and Anaxagoras, among others, bear witness.[123] Archelaus' genetic account of the development of the world led him to believe that men's notions, including the concept of justice (*to dikaion*), had developed gradually and variously; as Hecataius and later Herodotus

---

[122] See Cole (1972) 35 on the purpose of the *antilogiai*.
[123] On Archelaus, see DK 47 A 1, A 4, with Heinimann (1945) 113ff.

had demonstrated, a great range of customs now existed.[124] Archelaus
investigated the physical processes that resulted in the emergence of
man and, through man, civilization. But Archelaus' interest in prehistory, and even his conclusion that civilization – laws, cities, justice – is
man-made, do not warrant the inference that he and Protagoras were
engaged in the same endeavor.[125] Protagoras' story is not a naturalistic
account of the rise of human society. Protagoras was interested not in
how the world came to be, but in how it was. His account of the development of human society is analytic, not genetic.

Protagoras is made to say that Socrates' question about whether
excellence is something one can learn could be answered by means of a
story (*muthos*) or an argument (*logos*) (320c), which suggests that the
story he decides to tell is not intended primarily as a historical or
anthropological account of human society, but an explanatory one.
(The gods are mythological trimmings.) As in the fables of Aesop, the
historical/anthropological, as well as the divine, element in the
muthos is mythological.[126] That is, it is used to express insights into
man's present condition, not his origins. However, even those fables
which adopt the form of an explanation and most resemble, super-
ficially, Protagoras' *muthos*, are merely divine aetiologies for some
familar aspect of human experience.[127] By contrast, Protagoras'
account, despite the inclusion of the gods, is analytical; moreover, the
inclusion of animals is not a charming transposition of human concerns, but a means of identifying the uniqueness of the human plight.[128]
Thus, although it is true that the myth is not intended as a historical or
anthropological account of the origins of man or the *polis*, it is important that it is an account which could (minus the detachable involvement of divinity) describe the actual experience of the species and that

---

[124] According to Heinimann (1945) 120, Archelaus' emphasis on *nomos* was the result of the
        influence of Protagorean doctrines. Archelaus' emphasis on *nomos* may have been
        derived from Protagoras, but Archelaus shows no evidence of having considered the
        question which is, for Protagoras, the most important: not did men create laws, but why
        did they do so?

[125] As Kahn (1981) suggests.

[126] Winton (1974) 12f. suggests this parallel, citing especially Fables (in Perry's edition
        (1952)) 57, 100, 102, 103, 105, 108, 109, 240, 259, 266, 430, 444, 531. The genre, as
        he notes, existed in classical as well as archaic Greece. Cf. Plato, *Phaedo* 61b6, Ar. *Birds*
        651–3. See Hdt. 2.134 on Aesop's life.

[127] See, e.g., nos. 108, 159, 240, 266.

[128] Thus, despite certain resemblances, both Fables 311 and 181 differ importantly from the
        muthos: the first, because it fails to make anything of man's superiority to the animals,
        and the second, because the moral is not applied to man *as such* and explained in terms of
        certain necessary features of existence.

it not only illustrates how men do in fact behave, but also how it is necessary that they should behave.

Comparison with the modern genre with which it is frequently identified, social contract theory, helps to show that Protagoras' *muthos* is an argument, and what *kind* of argument it is. Social contract theory is not a naturalistic account of the rise of human society, but rather a theory about human nature and the necessary characteristics of human society.[129] Protagoras, like Hobbes and Hume, tells a humanly plausible story designed to illuminate and thereby shape the motivations and behavior of his contemporaries. The way in which Protagoras' theory aims to speak to contemporary man as he is differs from the approach of Hume as well as Hobbes, although it shares certain features of both modern accounts.[130] Like Hobbes's state of nature, Protagoras' picture of man's beastly prepolitical state would have had imaginative force for contemporaries because of the real danger of violent conflict and disintegration. However, while Hobbes's 'state of nature' is a state of relations (war) among solitary humans, Protagoras envisions man as not-yet-man. Unlike the seventeenth-century theorists, Protagoras does not appeal to a pre-civilized human condition because he regards man as essentially self-sufficient, his freedom as utterly unconditioned, and his ties to society, unlike his rights against it, as contingent and the product of agreement.[131] For Protagoras, society is constitutive of man's identity. The story is designed as a means of enlightenment; forceful presentation of man as not-yet-man helps man in society to appreciate that his humanity is social. Protagoras, unlike Hobbes, lived in a time in which reason was not yet widely perceived as a destructive instrument. He portrayed order in the *polis* as immanent; he did not regard the unity of society as dependent upon the authority of a 'supreme reason' which creates order by transcending the autonomy of 'private appetite' and 'private knowledge.'[132] In Protagoras' account, man in society relies upon what he himself knows. Social interaction organizes and shapes his beliefs in a way which enables him to interpret his experi-

129 See Hampton (1986) 266–79. I disagree with some basic aspects of Hampton's argument, but I have learned a great deal from her analysis. She seeks to show how social contract theories perform a 'joint explanatory and justificational task.' Note that the status of contractarian accounts as *history* is not irrelevant to all theories which include a description of the state of nature. See Tuck (1979) 43 on natural law theory and Dunn (1969) ch. 9 on Locke's religious interpretation of the state of nature.

130 I do not here have room to do more than make a brief (but, I hope, suggestive) comparison.

131 For a précis of the modern vision, see Taylor (1985) introduction and 248–88.

132 Hobbes, *Leviathan* 15, *De cive* xii, 6, cited by Wolin (1960) 258.

ence more knowledgeably and prudently. The content of Protagoras'
theory speaks to man as he finds himself in society; the theory promotes what it enjoins, namely the cultivation of the social virtues.

Together, the *muthos* and *logos* argue that (why) society is necessary to man's existence and flourishing *qua* man; they suggest that certain aspects of man's nature make social harmony difficult and
indicate how, nevertheless, it is possible. Protagoras did not design his
portrayal of prepolitical existence or the shift towards political society
as a blueprint for contemporary political action (as indeed the incorporation of a divine mechanism for the shift suggests). The story is
wholly an account of human nature, *not* an account of the society this
entails; it includes no naturalistic account of *how* men come to form
societies. Men live in 'scattered units'[133] and are unsuccessful in their
attempts to live in larger, more secure communities until they are
given respect (*aidōs*) and justice (*dikē*) by Zeus. In the *logos*, however,
there is an account of man's progressive adaptation to social life which
recalls those elements of Hume's vision of the analogous development
of species and person which are essential to his claim to be providing
an argument relevant to the situation of contemporary man.[134] Parents
teach their children about right and wrong from the time they are
small; teachers continue the process; 'and when they have left school
the city itself makes them learn the laws and live according to their
example' (326d). Such an account appears only in the *logos*, only in
Protagoras' discussion of how society makes social harmony possible,
and *not* in his story about man's need for society. That is, *aidōs* and
dikē are not adopted or deliberately fostered by solitary individuals;
society fosters these qualities and is held together by them.[135]

Protagoras' theory resembles Hume's. In both, it is the existence of
society that makes society possible. For Hume as for Protagoras, it
seems, society is transformational, in the sense that it requires and
fosters certain human qualities, e.g. *aidōs* and *dikē*. Hume's account
of progressive socialization suggests that society molds man's 'affections': it makes him different. And the implicit claim that the account
itself can persuade men of the point of society suggests that men can be
given new reasons for action which are not merely means to achieve

---

[133] See Taylor (1976) 84–5.   [134] Hume, *Treatise of Human Nature*, esp. II.2.
[135] So that what, e.g., Kerferd (1953) regards as a 'confusion' is in fact a meaningful clue to
the character of Protagoras' vision. Note that Protagoras' emphasis is on the survival of
the *species*, not – as in, e.g., Hobbes's account – on any particular man's desire to preserve his own life; the point is not only survival, but flourishing *qua* man.

ends posited by existing, and static, desires.[136] Yet Hume nonetheless regards man *qua* man as a being prior to society and motivated by fixed – and natural – affections. These assumptions undermine the plausibility of his theory as a theory about man as he is in society. In Protagoras' account society produces not only habits of self-restraint, but also enlightenment. All men are teachers of political virtue, but some men, like himself, are better teachers than others. What these accomplished teachers do is not only, like Hume's 'politicians,' to 'produce an esteem for justice'[137] but also to bring men to see that it is rational for them to esteem it. The *muthos* and *logos* are part of this process. (Protagoras also produces enlightenment indirectly, by training politicians to influence the perceptions of the citizens.) Unlike Hobbes and Hume, Protagoras succeeds in formulating a theory that speaks directly to contemporary man as he finds himself, because he assumes both that man is shaped by society and that society is shaped by man. The combination means that a social theory can have both access and influence.

The power of Protagorean theory to effect what it endorses is also a function of the kind of society it portrays and to which it is addressed. Like the eighteenth-century advocates of participatory democracy, notably Rousseau and Mill, and unlike Hobbes and Hume or theorists of the stable, bureaucratic, representative democracies of today, Protagoras believes that the integrity of the social order and the attitudes and character of individual citizens are interdependent, and that each shapes the other through the process of political participation.[138] The existence of society in Hume's sense, founded on 'natural justice,'[139] namely the ability to co-operate and to exercise self-restraint in the absence of civil authority is, for Protagoras, a necessary *and* a sufficient condition for the promotion of man's interests *qua* man. Man is a creature such that he must exercise self-restraint to co-operate with his fellow man, but *not* such that he must submit to him.[140] This

---

[136] See *Treatise* II.2 and MacIntyre (1967) 175.   [137] Hume, *Treatise* II.2.

[138] See Pateman (1970) ch. II, especially 22–3, 25. Note that Rousseau's state was not, unlike Athens, a democracy in the sense that the citizens executed the laws as well as legislated.

[139] Hume, *Treatise* II.1.

[140] Compare Hume and Protagoras on the link between waging war and political relations. In Hume's account, men who live in non-hierarchical concord must, in case of war, give authority to some single person who 'instructs them in the advantages of government,' *Treatise* II.8. For Protagoras, man is an animal who must by his very nature band together with his fellow man to wage war in his own defense. Natural order exists only when the *polis* exists – when man, as a species, is able to defend himself. Cf. analysis by Winton (1974) 18–19.

difference between Protagoras and Hume, and, even more starkly, Hobbes, is attributable to the fact that Protagoras' vision of political society does not divide society from government (or 'the state'). In the *polis*, and particularly the democratic *polis*, the citizens are autonomous and self-disciplining, and the policy-making power of the community is not regarded as external to the individual. Although democracy posited a discrete political realm of civic equality distinct from the realm of social and economic differences, it was through the political realm that men expressed and secured their interests and realized their identity. The *polis* is in Hume's sense a *society*; yet it is fully political in the sense that it legislates and enforces social standards and is capable of mobilizing its collective strength against external threats. Although there exist magistrates and generals, there is no question of the systematic submission of some men to the authority of others. Government is not 'coercive power,' but the direct expression of the collective good. Hobbes's view occupies the other extreme: society cannot exist without government in the sense of coercive power. It is because Protagoras does not regard political society as something extra, something external, that his theory succeeds in being humanly plausible. Society is social interaction, social harmony is the result of internal (not institutional) constraints, and social theory provides the citizen with his own, internal reasons for cultivating the social virtues. The political interaction characteristic of a direct, participatory democracy is self-sustaining, for it fosters the very qualities and attitudes on which free social order depends.

The root of the argumentative power of theories that analyze social man into his various elements thrives at the level of Protagorean theory, namely an analysis of the social character of human interests. It is this – and not the vision of man as constructing a political order external to and independent of himself – which gives such a theory plausibility for men as they are.[141] The analysis of man's social nature is not at base concerned with how men incur political obligations, but rather with the reasons why they should consider themselves obliged, reasons which do not invoke consent.[142] What is at issue for Hobbes and Hume, as well as for Protagoras, is not the legitimacy of any particular government, but the necessity of political society (which, for Hobbes, entails absolute sovereignty). Their theories are arguments for political obligation at its most general and basic level. Hume

---

[141] Cf. Hampton (1986) 270 who argues that social contract theories derive their force in part from representing the state as 'hired' by the subjects.

[142] See Dunn (1967) 156.

makes this explicit: he argues that it is not *consent* which underlies the legitimacy of government – certainly, as the history of the world demonstrates, it cannot account for the legitimacy of *actual* governments[143] – but rather man's interest in the security and protection which political society can offer.[144] Hobbes assimilated his account of sovereignty by acquisition to his model of sovereignty by institution; voluntary 'consent' in the one case seemed to him much like coerced 'consent' in the other. This is because it is not actually *consent* that interests him, but rather the way in which commonwealths – all commonwealths, whatever their history – serve real human interests.[145]

If even the modern theories are to be construed as analyses of man's interests *qua* man and not as claims about the relationship between citizens and rulers, yet it nonetheless remains true that for Hume and Hobbes political society is extrapolated from, and is external to, the individual human being.[146] But does such an individual exist? And can a society conceived in these terms survive? There is a sense in which the Hobbesian and Humean theories as theories – not in their characterizations of 'natural,' isolated man – are accounts of man as a social being. In the case of Hobbes, individual man is not merely fearful and self-concerned, but – in order that the society he *needs* may exist – he is rational and capable of interpreting his interests in terms of the existence, aims and characteristics of other men.[147] Hume thought in terms of individual man, his aims and desires, but argued that this abstraction could not in fact be found: men are naturally inclined to live in families, and the societies they form gradually shape their own sentiments.[148] Nevertheless, the very attempt to characterize man as an individual, outside society, and to build political society out of such individuals, results in theories which lack human plausibility, and are not relevant to the experience of particular men as they find themselves in society.[149] This may seem a paradoxical claim about Hobbes, since it is he who regards man as fundamentally the same within society as without it. Yet it is precisely because Hobbes's natural man

---

[143] Hume, *Of the Original Contract*, Hardie (1948) 360; cf. Dunn (1967) 177f.

[144] Hume, *Treatise* II.2.9, III.2.8.

[145] Hobbes, *Leviathan* ch. 20; see Dunn (1969) 98.

[146] See Altham (1979) 143; cf. MacIntyre (1967) 176, Hampton (1986) 270–1.

[147] See Skinner (1964) 326: to say that a man is obliged to obey the dictates of reason is 'simply to say that he fulfills the definition of being a man.'

[148] *Treatise* II.2: 'His very first state and situation may justly be esteemed social.' See Laslett (1956) 168.

[149] See MacIntyre (1967) 124, 134–5, Aron (1967) 169, Mackie (1977) 113, 120, Galston (1980) 4.

is consistently himself[150] – narrowly self-interested, with limited vision and sympathies – that the society he allegedly wants because he *needs* it may well remain external to the wants and needs felt by any actual person in society. Hobbesian society is, in fact, radically unstable. Once in society, man as conceived by Hobbes has no good reason not to exploit the general observance of the rules – if he can get away with it.[151] A theory that characterizes man as essentially asocial will either fail to address the concerns of man as he is in society, or if it does succeed in addressing them, will not provide the agent with a humanly plausible reason why he should act so as to preserve social harmony, and will therefore fail to *be* an argument for the necessity and possibility of political society. Although Hume appreciated the function of socialization in habituating man to social existence and disposing him to act virtuously, this approach mars his theory as well as Hobbes's. For Hume, man is affective and asocial man. Man *qua* man has no motivation to act justly. Hume argues that morality is the best means to an end which, as it happens, men desire. Man's attachment to society remains conditional, and his vision of himself that of an autonomous, self-sufficient agent. Yet the very capacity for autonomy and independent assessment of one's interests is itself not merely a social but a political artefact of a particular culture.[152] Compare Protagoras' *muthos*, which reveals that man is a political animal: analyzing his nature, as the story does, shows that man's existence is irreducibly social, and that no conception of morality or capacity to live by it attaches to men as individuals. This analysis serves to identify man's physical limitations and needs, and his inability, *qua* isolated head-of-household, to see beyond his own immediate and narrow self-interest. Political society overcomes these limitations, meets these needs, and supplies this inability; but it cannot do so *as* simply the combination of such stripped-down creatures.

Protagoras' version of a naturalistic account of political society[153] differs from the modern one in that the characteristic form of social life required for human survival is regarded as constitutive of a fully

---

[150] Cf. MacIntyre (1967) 139, 143, 176.

[151] His view of laws is what Hart (1961) 88 called 'external': he is 'only concerned with them when and because (he judges) that unpleasant consequences are likely to follow violation.' For a system of law to succeed, some significant proportion of the citizens must regard legal rules 'from the internal point of view,' i.e. not only voluntarily help maintain the rules, but also 'see their own and other persons' behavior in *terms* of the rules' (pp. 88, 189, 191, 197). See also Hampton (1986) 268, 270.

[152] See Taylor (1985) 204–8.

[153] Hart (1961) 189, following Hobbes and Hume.

human life. That is, political society is not merely instrumental but rather essential to human well-being, and it secures not man's mere persistence as a sentient creature, but his development as a creature capable of genuine autonomy and freedom. Protagoras' account differs from other *ancient* teleologies (e.g. Plato, Aristotle) in that its view of what it is to be (fully) a man is achievable by every citizen of a *polis*, and survival *and* flourishing are equally the product of politics. The very process that enables every citizen to *be* a citizen (and hence fully a man) enables him to be the best citizen and man he can possibly be. Every citizen is able to realize his capacities. This is suggested by the story of the flute-playing *polis*: if flute-playing, like the political virtues, were essential to the existence of the *polis*, and thus everyone taught everyone else what they knew, the result would be general competence and individual variation based on differences in natural talent (327c), not on the luck of having been born the son of an excellent flute-player, nor, it would seem, of having been born wealthy.[154] Thus Protagoras' conception of political excellence (*aretē*) includes both political success and power *and* basic political dispositions, as Plato's report suggests, but in a unified and coherent – not, as Plato would have it, a confused – account. Personal excellence (*aretē*) is defined in terms of one's contribution to a common project, the *polis*, and encompasses both the negative willingness to observe rules, or laws, or conventions which are the 'bonds of community,'[155] and positive participation in furthering the aims of the *polis* by contributing as best one can to the process of socialization and enlightenment in the interests of harmony and rational purposefulness. The natural qualities which correspond to innate musical talent are practical intelligence – the ability to interpret experience, generalize from it, appreciate its implications[156] – and the ability to communicate this understanding to others.

A political theory that sought to accommodate the realities of Athenian political life had to conceive politics and the *polis* as responsive to and expressive of the purposes of all citizens and yet explain why it would not dissolve into anarchy or incoherence. Protagoras met the challenge by combining an appeal to man's own understanding of his interests with a theory about the relationship between human nature and the requirements of society. Protagoras' theory does not refer to

---

[154] For a persuasive exegesis of the passage along these lines, see Winton (1974). Cf. Adkins (1973).

[155] See *Prot.* 322c: *aidōs* and *dikē* are *desmoi philias*. Cf. MacIntyre (1981) 141–2.

[156] See MacIntyre (1981) 145ff., on the relation between intelligence and the virtues.

all biologically-human beings as such, but to citizens or citizenship-
bearers (daughters or wives of citizens)[157] in communities ruled by
nomoi (i.e. not tyrannies). The idea of equality of worth across the
species or indeed outside the civic framework was alien to the
Greeks.[158] It was the achievement of democracy to secure the formal
equality within the civic structure of men who were patently unequal.
The attitudes characteristic of the ancient Greeks and their way of organizing privilege secreted a teleological view of man, the view that
men are to be judged and treated according to their realization of
human potential. No man was deemed to have rights or dignity simply
qua human being. Men were accorded respect and privileges, including political privileges, in line with their qualities, achievements and
contributions. Democracy's radical extension of such privileges, and
formal respect, to all members of a certain community, was confirmed
and emphasized by Protagoras. He sought to show that the highest
possible development of all individuals depended on the existence of a
political community all of whose members exhibited *aidōs* and *dikē*
and participated in politics. It is significant that Protagoras chose the
word *aidōs* to express one of the requisite qualities, for it is an archaic
and aristocratic term for other-regarding respect and a corresponding
sense of shame or self-respect.[159] This respect is now owed to all members of the community by all. What is at stake is not merely the
greatest possible exercise of freedom compatible with order, since evidently some men could hope to secure even greater freedom in a different political structure. Rather, Protagoras seeks to show that the
highest form of self-realization was to be achieved by means of the
constant interaction of men of all classes, since men of great natural
ability were to be found outside the aristocratic elite as well as within
it.

Like its epistemological counterpart, the political version of man—
measure is itself to be explored and debated. Protagoras' *muthos*
awakens the kind of reflections that lead men to perceive, on the basis
of their own experience, that their real interests are political, and that

[157] Protagoras nowhere says that slaves and/or aliens are excluded from his account: however, he refers to 'citizens,' and the society he analyzes is constituted by the interaction
characteristic of *political* relations. Slaves and metics may well be conceived as having
the potential for *aidōs* and *dikē*, but they are unlikely to realize it, except perhaps in the
minimal sense that they are subject to coercion (327d). Contrast Socrates (*Gorgias*
515a4–7, *Apol.* 29d–30b with Kraut (1984) 157) and Plato (*Rep.* 433d with Vlastos
(1968)); see below ch. 7.

[158] See Bordes (1982) 452.

[159] See North (1966) 6; Dreher (1983) 15. Cf. the role of shame in the development of value
as construed by Wollheim (1984).

democratic political order is both possible and desirable. Within society, men act according to their perceptions of their own interests, yet these perceptions are shaped by the broad process of socialization, which includes the sophist's own account of every citizen's nature and hence his interests *qua* man. The sophist, like the politician, must appeal to persons, and to what they can know. Protagoras' claim that there are interests constitutive of being a man is designed to speak to every man's experience of his condition. Every man can, by reflecting on his own experience via Protagoras' story, appreciate that life outside the *polis* would not only be exceedingly precarious, but not fully human. As Sophocles' Philoctetes insists, to be 'friendless, solitary, without a city is to be a corpse among the living.'[160] Furthermore, every man can understand, prompted again by Protagoras' account, what kind of behavior will preserve the *polis* and enhance his own well-being. He comes to recognize that he is a creature who both must (if he is to realize his own potential) and *can* live in a *polis* as a full, participating member. Bringing about this recognition is not merely a matter of altering the behavior of a renegade who does not appreciate the implications of his actions. Protagoras does not *predict* that all agents will adopt his theory as a way of understanding themselves and shaping their participation in society.[161] Yet Protagorean theory provides reason and incentive to believe that they *can* do so. It is the interaction of men who understand the necessity of cultivating *aidōs* and *dikē* (327a–b), an understanding itself cultivated through interaction, which constitutes the socialization that disposes and enables them to practice these virtues.

Protagoras' theory was not, of course, a glassy reflection of political relations in Athenian society: it was a *theory*, an argument. Protagoras himself was an outsider. He offered his theory as part of the process of socialization which he encountered at Athens and which, in his view, could be relied upon to bring all Athenians to a deeper understanding of their own interests, an understanding which would unify them despite (or perhaps even because of the awareness provoked by) factional strife. But the circumstances that may well have prompted Protagoras to formulate his theory also hint at a deeper divisiveness, and the conceptualization of goods independent of a practice formerly regarded as *the* form of life. Democracy embodied a distinction between the civic realm, a realm of equality, and a realm of economic and social differences. Protagoras' ability to formulate an argument

---

[160] Sophocles, *Philoctetes* 1018; see MacIntyre (1981) 127.
[161] Cf. modern critical theories, as characterized by Geuss (1981) 57f.

directed at the implications of this development may have derived
from his position as an outsider, and the argument itself, which laid
the foundations for a distinction between state and society, may have
promoted an external perspective among the members of the practice.
Protagoras, one of the first sophists, argued for what had previously,
it seems, been assumed: the *polis* was a 'necessary of life.'[162] What had
been assumed was that life in an autonomous community was essential to human well-being, but not that this life need be political in the
sense of requiring the active political interaction of all citizens. His
argument was addressed to man as he experienced life in the *polis*, and
challenged citizens to reflect on their needs *qua* men. Such 'subjective
reflection,' despite its original aims, may have led man to think first of
his own needs, and to begin to regard the claims of the *polis* as external. In its epistemological form, man–measure may have fostered the
idea that it is man *qua* man, not *qua* citizen, who measures. In Protagoras' analytical account, no conception of ethics attaches to man as
an individual. If man then comes to think of himself as first and foremost an individual – even a political one – then ethics is unleashed.
Protagoras' theory helped to bring about a loss of innocence. Hegel
remarked that 'a leading principle of the Sophists was that "man is the
measure of all things"; but in this, as in all their apophthegms, lurks
an ambiguity, since the term "man" may denote Spirit in its depth and
truth, or in the aspect of mere caprice and private interest.'[163] For Protagoras, 'man' did denote the deep aspect of spirit as it was manifested
in the flourishing *polis*. Yet it was in part in response to his formulation of a humanly plausible account of the necessity of society, which
appealed to man as he experiences himself and his potential *qua* man,
that others vaunted caprice and private interest.

[162] See Hegel (1956) 252–3.   [163] Hegel (1956) 269.

4   Man's measurings: cosmos and community

According to Protagoras, the form of life inhabited by man *qua* man is political, and so are human needs; criticism and enlightenment proceed within a shared and bounded consciousness. In politics conceived as the arena for the pursuit of the good life for man and the vehicle for increased self-knowledge and knowledge of the good,[1] men are made aware, through their participation in the *polis*, of the human interests which both constitute and are constituted by it. In the process of co-operating to achieve the goods specified by the *polis*, men enhance their own capacities and understanding; part of what they come to understand is how the *polis* is bound up with their own interests. A human practice, like the *polis*, that encompasses and expresses the good life for man can safely enlighten men about the character of that life so long as the practice *does* encompass what man takes to be his own good. External criticism, founded on conceptions of one's own good which are not defined by the practice, is both cause and consequence of disintegration. In the years after Protagoras offered his analysis of the *polis* and its relation to human needs and human awareness, and in part because of this analysis and the developments it reflected, the Athenians came to regard the political practice itself as external, no longer as expressive and constitutive of man's good and his freedom. Instead of viewing such order as there was in the world as something stable in which they participated, men increasingly construed it as something fragile, constructed by man and therefore vulnerable.

This subtle change in outlook is vividly portrayed in Euripides' *Hecuba* (produced in 425/4).[2] The queen of Troy, enslaved by the conquering Greeks, learns that her daughter has nobly confronted death at the hands of the army. Hecuba reflects on the constancy of human,

---

[1] See MacIntyre (1981) 204. MacIntyre sets out his concept of a 'practice,' which is said to include politics in the Aristotelian sense, on pp. 175ff.

[2] See Nussbaum (1986) ch. 13 to which I am indebted; translations are adapted from Nussbaum.

as opposed to inanimate, nature. Nobility, she says, 'is not corrupted in its nature by contingency, but stays good straight through to the end . . . To be nurtured well does offer instruction in nobility. If once one learns this well, one also knows the shameful, learning it by the measuring-stick[3] of the fine' (lines 592–602). Like Protagoras, and even in the face of great misfortune, Hecuba acknowledges that human values are grounded in nothing other than human practices, but that they are nonetheless – or rather, for this very reason – constant and deeply constitutive. Later in the play, however, she is deeply shaken by the news that an old friend, bound to her by the strongest social and personal ties, has cruelly, basely, betrayed her trust and killed the son she had left with him for safekeeping. Outraged, she appeals to her enemy, the leader of the Greek army, King Agamemnon, to avenge this violation of the deepest human values (lines 789–97). She herself is weak. But she says:

The gods are strong, and convention (*nomos*) which rules over them. For it is by *nomos* that we recognize the gods and live our lives, making our distinctions between injustice and justice. And if *nomos*, given into your hands, shall be destroyed [or corrupted] . . . then there is no equivalent [i.e. nothing equal to *nomos*] and nothing fair and just (*ouden ison*)[4] in human life. (lines 799–805)

The practices of men constitute *nomos* which governs even the gods, and human actions can destroy it. The degeneration of communal, political values is evident in Agamemnon's response. Hecuba is weak, a 'nothing,' and she relies on the king to champion the cause of justice (lines 843–4). He is sympathetic to her claim, for he considers her cause to be just (lines 850–3, cf. line 1247). But he is unwilling to risk the anger of his fellow Greeks, who regard Hecuba's enemy as their friend. In reviling him for his cowardice, Hecuba uses language that points beyond the dramatic context to the condition of the contemporary *polis*: 'Alas, among mortals is there no free man? To money or to fortune man is slave; the city's rabble or the provisions of the law constrain him to turn to actions that violate his judgment' (lines 864–7). Political interaction is no guide to right conduct, no expression of freedom. Agamemnon permits Hecuba to wreak her revenge, and expresses the hope that all may be well, 'for it is a common benefit for each individual and for the *polis* that the bad should suffer ill, and the good prosper' (lines 902–4). But the city itself and its leaders, here represented by Agamemnon and the Greeks, are corrupt and will not act

[3] The Greek term is *kanon*. Cf. Democritus' use of the term, below ch. 7.
[4] Literally, 'nothing equal'; see Nussbaum's note, Nussbaum (1986) 400.

to secure the common good. Persuasion and rhetoric are not means to express and secure common values, but rather to manipulate others in pursuit of one's private aims, often by appealing to the very values one is in the process of violating (see lines 816f., 1186f., 1246f.). Once communal trust and openness, and the sense of participating in a common project, have been corroded, the practices that comprise the political order created by man cease to be constitutive of his identity and become mere contrivances, ways of securing personal advantage within a system which can no longer secure the collective good.[5] Men are thrown on to their own resources and look to values or standards or goals independent of the political order.

As Euripides' *Hecuba* discloses, the political vision expressed by Protagoras was unstable. This vision marked the demise of a social characterization of order in terms of a concrete economic-cum-familial and religious hierarchy. The very act of distinguishing a political realm, a realm of formal equality secured by certain practices and institutions, from the world defined by social roles, itself secreted the distinction between man *qua* man and *qua* citizen which, combined with the experiences of Athenian democracy, helped to foster an external conception of the political order. This externalization prompted the appeal, formulated in various different ways, to personal rather than social or political qualities, or to social or political attributes construed in personal terms, that is to qualities deemed to be intrinsic to man and essential to his well-being.

The perception of the political order as external and contingent is described by Glaucon, Plato's brother, in Book Two of Plato's *Republic* as the prevailing view of 'the nature and origin of justice':

> When men have had a taste of both [doing wrong and suffering it] those who have not the power to seize the advantage and escape the harm decide that they would be better off if they made a compact neither to do wrong nor to suffer it . . . So justice is accepted as a compromise, and valued not as good in itself, but for lack of power to do wrong.[6]

This doctrine, readily mistaken for a discursive version of the Protagorean *muthos*, is in fact a radical deformation of the sophist's argument. Glaucon's story of the origins of justice portrays man as a creature who possesses in himself, in advance of the exercise of the

---

[5] See Nussbaum (1986) ch. 13, 406–18.

[6] *Republic* 358e, transl. Cornford. Cf. the formulation of a naturalistic basis for acting justly by the Anonymus Iamblichi, who stresses that no man is strong enough to dominate all the others; and Critias' claim that it is the belief in divine (i.e. inevitable) punishment that deters men from doing wrong even in secret. See Denyer (1983).

social virtues, the capacity to make decisions about his own interests, to weigh up the advantages and disadvantages of living in accordance with justice and law. Protagoras' was at once an agent- and an act-centered theory:[7] *aidōs* and *dikē* are characteristic of the just person; what such a person does is justice; yet the operation of the society created by just persons determines what it is to possess *aidōs* and *dikē* and fosters these qualities. By contrast, Glaucon describes an act-centered view, which portrays justice as a set of rules, arbitrarily imposed.[8] The *necessity* of living in society is not mentioned; the relative equality of men, which leads them to compromise, is regarded as a contingent, not a necessary, feature of the human condition. Here is the legacy of imperial power, power in a realm whose members, individual political communities, are not (unlike men) relatively equal in strength.[9] The extraordinary power of the Athenian empire offered a vivid example of the possibility of violating or even escaping social constraints through sheer strength.[10] If the universal force of a contract theory of justice depends on the inability of any one man to dominate others, then it is potentially vulnerable to the claims of, for example, the aspiring tyrant. In the quest for power,[11] man casts himself off from the practice, and regards himself as unbound. Thus Callicles, in Plato's *Gorgias*, speaks contemptuously of what is merely 'invented' by man – namely laws to constrain the strong – and formulates a moral standard based on the natural capacity to indulge extraordinary desires. Of course, as Callicles' analysis indicates, a group of individuals can also dominate the *polis* and impose its own exclusive interests in the shape of the law. Glaucon's portrayal of the norms of political society as the means to secure goods formulated (at least in theory) independently of political interaction reflects the growing power of the *demos* to pursue its interests both within and outside the *polis*. The flourishing power of the *demos* and of imperial Athens promoted awareness of the possibilities of self-aggrandizement, loosed from the force of those conventions once conceived as shaping and expressing man's freedom and autonomy. According to Aristotle, the Sophist Lycophron (a shadowy fourth-century figure) also offered an external conception of political order: *nomos* is 'a covenant, a guarantee that men will receive justice from one another' (*Pol.* 1280b11).

---

[7] For a discussion of this distinction, see Annas (1981) 157–69.

[8] Annas (1981) 267. Note *Rep.* 360e1 and Glaucon's interest in the 'external' fate of the just and unjust man.

[9] See Hart (1961) ch. X on international law, esp. 190–1.

[10] See Williams (1981a) 242, de Romilly (1963) 300f., 365; cf. Hart (1961) ch. X.

[11] On the ideology of power in this period, see Levy (1976).

Such a construal, Aristotle remarks, portrays society as no more a community than an alliance is, for in neither case does law educate and socialize those subject to it, but merely enforces the external forms of justice.

The transition to this external conception of politics, and its connection with the experience of Athens in the second half of the fifth century, is epitomized in the history of the term *autonomia*.[12] *Autonomia* is not attested before the middle of the century. It was at first applied to the independence and self-determination of the community as a whole, in both its external and its internal relations. As a term that signified freedom from external constraint, it came to be used most frequently and characteristically of the condition of some states in relation to their stronger and menacing neighbors. The eventual application of the term to the situation of a citizen within the *polis* is a sign that internal relations have come to be seen, as Aristotle noted in his reference to Lycophron, as if they were as distanced as external ones. The Hippocratic author of *Airs, Waters, Places* cited in chapter 2 declares that the Europeans, unlike the Asiatics, are independent (*autonomoi*) and act on their own behalf, because they are not ruled by despots (16.9, 16.35, 23.37).[13] The contrast is between despotism, i.e. external control, and self-determination. Although *autonomia* is sometimes used interchangeably with the term for freedom (*eleutheria*) (see, e.g., Thuc. 2.29, 2.96.1–4, 6.88.4; Hdt. 1.95–6, 8.140),[14] it seems likely that it was formulated to express a peculiarly political understanding of freedom, and one embodied in the capacity for self-determination exercised by the Athenians with the advent of democracy. Individual freedom is perceived as a function of collective freedom; the formula appears in Attic prose: because the *demos* rules, the city as a whole is free.[15] The city rules itself; it is free from any form of external control. The connection between *autonomia* and democratic freedom is implicit in Pericles' use of the term in his last speech as reported by Thucydides. According to Pericles, the men who shrink

---

[12] See Ostwald (1982), to whom I am indebted, although I disagree with some of his assumptions and conclusions.

[13] *Contra* Ostwald (1982) 11f. who contrives a distinction between being ruled by another power and by a tyrant within a state, when in most cases of rule by Asiatic powers both were involved. The reference is to despotic institutions, characteristic of Asiatics as opposed to Europeans. See Raaflaub (1983) 527.

[14] *Contra* Ostwald (1982) 15–16, no distinction is implicit in Hdt. 8.140. The Athenians will fight for the freedom of Greece and avenge the destruction of the temples.

[15] See Raaflaub (1983) 522, with references. Cf. Skinner (1984) on Machiavelli's reliance on the connection between internal and external freedom.

from action, who are unwilling to face up to the burdens of empire, that is the 'do-nothings' stigmatized in the Funeral Oration as men who take no part in political affairs and are regarded as 'useless' by the Athenians (2.40.2), would soon ruin a *polis* if their attitude were to prevail or if they were to live *autonomoi* on their own.[16] For, Pericles warned, the 'do-nothing' is not safe unless flanked by the man of action (Thuc. 2.63.2–3). Autonomy depends upon the active participation and daring willingness to take risks characteristic of men who prize self-determination. The democratic freedoms and responsibilities well expressed in the term 'self-rule' or 'giving laws to oneself' (*auto-nomos*) are deemed essential to the freedom of the city and all its citizens. Self-determination is the only form of rule compatible with freedom. The most frequent use of the term *autonomia* in surviving texts refers to a community's external relations,[17] to those elements of self-determination constitutive of the community's freedom yet compatible with belonging to the sphere of influence of a stronger power. *autonomia* in the relationship between one community and another is the capacity for self-determination, often in the context of participation in a larger order (an alliance or traditional hegemony). (See, e.g., Thuc. 5.77.5, 5.79.1, 1.97.1.) In the context of relations among Greek cities, it is characteristically guaranteed by treaty or agreement. *autonomia* is linked to the willingness to offer and respect 'fair and impartial judicial proceedings' (Thuc. 5.79.1, 5.27.2), i.e. not to resort to force before seeking a peaceful settlement of disputes.[18] In one case it is associated with participation in a common assembly (Thuc. 1.97.1). A word that refers to the absence of constraint by powers within or outside the community is used, in the Greek context, to identify how self-governing political communities can preserve their integrity in relations with other communities.

The growing power of the alliances in Greece, and particularly the Athenian empire, in the decades after the Persian Wars, posed a serious threat to the independence of individual communities and no doubt spurred concern to define *autonomia*. The claims of *autonomia* are formulated along the lines of political relations, but political relations in their most formal, external guise, held together by agree-

---

[16] *Contra* Ostwald (1982) this usage is not pejorative, and it makes clear the link between internal (political) and external freedom.

[17] See Ostwald (1982) for classification of the various constituents of *autonomia*.

[18] The ability to defend oneself is also important to *autonomia*. See Thuc. 1.139.3, 3.39.2, 6.89.3. The Aeginetans were exceptional in this respect: formal autonomy seems to have been thought compatible with the loss of ships and walls: Thuc. 1.67.3 with 1.108.4. See Ostwald (1982) 29f.

ments and institutions designed to prevent the coercive use of force. A similar attitude to power and freedom was eventually expressed within the community as well, in relation to an order deemed to be external. Thucydides, describing the reaction of the residents of Attica to the prospect of moving within the walls of Athens, refers to their traditional way of life in the country as *autonomos* (2.16.1). The attitude of the villagers to Athens itself was reminiscent, Thucydides suggests, of the relationship between a *polis* and an alliance (2.16.2). Whatever the accuracy of this characterization as a description of an actual long-standing attitude, it is significant that Thucydides chose these terms to portray the reaction of groups of Athenian citizens to the requirements of a policy designed to ensure the well-being of all Athenians, a policy which put strain on the idea that the good of every citizen, whatever his personal attachments, depended on abiding by the agreed means of furthering the common weal. More striking evidence of an external attitude to the norms of the political community occurs in Sophocles' *Antigone*, produced in 441.[19] The political will of the community is portrayed as narrow and partisan, not as the expression of collective values. Antigone resolves to defy the citizens and the order they secure (see line 78) and show respect for her dead brother, whose corpse has been left to rot outside the walls because he sought to conquer the city. As she goes to her death, condemned by Creon, the chorus declares: 'Power is not to be thwarted so. Your self-sufficiency (*autonomia*) has brought you down' (877). Self-rule and independence now mark a rebellion against standards once conceived as expressive of collective self-determination, and a resolute adherence to values which politics is deemed to have neglected. Self-determination is no longer political; democratic government is no longer seen to be self-government; *autonomia* is now a personal quality and achievement, as Democritus would later insist.

The Athenian experience prompted the reflection that the interaction of men pursuing what they took to be their own interests could not, via the process of socialization, secure the collective good or an order compatible with each citizen's freedom. Men came to doubt that any social processes were definitive of, perhaps even relevant to, the individual's attainment of his own good. The alienation of *nomoi* and

---

[19] See the discussion of this play by Nussbaum (1986) ch. 3. As Nussbaum points out, the play juxtaposes opposing sets of extravagantly simplified values. Creon supposes that human worth is entirely subject to civic standards so that (line 190) even friendship is a civic category. The play suggests the need for integration of the familial/social with the political and confrontation of the possibility of value conflict.

of the process of persuasion and argument on which the laws are founded is evident at the level of political interaction, as well as in interpretations of that interaction by Antiphon and Gorgias. Experience of policy-making in the assembly and the administration of justice by popular juries prompted the reflection that the decisions of the *demos* might be both arbitrary, whimsical, founded on nothing but men's beliefs, on the one hand, and on the other, coercive and not expressive of the collective interest, because of uneven enforcement of the power and influence of a few men or indeed of the majority. The demagogues were regarded in some quarters as manipulative wielders of arguments for their own ends,[20] the *demos* as partisan. The inconstancy of the populace is rebuked by both Pericles and Cleon, as portrayed by Thucydides, and condemned by the anti-democratic herald in Euripides' *Suppliants* (line 417). In 410, after the Athenians rejected an oligarchy which some of them, swayed by persuasion as well as terror, had voted in, they decided to codify the laws. This decision both reflected and prompted awareness of the arbitrariness and manipulability of the law. It is a subtle question – and probably, given the state of our knowledge, an unanswerable one – to what extent the Athenian citizenry shared the view of not unsympathetic as well as hostile observers that the laws were arbitrary and coercive, and political persuasion manipulative. However, the codification is one sign that the Athenian *demos* itself was aware of the need to ensure that political interaction expressed both freedom and order. The contrast between Aeschylus' *Suppliants* and Euripides' treatment, some forty years later, of the same theme, may perhaps[21] provide a further hint: while Aeschylus' king leaves the decision on the fate of the suppliants to the *demos*, which must determine for itself what risks it is willing to incur, Euripides' king asserts that the people will follow his lead, but that by involving them he will increase their loyalty to the cause.

nomos: the externalization of order

The process by which the boundary between 'internal' and 'external' was redefined so that law and social interaction joined divine rules on the far side of the line can be glimpsed in the writings of Gorgias the sophist. Gorgias' works suggest that man's pursuit of his own good, guided by persuasion, is neither an expression of his freedom nor a

---

[20] See, e.g., Eur. *Suppl.* 411f.; Ar. *Knights* 1211f.; [Xen.] *Ath. Pol.* with Meier (1970) 55ff.
[21] I do not wish to lay too much stress on this, in view of the many factors that may have influenced the dramatists' choice of emphasis.

means of attaining what is genuinely good for him. In the *Defense of Helen*, whose beauty caused the Trojan War, Gorgias makes a remarkable claim: persuasion, conventionally regarded as the expression of man's freedom and the order achieved through political interaction, as the antithesis of force and compulsion, is itself a form of coercion. Persuasion, he observes, 'has not the form of necessity, but it does have the same power.'[22] Gorgias argues that Helen was compelled to act as she did, and was therefore innocent of wrongdoing, because of the irresistible power of persuasion.[23] Gorgias' argument, as paraphrased by a recent commentator, is that: 'Persuasion by argument (*logos*) is equivalent to abduction by force, as nobody can fail to "consent to what is done" if he "agrees to what is said"; in other words, nobody can help acting in accordance with the considerations to which he has been brought.'[24] In Plato's *Gorgias* (452d–e) the sophist is made to describe the greatest good as the power to persuade with arguments, which secures power[25] by reducing others to slaves. Another Platonic passage (*Philebus* 58a–b) portrays Gorgias as distinguishing slavery achieved through force from that imposed by persuasion, through voluntary agreement.[26] Thus the man who is a master of persuasion seems to have taken the place of the gods: men are willing slaves, coerced by a vision of their own good or pleasure (see *Helen*, DK B 11 and 15). That is, they both do what they think best for themselves, and they are compelled to do so.

Yet Gorgias portrays Helen as an instrument, not as a participant in her own misdeed. The power of persuasion is not so much a secularized (politicized) version of the double causation of the world of Aeschylean tragedy as a reprise, in a different key, of the power of the Homeric gods. Persuasion has taken over that aspect of man which had constituted his consciousness and deliberate participation even when he was living out the plan of the gods; reason or argument is now the instrument of another's power. The spell cast by persuasion resembles divine delusion (*atē*), but with a potent new formula: the coercion is internal. Or rather, the conception of what was internal to the agent, which had gradually emerged as the instrumental view gave

---

[22] The 'sense' of DK B 11, 12 as given by Diels *ad loc*. See Morrison (1972) 52.

[23] On Gorgias and the treatment of persuasion, *peithō* (which is also personified as a goddess), in the discourses, see Calogero (1957), Segal (1962) and Buxton (1982).

[24] Calogero (1957) 13.

[25] The term used, *archē*, is also the word for empire or dominion.

[26] Cited, along with the *Gorgias* passage, by Calogero (1957) 16 with n. 24. But Calogero misleadingly (at any rate on the basis of this passage) refers to *peithō* as *bia di' hekonton*, when the passage contrasts these two terms with respect to the cause of enslavement.

way to conscious participation, has itself been alienated. The *peithō* which once expressed man's power and freedom in a world implicitly ordered[27] is now a form of coercion capable (unlike its divine analogue) of reducing men to the status of slaves.

In his discourse on Palamedes, Gorgias goes beyond the claim put forward in the *Defense of Helen* that persuasion compels men by manipulating their beliefs to the underlying assumption that men are compelled to act in particular ways by their own belief that to do so will benefit them. Palamedes contends that 'all things that men do, they do for one of two reasons, either pursuing gain or fleeing punishment' (*Pal.* DK B 11a, 19). The implication of both discourses is that man cannot do anything other than what he deems good; thus Helen is not responsible for having been seduced, for seduction is equivalent to abduction; and Palamedes is not guilty of treason, for he could not have done what he must have known would injure him.[28] The speech of Palamedes suggests that men act against their own interest only because of foolishness or madness: he himself is wise, and therefore cannot be thought to have been capable of acting imprudently (B 11a, 25). However, the *Defense of Helen* points to the flaw in this claim: persuasion succeeds by 'molding a false argument' (B 11, 11). Men are not omniscient, and find it difficult to 'recall the past or to consider the present or to predict the future. So that on most subjects most men take opinion as counselor to their soul' (B 11, 11). Ignorance, madness, the bewitching power of persuasion, or overwhelming desire, can cause men to act against their own best interests. What man takes to be good, his beliefs and desires, are portrayed as external. Men are coerced by appearances and incapable of discriminating among apparently good things.

Other sources also reflect the growing belief that all behavior is caused by human desire and therefore exhibits no order and cannot be shaped by social measures. Although, in a rather Anaxagorean portrayal of the world order, Euripides' Hecuba declares that the cumulative actions of men exhibit *dikē* because they are implicitly guided by Zeus, Zeus is construed as 'natural necessity or the mind of man' (*Trojan Women* 886–8). Hecuba suggests that order, guided as it may be, is not directly secured. In response to Helen's claim that Aphrodite, not Helen herself, had caused the betrayal of Menelaus, Hecuba retorts: 'Your own mind, seeing my son's supreme beauty,

---

[27] See Will (1972) 489.

[28] Calogero (1957) 14; see *Palamedes*, sections 13–19. This form of argument regularly appears in court speeches.

was made divine passion. Man's foolishness is his Aphrodite. Fittingly, the two words begin alike: *aphrosunē* and the name of the goddess' (*Trojan Women* 988–90). The gods are not responsible for man's actions, as in the *Iliad*, nor do they even share responsibility, as in Aeschylus' *Oresteia*.[29] Paradoxically, it is precisely because the gods are no longer thought to direct events through men that Helen can claim that she was merely an instrument, that the goddess, not she herself, must bear responsibility.[30] Aphrodite caused her to leave with Paris, and it is she who should be punished (*Trojan Women* 946–50).[31] The response to this claim is not, as in the *Iliad*, silent acquiescence nor, as in the *Oresteia*,[32] is it made clear that the agent, too, is responsible. (Note that the question of punishing the gods does not arise in these earlier contexts.) Rather, Helen herself acknowledges that her excuse may be thought 'specious' and she points instead to her own behavior in Troy as evidence that she had been coerced. Menelaus agrees with Hecuba that his wife 'willingly' abandoned him for Paris, and the goddess of love '(*Kupris*) for vain show fills out her plea' (1036–9). The touchstone of responsibility is consciousness and deliberation, but this is now deemed to be clearly incompatible with divine determination. If Aphrodite had caused Helen's action, the goddess would be fully responsible, indeed even liable to punishment. But divinity has been so far externalized, its powers so far internalized, that what once served as a partial reason for action is now merely an excuse. If one compares the portrayal of the conflict Orestes faces in Aeschylus' *Oresteia* and in Euripides' *Orestes*, the shift from a social or objective to a personal conception of the sources of human action is striking.[33] In the *Oresteia*, the conflicting demands on Orestes are external, and the resulting impasse can be resolved through a judicial process and the accommodation within society of the various claims on human motivation. Euripides, by contrast, emphasizes Orestes' own inner ambivalence; Orestes has internalized the conflict, which is in no way resolved, though its external manifes-

[29] Note Clytemnestra's exchange with the chorus after the murder of Agamemnon, in Aeschylus' *Ag.* 1372–76; N.B. 1487–8, 1505–8.

[30] Cf. Gorgias, *Helen*, DK 82 B 11 and 6.

[31] Cf. Euripides, *Orestes* 593–6, where Orestes suggests that it is Apollo who should be punished.

[32] See *Ag.* 1497–508: Clytemnestra acknowledges, indeed boasts, that she did the deed (1380, 1552f.); discussions of responsibility arise within the context of double causation. Cf. Orestes and Apollo in *Eum.* 462f. Also see Soph. *O.C.*, where the conflict is made explicit: Oedipus evidently acted deliberately and yet also unwittingly. In the *Trojan Women*, by contrast, Helen claims that she was nothing but an instrument.

[33] See Simon (1978) 104–13.

tations are ended by the machinations of Apollo, who appears at the
final moment to contrive a happy ending.

phusis: building up order from within

If such order as apparently exists in the world is perceived as in fact
external to the claims that move men, neither expressive of nor
capable of shaping man's aims, then how is the social world to be ordered? Are those qualities intrinsic to man, including his desires and
his perception of his own good, to be regarded as purely arbitrary and
manipulable, capable of providing no general standard, no basis for
social order? Before this sense that the laws were external and manipulable took hold, Protagoras had argued for a political version of
double causation, whereby what man takes to be good for himself is
precisely *nomos*. In Protagoras' theory, the appeal to individual
rationality is part of a claim that man's interests are defined and
shaped by political interaction. As this interaction came to be seen as
neither ordering nor expressing man's interests, and *nomos* seemed to
be merely what men took to be good for themselves, and this was
externalized, attempts were made to redefine what was in fact internal
and essential to man. Again, this parallels, but on a different plane,
developments of the archaic period. Man's status as a cause can no
longer be based simply on conscious participation or deliberate
action, but requires a more stringent account of the self. Euripides'
Hecuba suggests that the actions of men taken as a whole exhibit *dikē*,
because they are implicitly ordered by 'natural necessity' or 'the mind
of men.' Natural necessity expressed the simultaneous autonomy and
order characteristic of a world freed from divine intervention. If
human behavior could be understood as ordered in the same way as
the cosmos, by impersonal but intrinsic forces, then perhaps it would
be possible to account for both freedom and order in the political
realm.

However, theories which shed the ambiguities of the Anaxagorean
outlook, founded as it was on double causation, and argued that order
was constituted by unguided material interaction, were also capable
of poisoning man's understanding of his political condition. In a conflation of the various allegedly subversive beliefs of the wise men of
the fifth century, Plato declared that the doctrine that the universe
lacked transcendent design or purpose made it possible for men to
appeal to nature (*phusis*) as a standard that contradicted the precepts
of custom and law (*nomos*) (*Laws* 888e–890a). Materialist accounts
of the universe were not inherently subversive, as one would surmise

from the hostile and distorted picture offered by Plato and Aristotle. As teleologists who explained the world in terms of purpose they condemned the scientific philosophers for explaining the cosmos in terms of chance (*tuchē*) or the spontaneous *and* necessity (Plato, *Laws* 889, Aristotle, *Physics* 198b–199a).[34] The concept of 'necessary chance' appears in Attic tragedy,[35] where it seems to refer to the inexorable unfolding of the fate decreed by the gods. From the point of view of the teleologist, this is precisely what the alleged conjunction of necessity and chance in the writings of the scientific philosophers is *not* referring to: Plato complains that these men constructed a world composed of elements which combine 'in accordance with chance from necessity,' a world created and organized as it is 'not because of a mind . . . nor because of some god or by art, but . . . by nature and chance only' (*Laws* 889c). The cosmology offered by, e.g., the atomists, rests on both chance and necessity because it denies divine purpose or design.[36] As D. J. Allan observes in a discussion of the pre-Socratic attempt to explain cosmic order: 'Since purpose without a conscious agency did not yet appear to anyone to be conceivable, the alternatives which presented themselves were simply rational intervention on the one side and materialism on the other.'[37] In response not to teleology but to the notion of divine governance, the materialist attempted to show that the apparently purposeful and the apparently fortuitous were equally the result of unguided natural interaction. For Aristotle, chance and necessity are both characteristic of the materialist cosmos because it lacks (impersonal) regulating purpose. For the materialist, chance and purpose are both characteristic of the divinely-governed cosmos because it lacks (impersonal) regulating causes. Thus the atomist Leucippus (DK 67 B 2): 'Nothing occurs at random; but everything for a reason and by necessity.'[38] The atomists were challenging the conception of the world embodied in the phrase 'necessary chance': there is

---

[34] The fact that Plato and Aristotle have misrepresented the project of the scientific philosophers by criticizing them from a teleological perspective has been noted by many scholars, e.g. Barnes (1979), Vlastos (1975), Edmunds (1972).

[35] Soph. *Ajax* 485, 803, *Electra* 48, Eur. *I.A.* 511, cf. Aesch. *Ag.* 1042; the concept and the texts are referred to by Guthrie (1969) 415 n. 1 and dismissed too readily by Edmunds (1972) 350.

[36] See Barnes (1979) 123.

[37] Allan (1965) 4, see Balme (1940) 27, cf. Barnes (1979) 115.

[38] I agree with Barnes (1979) 111 that *ginetai* is not meant to limit the comment to generation, as Edmunds (1972) 343 assumes. Also, *matēn* means 'in vain' in the sense of 'for no reason,' not 'failing to accomplish an intended purpose.' See Guthrie (1969) 415. Aetius introduces this fragment by saying that 'Leucippus says that everything occurs by necessity and that that is the same as fate' – it is this later interpretation of atomism which I am trying to undermine.

no *tuchē* in the sense of what is mysteriously ordained;[39] what is necessary and patterned in the way the world is is a function of the nature of its constituent materials.

Various theorists sought to interpret human interaction, too, in terms of *phusis*. This tendency is evident even in theories, like that of Empedocles,[40] which have not abandoned the notion of transcendent ordering forces, but have interpreted these forces as at once impersonal and characteristic of human experience. Empedocles apparently described pleasure, like the sensory faculty of seeing, in terms of the proper balance or proportion of elements: 'Empedocles says that desires arise in living things from their deficiencies in the elements which make each other complete, and pleasures from what is appropriate, according to the mixtures of things which are like and of like natures, and pain and sufferings from what is inappropriate.'[41] Empedocles posits a normal or balanced state of the organism. The impulse to make up a deficiency in any one of the four elements is desire, and fulfillment of the desire is pleasurable.[42] Thus Empedocles' physical theory leads to a normative picture of human well-being akin to that depicted in fragments of the early medical writer Alcmaeon of Croton and implicit in various Hippocratic texts.[43] We do not know whether Empedocles proceeded to draw ethical conclusions from this view, e.g. that since pleasure marks the body's attempt to attain its own best condition, pleasure is always to be sought or, on the contrary, that since balance or equilibrium is the best condition, one should seek to cultivate a psychic state marked by the absence of desire and pleasure.[44] At the very least, it seems that consideration of man's interaction with the world on the basis of certain physical principles led, in Empedocles' theory, to conclusions about human well-being with evident implications for human behavior. Such a theory could provide criteria by which to judge human *nomoi*, as Plato suggests, but they need not have been subversive.

---

[39] The doxography which suggests that the atomists relied on chance is all post-Aristotelian. See Edmunds (1972) 249f. He does not, however, mention a fragment of Epicurus' *On Nature* which accuses the early atomists of explaining everything by *anankē* and *to automaton*. See Sedley (1983) 22–3.

[40] For a concise account of Empedoclean cosmological theory, see Hussey (1972) 130–3. Note that Empedocles' cosmos has a mind: DK 31 B 110.

[41] DK 31 A 95: transl. by Gosling and Taylor (1982) 21, based on text restored by H. Diels.

[42] See Gosling and Taylor (1982) 21, and on the physiological tradition of pleasure in general, see 19f.

[43] See discussion by Gosling and Taylor (1982) 23f.

[44] Gosling and Taylor (1982) 22.

And yet, as Plato observed in the *Laws*, when mind and purpose are banished from the cosmos and reside only in mortal man, then a gulf opens between the realm of natural, necessary and intrinsically ordered (i.e. caused but not contrived) interaction, on the one hand, and the creations of the human mind, on the other, between, that is, *phusis* and *nomos*.[45] This gulf is evident in Antiphon's attempt to interpret human experience in terms of *phusis*. Antiphon, a contemporary of Thucydides and Democritus and probably an Athenian citizen,[46] argued that nature provided a standard of human well-being, of man's intrinsic good as opposed to the good allegedly secured by social contrivances. Unlike Gorgias, Antiphon believed that man's understanding of his own good could constitute a reliable standard, but he agreed with Gorgias that social or political interaction could only distort that understanding. Antiphon's construal of order in the cosmos and among men is founded on a radical distinction between what is basic, persistent and constitutive of reality, and what is man-made or conventional. The only stable order exists at the most basic level; nature cannot, therefore, serve as the foundation of any *social* order, but can only provide a guide to the good of individual organisms. Antiphon's views on the nature of reality and man's access to it are expressed in a work whose title echoes that of writings by Protagoras and Parmenides: *Aletheia*, or *Truth*.[47] Fragments from the first book of this work include an excursus on justice, one on human nature, squaring the circle, time, and one on the issue addressed by Aristotle in his discussion of the materialists, namely that 'the nature and reality of natural things is the primary inherent stuff, unmodified and by itself' (Arist. *Physics* 193a9; cf. DK B 15). The connection among these

---

[45] A distinction about which a great deal has been written. See Heinimann (1945) and, for a recent discussion, Kerferd (1981) ch. 10.

[46] On the question of whether Antiphon the Sophist (author of the *Truth* and *Concord*, the man referred to in Xenophon's *Memorabilia* 1.6) and Antiphon of Rhamnus (author of the *Tetralogies* and other speeches, and a prominent oligarch) are two historical persons or one, I tend to the view expounded by Morrison (1961) and (1972) that the two are identical. But this conclusion is not decisive (one way or the other) for our understanding of the views expounded in the fragments of political/ethical theory, nor can our understanding of those views determine the identity of their author. The alleged conflict between a 'left-wing' and a 'right-wing' Antiphon (made much of by Guthrie (1969) 292–4) occurs within the fragments, between the *Truth* and the *Concord*. In part for this reason, some scholars have divided Antiphon up in other ways. (See Morrison (1961) 50 n.1.) For a recent discussion of the controversy, see Kerferd (1981) 49–51.

[47] See the fragments collected by Morrison (1972) 212ff. Translations used here are adapted from Morrison.

various topics is suggested by Antiphon's references to metaphysics and the theory of knowledge. The things we can see and know are not captured by language and the other conventional ways in which we organize the phenomena (B 1).[48] Time, according to Antiphon, 'is thought or measurement, not a real thing' (B 9). A sphere is conventionally regarded as generically distinct from, and irreducible to, a polygon; Antiphon attempted to show that the circle was in fact a polygon with an infinite number of sides (B 13). Men are by nature the same, despite the practice of dividing mankind into Greeks and barbarians (B 44, Fr.B, Col. 2). And what is real about a bed is its constituent material, wood, 'since the bed-ness is merely an incidental attribute, the customary construction and craftsmanship, whereas the reality is that which persists and is constant under these superficial modifications' (Arist. *Phys.* 193a15 = B 15). Although Antiphon is a materialist,[49] and surviving fragments suggest that he formulated a cosmogony based on the processes of separation and disposition (B 23; 24a),[50] there is no evidence that he based his account of man's nature on the interaction of the constituents of the human organism with one another or with the external world. Indeed the evidence, apart from Aristotle's inference, does not suggest that the distinction illustrated by the case of bed and wood was intended by Antiphon to apply to natural bodies (so that 'man' would 'really' be flesh and bone), but that it applied only to 'crafted' objects, furniture or a statue (B 15).[51] Antiphon's criterion of reality was persistence in the absence of (or even 'underneath') artificial, i.e. *man-made*, constraints. Thus man has a nature which is not reducible to the behavior of an agglomeration of flesh and bone.

Antiphon applies the criteria of persistence and constancy – as opposed to the customary and superficial – to human behavior, and arrives at a conception of what is beneficial to man by nature as opposed to what is demanded of him by law.[52] Because, unlike Empe-

---

[48] See Morrison (1972) 212f. The reflections on the inability of language to latch on to reality are perhaps to be understood as an instance of the contrast between (roughly) the real and the conventional, or between that which we organize or shape and unmodified reality.

[49] Note Origen's report (DK B 12) that in the *Truth*, Antiphon 'did away with *pronoia*,' referring perhaps to design in nature.

[50] See the fragments collected by Morrison (1972) 222–4.

[51] For Aristotle's use of the craft analogy, see Waterlow (1982) 71f. The references to tribes with 'shady-feet' and 'long-heads' (B 45 and 46) may be remnants of a discussion of the interaction of custom and nature. See Morrison (1972) 226.

[52] In what follows, I assume that Antiphon is not putting forward a theory of natural justice; this was argued by Kerferd (1959) and recently restated by Furley (1981).

docles, Antiphon interpreted the human *phusis* at the level of 'man' rather than 'combination of elements,' he looked to the most basic features of human behavior, those which persisted across the range of human cultures, to identify man's nature and his interests. Antiphon derived his conception of *phusis* by stripping away the layers of artificial acculturation, *nomos*: 'By nature we all have the same nature in all particulars, barbarians and Greeks. We have only to consider the things which are natural and necessary to all mankind' (B 44 Fr.B, Col. 2). Man's fundamental interest, he concludes, is self-protection, the avoidance of pain and damage. Unlike the law, which establishes arbitrary criteria of what man must and must not do, nature establishes a genuine distinction, between life and death. And 'life is one of the advantages at which men aim' (B 44 Fr.A, Col. 3).[53] Man ought therefore to do what he instinctively does, that is avoid harm (and attendant pain) and seek advantage (and attendant pleasure)[54] (B 44 Fr.A, Cols. 3–4). Local *mores* and laws are useless as guides to what man has good reason to do (B 44, Col. 3); indeed, what is defined as right by the laws is 'mostly an enemy to nature' (B 44 Fr.A, Col. 2).

nomos versus *phusis:* the dangers of socialization

In Antiphon's theory, in marked contrast to the vision of Protagoras, *nomos* is external and artificial, a set of rules which do not express, and often violate, the real interests of men. Men must accommodate themselves to the rules governing political society by observing them when necessary, when their actions are public and they risk being punished, but heeding the promptings of their own natures in private (B 44 Fr. A, Col. 1). It is the demands of nature, stringent and inescapable, which express man's autonomy and his interests, while law is both contingent and coercive: 'For the demands of the laws are imposed, but the demands of nature are necessary. And the demands of the laws are the result not of natural disposition but of agreement, but the demands of nature are exactly the opposite' (B 44 Fr.A, Col. 1). Whereas transgression of the law may or may not be punished – if an agent's behavior goes unnoticed, he escapes – any violation of 'the inherent demands of nature' invariably inflicts direct harm on the agent: 'The damage inflicted rests not on opinion but on truth' (B 44 Fr.A, Col. 2). And while the 'things laid down as good for you by

---

[53] See Furley (1981) 89.
[54] On this connection see Furley (1981) 89.

nomos are chains upon nature, those specified by *phusis* make for free-dom' (B 44 Fr.A, Col. 4).

Some indication of what the laws establish as advantageous is implicit in the extant fragments and evident if one considers Antiphon's attack on *nomoi* as in part a critique of Protagoras and of contemporary contract theory of the kind described by Glaucon in Plato's *Republic*. Justice is interpreted as obedience to the law, and the behavior which makes possible the enforcement of obedience is regarded as both just and 'useful for the various pursuits of men' (B 44, Col. 1). Presumably the rule of justice in relations among men is said to be useful because society takes over the individual's responsibility for protecting himself and, by demanding and enforcing obedience to the law, ensures that so long as an individual does not do wrong, he will not suffer any. (See B 44, Col. 1.)[55] According to Antiphon, if the laws succeeded in protecting those who obeyed and punishing those who did not, then obedience would not be disadvantageous (B 44 Fr.A, Cols. 5–6). The alleged advantages laid down by political society are chains on man's nature in part because, once transmuted into a system of justice founded on agreement, collective self-protection ceases to mean that any particular individual will in fact be protected. Those who adopt the habits of justice (*aidōs* and *dikē*) essential to the success of the agreed system are indeed less secure, because in doing so they make themselves vulnerable to those 'free-riders' who, since the sanctions of the law are collectively determined, dependent upon public notice, and therefore not inexorable, are able to get away with injustice:

And people who act in self-defense when attacked and do not take the offensive themselves, and people who are good to their parents even if their parents act badly to them, and those who offer the other party an oath for them to swear[56] but do not bind themselves with an oath, many of these cases are examples of conduct against nature, and lead to greater pain when less is possible and to damage which could be avoided. If, on the other hand, the laws afforded protection to those who surrendered their rights in this way and penalties to those who did not surrender them, but hit back instead, obedience to the law would have some <profitable aspect>. But as things are, it is clear that justice according to the law does not afford sufficient protection to those who submit in this way, since, in the first place, it licenses the sufferer to suffer and the doer to act . . . When justice is brought in to assist in punishment it is no more on the side of the sufferer than of the doer. (DK B 44 Fr.A, Cols. 5–6)

[55] For a discussion of the two aspects of conventional justice, see Furley (1981) 87–8.

[56] This was thought to offer one's opponent an advantage. See Aristotle, *Rhet.* 1377a8, cited by Morrison (1972) 220 n.11.

Far from expressing man's interest in his own security, the operation of the system of justice based on the principle that men who do no wrong suffer none, the basis of contract theory, depends on the systematic violation of this principle. The system requires that citizens harm one another and therefore put themselves at risk when their own interests are not directly involved. Antiphon observes that 'giving true evidence against one's neighbor is customarily considered [just] conduct' (B 44 , Col. 1). As he goes on to say, giving such evidence means causing harm to someone who has never done oneself any wrong, and incurring the accused man's undying hatred. Thus: 'It is clear that the administration of law and justice and arbitration with a view to a final settlement are all contrary to justice. For helping one set of people harms another. And in the process, while those who get help escape injustice, those who get harm are <treated unjustly>' (DK B 44, Col. 2).

Unlike Protagoras, Antiphon believes that man's interests are asocial. His interest in his own well-being is not furthered by the system of justice. The impersonality of law, embodied in principles of procedural justice, means that not doing any injustice is no guarantee that one will not suffer it. And the system requires that man take risks on behalf of interests that are not clearly his interests: he must harm a man who has done him no direct harm, and suffer the dangerous consequences. Man's genuine interests are those he has *qua* man, not *qua* man-in-society. The advantages promised by the rule of law are constraints on man's nature not merely because they are arbitrarily conferred, but because they induce men to adopt habits of justice and to act as if their interests are social, thereby endangering their well-being. It is no accident that the laws do not ensure, but in fact undermine, man's security. For because they seek to promote collective security, the laws are too loosely fitted to individual interests, too external, too general, to protect citizens at the level at which their security within the *polis* is threatened, namely in their relations with other individuals. In contrast to Protagoras, who analyzed man as 'not yet in society' to show that his interests are fundamentally social, Antiphon analyzed man's life in society to show that his interests are, at bottom, individual.

The system of political justice violates man's autonomy and constrains his nature; the laws even lay down 'what the mind must want and not want' (B 44 Fr.A, Col. 3). Man's freedom consists in heeding his nature and pursuing his own advantage. *nomoi* are contingent and arbitrary as well as coercive, and it is *phusis* which makes for order as well as freedom. The loose fit of the laws, and their inability to ensure that each man behaves in such a way that all men have good reason to obey, were features noted by other observers, who wondered why any man should refrain from doing wrong in private.[57] If society exists to further the interests of its members yet systematically fails to express or protect them, then every man in society is thrown back on his own resources and must decide for himself what behavior his interests dictate. Antiphon argues that this is precisely what men must do. But obedience to *phusis* as opposed to *nomos* is no license for unrestrained self-indulgence and self-assertion. The demands of *phusis* are more stringent than the law, and inescapable. Even when he is unseen (indeed, says Antiphon, especially then), man must act so as to secure what is good for him. It is not the case that what is painful is better for you than what is pleasant (B 44 Fr.A, Col. 4), as might be inferred from the demands of just behavior, which allegedly establish what is good for you yet increase pain and diminish pleasure (B 44 Fr.A, Col. 5).

Antiphon declares that 'whatever is in truth good for you should not be harmful, but should help' (B 44 Fr.A, Col. 4). The need to avoid harm may, therefore, dictate the restraint of immediate pleasures in the interest of longer-term well-being. According to Antiphon,[58]

The man who thinks that he will do his neighbor injury and will suffer no injury himself is a fool . . . Many people have been cast down by expectations of this kind into irreparable misfortunes. It has turned out that they themselves have suffered what they thought to inflict on their neighbors. Good sense might be said to belong to that man alone who makes himself withstand the immediate pleasures of his heart and has succeeded in overcoming and conquering himself. The man who intends to satisfy his heart's desire immediately intends what is worse rather than what is better. (DK B 58)

Man must regulate what he wants and does not want in accordance with nature's dictate that he pursue life and all that contributes to it. Antiphon's conception of prudent action might be expected, simply as a standard of individual benefit, to yield social order based on the maxim: do not do what you would not suffer. But Antiphon's theory

---

[57] See, e.g., Critias, DK 88 B 22; Glaucon and Adeimantus' demand to be shown why even Gyges, possessor of a ring which renders him invisible, should be just, Plato, *Rep.* 359b7–360d10; and the texts cited by Procopé (1971) 318.

[58] In a fragment cited by Stobaeus, often assigned to the *Concord* (see Morrison (1972) 228), rejected with the other Stobaeus fragments by Havelock (1957) 416. But the general point is confirmed by fragments preserved by other sources (DK 87 B 52, 59, 76) and is not inconsistent with the papyrus fragments. Antiphon apparently had some conception of the importance of inner 'balance' (B 61) or 'harmony' (B 59) but there is no evidence that he elaborated this into a theory of psychological well-being.

is formulated in response to a society which fosters antagonism and permits injury to the law-abiding, and its premise is: every man for himself. No socially-constructed order can secure each individual's good, and each man has overwhelming reason to ignore the laws when it is in his interest to do so. Antiphon assumes the existence of a social order, and the need to evade its dicta, and indeed he may have thought, though the extant fragments do not say so, that in general men profited from living in a regulated society. They must, however, avoid being shaped by its regulations, and maintain a watchful eye on its demands. The only secure standard of behavior is internal and individual; in a manner parallel to *nomos*, which had been internalized in Sophocles' *Antigone* as *autonomia, homonoia*, a word for social harmony or unity, is used by Antiphon as a description of a personal condition. Internal well-being was the aim, internal control the means, of achieving such order as was possible in human relations.

Antiphon's construal of the human good in the most basic terms is, from the point of view of social order, purely negative and essentially personal. The locus of control is entirely internal, i.e. *self*-control, and it is the self in the most primitive sense whose fundamental good is thereby secured. The grip of the theory is therefore extremely strong, and universal. Other thinkers, though equally convinced of the malign influence of existing political interaction, were unwilling to construe the human good so narrowly and negatively. While for Antiphon the salient consideration was that no social order is capable of expressing the personal interests of all its members, for thinkers as different as Socrates and Callicles the converse point was of greatest concern: no theory so closely tied to what actually motivates all men can possibly account for social order or indeed the scope of the good. The good, they suggest, exists at a greater distance from primitive, universal self-interest than Antiphon's theory would indicate. And indeed, some characteristic human goods are to be realized in relation to other men, in some form of society. Unlike Antiphon, Socrates and Callicles offer theories (in Socrates' case, only the groundwork of a possible theory) of justice. These theories are built on accounts of the good for man which seek to revise man's understanding of himself in society as it is, i.e. teleological accounts of the human good that point beyond present social relations. The teleological component is designed to provide a grip on human motivation as well as an objective criterion of the good for man. According to Socrates, man is his reason; according to Callicles, man is his desires. They believe that society, and particularly democratic society, corrupts man's understanding of his good. Each

man rules himself according to convention or whim, without any
guiding conception of what or who he is and might be.

In the *Protagoras*, Socrates describes his contemporaries as sharing
the view expressed in Gorgias' *Defense of Helen* and the *Palamedes*
that man is at the mercy of what he desires. According to Socrates,

> The opinion of the majority about knowledge is that it is not anything strong,
> which can control and rule a man; they don't look at it that way at all, but think
> that often a man who possesses knowledge is ruled not by it but by something else,
> in one case passion, in another pleasure, in another pain, sometimes lust, very
> often fear; they just look at knowledge as a slave who gets dragged about by all
> the rest ... The majority of people ... hold that many people who know what is
> best to do are not willing to do it, though it is in their power, but do something
> else. (*Prot.* 352b3–c1, d6–8)[59]

As Socrates' language suggests, at stake is the location of man's autonomy: is knowledge powerful, a ruler, he asks, or is it, as the many
think, dragged about by passion, a slave? Socrates' picture of this view
of motivation is also a picture of democracy itself, in which the forces
of order have no strength and the many, moved by momentary desires,
dominate the knowledgeable. Socrates ascribes to the masses the view
that men are incontinent, that is that they know a certain course of
action to be good (or bad) but nonetheless do not (or do) do it, because
they are moved by passion.[60] Although his portrayal of the opinion of
the many depicts the internalization and division of motives into
reason and desire, Socrates' own account preserves the outlook
expressed in tragedy and, in a different form, in the writings of Gorgias, namely that men desire what they believe to be good, and that it
is mistaken beliefs which lead men astray. In his argument on Helen's
behalf, Gorgias implies that firm belief might be proof against manipulation of one's wish to do what one believes to be good. The *Palamedes*, and briefly the *Defense of Helen*, introduce a distinction
between what is 'false' and 'true,' what is known and what is merely
believed, which served as the foundation of Socrates' attempt to rehabilitate the idea of man as a cause, not the plaything of persuasion or
circumstance. According to Socrates, the only voluntary act is an
action caused by knowledge of what is in fact good for you. Man's
autonomy rests with his reason. For Socrates, desire has no autonomous force. Socrates has altered Gorgias' claim that every man must
do that, and only that, which he believes to be good for him, to the

---

[59] Translation by Taylor (1976).
[60] For a very shrewd analysis of this issue in Greek thought, to which I am much indebted,
     see Irwin (1983). Irwin does not discuss Gorgias; see p. 190 n.19.

claim that all action is involuntary except action based on understanding of what is in fact good for him. Indeed, his own real interest is all that a man can be said genuinely to want. Thus no one voluntarily does what is bad for him. According to Socrates the man who acts in a way harmful to himself is not in reality acting at all: he is an unwitting instrument. When a man does act, that is when he acts voluntarily, there can be no question of his judgment being led astray or overwhelmed by desires, for the only thing that man can actually desire is what is in fact good for him.

The Socratic redefinition of man as a cause implies a new form of double causation: man deliberates about what he shall do, but he cannot do anything other than what is best for him, a necessity he discovers in the course of deliberation.[61] The participant in Socratic dialectic puts on the yoke of necessity, where necessity is no longer inscrutable but, because it concerns what will in fact turn out to be good for man, remains somewhat obscure. Whether we interpret the historical Socrates as having argued that the understanding promoted by dialectic enables accurate measurement of future pleasure and pains,[62] and is therefore sufficient for achieving the good, or, on the other hand, that such understanding is merely necessary, and external factors will continue to affect man's well-being in unpredictable ways,[63] in either case the Socratic project can be construed as in part an attempt to establish man's capacity for genuine autonomy, not the fake paraded as the pride of democracy. In the *Gorgias*, Socrates asserts that he is one of very few Athenians, perhaps even the only one, who 'undertakes the real political craft and practices politics' (521d6) because he does not seek to gratify his fellow citizens but to make them as good as possible (521a3, 521e1). The laws of Athens, as Socrates insists in the *Crito*, are entitled to obedience because they benefit the citizens and because the citizens have agreed to obey their just commands, and perhaps also in part because they constitute a way of life which makes Socrates' own activities possible.[64] But the version of contract theory which underlies the *Crito* commitment to obedience defines a purely external order. The laws do not provide criteria of justice, for lawful behavior does not constitute the virtue of justice. Men cannot rely on the political order to define or promote justice or the good.

[61] Cf. Williams (forthcoming).

[62] As in Plato's *Protagoras* 355a–357b.

[63] See Mackenzie (1981) 134–41, esp. 139 with n. 18, and Nussbaum (1986) ch. 4 on the science of measurement in the *Protagoras*.

[64] See Kraut (1984) especially 224–8, with Vlastos (1984), Irwin (1985).

If for Socrates the source of order was, to use Euripides' phrase, 'the mind of man,' then for Callicles it was 'natural necessity.' Callicles defined human agency in terms of the capacity to fulfill one's desires. The Protagorean claim that the way the world must be is tied to man's needs, aims and desires, is transmuted in the mind of Callicles into the notion that a man's raw desires define the way the world must be. Like Socrates, Callicles did not divide reason from desire; while Socrates assumed that men desire what they believe to be good for them, Callicles assumed that it was reasonable for men to want what they desire. The triumph of desire is not, for Callicles, incontinence. It is reasonable to want as much as one desires and can get. Reason, and the order associated with it, has no autonomous force. Here, as I noted earlier, is a conceptual offspring of the flourishing Athenian empire. Men (on the analogy of *poleis*) differ in strength and initiative, and they are prevented from exercising their powers to the full only by artificial constraints, the constraints of society as expressed in *nomos*, which enables the weak to fulfill their own desires so far as possible. *nomos* does not represent the collective interest, but the interests of the weak. Callicles interprets the indulgence of desire as the expression of man's freedom and his nature. Like Antiphon, he contrasts the claims of *nomos* with those of *phusis*, but *phusis* now dictates not mere survival, but domination. Man cannot realize his *phusis qua* man by observing the laws when necessary and heeding the promptings of *phusis* in private; he must shatter the *nomoi* that define society. The domination of the weak by the strong is naturally just. In a denunciation of the wise men of the fifth century which in fact suits only Callicles and his ilk, Plato declares that these men advocated 'the life that is right "according to *phusis*," which consists in being master over the rest in reality, instead of being a slave to others according to *nomos*' (*Laws* 890a). As Gorgias indicates, to act as one is led by the interaction characteristic of society to believe one wants to act is to be a slave. To act as natural desire dictates is to be a tyrant. Callicles' example of well-being is Archelaus, vicious ruler of Macedon.

At the level of political ideology, too, the opponents of democracy put forward a conception of what it was to be a man that pointed beyond democratic interaction.[65] Democracy had created a sphere of privilege, equality and freedom based solely on membership in the polity, not on personal or social qualities. Wealthy and aristocratic opponents of the democratic system claimed that this political attri-

---

[65] See Raaflaub (1983) 527–33.

bution of autonomy was responsible for licentious self-indulgence and the degeneration of social order as every man, whatever his background, education or character, could seek to realize his desires. Aristophanes provides a vivid glimpse of this attitude in his play *The Knights*, a comic defamation of the powerful demagogue Cleon, son of a successful manufacturer and known by the abusive epithet 'tanner' or 'leather-seller' (see *Knights* 136). In the play, two servants representing Nicias and Demosthenes (in real life Cleon's political competitors), conspire to promote a rival to Cleon ('Paphlagon,' a barbarian slave) in the affections of the sovereign people, Demus, their master. The man they choose to beat Cleon at his own demagogic game is a sausage-seller. They assure him that he shall rule Athens and her empire: 'You shall become, this oracle declares, a great man.' He is incredulous: 'Tell me, how could I, a sausage-seller, become a man?' (lines 176–9). Demosthenes insists that the sausage-seller's very baseness will ensure his political success, for leadership of the *demos* is no longer the privilege of cultured or worthy men, but is the province of the ignorant and coarse (lines 191–3; cf. 218–20). The sausage-seller's protest that he, low-born and unlettered as he is, cannot appropriately aspire to be a *man*, reflects the contemporary oligarchic view, founded in traditional and perhaps widely-accepted prejudices, that despite democratic ideology it is a man's personal and social qualities that determine his worth. Men of oligarchic sympathies at Athens seem to have deployed a notion of genuine human freedom against the democratic claim that citizenship itself constituted freedom and nobility. The articulation of social distinctions in terms of the concepts of truly free as opposed to dependent forms of work, of liberal education and the genuinely free as opposed to merely autonomous man, marked an attempt to undermine the democratic construction of a purely political identity and revert to a social definition of worth, power and order. The qualities of the free man were denied to the mass of citizens and reserved to the aristocrat.

Shifting ground: ordering the self politically

Protagoras' interpretation of the democratic city suggested that each citizen of the *polis*, tutored as he is by interaction with his fellow citizens, including the wise, has the competence, and together the citizens have the authority, to assess and realize the common interest. By the time Thucydides and Democritus undertook to analyze the political order, the ground had shifted. The social meaning of *nomos* had been affected by its epistemological status: it was condemned as malleable and subjective precisely because it was constituted by the interaction of men who themselves measured experience. Yet *nomos* was also condemned as external and coercive because man, aware of his status as 'measure,' came to regard his nature *qua* man not as a condition defined by social interaction but as something inward and at least partly independent of social convention.[66] Democracy no longer seemed to offer any stable criteria; interaction was no longer construed as constituting a stable collective good via what man took to be good, but seemed to have degenerated into the expression of ephemeral and conflicting desires. This condition is embodied in the experience of incontinence, of motivation without external sanction or inherent order. Incontinence or weakness of the will as described and rejected by Socrates[67] can be understood as the internalization of forces formerly regarded as external and liable to constrain man as a whole, wits as well as passions. As Dodds observed: 'The Greek had always felt the experience of passion as something mysterious and frightening, the experience of a force that was in him, possessing him, rather than possessed by him.'[68] The experience could still be described as infatuation (*atē*), but increasingly the desire to do wrong was portrayed, as often by Euripides, 'no longer as an alien thing assailing their reason from without, but as a part of their own being . . . Medea knows that she is at grips, not with an avenging deity (*alastōr*), but with her own irrational self, her *thumos*.'[69] Medea, contemplating the murder of her children, acknowledges that what she is about to do is bad, 'but the passionate heart (*thumos*) is stronger than my purposes' (line 1078).[70] Compare the incontinence described by Medea to the more Gorgianic observation of Hecuba, in Euripides' *Trojan Women*, that man's *aphrosunē* is his Aphrodite, i.e. that to be moved by lust is to be foolish. Implicit here, as in the discourses of Gorgias, is the assumption that the self is compounded of desires and beliefs, and that the wits of a man who does what is bad must be in some way deranged or defective. This assumption is also characteristic of the earlier tragedians' depiction of irrational behavior: men are deluded and infatuated, by *atē* or Aphrodite, and 'the evil appears good.'

---

[66] For a detailed account of this development, see Segal (1961).

[67] The concept seems not to have been articulated clearly before him, though it was probably recognized. See Irwin (1983) 184–9, 194.

[68] Dodds (1951) 185f.

[69] Dodds (1951) 186 with n. 17. See *Medea* 1078–80, *Hippolytus* 375f.

[70] Cf. *Hippolytus* 375f. and see Irwin (1983) 189f. on both passages.

Action under the influence is error, not incontinence.[71] The double causation which had tied human motivation, belief and desire together and into a structure of good and evil, could be analyzed in two ways: (1) man is overwhelmed, mind and all, by what he desires or (2) man is ruled, passions and all, by what he believes. Once this ambivalent concept of the sources of human action is reinterpreted as both fully human (*aphrosunē*, not Aphrodite) and fully internal (*thumos*, not *alastōr*), the self is divided into two parts, reason and desire. The first alternative then describes incontinence, the second one the ideal of self-control. Man's wits are no longer manipulated or overthrown from without, but are instead engaged in an internal struggle: either desires triumph over reasoned belief or reasoned belief rules desire.

The problem Thucydides and Democritus confronted[72] was how, in a society prey to primitive egoism and lust for power, to give all citizens internal reason to act in such a way as to promote the order and well-being of the whole community. They recognized that a theory of social order must appeal to the individual's assessment of his interests, and they were unwilling to construe man's real interests in teleological terms which threatened democracy by pointing to the imposition of order by an elite. Unlike Socrates, Thucydides and Democritus believed that reason must be both the means of achieving understanding and the means of controlling destructive impulse and desire. They both advocated self-control, the control of desire by reason, but self-control tied to stable, general criteria of well-being. In this way they sought to reconcile the personal and the political, by demonstrating that the capacity for ordered attainment of one's interests was *not* a function of personal power, or inherited qualities, or the capacity for dialectic. But how could insistence on individual well-being, the product of reflective distance from the norms of the community, be reconciled with the social order and commitment to the public good necessary for collective well-being? How could corrosive cynicism be neutralized?

---

[71] See Irwin (1983) 188. This does seem to me to rest on cognitivist assumptions.

[72] In a brief but provocative essay Hussey (1986) explores some affinities between Thucydides and Democritus. He suggests (p. 138) that Thucydides' approach to writing history was both 'literary' and 'scientific,' and that this fusion 'was possible only after a long process of criticism of particular facts in the light of general ideas,' including those of Democritus. Hussey does not discuss the possibility that affinities are in part the result of thinking about similar conditions, at a particular stage in Greek thought, in a democratically-minded way.

5   Thucydides: reflecting history – man and the community

Thucydides designed his history as a political argument, a justification of a certain kind of politics and political analysis. The form in which Thucydides expressed his political understanding was a deliberate response to the character of contemporary political life and attitudes. He was responding to concerns raised by democracy, and his response was democratic: that is why he chose to write history. History is a way of reflecting *within* society, of combining autonomy with order. It is also a *political* mode of understanding, capable of shaping as well as expressing the interests of all members of the political order through their participation in democratic interaction.

History as a way of understanding man and how he is to be understood

To see that Thucydides' *History of the Peloponnesian War* is in the same sense a response to political events and to reflections on those events as were the writings of those we conventionally call philosophers, it is essential to get beyond the appellation, 'Thucydides, historian,' or rather to arrive at a deeper understanding of Thucydidean history. Generic distinctions of this kind divide up the world in a modern way.[1] Among the Greeks, statesmen (e.g. Solon) sometimes expressed themselves in verse, as did those whom we would now call cosmologists (e.g. Parmenides); the men now known as philosophers articulated their ideas in, for example, fable (Protagoras) and dialogue (Plato). All of these thinkers, plus the dramatists and Herodotus, could be seen from a broad perspective as contributing to a single project, namely the understanding of man's position in the cosmos; from this perspective, their choices of modes of expression embody particular views of the character of that understanding and of how it is to be communicated. Thus, as I suggested earlier, Aeschylus and Sophocles

---

[1] See Fornara (1983).

were addressing some of the same questions as Protagoras. The exploration of those questions in dramatic form reflects a view of the human condition as riven by particular and competing demands, and of human understanding as achieved through participation, in the process of imaginatively working through concrete emotional and intellectual conflict.[2] Protagoras' choice of fable and analysis expresses greater explicitness and reflective distance, despite a continued commitment to the importance of securing the audience's imaginative participation (a commitment which persists in Socratic dialectic and at least in the early Platonic dialogues). To formulate the contrast more sharply than is strictly warranted, the tragedian's choice of genre *embodies* a particular understanding of the condition of man, while Protagoras' expresses one. To achieve even as much distance as does Protagoras from the representation of the human condition is to embody a view of the power of reason (enhanced by the consolidation of the effects of writing instead of oral performance)[3] but it is also to adopt such a view reflectively, with the consequences for subsequent self-understanding outlined in the last chapter. The dramatists embody a peculiar form of ethical understanding which they did not consciously adopt (though one might, on reflection, be tempted to do so). For all that it represents a particular (and not the only) mode of human self-understanding, the reflective understanding of man is the mode which speaks (now as then) to an irremediably self-conscious society.

Thucydides deliberately adopted history, or rather a particular kind of history, as the appropriate way to express an understanding both of man and of how he is to be understood. Herodotus' *Histories* embody a view of human nature and experience, but do not express a conception of how they are to be construed. Herodotus provided an account of the background, causes, and events of the Persian Wars; he traced the patterns of human triumph and destruction, and preserved for posterity the glorious achievements of men. Thucydides' transformation of the genre establishes his distance from his predecessor, who was eclectic, willing to entertain a number of different stories about an event and relatively unreflective about what historical narrative should be and what (if anything) it was *for*. Without citing Herodotus by name, Thucydides explicitly points to the different character of his own historical vision:

---

[2] See Simon (1978) ch. 7, MacIntyre (1981) 134, Williams (forthcoming), Nussbaum (1986) Introduction and Part I.

[3] See Havelock (1978), Simon (1978) 189–93.

It may well be that the absence of the fabulous from my narrative will seem less pleasing to the ear; but whoever wishes to search out the truth about events which have happened and about those which will one day, in accordance with human nature, happen again in the same or a similar way – for these to think my work profitable will be sufficient. And indeed, it has been composed not as a prize-essay to be heard for the moment, but as a possession for all time. (1.22.4)[4]

Thucydides' ambition to discover truths which would inform the future, as well as to render accurately (1.22.2) facts about the past, has earned him epithets ranging from pseudo-dramatist (Cornford) through moralist (Finley) and scientific historian (Cochrane) to pseudo (or social) scientist (Collingwood).[5] Again, such generic classifications fail to capture the distinctiveness of the Thucydidean project, which is shaped by the assumption that understanding of human nature and human interests is possible only through an accurate narrative embodiment of human experience. An interpreted, analytical history both expresses and embodies an understanding of the way men tend to behave, and the way they in fact have behaved, in particular circumstances. Thucydidean history combines and surpasses the virtues, as imaginative portrayals of ethical life, of drama and the philosophic fable. It demands both participation and reflection, and participation in and reflection on real experience, not a plausible or hypothetical tale. History could only serve as a form of political analysis and a way of living politically in so far as it was good history; for Thucydidean history appealed to what man is actually like, and the way the world actually is.

To what kinds of political developments was Thucydidean history a response? The challenge was posed by the experience of democracy; the task was to reconcile order with the exercise of autonomy and the elaboration of reflectiveness over time. In the latter years of the fifth century, politics was no longer seen to be a means of self-expression and tutor of self-restraint; *nomos* seemed an artificial constraint and political deliberation a matter of showmanship and manipulation, of self-promotion and self-indulgence. Under these conditions, reflection on human nature and human interests threatened on the one hand to sever man's self-understanding from and on the other to dissolve it in the realm of need and desire. From the point of view of Socrates, for example, politics at Athens simply was the indulgence of desire; he abandoned conventional politics as too vicious and dangerous, but boasted that 'of the men of our time I alone do politics' (*Gorgias*

---

[4] All translations of Thucydides are adapted from Smith in the Loeb edition.
[5] Cornford (1907), Finley (1968) ch. 4, Cochrane (1929), Collingwood (1946).

521d). What he meant was that he persistently questioned individual Athenians, in order to show that reasoned sifting of a man's beliefs commits him to certain behavioral principles (e.g. it is better to suffer harm than to do it). In the absence of the kind of political socialization of men's perceptions of their interests envisioned by Protagoras, ethics was gradually distinguished from politics and was entrusted with the task of securing social order. The interaction characteristic of the *polis* was no longer conceived as itself providing citizens with good reason to act in such a way as to contribute to communal well-being; to prevent men from taking advantage of their circumstances to gratify themselves, an external conception of man's good was proposed, a teleological vision of man as a rational creature. By contrast, the view of man which submerged him in the depths of need and desire portrayed him as the creature of his passions. Thus Callicles: the rules of society are designed to constrain men from indulging their desires to the full and thus realizing their true natures. Thucydides' *History* embodies the belief that neither account of human good will do. The desire of all men, or even members of the elite, to be tyrant cannot, in the world as it is, be sustained. However, as Socrates' confrontation with Callicles in Plato's *Gorgias* makes clear, an appeal to reason cannot in itself stifle such desires so long as individual men believe they can realize them.

Thucydides assumes, against both Socrates and Callicles, that reason and passion will often, particularly under certain circumstances and certainly in the world as it now is, come into conflict. No appeal to one or the other which fails to take into account the potential for conflict between them can define man's real interests, because it will blind him to significant aspects of his situation. The Socratic account, founded on the claim that man's only real concern should be the well-being of his soul, ignores basic human aspirations such as the desire to survive or the ambition to win power or glory. In large part motivated by the disintegration of socially-defined values, the Socratic appeal to principles of abstract reason is doubly unrealistic in that context. The Calliclean account of human interests and human freedom, apparently a realistic response to the perception that politics is merely a battle of interests for power, ignores the real constraints on any man's capacity to dominate others. Both accounts are conceived in response to conditions of ethical disarray, but both fail to – indeed, are too rigid to – grasp the real character and import of existing circumstances; in particular, Socrates and Callicles fail to appreciate the significance of social forces, which are stigmatized by both as corrupt and debilitating. Thucydides recognizes, and his *History* portrays, the effects of social and ethical disintegration; he observes the demise of the 'noble simplicity'[6] which secured social harmony and the advent, in conditions of insecurity and conflict, of constant suspicious calculations of advantage, which led to greater insecurity and more damaging conflict. Under such conditions, man's nature and his interests can no longer be conceived or defined strictly functionally, in terms of his place or role in society. A political understanding of man's interests must give way to a construal of the interests of men as individuals in particular circumstances. The teleological theories of man *qua* man, as essentially a rational soul or natural instinct, cannot meet this need because they increase man's reflective distance from experience and thus further undermine his capacity to act prudently to secure his real interests.

Thucydides' historical construal of man's nature and his interests acknowledges that men are now, irrevocably, reflective judges of their own well-being and suspicious of social constraints; and his history shows that under such circumstances well-being can be secured only in a political context and only by deploying principles of historical understanding. The problem is how, in a fractured society, to make men alert and responsive to the fact that their good is tied to acting responsibly, with a view to the well-being of the political community. Historical interpretation reveals that the behavior of the political community as a whole, as a unit in the world of communities of the late fifth century B.C., is an essential constituent of the well-being of its members. To have genuine force for men whose capacity for judgment or prudence[7] is obstructed by passions, such interpretation should ideally take the form of political interaction. Leadership which functions by offering and promoting historical understanding can reveal how men are constrained, and how their real interests are defined, by the way the world actually is, now. And it can foster the self-control which, as historical interpretation shows, is essential now to the realization of those interests. Leadership founded on principles of historical interpretation can thus secure both autonomy and order: the reflective agent is guided by political interaction, but a form of interaction responsive to and expressive of the agent's own reflection on his experience and his interests. Although history is most effective as a

[6] The term appears in the analysis of factional strife at Corcyra in Thuc. 3.82. See also the discussion of the quality as it is portrayed in Euripides' *Hecuba* in Nussbaum (1986) ch. 13.

[7] By 'prudence' I mean the quality of taking thought for the future and for the consequences of one's actions, with a view to securing the good.

guide to prudence when it is deployed politically, over time, yet a particular history could also, Thucydides believed, serve to teach individual men how to assess their own circumstances and identify their real interests. His own history is a 'possession for all time' not because history can be expected to repeat itself but because, presented in a certain way, history prompts identification and participation, and extends and sharpens the reader's ability to assess experience. Thucydides' analytical, reflective history of the Peloponnesian War is an answer to the challenge of his time both in content and form. It showed that the Athenians, powerful as they were, had good reason to exercise self-control. And it did so in a way which took into account both the force of human desires and the influence of context, circumstance and experience. The *History* constituted a way of thinking about the good for men – prudence – compatible with each man's constant reflection on his interests under changing conditions, and thus a way of thinking useful to all readers.

How does Thucydides achieve his aims?

How can an accurate rendering of particular events be useful, and useful not merely to those who experienced the immediate aftermath of those events, but to future readers? Thucydides' *History* is an argument: it both justifies itself (that is, shows that history is the proper way to think about – and in – politics, and that it makes historical judgment possible) and justifies also a particular set of actions in a particular context. For Thucydides, what there is to know about human nature can be known only historically. There are no static truths about men, only experience of them and understanding of particular situations. The *History* itself recounts the effects of reflectiveness on social order in circumstances which aroused doubts about the relation between the individual and the political good. This analysis shows that man should not construe who he is and what he should do in terms of social conventions or a static conception of human nature both of which are vulnerable because inflexible and unable to identify the good under changing circumstances. The reflective revision of human behavior is necessary for prudence. As a mode both of political action and of analysis, history cultivates social prudence and collective judgment, and shows the need for such cultivation. Thucydides did not seek to close off reflectiveness or the collective exercise of judgment, but to shape it.

How does Thucydides' argument work? How is the *History* structured as an argument? Thucydides offers a story of the actual experiences of persons placed in a context which, properly interpreted, reveals the connection between their actions and the reality of the situation. The power of such an account to cultivate prudence and self-control can be illuminated by comparison with the process of moral education and the goals of psychotherapy. Children learn what kinds of behavior are appropriate by being guided through a succession of experiences. They infer, over time, what principles of analysis are relevant and how to apply them in particular cases. Although experience yields no universally applicable abstract lessons and no precise parallels, children learn to exercise independent judgment of new circumstances. In psychotherapy, patients learn to interpret their own behavior, to perceive deeply-ingrained patterns of response to particular circumstances, i.e. to understand why their life keeps happening to them. In the process they come to see their personality and character, their 'nature,' as a historical artefact. Thus understanding reveals certain limitations on what is now possible, given who it is one has become, but it can also enable one to act with greater self-consciousness and to modulate if not avoid habitual, instinctive reactions. In an analogous way, Thucydides' *History* invites the reader to participate in a set of interpreted experiences which guide assessment of what is appropriate (prudent) under various circumstances and of how men tend to behave, so that he may learn how to judge for himself: how to understand his own situation and anticipate his own situation and anticipate his own likely responses to it.

The utility of the *History* thus depends on a synthesis of accurate reporting and interpretation. Thucydides integrates the interpretive tasks of the historian, the historical agents whose experience he records, and the readers who are expected to learn from that experience. The reader observes agents attempting to understand and interpret their situation in a context accurately rendered and rigorously interpreted by the historian and he learns how to interpret. Thucydides is not offering a realistic story or an argument about ideas imbedded in a realistic setting; he is making historical reality itself intelligible and illuminating. He selects from, condenses, organizes, simplifies, juxtaposes and synthesizes what (to the best of his knowledge, after thorough investigation) actually happened. His principles of historical interpretation and presentation are precisely those which an agent should use to make sense of his experience and to determine his actions.[8] The *History* does not merely express such principles; it embodies them. Thucydides does not invent. This claim may seem implausible in view of the fact that Thucydides incorporates speeches which are written in his own style[9] and which are said to express 'that which most befitted the occasion,' what was appropriate (*ta deonta*) (1.22.1).[10] Even in the speeches, however, Thucydides adheres to standards of accuracy as well as truth; his project requires that he do so. Unlike Homer and Herodotus, both of whom enlivened their narratives with speeches, Thucydides committed himself to keeping as close as possible to the general sense of what was actually said (1.22.1)[11] and to trying to meet an objective criterion of appropriateness to context. The structure and content of 1.22 make it clear that for Thucydides reconstruction of a speech was always a last resort.[12] Where reliable information was not available, or memory failed, reconstruction proceeded not on the basis of whim or prejudice but according to the historian's rounded and informed assessment of what the situation demanded (*ta deonta*)[13] where 'situation' includes historical circumstances, intellectual and emotional climate and a particular speaker's need to persuade a particular audience of a particular view under particular conditions.[14]

It is Thucydides' accurate and responsible presentation of a speech to bring out its significance, sometimes supplementing what he has heard in accordance with the criterion of appropriateness, which gives force to the speeches as interpretations and guides to it. For the speeches are useful to the reader in so far as they show men responding

[8] Cf. Cogan's discussion of history's relation to prudence, Cogan (1981) 182–3; and of rhetoric as the principle that structures Thucydides' inquiry, pp. 201f.

[9] But see Tompkins (1972). Note just how difficult it is to identify the stylistic differences Tompkins perceives.

[10] Collingwood (1946) 36 failed to conceal his irritation: 'Could a just man who had a really historical mind have permitted himself the use of such a convention?' It is hard to see why Collingwood counts Herodotus, who reports as genuine e.g. the Persian debate about constitutions, as a 'really historical mind' – unless 'historical' means 'uncritical' (which Herodotus was not, or not always). See Hunter (1982).

[11] See especially the *beginning* of 1.22.1. On the much-discussed issue of the meaning of 1.22.1, see now Dover (1981) 394–9, Cogan (1981) Introduction and the bibliography in Stadter (1973).

[12] Dover (1981) 394.

[13] Which is not to say that he may not have met this criterion rather better in some instances than in others. See Dover (1981) 394–9.

[14] See, especially, Dover (1981) 394–9, and Schneider (1974) 137–71, and Cogan (1981) ch. 6. For analyses of particular speeches conceived in this light, see Winnington-Ingram (1965), Macleod (1977) and (1978), and Cogan (1981) 3–119.

to real situations and reveal how – and how well – they manage to interpret events and exercise prudence. The actors and speakers in the *History* are interpreters: they do and say what they believe to be appropriate (*ta deonta*, in the complex sense adumbrated above) under the circumstances as they understand them. (Appropriateness does not entail rationality, but merely response to a perceived context.) They continually assess the likely course of events and the probable consequences of their actions. Like the historian, the agent reasons on the basis of the information he possesses and what he believes about the regularities of human experience, from what is or has been to what is likely to be. He may, again like the historian, seek to discover the truth (*to saphes*, see 6.33, 6.93). Thucydides selects and disposes antithetical speeches in such a way as to illuminate various – often the most general – aspects of particular decisions or circumstances; and the considerations raised in the debates are seen to be relevant (or not) to the outcome of events. Contrasting interpretations are presented as attempts to persuade others, and as such they appeal to what is usual, plausible, likely. Each speaker offers an assessment of a situation and its implications and of the motivation for and cogency of the other speaker's assessment. (See, for example, the speeches of Hermocrates and Athenagoras of Syracuse concerning the reported Athenian preparations to attack Sicily – 6.33, 6.36.) They in turn are part of a broader assessment by the historian, who places the conflicting and successive interpretations of historical agents in a context which reveals their adequacy or inadequacy. The relevant context is not simply the sum of actual events – what does happen, by way of contrast to the interpreter's assessment of what was likely to happen – but rather the historian's interpretation of what was actually possible for the agent at the time. Through his characterization of the context, the historian suggests an interpretation as a foil to the agent's. The *History* is not a series of predictions which are more or less accurate, but of interpretations which are more or less realistic, not a moral tale which teaches a universal lesson about behavior proper to all circumstances, but a realistic interpretation of a particular period of history which demonstrates what it is to be realistic. The reader of the *History*, at two removes, gains access to a reality which has been interpreted by historical agents and by the historian. He learns from a history of interpreted interactions and interacting interpretations.[15]

---

[15] For more detailed analysis of the interpretative unity, with respect to *to eikos*, of historian, agent and audience, see especially Hunter (1973) 23–42, 182–4, Schneider (1974) 125f., 171, of historian and audience, see Rawlings (1981) ch. VI and *passim*. His picture

What the historian offers in the narrative (speeches and actions) as a whole is precisely what the historical agent needs: an understanding of what is required in or appropriate to particular historical situations and the related ability to discern what events are likely to be associated with what others in accordance with the way men tend to behave,[16] itself an inference from the history of human experience and a regularity which underlies the existence of resemblances between one historical situation and another. Certain general features of man's nature remain constant, and are (in general) affected in the same or similar ways by similar events (1.22.4).[17] In his analysis of the civic strife in Corcyra provoked by the war between Athens and Sparta, Thucydides invokes the concept of human nature to explain the ferocious battles and the resulting calamities which 'happen and always will happen while human nature remains the same' (3.82.2).[18] He observes that the stress of war and want tend to undermine man's judgment (*gnomē*) and strengthen his passions (*orgē*). Not everyone is affected in this way[19] and the consequences of this general tendency 'are severer or milder, and different in their manifestations, according as the variations in circumstances present themselves in each case' (3.82.2). Human nature for Thucydides is not a fixed set of characteristics, neither basic, instinctual drives nor what man is at his best, but rather a psychological structure which underlies man's experience of the constant interaction of reason and desire. This interaction tends to be affected in regular ways by events. Thucydides' narrative not only provides illustrations of these regularities and variations in human

of the *History* as two wars each modeled on the other is overdrawn, though it produces some interesting insights. For a different view, see Edmunds (1975) 4f., 174ff., 205ff. Cf. Cogan (1981) ch. 6 on Thucydides' use of the principles of rhetoric.

[16] I concur with the view of de Ste Croix (1972) 32 that the phrase *kata to anthropinon* means 'according to characteristics of human beings which make for constancy in human affairs' and not 'in the conditions of human existence,' as Stahl (1968) 33 and Hunter (1973) 141–2 would have it; on Cogan's interpretation (1981) 186f., 234f. of *to anthropinon* as the peculiarly social aspect of man's nature, expressed by the principles of rhetoric, see below, nn. 18 and 22.

[17] Thucydides' use of the concept of human nature does not imply a belief in or a desire to affirm 'psychological laws,' as Collingwood (1946) 29 alleges. On this question see especially de Romilly (1956b) 56–63, esp. 62. The relationship between man's nature and historical events is not to be characterized deterministically. On *anankē* (necessity) in Thucydides, see de Ste Croix (1972) 60–1.

[18] The resemblance between 1.22.4 and 3.82.2 is one argument against Cogan's view (1981) 187–8, that *to anthropinon* is meant by Thucydides to refer to 'the human force that moves nations' as opposed to the 'physical or biological nature of people' signified by *anthropeia phusis* in 3.82.2 and 2.50.1.

[19] Note *tōn pollōn*, 3.82.2.

response; it also provides experience of them.[20] The reader is told, for example, of the degenerate way in which Athenian politicians after Pericles sought to manipulate the feelings of the masses; he also feels the power of their rhetoric. Or, in recounting the events which led in 425 to the Athenian fortification of a site on the Peloponnesian coast and the subsequent blockade of the troops sent from Sparta, Thucydides structures the narrative so as to arouse in the reader the surprise, confusion and alterations of feeling occasioned by these developments. Thucydides draws the reader into the emotional and intellectual responses which the *History* as a whole seeks to render intelligible. The reader is challenged to reflect on his[21] own reactions and helped to do so. The many echoes and recurrent patterns in the *History* are not meant to lull the reader into complacent certainty that he has grasped the inner workings of history; on the contrary, they challenge him to assess the genuine differences and similarities between two contexts, to think historically. An interpreted history, which itself depends upon and deploys judgments about appropriateness and likelihood, both supplements the reader's experience and sharpens his or her judgment.

By enabling us to experience and interpret a portion of human history, Thucydidean history cultivates judgment and fosters self-consciousness and self-control. Historical understanding of human psychological response prepares us to confront certain kinds of conditions in awareness of their likely consequences. The plague that ravaged Athens just after the outbreak of the war is a prime example of an unpredictable event. It fell upon Athens unexpectedly (2.48.2), and the doctors were helpless because of ignorance (2.47.4; cf. 2.48.3). The plague was unlike anything the Athenians had heretofore experienced (note 2.50.1): no human art or skill was of any use (2.47.4). 'The character of the disease,' Thucydides reports, 'was such as to baffle description; it attacked each person more harshly than was compatible with human nature' (2.50.1).[22] That is, the severity and

---

[20] See Connor (1984) 16.

[21] Or, now, 'her.'

[22] The usual translation of *kata ten anthropeian phusin*, 'beyond the capacity of human nature to endure' (Warner) does not make sense of the fact that it is preceded and followed by remarks on the utterly alien, unfamiliar character of the disease. Hobbes's 'being crueller even than human nature' could perhaps be construed in the sense I have suggested, *contra* Cogan (1981) 186–7, who restricts *anthropeia phusis* to 'the specific biological content of our natures.' The use of the term is comparable to 3.82.2; in both cases it refers to a constant feature of man's interaction with the world, though in the case of the plague Thucydides is suggesting that our understanding of human nature may require revision.

indiscriminateness of the plague contravened what men thought they knew about the effects of disease on human beings (see 2.51.3). Thucydides' account analyzes how this kind of calamity affected human relations in the city. Like war, and particularly in conjunction with it, the plague promotes indulgence in instinct and impulse, and shreds the fabric of society. But he also gave a detailed description of the disease itself, 'to enable men, if it should break out again, above all to have some knowledge in advance and not be ignorant about it' (2.48.3). For the plague was an utterly baffling and unfamiliar disease, and terrifying in part because it was so alien. It afflicted the healthy and strong as well as the weak, and no single remedy could be counted upon to bring relief to most sufferers: what helped one man harmed another (2.51). To have knowledge of the character of the disease would not enable future generations to prevent it or even perhaps to mitigate its violence, only to recognize it and anticipate its likely course; but even this level of understanding would help to stave off the terror which had so demoralized the Athenians, and perhaps diminish the devastating social consequences of despair. Throughout the *History*, in a variety of different contexts, Thucydides brings out the importance of mastering oneself psychologically in circumstances that tend to be undermining, and indicates that understanding of the nature of the situation and its likely effects can help to make self-mastery possible. (See, e.g., 6.34.6, 6.49.2.) Awareness of the range of conditions that men and women have endured, and how they have endured them, heightens the reader's self-conscious understanding of human – and, at a general level, his or her own – nature, and thus, in a way analogous to the awareness achieved through therapy, enhances the capacity for self-control. A historical understanding of human nature is also essential to the historical interpretations that underlie and cultivate judgment. In the process of reading Thucydides' *History*, as in the process of moral education, one picks up relevant principles of analysis, including how to understand human behavior under various conditions, and learns how to apply and, when appropriate, revise them in particular cases. An interpreted history shows us that certain elements of our experience may well imply others which we have not yet experienced or recognized and indicates where we should look for relevant considerations in assessing the particular reality in which we participate.

Historical principles: the Archaeology

Thucydides' own analysis of the early history of Greece, the so-called 'Archaeology' (1.2–19), itself serves this function of isolating relevant principles of analysis in a particular context which are then applied to the interpretation of events in the remainder of the *History*. To see the relationship between the Archaeology and the *History* in this way is also to appreciate an aspect of history's power to cultivate prudence which is somewhat obscured by the analogy with moral education. The *History* is not an assortment of interpreted situations; it is a connected narrative, a sequence of interpretations of (and in) contexts shaped by what has gone before. Judgment is therefore not simply a function of analytical powers honed by experience. Judgment rests on historical analysis, the capacity to perceive how the present has been brought about by the past. Only from a historical perspective is it possible to see what the present is actually like and how it is to be understood. Prudence, too, is historical. To seek to secure one's own good it is not enough to consider one's life as a whole, its entire length and range, as Aristotle encourages men to do, nor to consider it as psychoanalysis does (historically) as the development of a particular personality. Rather, one must view a life not just in the context of society but of the history of that society, or indeed of that civilization, and its likely future. Only thus can one come to understand one's own nature, the character of the world in which one lives, and what it is genuinely possible to be and to do in that world as it now is. Like the *History* as a whole, the Archaeology is an interpreted history. A highly analytical and dense account of the Greek world from the distant past to the present, the Archaeology provides both an analysis of human tendencies in response to the world as it was in the past, and a means of understanding what the present is like as a result of this particular history. The Archaeology is designed to show that the Peloponnesian War was a greater and more devastating war than any that had preceded it (1.2).[23] Thucydides is here asserting the importance of his

---

[23] Like Herodotus, Thucydides adopts the Homeric notion that 'great and noteworthy' deeds should be recorded and preserved (1.1.2). Precisely because he has been preceded by Homer and Herodotus, Thucydides argues in the *Prooemium* (1.1–23) that the events he has chosen to record are greater and more noteworthy than the Trojan and Persian Wars. Thucydides' proof of the greatness of the present conflict by contrast with the past does not depend on detailed comparisons of the size of armies or the wealth of rulers, but on principles of the acquisition and concentration of power which explain historically both the poverty of past encounters and the magnitude of the present one. On Thucydides' acceptance of convention and his self-conscious originality in delimiting his subject, see Immerwahr (1973), Parry (1972) and Connor (1984) 20–32.

history against the claims of Homer and Herodotus. But he is also making a point about the character of the world that made the Peloponnesian War possible and was shattered by it, and does so by placing the Trojan and the Persian Wars in a narrative which culminates in and explains the present conflict. For Thucydides, past is not precept: neither the world nor man remains the same. History discloses neither a set of abstract principles nor a static conception of human nature. The bulk of the *History* is structured by the principles of historical development set out starkly in the Archaeology. Yet as a particular moment in that development, the events of the *History* occur and must be interpreted in a context shaped by the specific consequences and implications of the events traced in the Archaeology.

Geographical, political, economic and psychological factors are invoked in Thucydides' analysis of the development of Greece from remote times (1.2–21). The naval power of Minos resulted in increased safety on the seas, which facilitated navigation, trade and communication. These in turn enabled the accumulation of capital and a more settled way of life. Those with large resources came to dominate those with few, and thus increased their power. The first common expedition mounted by the Greeks was the campaign against Troy which, says Thucydides, was made possible by the fact that Agamemnon 'surpassed in power the princes of his time' and not because these princes were bound by an oath (1.9.1).

In subsequent years, by land no wars arose from which any considerable accession of power resulted . . . Foreign expeditions far from their own country for the subjugation of others were not undertaken by the Hellenes. For they had not yet been brought into union as subjects of the most powerful states nor, on the other hand, did they of their own accord make expeditions in common as equal allies. (1.15.2)

The Persian invasion, which forced the Greeks to act together, did result in an accession of power to each of the two leading states, Athens and Sparta, the concentration of power in two camps and the polarization of the Hellenic world (1.18–19).

Thucydides' analysis of the accumulation of power in early Greece presents power in the form characteristic of the Athenians and their empire. The power that transforms Greece is founded on control of the seas.[24] And power is portrayed, in the Archaeology as in the Corinthian description of the Athenians, as the energy and drive for conquest.[25] Moreover, the desire and power to dominate others is

---

[24] De Romilly (1963) 64ff.; cf. Starr (1978).
[25] De Romilly (1963) 74; cf. Parry (1972), Immerwahr (1973).

linked in Thucydides' account with political liberty: only after the tyrants were expelled did the Greek cities realize their potential strength through the dominion of the more – and increasingly – powerful cities (1.17–19). In the period since the overthrow of the tyrants at Athens, the Athenian people, as Thucydides observes in a different context, 'had been not only not subject to anyone else, but for more than half of that period had themselves been accustomed to rule over others' (8.68.4). The freedom from domination which the Athenians enjoyed individually as citizens of the democracy was associated with the city's freedom of action and power (see 6.89.6; 7.69.21; cf. 2.36–43). It is precisely those aspects of power characteristic of the Athenians, including the constant search for more, which have in Thucydides' view been responsible for the historical developments that propelled Greece to the heights of strength and potency and made possible, even inevitable, the devastating conflict between Athens and Sparta. The truth about the distant past both reveals what is characteristic of men and demonstrates the peculiar – and historically sanctioned – greatness of Athens.

In addition to casting the principles of power in the form epitomized by the Athenian empire, the Archaeology construes concerted action as the mark of power. The enterprising spirit released by the overthrow of the tyrants resulted in the consolidation of power by certain states, which facilitated action in concert. Action in common was for Thucydides the hallmark of advanced power (1.3.1, 1.15.2, 1.17, 1.18.2). Indeed most of the Archaeology is concerned not with the power of particular cities but rather with the power of Hellas (e.g. 1.13.1). It is a sign of a period of Hellenic weakness that the only wars being fought were scraps among neighbors (1.15.2, 1.17) and a sign of strength that all of Hellas had been united under the two most powerful states (1.15.2–3). It also appears from Thucydides' account that for individual states as well as for Hellas as a whole, the disruptions arising from conflict are a hindrance to the acquisition or consolidation of power. The picture is complicated: Attica grew because she was a stable community, free from civic strife because she lacked good agricultural land. Communities which acquired power through their possession of fertile land soon lost it. They were ruined by internal conflict and plots from outside (1.2.4). One moral of this story is that power is neither confined to nor determined by natural resources. Moreover, factional conflict undermines power and power itself encourages such conflict. Although from one angle activity seems to be the essence of power as Thucydides conceives it, from another the absence of activity appears to be a prerequisite for growth and strength. Thus according to Thucydides it was only after Hellas recovered from the turbulence caused by the Trojan War and became 'securely tranquil,' when 'its population was no longer subject to expulsion from their homes' that it began to send out colonies (1.12).[26] The analysis of power in the Archaeology thus discloses an ambiguity: concerted action is the basis of power, and it requires peace; yet power is also portrayed as essentially activity. The ambiguity is resolved historically, in Thucydides' perception that it is the consolidation of power by the strongest states (as earlier by the strongest within states) which constitutes the growth of Hellenic power. Activity on the part of some states promotes general security and tranquillity (1.8.3–4). However, this can hardly continue to be the case once Hellas is polarized. The principles identified in the Archaeology take on a different orientation in changing contexts, and their implications for the present must be interpreted historically. The very development which has secured the growth of Hellenic power and which is associated with Athens has also created a conflict between the growth of that power and its security. The power of Hellas both must and cannot continue to grow. A conflict of the proportions of the Peloponnesian War would cause precisely the unsettled conditions and civic strife which Hellas had overcome in her accession to strength and power, and the conflict must be of these proportions because that is precisely what Hellas' accession to power has made possible.

Thucydides' account of motivation and rationality in the world-historical process involves the same ambiguity, and leads to the same dilemma, as his analysis of power. The historical process is not impersonal or mechanistic; power is the creation of human intelligence, the imposition of order upon the world. Yet the process is fueled by non-rational or irrational as well as rational elements in the human psyche. In the Archaeology, Thucydides is not concerned to distinguish or contrast rational and irrational motivations. They are complementary: daring, desire for gain and fear provide the impetus, and intelligence shows the way. No conflict between reason and emotion arises in the course of Thucydides' account. The desire for advantage, which powers the process, must – because the process is conceived as concentration and consolidation of power within Hellas – have two aspects. For some, advantage must reside in an assertion of power, for others

---

[26] Note the contrast between the chaotic dispersion of populations, a sign and source of weakness, and the dispatch of colonies, a sign and source of strength.

in acquiescence to it. The more settled life of Hellas, according to Thucydides, resulted from a desire for gain: 'Actuated by this, the weaker were willing to submit to dependence[27] on the stronger, and the more powerful men, with their enlarged resources, were able to make the lesser communities their subjects' (1.8.3). This process of assertion and submission organizes political life within the political community and among communities. It furthers the power of some individuals within the community which in turn makes possible the increased power of some communities within the group, and thereby promotes the power of Hellas as a whole. The rationalization (and therefore the growth) of power in political structures requires that some persons, and some political communities, for the sake of advantage to be gained through security rather than the constant pursuit of more (*pleonexia*), redirect their urge to act and expand. By submitting to active, organizing powers, the weaker elements not only secure safety but also share the benefits enjoyed by the newly-powerful community and group of communities as a whole.

Callicles' belief that the indulgence of the capacity to dominate others is natural and glorious and involves no conflict between the promptings of desire and the dictates of reason apparently finds confirmation in Thucydides' portrait of early Greece. Thucydides portrays the exercise of power by the strong over the weak. In their pursuit of the good, men are moved by fear, daring and the insatiable desire for advantage, and their actions are natural and prudent for them as individuals – some secure power, others safety – and beneficial for Hellas as a whole. But Thucydides' realism is historical: the motive forces in human history take on different aspects and come to have different implications as circumstances change. Eventually, as the rationalization of power proceeds, the tension between the real consequences of the historical process and its internal dynamic reaches the breaking point: one growing, organizing power confronts the other in a contest which can only undermine the process of consolidation. The consolidation and articulation of political power eventually bring it about that the principle which has fueled the development – namely that for the powerful, promoting their own interests means subjugating others – is the principle which strangles it. Once power is exhaustively divided between two alliances (or rather, as they now are, hegemonies, 1.19) the possibility of accumulating power disappears; expansion in one sphere is not, as previously, based on the consolidation of power in another, but instead threatens it.

[27] *douleia*, literally 'servitude' or 'slavery.'

Under these circumstances, the urge to acquire more cannot further the process of promoting the consolidation of power in Hellas, because any such attempt will undermine the solidity of subsidiary power structures, political community and alliance. The two aspects of gain – greed (*pleonexia*) and safety (*asphaleia*) – are no longer complementary, but antagonistic. Passions and instincts – fear, daring, ambition, desire for security – cease to promote well-being, to point to the prudent course of action. They must now be controlled by reason if the entire structure of mutually advantageous relations is not to collapse. Thucydides' analytical account of the progressive organization of political life in Hellas offers an interpretation of basic human motivations and their orientation in changing contexts which suggests that all men, in the world as it presently is, have good reason to restrain their pursuit of personal gain. Callicles' assessment of human motivation and his claim that the indulgence of the desire for power by a strong individual defines his good – attitudes at least in part inspired by the seductive success of imperial Athens – reveal their inadequacy as accounts of human nature and well-being when viewed in context. Callicles assumes a basic conflict of interests between the strong and the weak, who have banded together to enforce their will on powerful individuals. This assumption itself exemplifies the polarization which renders false any timeless construal of the Calliclean theory. As the Archaeology shows, men do aim to realize their own desires, and so long as the goods those desires identify are interdependent they may prudently pursue them. But once the ruling group, whether the masses, a junta, a monarch or a hegemon, begins to act tyrannically, that is to secure its own exclusive good, and interests within or between communities are polarized, then prudence dictates that reason must control passion.

Like Protagoras' *muthos*, Thucydides' *History* interprets the situation to which its own argument is a response. To cope with the Calliclean challenge, one symptom of the political developments which have brought men to regard law as external and man's nature and interests as somehow inward and not defined by social conventions, Thucydides acknowledges that reason is now at odds with desire. The split itself may have been engendered by reflective awareness that the demands of society or of those who rule society do not necessarily square with one's own needs or desires. Both those who concede the conflict, like Antiphon, and those who do not, like Protagoras, are concerned to show that the demands of one's own nature do not consist in the indulgence of untutored desire. Conflict, when it arises, may be construed as internal, between desire and prudence. Thucydides' identification of man's freedom and well-being as resting in the exercise of prudence as opposed to desire is not, like Protagoras' assimilation of the two, vulnerable to reflection on man's good *qua* powerful man or member of a powerful city; nor is it, like Antiphon's, content to see man's good as essentially what it seems to be under conditions of polarization. Thucydides' *History* depicts the debilitating increase in conflict among citizens and cities and the growing influence of the belief that men's interests are mutually exclusive, and shows that only historical interpretation can now, under these conditions, reveal what men, reflective as they now are, have good reason to do. Both Callicles' invocation of the tyrant Archelaus as the embodiment of human well-being and the contemporary glorification of the powers of imperial Athens reveal a dangerous situation and, aggravating that situation, utter blindness to reality.

Historical principles in context: polarization and tyranny

The analysis and representation in the *History* of the character and consequences of polarization is formulated in terms of tyranny. This phenomenon brings together questions of power and motivation and is, like them, analyzed in the Archaeology. The principles of analysis in one context, within the archaic community, are set out very briefly but penetratingly. The organization of power within Greek *poleis* had traditionally, according to Thucydides, taken the form of 'hereditary kingships based on fixed prerogatives'; the growing wealth of the cities eventually resulted in the establishment of tyrannies by powerful men (1.13.1). The tyrants in the Greek cities

> had regard for their own interests only, both as to the safety of their own persons and as to the aggrandizement of their own households, so they made security, so far as they possibly could, their chief aim in the administration of their cities, and so no achievement worthy of mention was accomplished by them . . . So on all sides Hellas was for a long time kept from carrying out in common any notable understanding. (1.17)

Whereas previously the desire to promote their own interests had prompted those who dominated their communities to subjugate other *poleis*, the two goals had come into conflict. Safety and glorious achievement were no longer compatible aims. Collective action by the political community was impossible because rulers and ruled no longer regarded their interests as interdependent. Tyranny was, it seems, both consequence and cause of a polarization in the interests of members of the *polis*. Mutual fear fed antagonism. To preserve his position – indeed, his very existence – the tyrant was compelled continually to seek safety, to secure his (now exclusive and private) interests. The overthrow of the tyrants and the development of free political interaction released energy for conquest.[28] Thucydides' account suggests that one man's capacity to wield power is complemented by another's need for protection or wish to participate in the benefits of hegemony; in order to wield greater power, the ruler of a political community must preserve a sense of social interdependence and harmony. And indeed, contrary to the tyrant's own instincts, it is by furthering common interests (through expansion), and avoiding further polarization, that the tyrant may perhaps safeguard his position in the community. The archaic tyrants were eventually overthrown with the help of the Spartans (1.18).

In the Archaeology, tyranny is represented as a hindrance to the power and glory to be achieved through collective action, because it promotes polarization. In the remainder of the *History*, which portrays the Hellas-wide polarization brought about by collective action over time, Thucydides analyzes the caustic effect of Athenian tyranny, the continuing drive for personal power within the confines of a polarized world, on the structures of Greek power. As the Archaeology intimates, the tyrant is obsessed with his own security, oppressed by fear and blind to reality. A similar enslavement to emotion and instinct in the pursuit of crude self-interest is evident at every level of Greek society once unifying political structures have begun to break down under the pressures of polarization. In political communities, and in the world of Greek communities, men act in ignorance of their own condition, unaware of the true implications of tyranny. Yet for all their blindness (indeed because of it) they are convinced that they see: alleged 'truths' of experience and 'truths' of human nature are invoked to defend a narrow construal of their interests. Like Callicles, agents in the *History* lay claim to understanding of the principles embodied in the Archaeology. By mistaking the import of historical interpretation and using it inappropriately, they unwittingly exemplify the true meaning of the process they claim to have understood. Thucydides' *History* shows how and why this has happened, and suggests that it was not inevitable. The *History* counsels what it itself offers:

---

[28] The Spartans became powerful early because they escaped tyranny (1.18.1); but it is the Athenian version of *dunamis* that structures Thucydides' analysis. See de Romilly (1963) 67 and 101 with 311–12.

understanding of human behavior and the course of events and judgment freed from the power of passion and fortune. In rejecting the conventions of the oral performance exploited by Herodotus, Thucydides sought to liberate his audience from the seductive appeal of rhetoric,[29] to enable them to judge and therefore act freely, in accordance with a true appreciation of their condition.

Thucydides' portrayal of the effects of polarization within the political community, including the consequences of failing to understand those effects, is set in Athens. After recounting the history of early times, Thucydides contrasts his own search for truth with the willingness of most men to make do with hearsay or current belief (1.20.1, 1.20.3). (Note *akoē*.)[30] The Athenians, for example, do not know the truth about the glorified tyrant-slayers, Harmodius and Aristogeiton: they believe that the slain Pisistratid, Hipparchus, was the tyrant. In fact, he was the tyrant's brother (1.20.2). This remark is not, as it may seem, a piece of pedantry. In Book Six, Thucydides declares that the violent fear and suspicion occasioned by the mutilation of the statues of Hermes just before the huge expedition against Sicily was due to embark, was promoted by the Athenians' traditional belief in the harshness of the archaic tyranny and the gallant but futile attempt by two young men to liberate their fellow citizens (6.53.2, 6.60.1).[31] He proceeds to discuss the affair of Harmodius and Aristogeiton at some length, to 'prove that neither men at large nor the Athenians themselves give an accurate account about their own tyrants or about this incident' (6.54.1). Thucydides' careful historical analysis (see esp. 6.55) shows that the plot against the tyranny was undertaken for the sake of love, not liberty, to avenge a personal affront by the tyrant's brother, not a political offense by the tyrant himself.[32] The plotters intended to overthrow the tyranny, in order to prevent the tyrant's brother from taking advantage of his power to secure Harmodius' favors by force (6.54.3). Moreover, they hoped that by portraying their actions as a fight for freedom and killing the tyrant himself as well as his brother, they would secure the support of the populace (6.56.3). The point of providing an accurate account of these events is to show that, contrary to popular belief, the actions of Harmodius and Aristogeiton were not a response to the harshness of tyranny, a

---

[29] See Hunter (1982) 289.

[30] See Rawlings (1981) 257f.

[31] Note the reference to hearsay, *akoē*. See Connor (1984) 178 with n. 52.

[32] They murder Hipparchus, the real object of their hatred, in a fit of *orgē* (6.57.2–3). Note also *alogistos tolma* at 6.59.1.

symptom of an attempt to end extreme polarization, but were rather the cause of oppression and divisiveness. Heretofore, according to Thucydides, the Pisistratid tyrants had not been oppressive. They exhibited excellence and intelligence,[33] ensured that Athens flourished (while exacting a small tax for themselves) and tolerated the continued (though supervised) authority of the traditional laws and constitution (6.54.5–6).[34] After this attack, however, Hippias' fear drove him to treat his subjects harshly and with suspicion, and to look outside the political community for sources of security (6.59.2–3; cf. 1.17). This polarization of political relations within Athens led eventually to the intervention of the Spartans at the behest of an exiled faction, and the flight of the tyrant to the court of the Persian king Darius, later Athens' deadly enemy (6.59.4).

On the basis of a misunderstanding of the Pisistratid tyranny, the Athenian people confirmed the implications of the archaic events by re-enacting them.[35] Motivated, like Aristogeiton, by fear of and antagonism to the upper classes[36] and by jealousy of the power of Alcibiades, the conspirators portrayed Alcibiades as a threat to freedom and democracy, a potential tyrant. They inflamed the people, who remembered what they had heard of the harshness of tyrannical rule and recalled that the tyrant-slayers had not succeeded, but that Spartan intervention had been required in the end (6.53.3, 6.60.1). Racked by fear, anger and suspicion, the Athenians acted with savage determination: they arrested many aristocrats and threatened Alcibiades himself, thus driving him, like Hippias, to conspire against Athens with her deadliest enemy.[37] The fact that what was dangerous in these circumstances was not the power of Alcibiades, but rather the consequences of heightening polarization, is brought out even more clearly by casting the Athenian people as Hippias, who responds to the killing of his brother with ruthless force, as if it had been a real political threat. Provoked by the mutilation of the Hermae and Alcibiades' 'undemocratic lawlessness' (6.28.2), the Athenians lashed out against the upper classes (see 6.60.1) thus bringing about not only Alcibiades' treasonous conspiracy but also, eventually, the factional strife of 411. Thucydides emphasizes the irony of the Athenians' belief that they were acting in awareness of historical precedent (6.60.1) by depicting

[33] *aretē* and *xunesis*, not *gnomē*.

[34] Thucydides describes Hippias as 'accessible' (*euprosodos*), 6.57.2.

[35] See Rawlings (1981) 257f.

[36] Note the description of Aristogeiton as *anēr tōn astōn, mesos politēs*, 6.54.2; cf. 6.56.1 and Rawlings (1981) 103f.

[37] See Rawlings (1981) 110f.

their misguided attempt to discover 'the truth' (*to saphes* 6.60.2, 6.60.4, 6.61.1, cf. 6.53.2) about the affair of the Hermae, and their pathetic certainty that they had done so (6.61.1). They are no true investigators: the truth about the archaic tyranny and about who committed the sacrilegious acts evaded them (6.60.2.); and no true interpreters: they do not understand the implications and dangers of polarization. Blinded by fear and anger, they bring about precisely what they seek to avoid: an oligarchic conspiracy, treason and Spartan intervention.

If the Athenian people failed to appreciate the import of the analysis of tyranny in the *polis* adumbrated in the Archaeology and illustrated in detail in the story of Harmodius and Aristogeiton, the Athenians as a community failed to follow out the implications of the analysis for the conditions of polarization within Greece described in the Archaeology and interpreted by Pericles. The Archaeology not only revealed what the contemporary world was like, but showed that the forces that had structured the world and which were now, as a consequence of these developments, to be seen as a threat to it, were the very qualities characteristic of the Athenians. Athens is the paradigm of the will to power which, in the Archaeology, appears as the motive force in history and the source of Hellenic greatness and, eventually, of Hellenic polarization. The Athenians secured power by gaining the leadership of an alliance (the analogue of the 'hereditary kingship' prevalent in early Greece) against the Persians; they extended it by gathering the naval and financial resources of the alliance into their own hands (1.19).[38] They thus acquired an empire, widely regarded, by the time of the Peloponnesian War (so Thucydides tells us), as a tyranny. The Corinthians prod their fellow Peloponnesians with the taunt that they are degenerate heirs of ancestors 'who liberated Hellas, whereas we, so far from making this liberty secure, are allowing a city to be established as a tyrant, though we claim the reputation of deposing monarchs in single states' (1.122.3).[39] Like the archaic tyrants, the Athenians were regarded as men pursuing their own (exclusive) interests;[40] they were the object of fear and hatred.[41] Within Hellas, Athens had no outlet for its expansive energies except an intensified assertion of control over its proper sphere and threats to the sphere

[38] Contrast the character of Spartan hegemony, 1.19. The Spartans were compelled by their situation to take account of their allies' views. See, e.g., 1.119–20.

[39] Cf. 2.63.2, 3.37.2, 4.85.5–86.11, 5.100, 6.85.1.

[40] Compare 3.10 with 1.120, 1.141.6; cf. 1.76.

[41] See, e.g., 1.75, 2.63.1, 5.95, de Romilly (1977) Part III, Pouncey (1980) 98f., Hunter (1982) 138.

dominated by Sparta. Both activities induced further polarization and incurred hostility. Athenian fear, in this polarized atmosphere, led them to tighten their grip (1.75); and it was Sparta's fear of growing Athenian power which, according to Thucydides, was the real reason, though not perceived as such by the men of the time,[42] for the outbreak of war. Like other tyrants, the Athenians were preoccupied with their own security, and eventually with their very survival.[43]

The pressures created by polarization broke down the political structures formed over time by the complementary desires for power and safety. The cities of the empire, the Athenian demagogue[44] Cleon asserts, submit to Athenian rule because of Athenian strength, not on account of any goodwill or common interest (3.37.2).[45] In the cities, the security achieved through political arrangements is dismantled by the conflict between Athens and Sparta. The Athenians' doomed search for security in the face of revolt within the empire led them, on principles expounded by Diodotus, to cultivate allies among the populace in the cities.[46] This ideological threat to the integrity of the political community was matched by the representation of Athens, by her enemies, as a mortal danger to Hellas as a whole comparable to the Persian menace, a danger so great that, according to Brasidas, the Spartan leader who sought to end Athenian control of the cities of northern Greece, those cities reluctant to abandon the Athenians must be compelled to do so, so that 'the Hellenes may not be prevented . . . from escaping bondage' (4.84.2–6). There was no longer any room for neutrality within the political community or in Hellas as a whole. Concern for personal survival was paramount, and survival both depended upon and was threatened by conflict. But the Athenians do not understand their own situation; they do not recognize that they are in the grip of polarization. In 415 B.C., an Athenian envoy in Sicily, seeking the aid of the men of Camarina against Syracuse, argued that the Sicilian expedition had been undertaken for the sake of Athenian security (*asphaleia*) (6.83.2–4): 'We are compelled to be active in many matters (*polla prassein*), because we have many dangers to guard

---

[42] See 1.23.3, cf. 1.88. Note 'cause least mentioned.'

[43] This progression is well analyzed and expounded by Cogan (1981) Part I, though he overstates the difference between an early materialist stage of the war and a later 'ideological' one. Note the comments of the Corinthians, the Athenians at Sparta and Pericles, esp. 2.63.3. Cogan does not discuss the Archaeology.

[44] The root meaning of the word is simply 'leader of the people,' but Thucydides views Pericles' successors, and particularly Cleon, as demagogues in the modern pejorative sense.

[45] Note the suggestion that only by harming herself could Athens do her allies any good.

[46] See Cogan (1981) 52ff. for his analysis.

against' (6.87.2).[47] Alcibiades, commending the idea of the expedition to the people of Athens, had expressed the same view:

> It is not possible for us to exercise a careful stewardship of the limits we would set to our empire; but since we are placed in this position, it is necessary to plot against some and not let go our hold upon others, because there is a danger of coming ourselves under the empire of others, should we not ourselves hold empire over other peoples. (6.18.3)[48]

Alcibiades invokes the achievements of Athenians of an earlier generation, who built the empire (6.17.7, 6.18.2). Understood as a timeless truth, the argument that Athens must continue to grow if she is to survive, that the pursuit of power and security are one, seems compelling; understood contextually, as it must be, it is blind and imprudent.

The Melian Dialogue exposes the Athenians' reckless ignorance of their condition. Melos was a small island in the Cyclades, sympathetic to Sparta but of no great strategic or material importance to either side.[49] The Athenians, conscious of their image as mistress of the seas, had tried to subdue Melos once before; they returned to the task in 416, determined to triumph. Why does Thucydides give such prominence to this apparently trivial encounter? Precisely because of its triviality. The ultimatum to the island of Melos reflects Athens' obsessive fear of her allies, her anxiety to eliminate all vestiges of opposition or neutrality,[50] although it is this very polarization which endangers her. Like the Pisistratid tyrant, like the Athenian populace in 415, Athens aggravates the danger by responding to it instinctively, without understanding. The Athenians react to evidence of allied and Spartan hostility by tightening their grip on power, thereby bringing about the very consequences they seek to avoid. The exercise of power, once power is exhaustively divided, regularly initiates this destructive cycle of instinctual responses, of antagonistic and futile attempts to secure safety.

And yet, again like the populace of 415, the tyrant city is confident that she possesses the truth about human nature and her own position. The power of historical interpretation is illuminated by Athens' fail-

---

[47] See Cogan (1981) 111f.

[48] See 6.18.6–7, 6.87.2, cf. 2.63.1, Cogan (1981) 98f.

[49] Except perhaps as a coasting-station to Sicily, but Thucydides does not concern himself with this possibility. See Thuc. 2.9.6, 3.91.1–3, 5.84.

[50] See Cogan (1981) 59, 89f. on the significance of this dramatization of a materially inconsequential event. Contrast Athens' behavior towards Melos in 426 (Thuc. 3.91). On the dialogue as a whole, see, e.g., Andrewes (1960), Macleod (1974), Méautis (1935), Wassermann (1947), Moxon (1978).

ure to exercise it. The tyrant's insight into her own condition as polarization progresses is, as the Melian Dialogue indicates, partial. She recognizes that she is a tyrant, but fails to comprehend the causes and implications of this in a polarized world. To the astonishment of the Melians, the Athenians invoke the principle, articulated in the Archaeology, that both Athens and Melos will benefit by this Athenian conquest (5.91–2). The claim is specious: it is *Athenian* violence, and not some common threat, that Melos will escape by submitting to Athenian 'protection' (5.93). The Athenians also distort another principle advanced in the Archaeology by failing to construe it historically: 'It is clearly true of men that, by a necessity of their nature, wherever they have power, they always rule' (5.105.2). They urge the Melians to be realistic, 'since you know as well as we do that what is just is arrived at in human arguments only when the necessity on both sides is equal, and that the powerful exact what they can, while the weak yield what they must' (5.89). These so-called truths of human nature, truths implicit in Thucydides' own Archaeology, are falsehoods when applied in this way to the situation in 416. If it is true that men always aspire to rule where they are able to do so, it is also true that this is no necessity, but a tendency which must be restrained, or redirected, when it ceases to be creative and turns corrosive. And if it is true that justice rests on relative equality and that the super-powerful, as Callicles insists, may do exactly as they please, it is also true that once the world is divided between two hegemons, something resembling the constraints of justice does apply even to the most powerful; the necessity on both sides is in fact, in a new way, equal. The Melians warn Athens that she ignores the common good at her peril (5.90). By blindly pursuing their own now-exclusive interest, the Athenians heighten the dangers of polarization. The Athenians refuse to see the point and heedlessly argue as if the danger from their own subjects were unrelated to the threatening power of Sparta (5.91). This complacency is soon blown apart by events in Sicily.

By the time of the Melian and Sicilian campaigns, Athens had good reason to restrain her pursuit of power in order to preserve the power she already possessed.[51] The Athenian *archē* both resembles the civic tyranny of the archaic period and, as a later stage in the development of Greek power, is defined by a different context. Thucydides' analysis

---

[51] This does not mean that we are meant to regard the Melians as noble; they, too, act imprudently. See de Romilly (1963) 291. Note that the Athenians also fail to comprehend the effect of polarization on Spartan behavior (5.109). What Sparta failed to do for Melos, a relatively insignificant island, she did in Sicily with devastating effect.

suggests that the position of the tyrant is constantly under threat, because tyranny involves a basic conflict of interests between ruler and ruled. This conflict may be masked temporarily by collective prosperity or the pursuit of a common aim (e.g. defiance of the Persians). The position of the archaic tyrant was not aggravated by world-wide polarization. On the contrary: the mistake of the archaic tyrant, oppressed as he was by instinctive fear, was to fail to see that his power could be shored up, at least in the short term, by leading the drive for conquest and collective advancement. But despite this implication of the analysis in the Archaeology, and despite Thucydides' detailed demonstration that Pisistratid rule need not have ended as and when it did, the civic tyrant, who sought to gather power into his own hands at the expense of others, was bound to be overthrown. At that stage of the progressive organization of power in Hellas, the subject peoples had the option of securing their own freedom (with the help of Sparta) and pursuing greatness on their own behalf.[52] While the archaic tyrant, rendered desperate by the polarization he had caused and was exacerbating, did not perceive that expansion might be prudent, the Athenians, equally obsessed and for the same reason, did not recognize that there was no longer any room to maneuver. There was no question, for the Greek communities, of securing freedom in the interest of glorious collective action. Now there could be only jockeying for position within an existing framework, with the consequence either of preserving the status quo or of dissolving the entire structure of Hellenic power.

The capacity to preserve power – to secure safety and greatness – under changing circumstances is not a function of excellence, intelligence and the toleration of formal laws or conventions while pursuing one's own interests, all features of Pisistratid rule and of the Athenian empire.[53] It is in part a matter of understanding the hostility which the exercise of power incurs and of acting on this understanding by avoiding giving unnecessary offense and resisting the pull of fear and suspicion. This requires the capacity for contextual interpretation, namely a historical understanding of human tendencies, one's present condition and what prudence dictates in the world as it now is, *and* self-control, the capacity to counteract human instinct and resist the temptation to ensure security by promoting one's own exclusive interests.

---

[52] Note 1.18.1, 6.56.3.
[53] See 1.76.3–77 and 2.37–41; cf. Hunter (1982) 265.

The priority of the *polis*

The level at which self-control was possible and at which the disintegration of Hellenic power could, perhaps, be halted, is the level of the political community, the *polis*. Here, the conflict of interests characteristic of polarized personal or national relations can be transcended, and the common good effectively expressed. The priority of the *polis* in this respect is a historical development. Thucydides does not regard the *polis* as marking a boundary between relations governed by morality and those motivated by expedience. To see that the *History* is an analysis of a particular moment in the historical process whose principles are laid bare in the Archaeology is to appreciate both that the line which divides men from one another at the level of the political community is a salient feature of Thucydides' account and that Thucydides draws no categorical distinction between the behavior of men to one another *qua* cities.[54] The same principles and methods of interpretation apply; the circumstances to be interpreted have changed. The Archaeology represents the development of Greek power in terms of man's desire for advantage, either security or power, and the personal domination and association spurred by these motivations, both among men organized as political communities and among the communities they constitute. In the *History*, Thucydides acknowledges the existence of the political customs and laws which come to express the force and character of common interests. These presumably evolved in tandem with the organization of Greece into *poleis* and alliances of *poleis*. Thucydides' account of the Peloponnesian War includes an analysis of the weakening of traditional norms brought about by the plague and by civil strife, and discussions about how states do and should behave. Some speakers in the *History* argue that laws or customs importantly constrain relations among citizens of a *polis*.[55] Other speakers refer to the laws of the Hellenes or discuss

---

[54] *Contra* de Ste Croix (1972) 136–7.

[55] Pericles, 2.37.3; Athenians with reference to the Spartans, 5.105.4; cf. 3.37.3 and de Ste Croix (1972) 19. Of the other passages cited by de Ste Croix (except for 3.83, discussed below), 7.86.5 – Thucydides' assessment of Nicias – shows only that Nicias ordered his life by the standard of conventional *aretē*. It is not clear that we should interpret *aretē* here as a peculiarly *civic* value. Cf. Edmunds (1975b) 141–2. The passage on the plague (2.53) is descriptive and analytical in tone. Thucydides *describes* men for whom gods, law, impiety and honor had meaning – but *that* is true also of accounts of the attitudes of men in confrontation with other *poleis*. In neither case is it evidence for Thucydides' beliefs about the appropriateness or inappropriateness of moral standards in a particular sphere. The existence of sanctions is not an important conceptual difference. See Hart (1961) esp. ch. 10.

excellence (*aretē*) as a virtue in relations with other *poleis*.[56] The distinction relevant to understanding Thucydides' realism is not a distinction between political and inter-*poleis* relations, nor between norms of human behavior operative in the development of Greek power and those characteristic of the contemporary functioning of Greek communities. The contrast is rather between two different social-cum-political realities, between on the one hand the interdependence in interests and motivations of the men who constituted political communities and groups of them and, on the other, the conflict which followed the culmination of that interdependence and undermined it. Polarization prompted reflection on the character and content of human interests and the extent to which they are reflected in political arrangements. Once these arrangements no longer clearly embodied a common good expressed in law and custom, reflection on whether and how this good was to be achieved was both inevitable and essential.

Thucydides' *History* is itself an expression of this reflective distance: the political community and its norms, once simply experienced as the embodiment of a collective good and complementary interests, are now analyzed and assessed as such. This analysis, if properly deployed, will not sanction man's increasing alienation from the *polis* and the indulgence of passion in pursuit of his exclusive interests, but will rather counteract the effects of polarization and show men that they do in fact have good reason to preserve the common life and social order fostered in the political community. Men will now act reflectively to secure the good once advanced by instinct, as in the case of the princes who followed Agamemnon because they feared his strength, and by custom and experience, as in the case of the political order that preceded polarization.

In the Archaeology, Thucydides analyzes the development of settled communities in Hellas in terms of the perceived needs and ambitions of particular groups and the constraints or opportunities posed by a particular level of political organization. He observes later that the war, and particularly the Periclean policy of gathering within the walls when the Spartans attacked, compelled the citizens of Athens, many of whom were accustomed to a relatively independent existence in the countryside, to face the consequences of membership in a particular

---

[56] E.g. the speech of the Plataeans (3.53ff.), Pericles (2.40.4). Also note Huart (1968) 447f. on *aretē*.

political entity.[57] The polarization of the Greek world made clear the dependence of human well-being on the integrity of the *polis*, an integrity to be preserved not by laws and conventions but by man's ability to reconstitute security under new circumstances, to reorient his understanding of his interests. One reason why the *polis* is so important is that it can foster this capacity for interpretation and self-control, thereby increasing the likelihood of its own survival and thus the survival and continued well-being of its citizens under the stress of war. When Sparta finally began the conflict, King Archidamus hoped to take advantage of the ties which bound many Athenians to their local communities. He would ravage Acharnia: 'The Acharnians were an important part of the *polis* . . . and he thought that they would not look on and see their fields ravaged, but would urge the whole people also to fight.' If not, 'the Acharnians, once stripped of their own possessions, would not be as eager to incur danger as before on behalf of the lands of the rest, and so conflict (*stasis*) would arise in the judgment (*gnome*)' of the Athenians (2.20.4). Thucydides' psychological-cum-political language reflects his assumption that the behavior of the political community is appropriately characterized both as the behavior of persons, of a collectivity, and as the behavior of a unit, an entity. *stasis* in the *gnome* of the Athenians refers to conflicting judgments by the citizens. The *polis*, like a man with conflicting intentions, cannot simply channel the aims of its parts but must reconcile them in a purposive whole. In polarized Hellas, this unity of intention is threatened by conflict between self-interest and prudence and between desire and reason, and the difficulty of resolving this conflict, as it must be resolved, through political reflection. If polarization and reflection had split desire from reason and necessitated prudent self-control on the part of the individual to secure his own good, this prudence dictated that the *polis* as a whole, itself polarized and part of a polarized world, had to restrain the indulgence of narrow self-interest and passion.

Within the *polis*, the public interest had to take priority over private interests; this unity in turn would enable the *polis* to pursue its own interests externally, interests which included establishing favorable conditions for internal stability. Once there ceased to be any room to maneuver, that is to expand collectively, the *polis* had to exercise self-

---

[57] According to Thucydides, the Athenians regarded the site of their households (*oikia*) and places of sacrifice as constituting their *polis* (2.16.2). Note the reference to independent (*autonomos*) habitation, 2.16.1.

control. It could no longer express the desire of at least some of its citizens to acquire more (*pleonektein*) or to secure their own at the expense of the collective good but had to control this desire, and therefore those citizens, in the interests of the well-being of the group. Thus Thucydides emphasizes the importance of leadership, directed not just outwards, to the preservation of power, but inwards, to the control of the desire to act and expand. The leader acts as mediator between the citizens and the entity they collectively constitute, by making possible reflective unity. When the Spartan king Archidamus ravaged the district of Acharnia, in full view of the Athenians within the walls, the prospect of conflict (*stasis*) in the judgment (*gnomē*) of the Athenians necessitated the exercise of Periclean *gnomē* to preserve a unified policy.

The *History* points to the necessity for and the means to civic self-control and judgment. The Peloponnesian War not only breaks down political structures and threatens security; it also tips the balance, already precarious because of polarization, between man's rational and irrational aspects. In his analysis of civic strife (*stasis*), Thucydides declares that 'in peace and prosperity both cities and individuals[58] have better *gnomai* (judgment) because they are not forced to face conditions of dire necessity; war fosters in most people passion (*orgē*) to match their condition' (3.82.2). The account of Corcyrean *stasis* reveals the vulnerability of social conventions to the persistent and, under these conditions, desperate pursuit of individual good. Yet it also reveals that the indulgence of crude instinct cannot secure the safety and well-being to which it appears to aspire. The well-being of the members of society depends upon collective guidance by judgment, i.e. both historical understanding and the capacity for self-control. Both cities and men, according to Thucydides' formulation, exhibit (or possess) judgment (*gnomē*) and passion (*orgē*). *gnomē* is Thucydides' term of art for the intellectual quality, judgment, and it is often contrasted with, and portrayed as restraining, *orgē* (not merely anger, but the entire range of impulsive, instinctual, emotional behavior).[59] In Thucydides' use of the term, *gnomē* is both the capacity

---

[58] *hai te poleis kai hoi idiotai.* For other formulations indicating a parallel between cities and individuals, cf. 1.82.6, 1.124.1, 1.144.3, 2.8.4, 2.64.6, 4.61.2.

[59] See Huart (1973), *passim:* according to pp. 12–13, the word *gnomē* signified from the first both the capacity to know and the result of exercising that capacity; it was applied to practical rather than theoretical questions. Thucydides' emphatic use of *gnomē* indicates his desire to study reason not in the abstract, but in the context of human action. Thucydides virtually ignored alternative words for mind or thought. The interaction of *gnomē/orgē/tuchē* structures the *History.* Cf. Huart (1968) esp. 501–7, de Romilly (1956a) 50ff.,

to assess reality and what restrains man's impulsive and superstitious tendencies. (I shall use the word 'judgment' to translate *gnomē*.) *gnomē* is also regularly and significantly contrasted with *tuchē*. For Thucydides, *tuchē* does not mean fortune in the sense of providence, but rather chance, the (apparently) unpredictable. The exercise of judgment reduces the scope of *tuchē* and man's vulnerability to it. Chance, of which the plague is a prime example (see 2.64.1), tends to undermine judgment, often through its effect on the passions. The power to maintain stability rests on understanding and self-control, i.e. *gnomē*, in the political community and in the individual. The connection revealed in Thucydides' phrase about the effect of war on the *gnomai* of communities and individuals is both an analogy between the mechanisms of individual and social self-control and a causal link. The *gnomē* of the city as a whole, especially in a democracy, depends directly on the *gnomē* of its citizens, and both depend upon the judgment – intelligence, foresight, incorruptibility, persuasiveness – of the city's leader(s). The leader's awareness of the influence of internal stability on external power (and vice versa) and his ability to shape the attitudes of individuals in accordance with his own *political* vision, determine how the *gnomai* of the citizens will be reflected in the response of the *polis* to the vicissitudes of history.

Thucydides' appreciation of the importance of judgment for the preservation of a dynamic equilibrium between citizens and the world they now encounter as a political community is bound up with his admiration for the achievements of Athens, and his concern to explain why those achievements were tarnished by disunity and defeat.[60] The model of a *polis* which evinced intelligence and could potentially be ruled by it was the Athenian *polis*. The contrast between the two aspects of the *polis*, as a collectivity and as an entity, is starkest for the Athenians. Yet the intelligence, independence and ambition of the Athenians, which could cause disintegration, could also, when the citizens were united, make possible a flexible, realistic, prudent response to changing circumstances. The historian's admiration merged with

123–6, 132, 153, 165, 172, Edmunds (1975) esp. ch. 1, Parry (1957), who associates *gnomē* with the *logos* side of the *logos–ergon* antithesis, Woodhead (1970) 51–2, 71, 90ff., 109, 134, who discusses the relationship between *gnomē* and power, Zahn (1934) on *gnomē* as used by Pericles and Mittelstadt (1977) on Huart's discussion of *gnomē* as a psychological term.

[60] Admiration of the Athenians is evident throughout the extant *History*; concern to explain Athens' disunity and defeat was necessarily a relatively late intention. But the two are not at odds. See de Romilly's discussion of this question and its significance for the composition problem, in de Romilly (1963) *passim*. See also Pouilloux and Salviat (1983) 392f.

historical realism. Just as knowledge about the remote past served to demonstrate as well as to explain the force and scale of the present conflict (cf. 1.2–21), so too a proper contextual understanding of the behavior of political communities which lacked judgment would show that and show *why* Periclean Athens was superior. The interpretation of the events of the Peloponnesian War as a history of judgment and a history that cultivates it, is (at the level of the *polis*)[61] achieved by way of two related contrasts: (1) with respect to judgment as a means of ordering the political community, between Pericles and his successors and (2) with respect to judgment as a means of ordering the world, between Athens and Sparta.

The rule of reason: leadership and democracy

Thucydides' characterization of Pericles' role in the Athenian *polis* has two aspects, which correspond to the two aspects of the political community, entity and collectivity. *gnomē* rules both as reason (Pericles is Athens' *gnomē*) and through reason, by shaping the attitudes of the citizens and promoting their own self-control. In the latter role, Pericles serves as interpreter and historian; he participates in the *polis* as one *gnomē* among others, as a leader who tries to persuade his fellow citizens of the rationality of a particular view and a particular attitude. He teaches them how to interpret. Under the guidance of such a leader, the democratic *polis*, marked by personal freedom rather than discipline, and ruled (*de jure*) by all the citizens, could realize both autonomy and order. Pericles' function as historian and guide to interpretation consists of four related tasks. In the first place, he analyzes the present situation, reveals the relevant principles of interpretation and uses them to sketch out the likely course of events, and identifies and explains the policy that commends itself as prudent under the circumstances. Thus in his first speech,[62] in urging the Athe-

---

61 As, e.g., de Romilly (1956a), Stahl (1968) and Hunter (1973) have shown, the interaction of intelligence and circumstance occurs throughout the *History*. I have concentrated on the political speeches, to the (virtual) exclusion of the military ones, but the character and the force of the distinctions which shape the political speeches depend in part on the consistent reiteration of similar themes throughout the *History* (and not just in the speeches), and particularly in the military encounters.

62 The historian's Pericles speaks to the audience of the *History* as a leader who spoke in that way, on such occasions, to his historical audience. That is, Pericles' significance as an actor in history – a significance portrayed in the *History* – is for Thucydides indivisible from his ability to respond appropriately to particular circumstances, to know and expound and act upon *ta deonta*. If Pericles is made to speak in prophetic, tragic or abstract and reflective phrases and concepts, that is because in Thucydides' view, this was

nians not to back away from the impending conflict with Sparta, Pericles analyzes the strengths and weaknesses of Sparta and the Peloponnesian alliance in comparison to Athens and her empire (1.141f.). He applies this analysis to the possible courses of action the Spartans might adopt and shows that, and how, the Athenians can render themselves invulnerable:

If they march against our territory, we shall sail against theirs; and the devastation of a part of the Peloponnesians will be quite a different thing from that of the whole of Attica. For they will be unable to get other territory in its place without fighting, while we have an abundance of territory both in the islands and on the mainland. A great thing is the control of the sea. Just consider: if we were islanders, who would be more unassailable? So even now we must, as near as may be, imagine ourselves such and relinquish our land and houses, but keep watch over the sea and the city; and we must not give way to anger against the Peloponnesians on account of our losses and risk a decisive battle with them, far superior in numbers as they are. If we win we shall have to fight them again in undiminished number, and if we fail our allies, the source of our strength, are lost to us as well; for they will not keep quiet when we are no longer able to proceed in arms against them. (1.143.4–5)

In arguing for this policy, Pericles points to the sources of Athenian strength (see also 2.13) and to the position of Athens in a polarized world. The allies are waiting for an opportunity to revolt (see also 2.63.1). Athens, Pericles asserts in his final speech, is 'like a tyranny' (2.63.2), and she must recognize and accept the implications of this fact. Her interest lies in preserving the status quo. Athens must go to war in order to demonstrate that she is Sparta's equal (see, e.g., 1.141.1). Her power rests on naval strength and her control of an empire. She must not seek to contest Spartan power on land nor to pursue further conquests. In his first speech, Pericles admonishes the Athenians: 'We shall prove superior, if you will not consent to attempt to extend your empire while you are at war and not to burden yourselves needlessly with dangers of your own choosing' (1.144.1). To do so, he warned, would be disastrous.

In showing the Athenians how to analyze their present circumstances and what conclusions to draw concerning present policy, Peri-

appropriate to the task of leading Athens effectively under the circumstances as he and/or Thucydides interpreted them. Cf. Gomme (1956a) 81. For an acute discussion of the general issues concerning the status of these speeches see Dover (1981) 393–9. Extensive bibliography in Stadter (1973). For a review of the debate about alleged anachronisms and their function in these speeches, see Ziolkowski (1963) esp. ch. 9. For a range of views, see, e.g., Parry (1972) 61 with note, Andrewes (1960), Strasburger (1958), de Romilly (1963) esp. 110–55, Gomme (1956a) *ad loc.*

cles also, as the cited passages from his speeches indicate, performs his
second task: he helps the Athenians to appreciate the force of human
instincts, the characteristic interaction of *gnomē–tuchē–orgē* under
various conditions, and thus to prepare them for the challenge of exercising self-control. The policy appropriate to an imperial power determined to maintain her position against the other hegemon in a
polarized world would require great self-control to resist the temptation to indulge feelings of resentment (*orgisthentas*, 1.143.5) and
risk battle with the Spartans and to refrain from seeking to secure even
greater power. In his first speech, before the outbreak of open war and
in response to Spartan embassies offering peace on certain conditions,
Pericles informed the Athenians of his insights regarding the likely
effect of war on their resolution:

I hold, Athenians, to the same *gnomē* as always, that we must not yield to the Peloponnesians, although I know that men are not moved by the same *orgē* when they
are actually engaged in war as when they are being persuaded to undertake it, but
change their *gnomai* in accordance with events. (1.140.1)

Pericles' judgment remains firm – Athens must go to war – although
he knows that even if the Athenians are now persuaded of the correct-
ness of that view, they may well, in the course of the war, *change* their
judgments (thereby affecting the likely outcome of the war, and therefore the prudence – in anticipation of this likelihood – of undertaking
it in the first place). By making the Athenians aware of the likely effect
of war on their own resolution, Pericles hopes to bolster the value of
his own advice: if the Athenians consciously decide *now* that they will
continue to support the common decision (even if events should by
any chance take a turn for the worse), their fortified determination
will increase the likelihood of success. In his speech to the assembly
after Athens had suffered the plague and a second Spartan invasion,
Pericles sought to 'remove the passion (*to orgizomenon*) from their
gnomē' (2.59.3). He again interpreted the behavior of the Athenians:
he pointed out that they were acting in just the way he had initially
warned them against (see 2.59.3). As Thucydides himself remarks, the
Athenians 'had been changed in *gnomai*'; they sent envoys to the
Spartans to treat for peace, but to no avail. They were 'altogether
without resources of judgment'[63] (2.59.1–2). Pericles reminded them
of the terms under which they had determined to go to war, again
evincing his own understanding of their actions (2.60.1; cf. 2.60.4,
2.61.2, 2.64.1). He asks the Athenians to regard their own behavior in

[63] Literally, 'helpless in judgment' (*gnomē*).

the way that he perceives and interprets it. The purpose of enlightening them about the causes and character of their responses is again – now in a different context – to enable them to persevere. Pericles observes that 'those who in the face of calamities show least distress in *gnomē* and in action make most vigorous resistance, these are the strongest whether they be political communities or individuals' (2.64.6). He suggests a reason why the Athenians have allowed their judgment – their capacity for interpretation and self-control – to be sapped by misfortune:

For it has happened, now that you are suffering, that you regret having been persuaded when you were still unscathed, and in your weakness of *gnomē* my advice now appears wrong. The reason is that each one of you is already feeling his hardships, whereas the proof of the benefit is still lacking to all, and now that a great reverse has come upon you suddenly, you are too dejected in mind to persevere in the policy you decided on. (2.61.2)[64]

The Athenians, he argues, should recognize that they still have good reason not to be afraid (2.62.1) and should be convinced by their *gnomē* that they are indeed superior to the Spartans (2.62.4). He maintains not only that it is possible for the Athenians to triumph over their present hardships, but also that it is reasonable, and prudent, for each of them to attempt to do so. The Athenians are downcast because each is sensible of his own present suffering; Pericles assures them that there are benefits to be gained by looking beyond immediate troubles and beyond private concerns.

Pericles' third task is, therefore, to show the Athenians that the *polis* whose unity he expresses makes legitimate demands upon all its citizens as a *whole*, demands which it is genuinely prudent for them to fulfill. Prudence in the world as it presently is dictates that the public weal take priority over individual self-interest, now that the two often appear to be at odds. Pericles seeks to prevent the indulgence of exclusive, partial interests by showing that such behavior, based on a narrow perspective, is inimical to the continued well-being of the *polis*, and that the public interest does genuinely embody the real interests of all citizens. In his last speech, Pericles asserts that:

A *polis* confers a greater benefit on individuals when as a whole it is successful than when it prospers as regards each citizen but fails collectively. For even though a man flourishes in his own private affairs yet if his *polis* goes to ruin he perishes with it all the same; but if he is in evil fortune and his *polis* in good for-

---

[64] Note 2.61.3: 'the mind is enslaved' by that which is sudden and unanticipated. Cf. 1.140.1.

tune he is far more likely to come through safely. Since, then, the *polis* may bear
the misfortunes of its private citizens but not vice versa, surely all men ought to
defend it, and not do as you are doing: proposing to sacrifice the safety of the community because you are dismayed by domestic hardships. (2.60.2–4)

Each individual might, especially under the stress of war, be tempted
to *think* that his own prosperity is an independent variable and therefore, in making decisions, even as part of a group, take into account
only the state of his own fortunes. Yet, Pericles insists, in fact the *polis*
as a whole is an entity, though it is characterized as a collectivity: its
well-being as a collective entity does not consist in the private prosperity of each of its members. Thus each citizen should 'put away grief
for private matters and devote himself to the safety of the community'
(2.61.4).[65] As the analysis in the Archaeology suggested and Pericles
stresses here, it is not material resources that constitute power (see
(1.143.5, 2.62.3), but rather the capacity to act collectively, as one.

In this speech – and at greater length in the Funeral Oration – Pericles argues that the fate of the *polis* must be every citizen's first priority, not only because his own survival directly depends on the
safeguarding of the whole, but also because the *polis* itself is great,
magnificent, powerful and worth suffering for (see 2.61.4, 2.62.3,
2.63.1, 2.64.3). In the Funeral Oration, Pericles praises the dead war-
riors who 'bore themselves in a manner befitting the *polis*' (2.43.1).
He observes that the courage which motivated these men, and which
enables the Athenians to ward off their enemies, is evidently advantageous (2.43.1). Yet the advantage is not directly material: it consists
of participation in Athenian power. Pericles exhorts the Athenians to
fix their gaze 'upon the power of this *polis* and become lovers of the
polis' (2.43.1). To praise the city is to praise the men who have made it
great (2.42.2). Any particular man may fail but the courage of every
citizen, a general willingness to die for the *polis*, is advantageous
because it underlies the success and greatness of Athens, and that
greatness in turn inspires the sacrifice. The attitude proper to an
Athenian, maintains Pericles, is to regard courage as freedom, and
freedom as well-being (2.43.4). Athenians ought to be willing to offer
up their lives precisely because their lives are so worth living: it would

---

[65] *To koinon*, from what is common or shared, as opposed to *ta idia*, private things. Cf.
2.44.3, where Pericles argues that citizens should have more children, both to provide the
city with its life-blood, but also as a bond between each citizen and the ongoing task of
protecting the city. Only those who have a personal stake in the city's policies can offer
good advice, he maintains. Again, but this time from the opposite direction, Pericles is establishing a connection between every person's interests and the fate of the *polis* as a
whole.

make a great difference to them if they should suffer a disaster (2.43.5). Hazarding one's life for a *polis* like Athens is glorious and more to be valued than the continued enjoyment of personal wealth (2.42.4). Pericles declares: 'It is for this reason that I have dwelt upon political matters' – i.e. the different aspects of Athenian life and power – 'for I have desired to show you that we are contending for a higher prize than those who do not enjoy such things in like degree' (2.42.1).

Pericles not only explains the ways of men to men and articulates the proper relationship between private concerns and the public good; he also interprets the political implications of the freedom which characterizes Athenian life and offers particular criteria – shaped by the need for judgment and the priority of public over private concerns – for the valuation of leadership under such conditions. In the Funeral Oration, describing 'with what political system and as the result of what way of life Athens became great,' Pericles refers to the Athenian political system as *demokratia*, because administration of the *polis* is 'in the hands, not of the few, but of the many' (2.37.1). The key to this portion of the Oration is Pericles' observation that in Athens they engage in politics, or govern themselves, freely (2.37.2). The freedom of Athenian *polis* life includes the freedom of the many from domination by the few, and the freedom of the few to achieve distinction; freedom from constraint in personal relations: 'We do not feel *orgē* towards our neighbor if he does as he likes', and self-restraint: 'We render obedience to those in authority and to the laws' (2.37.2). Pericles' account is not straightforwardly a description of Athenian democracy, but an interpretation: the primary value is not equality, but freedom; public inequalities are the legitimate consequence of free (not class or wealthbound) competition 'to do the *polis* some good' (2.37.1).

In his last speech, Pericles (and this is his fourth task) tells the Athenians what he has all along shown them by example, namely what kind of leadership is appropriate to and required in such conditions of freedom. He enumerates his own virtues as a leader, which together describe a consistent dedication to the public point of view: 'I, with whom you are angry, am as competent as any man, I think, both to determine what is required (*ta deonta*) and to expound it, and as good a patriot and superior to the influence of money' (2.60.5; cf. 2.65.8). Caring properly for the good of the *polis*, according to Pericles, requires *gnomē*, powers of expression and persuasion, and devotion to the *polis* as a whole, untainted by petty self-interest. *gnomē* about civic policy is tied to personal disinterestedness, as is the ability to lead a *polis* according to *gnomē*. The citizens must not be encouraged to believe that politics consists in the pursuit of private interests, for commitment to the pursuit of narrow self-interest distorts both the leader's and the city's understanding of the sources of collective well-being and their capacity to act on that understanding. Pericles' *gnomē* enabled him to explain to the Athenians that – and why – they should look at their own behavior and policies from the public point of view and that as free men they should trust and respect leaders – like himself – who had the intellectual and personal qualities necessary for consistent, effective, devoted promotion of the viewpoint and interest of the whole *polis*. As portrayed and described by Thucydides (2.54.1–4), Pericles' last speech was both an attempt (unsuccessful in the short term but ultimately effective) to quell Athenian *orgē* against him and an effort to increase their willingness and capacity to endure the war. Pericles succeeded in withstanding the anger he had provoked by arguing for the priority of the public good over private suffering because, in the end, he persuaded the Athenians that his view – the public view – was the appropriate one and that it was leadership of the kind he represented which would best serve the needs of the community (2.65.4–5).

If Pericles ruled the collectivity through *gnomē*, by acting as guide to interpretation and goad to self-control, he also ruled as the *gnomē* of the *polis* conceived as an entity, by opposing his judgment to the passion of the citizens. This aspect is well illustrated by the incident mentioned in the preceding section: in order to prevent the Athenians from doing something rash, seized as they were with *orgē* at the sight of the Spartan invasion of Attica, Pericles substituted his judgment for theirs; he refused to convoke any formal or informal meeting of the citizens, in the fear that a discussion animated by *orgē* rather than *gnomē* would lead to a serious policy mistake (2.22.1). Pericles' power to control the responses of the Athenians is also manifest in the intentions which inform his speeches to them, and which are described by Thucydides in his retrospective assessment of Pericles' eminence:

Whenever he saw [the Athenians] unduly confident and arrogant his words would cow them into fear; and, on the other hand, when he saw them unreasonably afraid he would restore them to confidence. And so what was in name *demokratia* [i.e. rule by the *demos*] was becoming in fact rule by the foremost man. (2.65.9)

Did Pericles manipulate the Athenians? Was Athens in no real sense a collectivity, but rather an entity whose citizens are ruled, as the desiring parts of individuals are ruled, by one reason? Consider a portion of Pericles' final speech which seems to confirm that this view is the only adequate one:

There is one point I propose to lay before you on which, I think, you have never yourselves as yet reflected, in spite of the advantage it gives you as regards your empire and its greatness, and which I have never previously dealt with in my speeches, and should not have done so now – for it makes a somewhat boastful claim – had I not seen that you are unreasonably dejected. (2.62.1)

The claim in question is that the Athenian naval empire could without hindrance, either from the Great King or any other nation, span the length and breadth of the world's oceans (2.62.2). Pericles here acts to boost the sagging morale of the Athenians, not by helping them to see their situation more realistically, but by magnifying Athenian power to inflate their self-confidence, in ways which would be dangerous if construed as having implications for Athenian actions in polarized Greece. But – and it is an important caveat – Pericles tells the Athenians that this is what he is doing. He tells them that in this context it is appropriate for him to prompt, and for them to engage in, reflection on the sheer power of Athens. Pericles' rhetorical strategy rests on the assumption that its transparency will not cancel its power to boost morale, but will limit its range: reflection will persuade the Athenians that confidence is warranted, but that its content and implications are always to be construed historically, contextually. The Athenians are not being manipulated. They are being led, and taught. Pericles gives the Athenians enough guidance to enable them to assess his leadership; and Thucydides' portrayal of leadership enables the reader to compare other leaders to Pericles.

The contrast Thucydides draws between Pericles and his successors, and between Periclean Athens and Athens after Pericles, emphasizes the uniqueness and the normative significance of Periclean leadership. The politicians who led Athens after the death of Pericles were not equipped to promote the good of the whole *polis*: they lacked *gnomē*. They all lacked the ability to act as the *gnomē* of the *polis* in tempering and channeling the *orgē* of the Athenians. Each also lacked the capacity, as one leader among others in a free and democratic *polis*, to interpret circumstances, determine and expound the prudent course of action, and to persuade the Athenians of the rationality of a *political* perspective. In the absence of effective leadership, the Athenians gradually succumbed to the strains of war and to the divisive forces of polarization and ceased to be able to pursue prudent policies as a collective entity. The Athenians, says Thucydides, ignored Pericles' advice – advice based on foresight which was justified in the event (2.65.6, 2.65.13) – that they should remain quiet, 'and not seek to extend their sway during the war or do anything to endanger the *polis*' (2.65.4).

[They] not only acted contrary to his advice in all these,[66] but also in matters that seemed generally to be foreign to the purpose of the war[67] they administered the affairs of the *polis* in ways injurious to themselves and to their allies, in accordance with private ambition and private greed. These policies, so long as they were successful, merely brought honor or profit to individuals, but when they failed proved detrimental to the *polis* in the conduct of the war. (2.65.7)

The reason why this happened, in Thucydides' view, was precisely because there was no leader who could or would mediate the purely personal desires of the Athenians;[68] indeed, the leaders participated in the indulgence of crude self-interest and they fell victim to the polarized atmosphere they helped create. Pericles had been more concerned about promoting the policy most prudent for the *polis* than about safeguarding his own position. He was not constrained by the

---

[66] An exaggeration; Thucydides is probably thinking primarily of the Sicilian Expedition. See Gomme (1956a) 191. Some scholars have criticized Thucydides' account of Periclean strategy, particularly the likelihood of its success, and have challenged the contrast he draws between that strategy and the one followed by Cleon. See Kagan (1974) esp. 350–62. According to Thucydides, Pericles thought and was right to think that the war was being fought to demonstrate Athenian equality, and that Cleon, for example, was wrong to persuade the Athenians to reject Spartan peace offers after the battle of Sphacteria. The key to the survival of Athenian power is the maintenance of an equilibrium, which requires the unity and integrity of the *polis* and the dispassionate assessment of particular policies – two related features, both dependent on Periclean leadership. Thucydides offers a systematic analysis of the realities of power in Greece along these lines. A challenge to this view would have to be equally systematic and interpretative, offering a rival account of the way the world is which appeals to historical experience. The great failing of Pericles' successors was not so much the content of their strategy as their incapacity to embody it in leadership that promoted unity and level-headed judgment. The two are not, for Thucydides, unrelated: an acquisitive, power-hungry strategy tended to undermine the possibility of unity and prudence, which were essential in his view to the success of any policy, and particularly important given the polarization of power in Greece. What is at issue, then, is not simply an alternative strategy, but an alternative history and understanding of leadership.

[67] Gomme (1956a) 192. Cf. his discussion on p. 191: it is not clear whether Thucydides is referring to military expeditions or internal rivalries; I incline to the latter. In either case, it appears that they are distinct from the items already listed as 'contrary to Pericles' advice' because, although they imperiled the city, they were not specifically anticipated by Pericles.

[68] See his account of the motivations which prompted enthusiasm for the Sicilian Expedition, 6.24.3–4. On 2.65 as a reflection of Thucydides' confidence in Pericles, Athens and reason, see de Romilly (1965) *passim*.

petty desire for acclaim: 'He restrained the masses freely[69] and led them rather than was led by them, because he did not speak to please them, pursuing power by improper means, but having power he, on the strength of his reputation, even spoke *pros orgēn* (i.e. so as to provoke their anger)' (2.65.8). Pericles risked opposing the desires of the people in an attempt to educate or temper them. By contrast, his successors were constantly competing for personal influence, since they were 'more on an equality with one another.' They each sought popular favor, so they were 'prepared to surrender public matters to the people according to their pleasure' (2.65.10).[70] No consistent, rational and *polis*-based policy was possible. One disastrous consequence of 'personal intrigues for the sake of gaining the popular leadership' (2.65.11) was the fate of the Sicilian Expedition. The error of the expedition

was not so much a misjudgment [an error of *gnomē*] of the enemy as a mistake on the part of those who dispatched the expedition, who did not decide on suitable measures for those who were sent out but instead engaged in personal intrigues for the sake of securing the popular leadership, and thus 'blunted' the military campaign and also brought about for the first time civil discord at home. (2.65.11)[71]

Political disunity weakened Athenian power and eventually destroyed it (2.65.12).[72]

In his account of Athenian politics after the death of Pericles, Thucydides dramatizes the degenerate relationship between the Ath-

---

[69] I am persuaded by the argument of Edmunds and Martin (1977) 187f. in support of the view also expressed by Gomme (1956a) *ad* 2.65.8, that *eleutherōs* refers to 'the freedom of Perikles himself in the conduct of his office.'

[70] See Gomme (1956a) *ad* 2.65.10.

[71] See paraphrase by Dover (1981) 423ff. As Dover argues, p. 427, this marks a departure from 6.1, where Thucydides suggests that Athens did underestimate the enemy and was undertaking too much. According to Dover, what Thucydides has in mind in 2.65 is the decision to recall Alcibiades. Note 6.15.3, where Thucydides emphasizes the importance of the loss of Alcibiades; this may refer not just to what he could have contributed to Athenian military policy, but what he did contribute to the Spartan. The language of 2.65.11 seems more general, however, and may (despite the absence of firm indications in the narrative (see Dover (1981) 23)) refer to the fact that the Athenians permitted Nicias to flounder (see 7.8.1). Thucydides' point in 2.65.6–13 seems to be that Athens did not lack the material resources required to subdue Sicily (and that this was not primarily what Pericles was concerned about, 2.65.6, cf. 1.144.1) but that she could not stand the strain imposed (in part because of its effect on the allies and on Sparta) by the attempt to extend her empire in wartime. The strain was caused by civil strife and exacerbated it.

[72] See Dover (1981) 424; Thucydides has given the theme of political disunity such prominence that 'the destruction of the Athenian fleet and the subsequent reduction of Athens by starvation are entirely suppressed.'

enians and their leaders[73] and the disappearance of those qualities which became increasingly essential as they were stamped out or distorted. *orgē* had become the instrument for winning popular support for a policy. The people, encouraged to act on the basis of passion, not judgment, vented their *orgē* at leaders they resented or whose policies failed to live up to their unreasonable expectations. In 425, the Athenian generals sent on a mission to Sicily returned to Athens. They had been excluded from involvement in the affairs of the island by a reconciliation among the warring cities. The Athenians were enraged, and they lashed out at the generals, exiling two and fining one.

To such an extent [commented Thucydides] because of their present good fortune (*eutuchia*) did they expect to be denied nothing, and believed that no matter whether their resources were powerful or deficient, they could equally accomplish what was possible and what was impracticable. The cause of this was their amazing success, which inspired them with strong hope. (4.65.4)

The Athenians had lost touch with reality; they were incapable of realistic interpretation and incapable of exercising self-control. This was both cause and consequence of the failure of leadership. Neither those men who were blinded by ambition nor those who struggled to maintain their integrity were capable of providing what the Athenians needed, namely a purely and persuasively public perspective, interpretative abilities, the capacity for self-control and the personal qualities necessary to inculcate both. They also lacked a vision, a historical vision of the kind of leadership the Athenians needed and should have valued in the circumstances.

The deterioration in the character of Athenian leadership – that is, the character of the interaction between leaders and people – is dramatically illustrated by the debate between Cleon and Diodotus. For the present argument, the most significant aspect of this much-discussed debate[74] is what it reveals of Thucydides' perceptions of politicians and politics in post-Periclean Athens. Under the pressure of war and polarization, with no powerful *gnomē* to unify it, Athenian politics turned into a fragmented, contentious, self-interested game. The change is portrayed by Thucydides as a shift from policy-making to politics.[75] At the assembly called for the purpose of reconsidering

---

[73] Cf. de Romilly (1965) 566. Parry (1957) 189 cites the 'dissociation of *logos* and *ergon* which marks all the *History* after 2.65.'

[74] See, e.g., Andrewes (1962), Bodin (1980), Karavites (1979), Wasserman (1956), Winnington-Ingram (1965). See the extensive bibliography in Stadter (1973).

[75] Both Cogan (1981) 98f. and Pouncey (1980) 105f. chart the reduction of public to private at Athens, but neither characterizes the Mytilenean debate in these terms.

the decision to put the rebellious Mytileneans to death, various *gnomai* were expressed (3.36.6). Finally, the man who was 'by far the most influential with the people' (3.36.6) came forward to speak. Yet in contrast to his portrayal of the occasions on which Pericles addressed the Athenians, Thucydides reports *two* speeches, not merely the view of the most influential leader. The *gnomai* of Cleon and Diodotus were 'expressed with nearly equal force, one against the other.' In response, the Athenians 'experienced such a conflict of opinion that in the show of hands they were almost equally divided' (3.49.1). In Thucydides' characterization of post-Periclean politics, neither Cleon nor Diodotus nor anyone else had sufficient influence or ability to raise his judgment to the level of unified policy. The intended comparison with Pericles is implicit, but unmistakable, in the echoes of Periclean language and ideas in the speeches of both men.

The speeches of Cleon and Diodotus both exemplify and describe the disintegration of Athenian politics. In his speech, Cleon claims that intelligence is manipulative and dangerous: it is merely playful and misleading wit, and each Athenian tries to outdo the 'dealers in paradox' (3.38.6). He has no patience with or faith in the Periclean ideal of wisdom without weakness (2.40). He invokes a standard associated, in the *History*, with the Spartans: 'Ignorance combined with self-control is more useful than cleverness combined with licentiousness' (3.37.3–4). These are, it seems, the only alternatives. Although he praises ignorant self-control, Cleon himself exhibits the clever intemperance which, as he rightly says, is dangerous. Cleon is introduced by Thucydides as 'the most violent of the citizens' (3.36.6). He appealed to the passions of the people. At the first assembly, Cleon had persuaded the Athenians to condemn, in anger (*hupo orgēs*), the entire population of Mytilene (3.36.1–2). At the second, he called upon the Athenians to remember 'as nearly as possible what [they] had suffered' (literally 'becoming as near as possible in *gnomē* [or by means of *gnomē*] to what you suffered') at the hands of the Mytileneans, and urged them to strike back (3.40.7; cf. 3.38.1). Yet, in warning the Athenians not to reverse their earlier decision under the influence of pity or remorse, Cleon seems to be filling the role so valuably played by Pericles: he opposes his judgment to the whims of the people. Like Pericles, he asserts: 'I am the same in *gnomē*' (3.38.1, cf. 2.61). Moreover, again echoing Pericles, he tells the Athenians that their empire is a tyranny over subjects who remain obedient because of Athenian strength, not out of good will (3.37.2–3, cf. 2.63), and that if they wish to maintain the empire they must do what is necessary without flinching, or else give it up 'and in discreet safety practice the fine virtues' (3.40.4–5 with 2.63.2). These echoes challenge the reader to consider whether the similarities are genuine or merely rhetorical. The original decision was, Thucydides makes clear, made under the influence of passion; what Cleon wishes to prevent is not the impulsive overthrow of a policy arrived at deliberately and reflectively, but the reflective reconsideration of an impetuous decision. Delay, he insists, will 'dull the edge of wrath (*orgē*)' (3.38.1). If, as Cleon charges, the democracy seems to be incompetent to govern others (3.37.1) because it cannot stick to its decisions, that is because the citizens have not been encouraged to deliberate properly, and not because they have deliberated too much. Moreover, he diminishes the likelihood of prudent deliberation and collective resolve by encouraging the belief that those who oppose his view must either be corrupt or irresponsibly sophistical (3.38.2–4, 3.40.3). He thereby fosters the very 'fear and intrigue' which he believes is characteristic only of imperial relations, and not of relations within the *polis* (3.37.2).

Cleon's understanding of the phenomenon of polarization and of Athens' position in relation to her allies is merely apparent. He argues for rigidity and inflexibility, which can be dangerous in circumstances that require prudence and sensitivity. As Pericles had argued, Athens must be prepared to do what is necessary to preserve her empire; in the guise of advocating just this, Cleon proposes measures which would increase the danger to the empire by promoting further polarization. Cleon's own words, used with respect to the Mytileneans, can be seen by the reader, in the context of the *History* as a whole, to apply to Athens herself and to cast doubt on the prudence of Cleon's policy. It is indeed those communities that 'came to great prosperity most unexpectedly and suddenly which turn to insolence,' and 'adversity is more easily repelled than prosperity maintained' (3.39.4). Furthermore, Cleon argues, with unintended implications for his own plan to put to death all the Mytileneans, guilty and innocent alike, that

it is generally those who wrong another without cause that follow him up to destroy him utterly, perceiving the danger that threatens from an enemy who is left alive; for one who has been needlessly injured is more dangerous if he escape than one avowed enemy who expects to give and take. (3.40.6)

It was necessary to punish Mytilene, but not to 'destroy a whole *polis* instead of merely those who were guilty' (3.36.4). To do so would, as

Cleon acknowledges, be 'unreasonable'[76] and it is a mistake to think, as he does, that it is in the interests of Athens to do what is unreasonable.

Diodotus, by contrast, argues for restraint, and for the virtues of wise counsel as opposed to brute force (3.48.2). His description of the complicated process of decision-making, in which orators try to second-guess the people and members of the assembly suspect the motives of every speaker, reveals the corrosive effects of the skeptical attitude to the role of reason and judgment in Athenian politics evinced by Cleon. Because of its citizenry's 'excessive cleverness,' says Diodotus, Athens is 'the only *polis* which a man cannot serve openly and without deceiving it, for whenever he openly offers [the citizens] something good he is suspected of secretly profiting by it in some way' (3.43.3). The citizens believe that politics has become essentially self-interested. This perception is extremely damaging, as Diodotus observes: it feeds upon itself, and results in a vicious interplay between suspicion and deceit which undermines the ability of the Athenians to devise or execute policy. Even a man with public-minded motives must practice deception. And indeed, even such a man, as Diodotus appears to be, is prey to the prevailing atmosphere of distrust; he alleges that anyone who contends that discussion (*logoi*) should not guide action is either stupid or 'has some private interest at stake' (3.42.2). Diodotus himself does attempt to tell the citizens the truth about their own behavior, and – like Pericles – to help them perceive and understand the implications of their actions. He implies that the citizens ought only to consider whether a man offers good advice to the *polis*; the issue of corruption, or motivation, ought to remain separate: 'If a man be suspected of giving even the best advice on account of a desire for gain, we bear a grudge, and thus deprive the *polis* of a manifest advantage' (3.43.1). Yet for Thucydides, in part because self-interested political rivalry encourages the notion that all advice is suspect, an ability to formulate and expound policy which is not founded on incorruptibility and public-mindedness cannot yield good advice, or at least not good policy. For the point of good policy is the integrity and prosperity of the *polis*.

Arguing for his view that only those who initiated the Mytilenean revolt should be put to death, Diodotus analyzes human nature (3.45.3f., cf. 4.108.4) and the present situation of Athens, and shows that it is imprudent to indulge the self-righteous desire for revenge

---

[76] *para to eikos*, i.e. contrary to what men would regard as likely or in accordance with reason.

promoted by appealing, as Cleon had done, to the 'more legal aspects of the case' (3.33.3). Law is too crude and inflexible an instrument to cope with the complexities of human psychology. Like Thucydides, Diodotus recognizes that prudence must replace reliance on social and legal conventions and that prudence, under present circumstances, dictates moderation:

> We must not, therefore, be such rigorous judges of the delinquents as to suffer harm ourselves, but we must rather see how for the time to come, by punishing moderately, we may have at our service dependent cities that are strong in material resources; and we must deem it proper to protect ourselves against revolts not by the terror of our laws, but rather by careful attention to events . . . We ought, instead of rigorously chastising free peoples when they revolt, to watch them rigorously before they revolt, and thus forestall their even thinking of such a thing; and when we have subdued a revolt, we ought to put the blame on as few as possible. (3.46.4–6)

Diodotus goes on to point out that to punish the innocent as well as the guilty would be to provide ammunition to those who hate the Athenians (3.47.3). However, this reasonable observation is succeeded by an imprudent one: whatever the people of Mytilene did or did not do, they should be treated as innocents, because the masses in the cities, as a group, are sympathetic to Athens and must not be alienated (3.47.4, cf. 3.47.2–3). To take up the cause of the people against the oligarchs in this way could perhaps be advantageous to Athens in the short term. But the attitude from which this suggestion proceeds is a product of polarization, and the policy it points to will aggravate that condition; it will promote class conflict dangerous for Greece as a whole and for the integrity of every *polis* including Athens. It resembles, in these respects, Diodotus' attitude to the attribution of self-interest to those who attempt to guide the community: he recognizes the deleterious effects of this climate of suspicion, yet thinks the symptoms can be alleviated without rooting out the cause, and himself indulges in the kind of accusation he deplores. As his discussion of human psychology reveals (see 3.45.3), Diodotus did not make Cleon's mistake of divorcing the basic character of political relations from that of relations between communities. In both realms, Diodotus' understanding of the nature and sources of polarization and of its effect on his own attitudes is only partial.

The portrayal of the two protagonists in the debate over the Sicilian Expedition reveals that eleven years after the punishment of Mytilene, after Cleon had persuaded the Athenians to refuse to make peace from a position of strength (425 B.C.) and Nicias had persuaded them to make a peace which held out little hope for stability (421 B.C.), it had become even more difficult, perhaps impossible, in the political atmosphere of post-Periclean Athens and war-torn Greece, for a politician to be in Thucydides' terms a good policy-maker, i.e. a leader who does the right thing, in the right way, for the right reasons. Nicias, as Thucydides presents him, echoed Periclean sentiments and his policy of not seeking to extend the empire (6.10.11),[77] and appealed to foresight (*pronoia*) (6.13.1); he tried to oppose the whims of the people, but although he was patriotic, incorruptible and often able to formulate correct policy, he was unable to guide and control the *demos*. He participated in the tendency to launch personal attacks on opponents: he accused Alcibiades of pursuing his own exclusive interests (6.12). After the Athenians had ignored his warnings against the Sicilian Expedition, Nicias tried once again to deter them, by dramatizing the extent of the resources required. True to Diodotus' portrayal of post-Periclean Athenian politics, Nicias resorted to trickery in a final attempt to persuade the people to abandon the expedition.[78] However his stratagem achieved only his secondary, not his primary object. As one of the leaders of the expedition he opposed, Nicias secured what he considered to be adequate resources (6.24.1) for the limited campaign he favored (6.47). However, the very size of the expedition increased Athenian confidence and expectations (6.24.2–3), made a more ambitious and strenuous campaign all but inevitable and magnified the scale of the eventual disaster. In response to Nicias' cautious plan of operations, Alcibiades 'insisted that they ought not, after sailing out with so great an armament, to go back in disgrace without effecting anything' (6.48). Once engaged in the siege of Syracuse, without Alcibiades, Nicias was plagued by all the difficulties of, as he had warned, founding 'a city amidst alien and hostile peoples' (6.23.2). Worn down by the energetic intervention of the Spartans, Nicias tried to persuade the Athenians to act on his assessment of the disparity between the policy he was expected to carry out and the resources, including the personal resources, now available to him. He wrote a letter to the Athenians explaining his own judgment

[77] *Contra* Edmunds (1975b), who entitles a chapter 'The Spartan character of Nicias.' Edmunds has, in my view, been led astray in this as in some other areas by blurring the radical difference between Periclean and post-Periclean Athens, particularly in terms of leadership and the distinction between the Periclean ideal and the representative Athenian portrayed by the Corinthians, and by misinterpreting the Periclean view of *tuchē*. Cf. Rawlings (1981) 127–58.

[78] Cf. Nicias' behavior at 4.28 and the stratagems adopted by Cleon, 4.27 and Alcibiades 5.45.

that they should either recall the expedition or send reinforcements, and in any case relieve him of command, as he was seriously ill. He provided them with sufficient information to make a reasonable, realistic judgment (7.8.2, 7.14.4, 7.15). He urged the Athenians to use their intelligence and to base their decision on the hard facts. He wrote, rather than transmitting a message orally, because he feared that the messengers 'might not report the actual facts . . . because they wished to please the multitude' (7.8.2). Nicias was willing to speak the unpleasant truth. In his first speech against the expedition, he claimed that he had never, 'for the sake of being preferred in honor, spoken contrary to [his] judgment (*para gnomēn*)' (6.9.2–3).

Nicias understood the nature of post-Periclean Athens, a democracy drunk with success (see 7.14.4). Yet he could not stem the tendency of the Athenians either in the assembly or in the army in Sicily (7.14.2, cf. 7.72.4) to react with passion rather than judgment to any frustration of their hopes.[79] In the end, afraid of the anger of the *demos*, Nicias allowed the strain of events (no doubt compounded by ill health, his private fears and desires, and superstition) to overcome his judgment (see 7.48; 7.50.4). Although he had opposed the expedition from the start, appreciated the risk of disaster, and knew he was no longer fit to command, Nicias insisted in the end on remaining in Sicily. His fears rendered him gullible and inadequately sensitive to circumstances.[80] His final speech to the Athenians was, in part, a desperate effort to be Periclean, to encourage his men when they were disheartened by appealing to the power of knowledge (7.63.4, 7.64.2). But it also reveals his unreasonable determination to die in the line of duty rather than confess defeat (7.77.3, 7.48.4). Nicias had lost touch with reality. A man who was unable either to withstand the force of events or to assess it, he unreasonably ignored the dire prospects and led many Athenians to their deaths, fearing personal humiliation and punishment more than the devastation of Athenian power. Thucydides' comment on Nicias' death at the hands of the Spartans is a precise assessment of the man's qualities and limitations, formulated as it is in terms of conventional categories: he was the 'man who, of all the Hellenes of my time, least deserved to meet with such a misfortune because the whole of his life had been regulated in accordance with

---

[79] Cf. the punishment of the generals who in 424 had ended the earlier campaign against Sicily by agreeing to a peace treaty, and Thucydides' comment on Athenian confidence.

[80] Even such partial but accurate knowledge as he did have of Syracusan affairs, 7.48.2–3, 7.49.1 (note *akribōs*), laid him open to manipulation on a matter of great importance to Athenian safety, namely the timing of the retreat; see 7.73.3–4.

excellence (*aretē*)' (7.86.5). Nicias lived in a world which expected *tuchē*, like a benign divinity, to reward those who lived up to conventional standards. But the world had changed, and *aretē* was no longer enough.

Alcibiades, an altogether different figure, resembled Nicias in lacking *gnōmē*; the defect manifested itself in different ways. Alcibiades did not even attempt to appeal to reason when trying to influence the people.[81] Eventually, he himself was victimized by Athenian *orgē*.[82] In politics he pursued his own interests, whether or not they clashed with the interests of the city:

> Most zealous in urging the expedition was Alcibiades son of Cleinias, wishing as he did to oppose Nicias because, along with their general disagreement with regard to public policy (*ta politika*) Nicias had made invidious reference to him, and above all he was eager to be made general and hoped thereby to subdue both Sicily and Carthage, and in case of success to promote at the same time his private concerns in wealth as well as in glory. (6.15.2–3)[83]

Pericles exploited his reputation to chastise and guide the people; Alcibiades, to indulge his desires beyond his means (6.15.3 with 2.65). As I suggested in discussing the polarization in Athens in 415 B.C., his private self-indulgence rendered him an object of suspicion (6.15.4) and undermined his ability to contribute to the public good: 'Though publicly he managed the affairs of the war most excellently, in his private life every man had been offended at his practices' (6.15.4). Again, Thucydides' language emphasizes the importance of an exclusively 'public' attitude on the part of a democratic leader. Treason was only a quantitative step for a man who, according to Thucydides' portrayal, acted as if he owed allegiance only to himself. His cynical claim that he was indeed an Athenian patriot, made in a speech to the Spartans when he was seeking to advise them in the war, reflects his belief that his own needs constitute the standard of statesmanship: 'It is not . . . against a country still my own that I am going but rather one no longer mine that I am seeking to regain' (6.92.4).

The loss to the *polis* represented by Alcibiades' failure to make

---

[81] Alcibiades' persuasive techniques relied on promoting *orgē*, not *gnōmē*. Cf. 6.88.10, 6.17.1. Edmunds' interpretation (1975b) 124–8 of Alcibiades suffers from the problems cited in n. 77 above. Moreover, he does not appreciate the importance of the fact that (as he notes, p. 127), Alcibiades lacked 'Pericles' moderation.'

[82] See above on the digression concerning the Pisistratids and Rawlings (1981) 76f. and 100f.

[83] Note Alcibiades' claim, 6.16.3–4, that his extravagance benefited the city as well as himself.

proper use of his gifts[84] is suggested in Thucydides' account of one occasion on which Alcibiades behaved like Pericles:

> When the Athenians at Samos [in 411] were bent upon sailing against their own
> people . . . it was he who prevented it. And in that critical moment no other man
> would have been able to restrain the crowd[85] but he stopped them from sailing,
> and reproaching those who were on their own private account angry (*orgizo-
> menous*), he caused them to desist. (8.86.4)

By this action, according to Thucydides, Alcibiades 'seems in an eminent degree, and more than anyone else, to have benefited the *polis*'
(8.86.4). Thucydides' earlier assessment of Alcibiades' motives – his
self-indulgence and private ambition – is of a piece with the subsequent[86] judgment that this sort of behavior was primarily responsible for the destruction of the Athenian *polis*:

> For the masses, afraid of the greatness of his lawless and sensual self-indulgence in
> his manner of living, as also of his designs as revealed in every single activity in
> which he was involved, became hostile to him on the ground that he was aiming at
> a tyranny . . . and so, entrusting the city to other hands, after no long time brought
> it to ruin. (6.15.4)

Thucydides' favorable assessment of Alcibiades' military capabilities
and of his capacity to contribute to the well-being of the *polis* (cf.
2.65.11, 6.15.4) seems to have been formulated with regard to the
period after 411, without altering either his opinion of Alcibiades'
policy for Sicily or of his motives in 415.[87] The events of 411 and their
aftermath evidently persuaded Thucydides of Alcibiades' great potential as a leader, potential which – as Thucydides appreciated early on –
was undermined by his extreme egoism and destructive passion, and
the corresponding features of Athenian political life.[88]

As Thucydides' portrayal of post-Periclean Athens indicates, the
primacy of private passions causes individuals and the city to respond
irrationally to experience, thus exacerbating antagonism within the
polis and the imprudent pursuit of exclusive interests. Self-control
affects the possibility of realistic understanding, and vice versa. The

---

[84] On Thucydides' assessments of Alcibiades, see de Romilly (1983) 196f., Pouncey (1980)
105f., Pouilloux and Salviat (1983) 398–400; note Alcibiades' galvanizing effect on
Spartan policy, Rawlings (1981) 185f.

[85] Cf. description of Pericles, 2.65.8.

[86] Dover (1981) 427.

[87] Dover (1981) 424–6. Cf. Brunt (1952), who argues that Thucydides' information was
biased in favor of Alcibiades.

[88] On Thucydides' presentation of Alcibiades' persecution by the people, see Rawlings
(1981) 100f. and Pouncey (1980) 105f.

power of reason to maintain the stability of the Athenian democracy entails both understanding and self-control on the part of its leaders and the propagation of these virtues among the citizens. The speeches of Pericles suggest that self-control can be fortified through understanding of the character and powers of reason, including its vulnerability to chance (*tuchē*) and passion (*orgē*). The primacy of reason involves awareness that the role of chance is restricted: the influence of chance on judgment and morale even in the limited Thucydidean sense (what cannot be anticipated) is potent, but can be resisted. The primacy of reason also involves awareness that control of passion is essential to the capacity to assess and respond rationally to events. In Democritus' view, as I shall indicate in the next chapter, chance takes hold in man's nature through indulgence in crude pleasure and sensation. For Thucydides, indulgence in passion undermines the ability of the *polis* to withstand the fluctuations of history.[89] In both cases it is reason which, by asserting control, restricts the power of crude sensation and thereby expands its own sphere of influence.

The dangers of freedom: Athens versus Sparta

Thucydides' exploration and analysis of the capacity to respond realistically and prudently to historical circumstance takes the form not only of a characterization of Athenian politics during and after the hegemony of Pericles, but also of a portrayal of Athenians and Spartans. The contrast between the two poses concretely the question left hanging at the end of the Archaeology: is it possible to achieve or to preserve both safety and greatness, in the world as it now is? In the *History*, Thucydides dramatized and interpreted the confrontation of two radically different military and political systems, temperaments and views of the world. This dramatic contrast is evident in the counterpoint of speeches and narrative, as well as in Thucydides' own comments and the overall framework of the *History*, which is the tale of two great cities at war, each playing a distinctive role. The attitudes, way of life and behavior of the Spartans point up the weaknesses, and the strengths, of the Athenians. Thucydides' analysis of the confrontation between the two provides both a conceptual framework for interpreting the behavior of political communities in response to experience and a historical context for assessing the reality to which each city had to respond. The speeches indicate the terms in which

[89] See e.g. Thucydides' account of the decision regarding the rebellious Mytileneans, with Edmunds (1975b).

Thucydides analyzed the conflict: the words and concepts are Thucydides' own, and they express what was appropriate (*ta deonta*). They echo and derive added meaning from the use of the same ideas in other contexts in the *History*. Moreover, the terms of analysis are justified in the event; they make sense of the behavior of the two communities in the course of the war, as Thucydides perceived it.

The speeches provide a picture of the difference between Athenians and Spartans cast in terms of those factors which are shown in the *History* to be decisive for human behavior and well-being, namely *gnomē, orgē* and *tuchē*. In 432 B.C. after the Athenians had laid siege to Potidaea, the Spartan allies gathered in Laconia. Various cities voiced their complaints, but Thucydides reports only the speech of the Corinthians, who urged Sparta to take up arms against Athens. Corinth portrayed the Athenians as insatiable imperialists and the Spartans, who alone could prevent Athens from subjugating Greece, as ineffectual stay-at-homes. The Athenians, they said, were 'bold beyond their power, daring beyond their judgment (*gnomē*) and sanguine in the presence of dangers.' The Spartans, on the other hand, 'do less than [their] power justifies, do not trust even the certainties of judgment (*gnomē*) and despair of deliverance from dangers' (1.70.3). This comparison incorporates the major themes of Thucydides' narrative: power, chance and judgment. The Corinthians refer indirectly to the interaction of *gnomē* and *tuchē* when they assert that the Athenians remain 'sanguine in the presence of dangers,' while the Spartans 'despair of deliverance.'

The contrast between Spartan and Athenian perceptions of *tuchē* emerges in greater detail from a comparison of the Athenian speech at Sparta in 432 with the Spartan peace mission to Athens after the Athenians had blockaded the men on Sphacteria in 425. In 432, a group of Athenians in Sparta on other business, Thucydides reports, requested an opportunity to address the assembled Peloponnesians; they warned the Spartans to 'take counsel slowly' and to use their own judgment rather than allow themselves to be persuaded by the judgments of others (1.78.1). In seeking to persuade the Spartans, who were renowned for their caution and unwillingness to take risks, the Athenians stress the overwhelming power of chance: 'Understand thoroughly before you become involved in it how great is the role of the incalculable in war,' they advised the Spartans. 'For when war is prolonged, it usually becomes a mere matter of chance (*tuchē*) and from chance neither side is exempt, and what the outcome will be is unknown and hazardous' (1.78.1–2). In making this argument, however, the Athenians reveal their own attitudes: it is precisely because chance affects both cities and is unpredictable that man must rely upon his intelligence. According to the Athenians,

Most men go to war and resort to deeds first ... and then, when they are suffering, at length engage in words. But [they said] since we ourselves are not as yet involved in any such error and see that you are not we bid you, while good counsel is still a matter of free choice to both of us ... to let our differences be settled by arbitration according to our agreement. (1.78.3–4)

The Athenians acknowledge the role of chance, particularly in military conflicts, but emphasize that human reason can be effective in avoiding the unknowable, risky consequences of war. And since neither side can control chance, superiority will be determined in the realm of human intelligence: wise counsel and free choice.

Similarly, the Spartan envoys sent to Athens in 425, after the capture of the men on Sphacteria,[90] both speak to Athenian values and reveal their own. They urge the Athenians to choose peace, and to regard their speech 'as a reminder about how to come to a good decision, addressed to intelligent men.' By turning their 'present favorable fortune to good account' the Athenians would leave 'to posterity an unendangered reputation for both strength and wisdom' instead of being 'credited with having won even [their] present advantages by means of fortune (*tuchē*)' (4.17.3–4, 4.18.5). Yet, in contrast to the way in which the Athenians at Sparta described the power of chance in order to define the influential role of human reason, the Spartans at Athens manipulated the concept of the power of human reason in order to clarify the influential role of chance. The Spartans warned the Athenians to use their intelligence and thereby recognize that intelligence is of no use. Describing their own bad luck, they claim 'it was neither through lack of power that [they] experienced this misfortune, nor because [their] power became too great and [they] became reckless.' Rather, their resources were what they had always been and '[they] simply erred in judgment (*gnomē*) – a thing to which all are alike liable' (4.18.2–3). *gnomē* for the Spartans, like *tuchē* for the Athenians, is a factor which affects all states equally, and is therefore *not* a critical element in assessing the prudence of a policy. The Spartans argue that fortune, not intelligence, determines superiority. Even Athenian strength cannot ensure that '*tuchē* will always be with [her].' In war, men must 'follow where [their] fortunes (*tuchē*) lead' (4.18.2–4).

[90] See Cogan (1981) 74–6.

Together, these three speeches not only articulate the contrast between the temperaments, as well as the values, of the two powers, but also serve as a commentary upon this contrast, placing it in context and revealing its ambiguities. Before the war, in an attempt to calm Spartan fear of what the Corinthians had portrayed as innate aggressiveness,[91] the Athenians emphasize the reassuring aspect of their reliance on intelligence, namely their capacity for self-control and deliberation. By 425 B.C. the Athenians themselves, encouraged by the self-seeking Cleon (4.21, 5.16) have been seduced by *tuchē* into insatiable greed (4.21.2, 5.14.1; cf. 4.17.4) and are deaf to the Spartan invocation of the value of exploiting *tuchē* through intelligence. For their part, the Spartans were deaf to the Athenian appeal to the riskiness of war. Having departed, under the influence of fear and Corinthian pressure, from their characteristic risk-aversion, the Spartans lived up to the Corinthian portrayal once the conditions predicted by the Athenians had come about: the unexpected, the fortification of Pylos, cowed them into suing for peace. In the early years of the war, under the influence of Pericles, the Athenians exhibited self-control not envisioned in the Corinthian portrait. As the years passed, they became intoxicated by success and lived up to the Corinthian characterization (note 1.70.3 with 4.17.4, 1.70.8 with 4.21.2). Thucydides thus exhibits the weaknesses of the Spartan character while presenting them as a necessary corrective, under certain circumstances, to Athenian self-confidence. Athenian inventiveness and self-reliance were the sources of greatness; in the form of recklessness, they were the cause of devastation. By refusing the Spartan peace offer, the Athenians abandoned the limited aims which were, in Pericles' view, necessary and sufficient for the maintenance of a balance of power in Greece, and committed Hellas to the destructive, bitter spiral of conflict (see 4.19.20).[92]

Thucydides' account of Spartan and Athenian behavior under the stress of war confirms the ambiguities implicit in the speeches. The qualities characteristic of each could be construed either positively or negatively, depending on the context in which they were expressed and shaped. Sparta could be regarded as stable and cautious, or stolid and rigid; Athens as rash and undisciplined, or enterprising and intelligent. The qualities of the Spartans were a function of the training and discipline characteristic of their way of life. Reliance on discipline was

[91] See the discussion by Cogan (1981) 25f.
[92] See Cogan (1981) 75–6, with n. 31. The Spartan predictions about the consequences of refusal are confirmed by the remainder of the *History*; see 5.14.2; cf. 2.65.11.

the source both of Sparta's strengths and of her weaknesses. At Mantinea, Thucydides relates, the Spartans 'proved inferior with respect to experienced skilfullness (*empeiria*).' Sparta triumphed by means of courage (*andreia*) (5.72.2–3). They were trained to be brave rather than resourceful, stalwart rather than enterprising. This lack of resourcefulness emerges in Thucydides' account of the naval confrontation at Rhium in 429. The Spartans, in their initial departure from the tradition of land warfare, lost the sea fight to a few Athenian ships. They could not comprehend their defeat (this incomprehension was itself due, says Thucydides, to lack of experience) and 'thought that there had been cowardice somewhere, failing to consider the long experience (*empeiria*) of the Athenians as compared to their own brief practice' (2.85.2–3). In their speech to the troops, the Peloponnesian commanders argued that they ought not to be afraid of further naval encounters: there were reasons why they had been defeated in the first battle. These reasons – lack of preparation, the purpose of the expedition (namely to fight on land rather than at sea), the vagaries of war and inexperience – are adduced not primarily because the Spartans can hope to alter these factors significantly (though note 2.85.3, 2.87.5) but rather as evidence that it was at any rate not cowardice that caused their defeat (2.87.2). It was not right, the commanders continued,

that the *gnomē* which was not then beaten [in the previous battle], but has some answer yet within its power,[93] should be blunted by the outcome of the event; rather [they] ought to consider that although men may suffer reverses in fortune (*tuchē*) yet brave men are always the same in judgment (*gnomē*). (2.87.3)

gnomē, in the sense of the self-control which resists demoralization – determination – was essential to courage, and could, according to the Spartan generals, be divorced from experience or skill. Courage, they argued, was far more important to success than skill, knowledge or experience; as Phormio, the Athenian general, remarked to his men, the Spartans relied chiefly on courage in their encounters with the Athenians, 'as if it were their peculiar province to be brave' (2.89.2). The Spartans were proud to declare that their discipline and courage, and not the cleverness and resourcefulness characteristic of the Athenians (see 2.87.4) were the source of their strength.

The bravery and wisdom of the Spartans, King Archidamus argued, sprang from their 'well-ordered temper.' They were brave in war

---

[93] Translation relies on formulations suggested by Gomme (1956a) *ad loc.* Cf. the language of 5.75.3.

'because self-control (*sophrosunē*) is the chief element in a sense of shame and a sense of shame, in turn, is the chief element in courage' (1.84.3). The Spartan 'temper' was not founded on intelligent self-reliance, but on training. In fact, the Spartans were wise in counsel, according to Archidamus, because of ignorance, having been 'educated too rudely to have contempt for the laws and with too much rigorous self-control to disobey them' (1.84.3). Spartan power, courage and confidence rested on education and training. The Spartans did not 'believe that man differs much from man, but that he is best who is trained most severely' (1.84.4). Archidamus encouraged his fellow-citizens not to be ashamed of their reputation for slowness and dilatoriness: 'This trait in us may well be in the truest sense sensible self-control (*sophrosunē*). For by reason of it we alone do not become insolent in prosperity or succumb to adversity as much as others do' (1.84.1–2). Spartan resistance to the oscillations of *tuchē*, as the commanders at Rhium also noted, depended not on intelligent resourcefulness but on stolid self-control. Thucydides himself confirms at least part of Archidamus' claim: in praise of the Chians, he likens them to the Spartans, who are 'at once prosperous and self-controlled, and the greater their city grew the more securely they ordered it' (8.24.4). *sophrosunē* is the quintessential Spartan virtue, and it persists through good times and bad; in this sense, Sparta is invulnerable to *tuchē*.

But Spartan discipline not only fostered fortitude and bravery; it also, under changing conditions, rendered Spartan courage, policy and well-being vulnerable to *tuchē*. For Spartan *sophrosunē* is self-control in its most restrictive sense: an unchanging, static way of life. Spartan inwardness, isolation and caution limit exposure to extremes of *tuchē* and make *sophrosunē* possible. When forced by circumstances to expose themselves to risk, the Spartans were therefore extremely vulnerable. According to Thucydides' commentary on the Spartan state of mind after the Athenian capture of Sphacteria,

> The reverses of fortune (*tuchē*) which had befallen them unexpectedly in such numbers and in so short a time, caused very great consternation and they were afraid that some time a calamity might again chance to happen like that which had happened on the island; and on this account they showed less spirit in their fighting, and whatever move they might make they thought would be a failure, because their *gnomē* had become unsure as a result of having been hitherto inexperienced in adversity. (4.55.1–4)[94]

The Spartan response to the threat of Athenian invasions is not to send

[94] Cf. 1.69.5.

forces to meet them but to post garrisons for fear that some innovation may undermine their institutions (4.55.1; cf. 1.70.4, 1.102.3). Implicit in this comment on Spartan behavior is Thucydides' awareness that preserving the shape of Spartan life requires constant vigilance on the part of the Spartiates; when the deadliest enemy is internal, defensiveness takes precedence over initiative (cf. 5.14.3, 1.118.2). Dependent as her way of life is on the continued subjugation of the helots, Sparta is permanently polarized internally. Like the tyrants mentioned in the Archaeology, she is intent on safety. As the Athenians remark to the Melians, 'advantage goes with security (*asphaleia*), while justice and the noble are practiced with danger, a danger which the Lacedaemonians are in general the least disposed to risk' (5.107). The Spartans, as all acknowledge (see 1.68, 5.105.3), exhibit great nobility and excellence in their relations with one another; these relations are both made possible by and directed to control of the helots. In their external relations, as a result, the Spartans (like the tyrants) are suspicious of entanglement, leery of taking risks, and, as the Athenians observe, 'consider what is agreeable to be honorable, and what is advantageous just' (5.105; cf. 1.68.1–2). The peculiarities of Spartan society – its remarkable internal orderliness and discipline, and externally, its unwillingness to take action and its vulnerability to the unexpected – are all due to the fundamental instability created by Spartiate domination of the non-Spartans who make their way of life possible. *sophrosunē* cannot enable the Spartans to respond and adapt to changing external circumstances, for it is precisely change and adaptation which *sophrosunē* is intended to prevent.

The portrayal of the Athenian character and its manifestations in internal and external relations also has two aspects. In contrast to Spartan stability – which the Corinthians, in their desire to prod their ally into action, interpret as stolid passivity – the Athenians are 'given to innovation and quick to form plans and to execute their decisions' (1.70.2). Spartan practices, the Corinthians insisted, are

old-fashioned as compared with theirs . . . It is true that when a *polis* is at peace unaltered customary practices are best, but when men are compelled to enter into many undertakings there is need of much improvement in method. It is for this reason – because of their great experience – that the practices of the Athenians have undergone greater change than yours. (1.71.2–3)

The Athenians deliberately seek the experience and activity which require that they constantly alter their practices: 'They regard untroubled peace as a far great calamity than laborious activity ... They were born neither to have peace themselves nor to let other men have it' (1.70.8–9). Despite the Corinthians' evident – and instrumental – respect for Athenian attributes, their characterization reveals the negative aspect of the Athenian personality: the desire for constant innovation and activity has led them to prey upon other Greek cities. They are 'always seeking more' (1.70.8). The Athenians are daring 'beyond their strength,' venturesome 'beyond their better judgment' (*para gnomēn*) and 'sanguine in the face of dangers' (1.70.3) – all dangerously destabilizing qualities, as Thucydides' account of post-Periclean Athens reveals. Rashness and lack of discipline constituted the weak profile of qualities which, viewed from another angle, were Athens' best features: self-reliance, energy, resourcefulness and the spirit of enterprise founded on a system which expressed the collective interest. Contrast Thucydides' account of the Spartan response to the occupation of Cythera and the capture of Sphacteria with his description of the Athenians' reaction when they realized that the entire expeditionary force to Sicily had been destroyed (8.1.1–4). Like the Spartans, the Athenians experienced fear and consternation. But they recovered themselves and acted assertively to meet the impending crisis. They were not, it seems, cowed or demoralized, nor did they retreat within themselves, guard against internal disorder, and batten the hatches, as the Spartans instinctively did: 'In the panic of the moment they were ready, as is the way with the *demos*, to observe discipline in everything. And as they had determined, so they proceeded to act' (8.1.4). Democratic rule was erratic; but the citizens of a democratic *polis* were capable of appreciating the need for discipline and of acting to secure it.

The ambivalence about Athenian power manifested in the Archaeology re-emerges in the contrast between Athenians and Spartans. *sophrosunē*, for which the Spartans were renowned, was not an attribute of Athenian democracy, even as it is portrayed by Pericles in the Funeral Oration, and Thucydides evidently admired *sophrosunē*. *sophrosunē* could hardly be said to characterize the citizens of democratic Athens as a whole, since it was a way of life as much as a quality of character, and a way of life associated with oligarchy.[95] The contrast between Athenians and Spartans implies that the choice is a unified and complete one: *sophrosunē* is associated with a particular kind of social system and foreign policy, and so, too, is intelligence (*xunesis*). Thucydides' ambivalence, implicit in the static contrast be-

[95] See 8.64.5, 8.53.3. Cf. North (1966) 100, Gomme, Andrewes and Dover (1981) *ad* 8.64.

tween the temperaments of Athenians and Lacedaemonians, is to be construed historically. Before the period of which Thucydides is the historian, the qualities described by the Corinthians enabled the Athenians, on the one hand, to secure and consolidate imperial power, and the Spartans, on the other, to extend and preserve control of their own sphere of influence while avoiding internal disruption. By the time of the Peloponnesian War, however, the maintenance of an equilibrium between the traditionally stable internal order and the demands of power depended upon limiting external responsibilities to whatever was necessary to defend and consolidate Sparta's existing strength.[96] Sparta's lack of experience, and her inflexibility, crippled her capacity to initiate glorious enterprises or to respond to the eventual encroachments of an active, innovative power. And Athens' very success created a tension between active and free-ranging ambition and the necessity of taking into account the existence and aims of other *poleis* in a world polarized by Athens' own power and strength. The Athenians retained in a new context the attributes which had brought about their rise to power. The combination of an energetic, ambitious citizen body and the demands of the increasing power secured by its activities make the achievement of stable political equilibrium in a city like Athens extremely difficult. The risks are far greater for Athens, but so is the potential.

Thucydides' ambivalence points to the need to control Athenian desires and unify and stabilize its policies without smothering the energy, intelligence and capacity to respond creatively to experience which had built Athenian power and remained its greatest resource. Yet the inflexibility and ignorance evinced by the Spartans is evidently not the answer. The Spartan virtues were invoked at Athens by Cleon (3.37.3; cf. 2.87.3). From the perspective of the historian Cleon can be seen to be aggravating the weaknesses of Athenian society and stifling its strengths. A different kind of institutional structure could perhaps provide more consistent discipline. Thucydides seems to have regarded the institutions associated with the Five Thousand at Athens, the moderate oligarchy or conservative democracy which paved the way for a return to full democracy after the oligarchic revolution of 411, as an improvement over the radical democracy (8.97.2).[97] How-

---

[96] Thucydides would have been confirmed in this view by observing Sparta's behavior as an 'imperial' power after 404. See Pouilloux and Salviat (1983) 395.

[97] Cf. Gomme, Andrewes, Dover (1981) *ad loc*. The meaning of *eu politeuein* is unclear. But Thucydides' reference to a blending of few and many indicates that he had in mind institutions or a 'constitution,' not merely the day-to-day management of affairs.

ever, institutional answers – like the extreme case of the Spartan social system – risked blunting the self-reliance of the citizens and their adaptability. Thucydides did not in the first instance look to institutions, but to leadership: Pericles led the *polis* moderately (2.65.5). The moderate blending achieved by the Five Thousand was, I would argue, an institutional approximation to this virtue, to the power of aristocratic leadership in a democracy. When he says that Athens 'though in name *demokratia* was in fact becoming rule by the foremost man' (2.65.9–10), Thucydides is not praising monarchy, but rather a singular kind of aristocracy whose force is not institutional but psychological. Equality in the sense of the absence of a guiding *gnomē* was, in Thucydides' view, no virtue. Yet the triumph of Periclean leadership was *not* replicating *sophrosunē* in a democracy, but guiding and channeling the quintessential Athenian virtues, epitomized by the capacity to act both boldly and reflectively. As Pericles declares in the Funeral Oration:

In the same men are united a concern for both domestic and political matters, and notwithstanding our various occupations there is no lack of insight into politics. For we alone regard the man who takes no part in public affairs not as one who minds his own business, but as good for nothing; and the same individuals [i.e. the Athenians generally] either decide on or originate public proposals, in the belief that it is not discussion that hinders action, but rather not to be instructed by discussion beforehand. We have this point also of superiority over other men, that the same group of individuals is at once most daring in action and most given to reflection on the ventures we undertake; among others, boldness implies ignorance, and reflectiveness produces hesitation. (2.40.2–3)

The point being stressed in this passage is that the Athenian populace does not rely on a division of labor: each citizen is competent publicly as well as privately, each acts as well as judges. The ability of every individual Athenian to be bold and reflective in serving the ends of the whole *polis* as well as his own is the source of the city's greatness (2.41.1–2).

The historian's ambivalence – self-control or intelligence, safety or greatness – which emerges in the contrast between Athenians and Spartans and is deepened by Thucydides' historical understanding of these characteristics and aims under changing conditions, is resolved in his interpretation of Periclean Athens. The more a *polis* resembles a collectivity, the riskier, and – if it succeeds in acting as an entity – the better. The Athenian democracy represented the possibility of the free exercise of intelligence, freed from and indeed superior to the power of *tuchē* and *orgē*. Under Pericles, the Athenians were as bold as their power warranted, venturesome in accordance with *gnomē* and hopeful when it was reasonable to be so: 'Intelligence . . . trusts not so much in hope, which is strongest in times of perplexity, as in *gnomē* based on existing circumstances, which gives a more certain perception of the future' (2.62.5). By means of his ability to determine what was appropriate (*ta deonta*) and to persuade the Athenians of the wisdom of his determinations, and through his capacity to moderate and unify their behavior in accordance with those determinations, Pericles made possible intelligent self-control and thereby preserved for a time both the security and the greatness of Athens. Thus, says Thucydides, 'he kept the *polis* in safety and it was under him that it became greatest' (2.65.5). The Athenians should not yield; neither should they expand. They had attained the height of their power. In a world shaped by the existence of that power, greatness consisted in preserving it.

History and leadership

Kierkegaard observed in his journal that although 'life must be understood backwards [it] must be lived forwards.'[98] Thucydides' belief that history, or more specifically the kind of history that exhibits and fosters judgment, is the way to understand who we are and what we have reason to do, rests on the assumption that we can understand life as we live it, by viewing it historically. Pericles' capacity to lead is the capacity of a historian who constantly construes events, casts prudence in terms of historical analysis and teaches the citizenry to do so. It is not appropriate, though it might be tempting, to contrast the agent Pericles, who moves forwards and experiences life from the inside, with the historian Thucydides, who thinks backwards and reflects on life from the outside:[99] Thucydidean history integrates the interpretative tasks of historian, historical agents and reader. But was not Thucydides' achievement a triumph of pure insight, whereas Pericles' consisted in part of the constant modulation of understanding in response to experience? No: Thucydides not only helps the reader to interpret, by doing so himself and exhibiting his own judgment; he also fashions the *History* so that the reader responds not just intellectually but emotionally (with surprise, dismay, sympathy) to the events being interpreted and he thereby controls, in some measure, both the response and the interpretation. Like Pericles, Thucydides achieves this control through self-effacement and rendering an objective

[98] See Wollheim (1984).
[99] Cf. Beiner (1983) 107–8.

account. But, again like Pericles, he does not substitute his analysis for our own. In controlling our interpretation, he helps us to interpret. He demands, and challenges, an audience of independent judgment. Just as Pericles tells as well as shows the Athenians what kind of leadership to value, so, too, Thucydides both shows and tells the reader what kind of history to value. The role of the agent, who reasons prudentially about the future, with purpose, drawing on substantive experience, can be distinguished in theory from the role of the critical spectator, who reasons historically and discusses the meaning in and bestows dignity upon political events from a distanced, disinterested perspective;[100] but the two roles are not in fact, or so the *History* suggests, separable. Prudence is historical and history prudential. The historian and the agent perform the same functions, with the same skills, combining reflective distance and imaginative participation in the same way.

Yet we are left with the sense that there are significant differences between Pericles and Thucydides which are obscured by this assimilation. Pericles' arguments, and his example, are addressed from within a community to individuals who share a political life; Thucydides', by contrast, are addressed to individuals either temporally or spatially, but in either case psychologically, outside the community whose experience he interprets. This distinction raises important questions about the character of the Thucydidean project, but it does not shatter the symmetry between Thucydides and Pericles. To the extent that Pericles and Thucydides were both addressing their contemporaries, they were both speaking from within a political practice to those who shared their assumption and habits of thought. To the extent that they were both addressing men who had, like Callicles, begun to question the status of a shared life and to view politics externally, they were both arguing for and exemplifying the virtues of community to those who felt themselves to be removed from it. Both tried to persuade their audiences to acknowledge and imaginatively to participate in the goods internal to the political practice. By 'practice' I mean a

coherent and complex form of socially established cooperative human activity through which goods internal to that form of activity are realised in the course of trying to achieve those standards of excellence which are appropriate to, and partially definitive of, that form of activity, with the result that human powers to achieve excellence, and human conceptions of the ends and goods involved, are systematically extended.[101]

[100] See Beiner (1983) 159–61, 166–7.
[101] MacIntyre (1981) 175.

Goods external to a practice are 'externally and contingently attached' to the practice (e.g. prestige, status, money) and can be achieved in other ways than by participating in the practice, whereas internal goods cannot be secured in any other way, and can only be specified in terms of the practice itself and only be 'identified and recognised by the experience of participating in the practice in question.'[102] Pericles and Thucydides seek to patch a leaky practice not, like Plato, by formulating a vision of human well-being that gives each individual, whatever his circumstances – even Gyges, possessor of a magic ring – reason to behave in ways consistent with social order, a vision realizable only in a political community very different from the existing one, but rather by offering a mixture of external reasons for reconstituting the practice and an evocation of the goods internal to it. Thucydides does not attempt a radical solution to the problem posed by the free-rider; he seeks to restore those conditions of communal life which make such behavior seem self-defeating. For this task, in relation to his contemporaries, he is not so well placed as Pericles. Men need not just to understand and imagine; they need to be led. The conditions of life must be such as to foster the vitality of the practice, and a leader has more influence over this than an historian.

Leaders die. So do practices. It might therefore be objected that reliance on historical judgment within concrete practices, instead of on rules or abstract standards of rationality or obligation, is insufficiently binding. A version of this objection is implicit in Thucydides' ambivalence about Athens and Sparta: it is dangerous to depend for order on the constant exercise of collective judgment. Thucydides is in fact tempted to modify this aspect of Athenian life, through institutional reform along the lines of the regime of the Five Thousand. But as Thucydides' portrayal of the weaknesses of Sparta and the strengths of Periclean Athens indicates, he acknowledged that reliance on judgment was the only way to maintain flexibility, adaptability and the capacity to respond to changing circumstances. It is, moreover, as Thucydides' own decision to write history reveals, the only way to meet and neutralize cynicism, namely the separation of the reflective assessment of men's needs and interests from the structures imposed by social institutions and social conventions. Thus in an important sense the standards of judgment are more binding than those of custom, since they grip reflective man.

But is this way of thinking about ourselves and about politics insufficiently binding in another way, namely insufficiently demanding?

102 MacIntyre (1981) 176.

Does it not leave too much room for self-delusion, complacency and parochialism? Thucydides' *History*, at any rate, construes the present and the future not as images of the past, but as shaped by past events. A historical analysis of the present therefore challenges men constantly to assess how they are actually situated now, how circumstances have changed. Like Periclean Athens, Thucydidean history faces the future as well as, and in the presence of, the past, and is similarly subject to deterioration (see 2.64.3). What Geertz says about cultural theory fits Thucydidean history as well:

It is directed toward the task of generating interpretations of matters already in hand, not toward projecting outcomes of experimental manipulations or deducing future states of a determined system. But that does not mean that theory has only to fit (or, more carefully, to generate cogent interpretations of) realities past; it has also to survive – intellectually survive – realities to come.[103]

Because it faces the future in construing the past, Thucydidean history clearly points beyond itself. Thucydides recognized that the need for history, including his own history and the historically-minded leadership of Pericles, was a cultural artefact, although he also seems to have believed that some men, including himself and Pericles, possess a capacity for judgment not vulnerable to the pressures of circumstance. Thucydides also recognized that the *polis* itself and the polarization of the world of Greek communities were the product of historical forces. It seems to me unlikely that he believed that this polarization was the end-state of history, and could only be alleviated or exacerbated, that the Greek world was for all intents and purposes the only world to which prudence would ever have to attend. The likely shape of the future is implicit in Thucydides' history of past and present. Polarization was certainly the salient fact of experience. But Thucydides' portrayal of the transformation of Sicily under the pressures of war, while it fits the analysis of the effects of polarization, also hints at the possibility of changes in the structure of power within Greece, namely challenges to the hegemony of Athens and Sparta. As a move outside Athens' traditional sphere of influence, the attack on Syracuse also suggests the possibility of even wider Athenian ambitions, for example designs on Carthage.[104] And the emphasis in the Archaeology and throughout the *History* on action in common could be extrapolated to an eventuality certainly contemplated by others in the fourth century, namely a campaign by a united Hellas against Persia.[105]

[103] Geertz (1973) 26.   [104] See the comments of Alcibiades, Thuc. 6.34.
[105] E.g. Isocrates, *Panegyricus, Philippus*.

As a way of thinking about human interests, Thucydidean history, unlike the purportedly more stable kinds of theories explored by Democritus and advanced by Plato and Aristotle, discourages both cynicism and complacency. As a way of living politically, it encourages reflection within a social context, and facilitates the achievement of both autonomy and order: it binds men to a political understanding of their own good and challenges them constantly to revise and extend that understanding by examining the world and themselves. Thucydides' successors as political analysts, like Pericles' political successors, lost their nerve and succumbed to the degenerative force of circumstances; they turned away from the demands of leadership and history.

6 Democritus: reflecting man – the individual and the cosmos

While Thucydides argued that only as the citizen of a particular kind of social order could man come to understand the constraints on his ability to attain well-being and to act on that understanding, Democritus maintained that the way for the individual to secure his own good was to attend to his nature *qua* man. For Democritus, the order that shaped and expressed the exercise of human autonomy was not political, but cosmic. Man was part of nature. He must heed the stringent requirements of basic, physical well-being. Yet these requirements, though fundamental, were not, in the style of Antiphon, primitive. Atomism did not enjoin mere survival and the avoidance of physical harm, but a rich structure of behavioral and ethical norms tied, by a construal of human nature grounded in the nature of the cosmos, to intrinsic well-being. Because the normative constraints postulated by atomism, the view of the world as consisting of atoms and void, operated at the level of particles, they could serve as the foundation of order across the whole range of complex human behavior and interaction. The atomist did not need to appeal either to a crudely primitive or a socially determinate concept of man's nature and his good. That is, Democritus' account provides man with a way of understanding himself and his interests which is not defined in terms of those qualities associated with social status nor those required for and shaped by democratic political interaction. The norms postulated by atomism apply to all men *qua* human beings, not merely *qua* members of a social order or citizens of a democracy. Like the democratic vision of civic equality, atomist ethics rests on a concept of personal autonomy not limited to those with superior social resources and privileges. Atomism gives men reason to act in certain ways that are internal and yet more objective and stable than those established through political interaction. As an account of what the world is like at a level below, and underlying, the categories of human experience, atomism posits a form of double causation that does not interfere with man's conscious, and extensive, autonomy.

Atomism explains and legitimates the world as it appears to man, his access to understanding, his autonomy and his good, in stable objective terms by appealing to a non-phenomenal reality. This approach is centered on the attainment of personal well-being; it is at this level that the good can be secured. Unlike Thucydides, therefore, Democritus stresses man's capacity for self-sufficiency and reinterprets constraints usually conceived as social or political as inherently personal. As a result of this emphasis on individual good, and despite the flexibility and complexity of his conception of that good, Democritus has difficulty establishing a strong connection between personal well-being and a genuinely political order.

Assembling the pieces

Before I attempt to fill in this sketch of Democritean theory, I must defend the attribution to Democritus of any ethical or political theory whatever. While the principles of atomist physics are referred to and discussed by relatively early and reliable sources such as Aristotle and his student Theophrastus, as well as the late fourth/early third-century atomist philosopher Epicurus, Democritus' ethical reflections exist only as maxims preserved by much later epitomators under the name of Democritus (in the collection by Stobaeus) or Democrates. As a source, Stobaeus is probably somewhat more reliable than the compiler of the sayings of Democrates.[1] But the character of the two collections provides no basis for certainty that they include only genuine Democritean doctrine. We also have no general criteria for separating the authentic from the inauthentic – a very few fragments are confirmed by other more reliable sources (see B 188 with B 4, B 3; B 119). Echoes of ideas we associate with Socrates or Plato are not to be dismissed as inauthentic: Democritus was a contemporary of Socrates, and these could be genuine echoes[2] or independent and differently-oriented views lifted out of context precisely because they resembled the ideas of other philosophers. Other considerations of content are no more satisfactory as independent criteria of authenticity. Thus correspondences between certain fragments and the doctrines of later atomists could be the result of forgery rather than continuity.

Distinctions based on the form rather than the content of the frag-

---

[1] See Procopé (1971) xvii. 31 of the 81 sayings preserved in the Democrates collection appear in Stobaeus, and comparison of the two versions indicates that Stobaeus was drawing on a fuller account (see B 84, 264, 284). (The cited example also suggests that various collections of maxims were already in use by the time Stobaeus and the compiler of the *Sayings* assembled their versions. Stewart (1958) 180.)

[2] See Gosling and Taylor (1982) 28.

ments could prove more useful, not in providing an exhaustive division of the fragments into the authentic and the inauthentic,[3] but in identifying at least some fragments which can confidently be attributed to Democritus. The character of many of the fragments suggests that they were not originally designed as maxims. Some are syntactically incomplete:[4] others, though formally complete, are hardly self-explanatory. They are obscured precisely because they are not inward but point beyond themselves to contexts not supplied by the remaining fragments. The fact that Stobaeus does not designate the titles of the Democritean works from which he is quoting suggests that even the shorter, more epigrammatic fragments may derive not from a Democritean collection of sayings, but from a later compilation of extracts from various works. This hint is strengthened by an argument from silence: if a collection of maxims had existed among the genuine works of Democritus, quotations from it would appear in the doxographers, including Sextus Empiricus and Diogenes Laertius. The reference to 'pieces of advice' by Dionysios, the Bishop of Alexandria (DK B 118–19) does not undermine this inference, since he could well be referring to a post-Democritean collection of extracts. After listing the titles of the various works of Democritus known to him, Diogenes Laertius remarked (49): 'As for the rest, of those which some ascribe to him, some are furnished from his own [works], some are agreed to be from other [sources].' The first set of writings ascribed to Democritus by 'some men' may be the fragments preserved for us by the later epitomators.[5] The majority of extracts have evidently been abbreviated and deformed in the process of transmission (note the bare infinitives in B 41, 67, 74;[6] and the different versions of the same thought: e.g. B 84, 244, 264; B 44, 225).[7] By contrast, the longer fragments – including a number with social or political themes – seem to have been better protected, perhaps because they aroused less interest and therefore passed through fewer anthologies.[8] Thus interpretation of Democritus' ethical reflections should be grounded in the long and the best-attested fragments, and build from these a conceptual framework which can then be supplemented by those fragments which are less secure.[9]

Even this cautious procedure assumes that the fragments, in spite of

[3] See Procopé (1971) xxiii-xxiv on Laue's misguided attempt to do this.
[4] E.g. B 257, apparently the *de* portion of a *men/de* construction.
[5] Philippson (1929) 409, Stewart (1958) 187, who identifies 'some' (*tines*) as the cynics.
[6] Procopé (1971) xxxii.
[7] See also B 297 with Stobaeus 4.34, 62; B 187 and B 36; Stobaeus 3.17, 39 with B 214.
[8] The suggestion is Procopé's (1971) xxxiii n. 1; cf. Stewart (1958) 188 and 191 n. 44.
[9] Procopé (1971) xlii, Stewart (1958) 191 n. 44.

having been extracted from a number of different works, can legitimately be used to illuminate and supplement one another, i.e. that at
least the ethical fragments are discrete parts of a unified outlook. The
character of the fragments themselves (e.g. B 43, 45, 69, 107, 171,
214, 255, 257, 267, plus the long and/or well-attested fragments B 3,
188, 191, 266) suggests not merely that this assumption is warranted
(which would in any case be prima facie likely for a thinker as daring
and systematic in other realms as Democritus) but also that his ethical
theory was an extension of his views about nature, knowledge and the
soul. In sum, it seems plausible to suppose that Democritus composed
essays on ethical themes, and that these accounts were self-
consciously based on views about human nature and human well-
being. The combination of banal, conventional moralizing and
unusual claims and insights, both of which were probably incorporated in works of connected prose, suggests that Democritus was engaged in the project of providing new grounds for conventional
values.[10]

Democritus was a contemporary of Thucydides, a generation
younger than his fellow citizen of Abdera, Protagoras. According to
Democritus himself, in his treatise on the small world-order, he was a
youth when Anaxagoras was an old man.[11] One fragment reveals that
he visited Athens, where, he says, no one knew him (B 116). We know
nothing whatever about his sojourn in Athens (though it is reasonable
to suppose that he was exposed to the intellectual ferment excited by
Socrates, Anaxagoras, the sophists and others) or about his involvement, if any, in the politics of Abdera, about whose constitution at this
period we also know nothing.[12] Nonetheless, there is good reason to

[10] *Contra* Procopé (1971) xl.

[11] DK A 1. Diogenes also reports the tradition (preserved by Apollodorus, *FGrHist* 244 F 36
II 1030; see DK A 2) that Democritus was born in the 80th Olympiad (460–457). See
Bailey (1928) 109. Suidas (DK A 2) places his birth in the 77th (472–469), making him
Socrates' contemporary. Thrasyllus asserted that Democritus was born in the third year
of this earlier Olympiad (470) one year before Socrates (DK A 1). Both dates are compatible with Democritus' comment about his age relative to Anaxagoras; the later date is perhaps somewhat preferable, especially given the evident temptation to classify Democritus
as older than Socrates on generic grounds, i.e. that Democritus was the last 'scientific'
philosopher, Socrates the first 'ethical' one: Ferguson (1965) 18. Various sources assert
that he lived to a great age (DK A 4, A 5, A 6). It seems likely that he was a man of about the
same age as Thucydides and that he lived into the fourth century, perhaps long enough to
read some of the works of Plato.

[12] Abdera was on the coast of Thrace, a trading port and one of the richest cities in the Athenian League or Empire. Thuc. 2.29.1 indicates the presence of an Athenian representative
(*proxenos*), a prominent local personage at Abdera, and suggests a relatively close political relationship. Philip II absorbed the city state into the kingdom of Macedonia in the
mid-fourth century.

include him among those thinkers who confronted the issues raised by
the operation of a democratic *polis* and addressed them in a manner
sympathetic to democratic aspirations. The extant fragments include
reflections on the functioning of a system in which officials are responsible to the people (B 266), and a declaration that poverty in a democracy is evidently preferable to wealth in a city ruled by a junta
(*dunasteia*).[13] Democritus also reconstrues aristocratic values – good
birth and courage – in terms of self-control and prudence (B 57, B
214). More generally, the approach to prudence and social order
reflected in the fragments seems to be of a piece with the attempts of
Protagoras and Thucydides to interpret political order, unity and stability in terms not of the institutional dominance of a hereditary or propertied elite, but as the product of interaction between an elite of merit
(which tends, of course, to overlap with the above) and the mass of
citizens who must be brought not simply to submit to or recognize but
to *exhibit* prudence.

To notice the broad similarities in approach between Protagoras
and Thucydides, on the one hand, and Democritus, as represented by
the longer ethical and social fragments, on the other, is to begin to
specify the general context in which Democritean thought belongs,
and to understand Democritus' peculiarities, in particular his reliance
on an underlying cosmic structure. Protagoras and Thucydides, I have
argued, were influenced by contemporary developments in the understanding of both cosmos and *polis*, namely the attempts to explain
change and order in a world liberated from man-like divinities and traditional rulers. In the shadow of Parmenides and democracy, the
cosmos was characterized in such a way that order and change were
compatible. The sources of order were located in the world as it regularly and perceptibly is, and the sources of order in human affairs
within and among men. Free interaction resulted in order, in cosmos
and *polis*. This unified approach to the conception of order may be regarded as linking cosmos and *polis* merely by analogy. Indeed, Protagoras and Thucydides privileged the political conception of order,
associated as it was with divine providence, and regarded the question
of cosmic order as a threat to human autonomy. Until Aristotle introduced the idea of purpose without conscious agency, cosmic order had
to be explained either in terms of rational intervention or in terms of
materialism.[14] Thucydides excludes the possibility of double caus-

[13] The language of the comparison ('it is as much to be preferred as freedom is to slavery') is
one indication that this is not the utterance of someone who, like Plato, despises both
democracy and oligarchy, and for whom both are slavish.

[14] Allan (1965) 4; see Balme (1940) 27; cf. Barnes (1979) 115.

ation in the form of rational (i.e. divine) intervention and regards order in the world as the product of the pursuit of human purposes. Protagoras rejected the materialist explanation of cosmic order offered by Parmenides because it alienated the sources of order and stability from human experience and human purposes by postulating a world without change. Protagoras' man–measure doctrine forfeits the security of a perfectly stable, objective reality in order to secure the integrity of human understanding and humanly-contrived order. Atomistic materialism, however, seeks to make it possible for the ordering of the two realms, cosmos and *polis*, to be welded together, without sacrificing the stability and objectivity of the one or the autonomy of the other. Democritean realism depended upon a realist metaphysics, but a metaphysics that attempted to explain – not dismiss – appearances and man's experience of himself and the world. By uniting atomism and anthropology, Democritus reveals man's nature as a creature of both cosmos and *polis*. His theory proceeds at two levels, integrated by a conception of human nature: atomism is an investigation of the cosmos, an explanation of the existence, unity and continuity of the world we experience, including ourselves; anthropology is an exploration of man's needs, of what it means to experience that world as the creatures we are, both atomistically and phenomenally. Each level shapes and confirms our understanding of the other.

Appearance and reality

Democritean atomism succeeds in tying the autonomy and order in human existence to a cosmic reality by invoking the non-phenomenal to ground and explain the phenomenal. As a theory of cosmic order – a response to Parmenides – and of the order in human experience, atomism explains the world as it appears to us, a world of change and stability, in terms of an underlying, objective reality. Atomism was conceived by Leucippus as a solution to the problems raised by Eleatic musings on being.[15] Unlike Empedocles and Anaxagoras, who also struggled to transcend Eleaticism, Leucippus succeeded in formulating a pluralism which preserved both the unity of the cosmos and the reality of change and multiplicity.[16] He argued that the world was constituted by elementary, indivisible particles and the void. The particles differed only in size and shape. The things of the visible world therefore varied according to the size, shape, position (*tropē*) and

---

[15] See Furley (1967) and Mourelatos (1974) 17.
[16] See Arist. *GC* 325a23–8.

arrangement (*diathigē*)[17] of their constituent atoms. The atomists
were, therefore, in a position to explain the existence and behavior of
stable, self-reproducing compounds in terms of their components.[18] A
combination of circumstance (collision, a vortex, proximity) and the
character (size and shape) of the atoms results in the appearance of a
large variety of compounds (note that compounds differ from one
cosmos to the next).[19] Once together, the atoms of the compound stay
together because they interact so as to cohere in a stable synthesis.[20]
An account of the behavior of the compound must appeal not just to
the autonomous character of each constituent atom – though this persists – but to the structure of the configuration. Both fire and the soul
are made up of small, spherical atoms[21] yet each has a different, and
persistent, nature.[22] Moreover, the behavior of the compound – and
its stability – will continue to be affected by external circumstances,
e.g. whether it is the sort of compound which can survive and repro-
duce in the cosmos as it is. And the generation of worlds from particular collections of atoms in space introduces a conservative element
which makes the atomist account of order even more plausible: the
compounds characteristic of the cosmos we know are likely to remain
fairly constant and stable just because the rest of the (finite) cosmos
precipitated out of the vortex as it did.[23]

So far as we can tell, it was Leucippus who formulated the atomist
solution to the Eleatic paradoxes of being by reconciling multiplicity

[17] The term for particles is *atoma*, for shape *rhusmos*, for position *tropē*, for arrangement
diathigē. DK 67 A 6, Arist. *Met.* 985b4. Aristotle does not here mention differences in
size. See DK A 60a, and Arist. *GC* 325a30–3.

[18] Unlike the elemental materialists. See Waterlow's brilliant analysis of Aristotle's critique
of the materialists, in Waterlow (1982) chs. I and II, especially 81ff.

[19] DK A 40.

[20] See Waterlow (1982) 79 describing the materialist project which could not succeed
because of the elemental theorists' belief in natural motion. The atomists do not share Aristotle's view of elemental locomotion (see Englert (1981) 45ff.) and are therefore not, I
would argue, bound by the consequences of his argument. Atoms possess no qualities, differing only in shape or size. See A 49, 123, 125, 126, *contra* Arist. *De caelo* 326a, probably an inference from the fact that Democritus identified hot things as consisting of
small, spherical atoms. See Cherniss (1964) 120, 262 n. 181, 289f. with n. 3. On the contentious question of whether atoms have weight, see Englert (1981) 47–9, Kirk, Raven,
Schofield (1983) 421–3.

[21] DK A 106; Arist. *De an.* 404a1–7.

[22] *Contra* Aristotle's implication. See Cherniss (1964) 289f. with n. 3. For the atomistic
account of the soul as revealed and misinterpreted by Aristotle, see Arist. *De resp.*
482a25–30, *De an.* 403b29–404a16, 405a5–13, 409b17, *De caelo* 307a16.

[23] The peculiar theory of action and passion attributed to Democritus by Aristotle (*GC*
323b10) also has conservative implications for the world as it has arisen; cf. *Phys.*
252a34.

and unity, change and continuity in terms of the interaction of atoms in the void, while it was Democritus who elaborated and systematized the atomic world-view.[24] Democritus' eagerness to adapt atomic principles to the phenomena and to imbue those principles with a vividness which masked their stark remoteness from the world of experience[25] emerges clearly even from the fragmentary remains of his writings on atomic theory.[26] According to Aristotle, Democritus came closer than any of the other scientific philosophers to appreciating the formal as well as the material aspect of scientific explanation,[27] precisely because atomism attempted to do what Aristotle regarded as prima facie impossible, namely provide a causal explanation of the phenomena we experience in terms of a realm of inaccessible, unqualified, insubstantial particles. For Democritus, both levels of analysis were necessary; the material was invoked to explain the formal, but the formal might also serve as a guide to the interpretation of the material, given atomist assumptions. So, for example, the soul is essentially the source of bodily motion, perception and life; materially it is a configuration of small, mobile atoms, said to be such because of its essential features.

To explain how there could be order and regularity in the world as we know it without invoking any external ordering forces,[28] the atomists resorted to a non-phenomenal reality. They were not arguing either that the regularities of the world as we know it are simply the arbitrary consequence of real events at the level of atoms and void or that atomist theory could provide an adequate account of observable regularities and complexities solely in terms of the behavior of individual atoms. Democritus tried to indicate how an entity consisting of constituent bits of matter behaves as a unity, with its own complex and persistent nature and requirements.[29] Phenomena behave as they do because their atomic constituents are as they are, given that those

---

[24] See material collected by DK under Leukippos, Bailey (1928) 66f. Von Fritz (1963) 12f.; Aristotle, *De an.* 404a, says that Leucippus and Democritus gave similar accounts of the constitution of nature out of atoms. Furley (1967) 508 ascribes the argument for indivisible magnitudes (*GC* 316a11–34) to Democritus.

[25] *Contra* Brunschwig (1984) 120.

[26] von Fritz (1963) 19.

[27] Arist. *PA* 642a25–8 with *De an.* 404a9; *Met.* 1078b19–20; *Phys.* 194a20; cf. *De caelo* 306b30–307b18. Democritus combines the virtues of the *phusikos* and the *dialektikos* as described by Aristotle at *De an.* 403a29–b6. See also *GC* 315a35–b7, 315a13.

[28] See DK A 40, perhaps a response to Anaxagoras, B 4; cf. Kirk, Raven, Schofield (1983) 420 n. 6.

[29] See Waterlow (1982) 67, on Aristotle vs. the materialists. Again, the atomist escapes the Aristotelian objection.

atoms happen to constitute a particular thing, e.g. a soul in a human body. There is a causal, non-arbitrary connection between the behavior of atoms and the constitution or condition of persons. Democritus wrote on a wide range of topics, including not only ethics and politics but also astronomy, zoology, geology, mathematics, and musical theory (DK A 33). Whatever it might mean to say that these writings were the work of an atomist consciously working out the implications of a theory, it is evident that Democritus' desire to make sense of the phenomena in atomist terms extended to an account of human nature. He sought to explain phenomenal features of human nature – respiration, the capacity to initiate action, as well as features peculiar to man among ensouled animals, such as thought – in terms of man's atomic and organic make-up. Democritus invoked atomism to explain the behavior of human beings without *reducing* the phenomenal to its non-phenomenal constituents.[30] Perhaps particularly to a modern critic it might seem implausible that a materialist account of man could be intended to underpin, not undermine, man's capacity to understand and shape himself and his responses to experience. Does not materialism tend to secrete a host of other '-isms': reductionism, determinism and skepticism? To appreciate the character of the Democritean project, it is important to recognize that Democritus sought to account for the characteristic formal features of human experience: he was not a reductionist. He offered a theory of the world which is accessible to human reason via experience: he was not a skeptic. And his theory demonstrated and undergirded human autonomy: he was not a determinist.

To see that this is so, it is helpful to begin not with the fragments, but with Epicurus. For Epicurus espoused both atomism and human freedom, and he explicitly argued against reductionism, determinism and skepticism.[31] His allusions to Democritus in this context are revealing. In his treatise *On Nature*, Epicurus argues that skepticism, which follows from reductionist atomism, is self-refuting.[32] Epicurus' criticisms are not directed against Democritus himself, but against the

---

[30] Cf. modern hierarchical models of explanation in, for example, evolutionary theory, which 'recognize genes, organisms, and species as legitimate entities in a sequence of levels with unique explanatory principles emerging at each more inclusive plateau,' Gould (1983a).

[31] For what follows on Epicurus see Sedley (1983), which includes a re-edited and reinterpreted text of a portion of *On Nature* concerned with these questions.

[32] Sedley (1983) 34f.

implications of his doctrines, implications revealed not only by the teachings of his disciples but also by the practical consequences of attempting to live in accordance with those doctrines:[33]

The first men to give a satisfactory account of causes, men not only much greater than their predecessors but also, many times over, than those who came after, turned a blind eye to themselves (although in many matters they had alleviated great ills) in order to hold necessity and accident responsible for everything. Indeed, the actual account promoting this view came to grief when it left the great man blind to the fact that in his actions he was clashing with his doctrine; and if it were not that a certain blindness to the doctrine took hold of him while acting he would be constantly agitating himself. Wherever the doctrine prevailed he would be falling into desperate calamities, while wherever it did not he would be filled with conflict because of the contradiction between his actions and his doctrine. (lines 16–114)

Leucippus and Democritus, unlike the thinkers whom Epicurus has been criticizing in the earlier portion of the book, are not castigated as determinists who deliberately interpreted human behavior, including their own, solely 'in terms of material changes' and regarded 'talk of "intention," "desire," etc. [as] superfluous, with no additional descriptive or explanatory force.'[34] Rather, the first atomists are described as blind to themselves, that is to the devastating consequences for their own actions of a determinist doctrine. Democritus, the 'great man' of Epicurus' account,[35] was unaware of any conflict between his analysis of the world in terms of atoms and void and his own autonomy. The implication of Epicurus' comments is not that Democritus was simply ignorant of an obvious conflict but rather that he was blinded by his own doctrine, that the doctrine itself obscured the contradiction which Epicurus identified and, as he thought, dissolved in his own version of atomism. Democritus was not, in fact, 'constantly agitated'; there was for him no question of having to decide between, on the one hand, letting atoms rule by ceasing to make decisions and, on the other, making decisions and thereby flouting his doctrine. Epicurus, it has been argued, rejected reductionist atomism;[36] Democritus, I suggest, never adopted it. His doctrine was formulated in part as a vindication of human autonomy by means of an account of the internal determinants of human action. It was not absence of antecedent causation but absence of external coercion which was deemed essential to human freedom and autonomy. The

---

[33] Sedley (1983) 31f.   [34] Sedley (1983) 31f.
[35] Sedley (1983) 30.   [36] Sedley (1983) 34f.

'internal necessity' regarded by the Epicureans as the antithesis of free-dom was originally its hallmark.[37] Leucippus and Democritus were not physical determinists in the modern sense, nor did they construe their theory as a threat to autonomy via reductionism. In invoking the uncaused swerve of an atom to explain the mind's autonomy, in response to the reductionist psychology of the followers of Demo-critus, Epicurus was *not* responding to a vision of the cosmos as 'a mechanist world in which the behavior of the mind is inexorably de-termined from the moment of its birth, but one in which it is inexor-ably determined from moment to moment.'[38] Determinism as we know it 'depends on a belief that the further effects of a cause are as precisely regulated as the nearer effects, that transmitted motions are quantitatively determined – in fact, on an assumption of the principle of inertia.'[39] But the atomists, early and later (and their contempor-aries), and Aristotle assumed that this was not the case: 'Motions die out.'[40] Leucippus and Democritus were concerned to overturn *tuchē* (the uncaused, the purposed) and install intrinsic, natural causation in its place.[41] Aristotle's teleological critique of materialism's reliance on necessity and coincidence is not an attack on a universal, orderly nexus of causes, that is, *not* an attack on 'mechanistic determinism.'[42] For Democritus, atomic 'necessity,' the explanation of internal caus-ality, grounded man's freedom. He was not burdened by the trouble-some implications of the reductionism which concerned Epicurus.

For Democritus as for Epicurus, explanation of phenomena at the atomic level was insufficient.[43] The implication of Democritean doc-trine, whether or not Democritus ever explicitly addressed the question, is that phenomenal experience is also a particular configur-ation of atoms and void, and any change in the former must also be a change in the latter ('supervenience'); but the mind is nevertheless autonomous. The basis for this assumption can best be revealed by referring to Epicurus' attempt to establish, against the reductionism of the Democriteans, that man's 'self' is not reducible to his constituent

---

[37] It may perhaps have been a consequence of the early atomists' internalization of auton-omy that later thinkers sought a further, deeper definition of human freedom.

[38] Balme (1941) 27. Bailey (1928) 187f. and Barnes (1979) 232f. portray Democritus as a physical determinist.

[39] Balme (1941) 23, cf. 26. Cf. Sorabji (1980) 62.

[40] Balme (1939) 138.   [41] See Allan (1965) 15 n. 9.

[42] See, in general, Balme (1939) and (1941), esp. (1939) 137.

[43] See Sedley (1983) 34.

atoms and that man's character, not his atomic make-up, is responsible for his actions. According to the *On Nature* text, when, for the self-determining animal,

a development occurs which takes on some distinctness from the atoms on the basis of some discriminatory mode – not the mode which resembles viewing from a different distance – he acquires responsibility which proceeds from himself; then he straightaway transmits it to his primary substances and makes the whole of it into a 'yardstick' [*kanon*, reading conjectural].[44]

This account has been compared to the 'modern notion of "emergence"': 'In Epicurus' view matter in certain complex states can take on non-physical properties which in turn bring genuinely new behavioral laws into operation.'[45] The difference between Epicurean and Democritean non-reductionism is, I think, suggested by Epicurus' own distinction between a 'discriminatory mode' (an emergent feature of the mind or character) and a mode whose distinctness from the atoms rests in 'viewing from a different distance.' The 'different distance' is the phenomenal as opposed to the atomic scale, which registers the behavior of bodies as the behavior of persistent compounds, not as the interaction of constituent atoms. Epicurus thought it necessary to invoke a 'discriminatory mode,' to 'drive a wedge between causation by the self and causation by the atoms.'[46] Democritus did not see any reason to do so. For the acceptance of supervenience need not entail a *mechanist* or reductionist account,[47] and can explain how 'the self and its mental states, being secondary properties parasitic on configurations of atoms, could . . . control the motion of those configurations,' without invoking 'non-physical properties' or an 'external antecedent cause' like Epicurus' swerve.[48] As has been pointed out,

There is no reason in principle why secondary properties of configurations of atoms should not affect their motions. After all, the density of a stone is a mere secondary property of its constituent atoms, yet is capable of determining that the stone will move down when it is dropped in water . . . Although the motion of a single atom is fully accountable for in terms of primary physical laws, it seems perfectly correct to invoke secondary properties as causes of the corporate behavior of atomic compounds.[49]

---

[44] *On Nature* 27–35, Sedley (1983) 37.
[45] Sedley (1983) 39.   [46] Sedley (1983) 41.
[47] Compare Sedley (1983) 41 on the correlation of supervenience and mechanism with both his earlier discussion (pp. 39–40) and his later reference to Carneades' criticism of Epicurus (49f.).
[48] Sedley (1983) 39–41, 49–50.   [49] Sedley (1983) 39–40, cf. 49–50.

Democritus, I suggest, assumes some such account of the human configuration, which, like the stone, possesses properties not adequately explained as the sum of the properties of individual atoms, properties like 'soul' or 'mind' which serve as causes of the configuration's corporate behavior. The autonomy of the embodied soul resided in its distinctiveness as a phenomenal entity, in its capacity to affect itself as a whole and in relation to other compounds, in the possibility of organizing but not overriding or transcending its constitutive atoms, in short in 'the mode which resembles viewing from a different distance,' not 'some discriminatory mode.' It seems plausible to suppose that Epicurus is, in this passage, explicitly rejecting the Democritean version of non-reductionism, a materialist doctrine which assumes supervenience, and proposing instead a doctrine of emergence and transcendence of atomic motion. This supposition would help to explain why Epicurus resorted to the swerve instead of simply declaring, as Carneades in the second century B.C. suggested he should have done, that 'as a datum of experience . . . volitions do somehow exert an independent causal influence on matter.'[50] Democritus had already put forward such a view, based on a distinction between the atomic and the phenomenal.[51]

Although Democritus may well never have explicitly confronted the possible reductionist and determinist implications of atomism spelled out by his followers and attacked by Epicurus, he was, it seems, aware of the epistemological difficulties posed by a theory which divorces sensible phenomena from the imperceptible stuff of which they are composed. The threat of skepticism resided, for Democritus, in the gap between the phenomenal and the atomic and not, as may have been the case for the 'Democriteans' and Epicurus,[52] in the close connection between the two which accompanies a reductionist and determinist outlook. Whatever may have been the case with the

[50] Sedley (1983) 49–51.

[51] It was, I think, the early atomists' reliance on this distinction – on maintaining a significant gap between the two levels – which rendered them, in Epicurus' view, 'blind' to themselves, that is to the fact that phenomena, including the 'self' or the 'soul,' not only were atomic states but could be reduced to and were determined by interaction at the atomic level. Reductionism and determinism are not entailed by Democritean theory. But once these potential interpretations of the theory had been realized by the fourth-century Democriteans (Sedley (1983) 33), the delicately balanced view held by Democritus seemed 'blind.'

[52] Sedley (1983) 32–3, who suggests that Democritus himself was 'inclined to suppose that the atoms and void were real while the phenomenal objects and properties were no more than *arbitrary* constructions placed upon them by human cognitive organs.' *Contra*, see below pp. 211–15.

'Democriteans,' Democritus did not doubt the existence and regularity of phenomena, and his formulation of atomism depends upon the belief that the senses, and argument from analogy based on sensory experience, can provide clues to the nature of the regular relations between atomic constituents and phenomena. But precisely because of the distance between atoms and phenomena, Democritus did occasionally doubt the possibility of access to truth about the nature of the cosmos. It has been argued by some scholars[53] that these doubts amount to skepticism and disclose Democritus' deep misgivings about the status of his own theory. However, I maintain that Democritus does not reject sense perception and that despite his skeptical musings, he believed in the capacity of the human mind to know truth as well as to act autonomously.[54]

Not surprisingly, the two capacities are connected. Man's mental states – his thoughts, beliefs, reasoning – are atomic configurations. In a series of fragments preserved by Sextus Empiricus, himself a skeptic inclined to emphasize the skeptical aspects of Democritean thought, Democritus states (as the conclusion, apparently, of an argument)[55] that belief is for each man an alteration of constituent atoms,[56] an alteration which proceeds, another fragment suggests, according to the 'constitution of the body and of those things which flow into it and those which counteract.'[57] The corollary of this fact is that 'we know nothing in reality (*eteēi*) about anything'; we 'in actuality grasp nothing firm (*atrekes*)' (B 7, 9). And again:

A man must understand by this *kanon*, that he is removed from reality (*eteē*). B6[58]

Yet it will be clear, that knowledge of what each thing is in reality (*eteēi*) is inaccessible. B8

That in reality (*eteēi*) we do not grasp of what sort each thing is or is not, has been made clear in a number of ways. B10

[53] E.g. Barnes (1979) 258f. Cf. Sedley (1983) n. 41.
[54] E.g. Taylor (1967), Hussey (1972), von Fritz (1963) 21–3, Vlastos (1945/6) 389 with notes.
[55] See B 10: *pollachēi dedelotai*, B 7: *houtos ho logos*, Barnes (1979) 258.
[56] Reading *ameipsirusmiē* in B 7, with de Ley (1969) but the interpretation is not affected if *epirusmiē* is retained and read, as it is by, e.g., Langerbeck (1935) (cf. Kapp (1936)) and von Fritz (1963) 37, as meaning 'reforming' or 'reshaping'.
[57] B 9; Barnes's (1979) reading of *diathigē* (see p. 257 with n. 19) is an unnecessary and gratuitous change. On the relevance of *diathekē* in this context, cf. Theophrastus, *De sens.* 64.
[58] Barnes (1979) 258 translates without a comma: 'A man must know by this [i.e. the preceding] rule that he is separated from reality.' Given that the fragment is torn from context, I don't see how to choose between the two or to know what rests on the choice.

These fragments[59] have been torn out of context; it is difficult enough to assess their import but impossible to determine with any certainty their place in Democritus' theory. It is *possible* that Democritus prefaced statements which he understood to be devastating to the status of all human beliefs[60] including atomism with the comment that the statement is 'clear' (*delon* – B 7, 8, 10) or that man must 'understand' or 'know' according to the conclusion embodied in the statement (B 6). Perhaps he was simply being inattentive or deliberately paradoxical and ironic. It is, however, rather more likely that Democritus' observations in these fragments are, and were in his view, consistent with the belief that the mind can have knowledge of the world and of itself just as – and for the same reason that – it can act autonomously.

On such a view, the fragments can be read as reflections on the implications of a theory which relies on a qualitative gap between the phenomenal and the fundamental. The fragments are certainly open to this interpretation: what man is removed from, what he cannot know, what is inaccessible, is that aspect of reality summed up here, as in other fragments, by the Democritean term of art *eteē*, namely atoms and the void. That is, we do not 'grasp' the basic, unchanging substance and nature of reality (B 9, 10) because the very act of 'grasping' or perceiving is itself a change, in us and in the object.[61] As we ourselves are a particular and complex kind of atomic configuration, we are 'removed' from the level of atoms and void (B 6). This does not, however, mean that we are barred from all understanding of the external world. It has been argued that the Abderite arguments concerning the possibility of knowledge *eteēi* 'are equally arguments against reasonable beliefs . . . being atomically caused, [our beliefs] are not founded on reason; and the physics of the cognitive processes assures us that no impressions of external reality are accurate.'[62] This claim receives support from Epiphanius' account of the views of Leucippus, who allegedly said that we have belief, but nothing in accordance with truth (*kata aletheian*).[63] However, Epiphanius' chosen illustration, that everything 'appears like a stick in water,' i.e., presumably, bent

---

[59] See also B 117: *eteēi de ouden idmen. en buthōi gar hē aletheia.*

[60] As, e.g., Barnes (1979) 260–1 interprets these fragments they 'leave no room for any knowledge at all'; cf. Sedley (1983) n. 41, Taylor (1967) 19.

[61] Barnes (1979) 261 briefly raises the possibility of this kind of interpretation, only to reject it. See von Fritz (1945/6) 77. Cf. Taylor (1967) 23 on the 'limitations of knowledge.'

[62] Barnes (1979) 266.

[63] Barnes (1979) 260.

when it is in fact straight (67 A 33)[64] suggests that our impression of reality is not a delusion, or without content, but a distortion for which it is possible to correct. We cannot in any case directly apprehend atoms and void; nor can we rely unthinkingly on the validity of those things we do happen to apprehend; but we are capable of drawing reasonable inferences about the nature of reality on the basis of what we regularly sense or experience.[65]

Even the comments and citations of Sextus, committed though he is to interpreting Democritus as a skeptic, confirm this view. Introducing fragments B 9 and B 10, Sextus says that they are excerpts from a work entitled *The Strengthenings* in which Democritus 'promised to assign to the senses the power of evidence'[66] though 'he is nonetheless found condemning them.' The title of the work is itself revealing.[67] Diogenes Laertius remarks that the book was 'critical of what had previously been said.'[68] 'The strengthenings' may have been intended as a contrast to the title of Protagoras' book, *The Downthrowers*, in which case the criticism 'of what had previously been said' may refer to a critique of Protagorean doctrine.[69] Yet it was not the senses *per se* which Protagoras 'threw down,' but rather the capacity of the senses to attain knowledge of an unchanging, independent reality, so a critique of Protagoras which aimed to uphold the senses must have upheld them *as* enabling knowledge of the structure of the cosmos. B 10 indirectly bolsters this suggestion: in form, it evokes the man–measure doctrine ('we do not grasp how a thing is or is not'). The fragment, as Sextus notes, diverges from the main current of the argument of the book to (I have suggested) point out that we do not have direct access to the basic reality of things. Democritus may be alluding to Protagoras here in order to emphasize the rather different shape of his own agnosticism: there *is* a basic reality (*eteē*) which eludes and must elude man's direct 'measurement.' Whatever the exact content or focus of *The Strengthenings*, it seems that Democritus set out to demonstrate

---

[64] Which Barnes (1979) does not cite.

[65] See Taylor (1967) 22, for a possible description of this process; cf. Barnes (1979) 261.

[66] See Vlastos (1945/6) n. 60.

[67] The Greek term is *kratunteria*, or 'confirmations': the senses confirm the theory. See Taylor (1967) 21–2, Kirk, Raven, Schofield (1983) 412–13.

[68] DK A 33 cited and discussed by Taylor (1967) 22. Note Taylor's suggestion that Democritus is referring to his *own* previous arguments.

[69] Note that Democritus was said to have criticized Protagoras' theory of truth: B 156 and A 114, which reports that Democritus used a self-refutation argument against man–measure. In Democritus' view, Protagoras *must* appeal to the way the world is in itself, for otherwise the senses have *no* grip; to speak as if what the senses can pick up is all there is to reality is incoherent. See also note 97 below.

that the senses can provide evidence of the basic structure of the cosmos, if not 'grasp' the elements of any particular portion of it.

While Sextus concludes that 'in those passages [Democritus] pretty well destroys apprehension in its entirety, even if he explicitly attacks only the senses,'[70] he goes on to provide further evidence of Democritus' reliance on the senses supplemented by the power of the mind:

But in the *kanons* he says that there are two kinds of knowing, one through the senses, the other through the intellect; he calls the one through *dianoia* 'legitimate,' ascribing to it reliability for the judgment of truth, and he dubs that through the senses 'bastard,' denying it inerrancy[71] in the discrimination of what is true. These are his words: 'Of knowledge (*gnomē*) there are two forms, the one legitimate, the other bastard; and to the bastard belong all these: sight, hearing, smell, taste, touch. And the other is legitimate, and separated from that.' Then, preferring the legitimate to the bastard, he continues: 'When the bastard can no longer see anything smaller, or hear, or smell, or taste or perceive by touch, but more fine (*epi leptoteron*)'[72] . . . Thus according to him too, reason, which he calls legitimate knowledge, is a criterion. (*Adv. math.* 7.138–9)

This fragment has been said to reveal 'an empiricist Democritus rising in revolt against the sceptic.'[73] But here again, the passage is better interpreted as part of a consistent, if complex, set of beliefs. Note first that both 'forms,' legitimate and bastard, are described as forms of knowledge. The bastard form is not denied all access to truth but only, in Sextus' paraphrase, 'inerrancy.' Moreover, it is Sextus who divides the two forms of knowing into 'sensory' and 'intellectual.' Democritus himself in this fragment merely associates the 'bastard' form with the five senses, and says that the legitimate form is 'separate' and capable of making finer discriminations, but not that the two modes represent, for example, different 'organs' of perception: rather, the 'legitimate' form resembles, to use Epicurus' language, 'viewing from a different distance.'

Mind (*nous*) is, for Democritus, a particular condition of the soul and reflective understanding is a form of perception. Soul and mind are not *identical*,[74] but they are materially uniform or continuous. According to the doxographer Aetius, Democritus said that 'all things share *psuchē* of a sort, even corpses, since they share in some heat and

---

[70] Sextus, *Adv. math.* 7.

[71] *aplanes*; cf. *atrekes* B 9.

[72] B 11. See Barnes (1979) 258.

[73] Barnes (1979) 261.

[74] *Contra* Aristotle's inference, *De an.* 404a27–30; cf. 405a8–12; explicated by Philoponus, A 113; cf. A 105.

sensation' (A 117).[75] Aristotle associates Democritus with those thinkers who 'suppose thought to be perception and this to be (physical) alteration' and conclude accordingly that the phenomenal is true (A 112). Democritus did suppose that thought was a kind of perception, and that it involved physical alteration; but although all sensation is genuinely a perception of something, of some interaction of atomic configurations, not all sensations are equally discriminating. Not all creatures with souls have identical perceptual capacities: creatures which exercise reason can discriminate among the mass of perceptions[76] and the wise have more perceptions than animals without reason, just as gods have more than wise men.[77] It is precisely the material continuity of soul and mind, and the fact that perception is affected by physical alteration, which make the attainment of a discriminating distance possible. The 'legitimate reason' which supplements the five senses (B 11) is, as the fragment trails off, modified (in what way we do not know) by the phrase *epi leptoteron*, 'finer.' I suggest that this may refer not just to the scale of the object to be perceived[78] but also to the condition of the perceiving soul. The characteristic features of the soul are, for Democritus, as a variety of sources attest, due to the 'fineness' or subtlety (*leptomereia* – A 101) and mobility of its constituent atoms. Theophrastus reports that in Democritean theory, 'what is subtle (*lepton*) is hot' (*De sens.* 75). Here 'subtlety' may refer not to the atoms but to the character of an atomic configuration as a whole, in this case 'fire' (cf. A 73: the top of a flame contracts as it cools). So *leptoteron* in B 11 may perhaps be a reference to the feature of soul atoms which makes both perception and thought possible *and* (and in the context more appropriately) to a greater diffusion, quickness and extensiveness of motion which enable the soul to surpass mere sensory receptivity and is characteristic of it when it does so.

However Democritus may have visualized the details of the process – and the above suggestion is no more than merely a plausible and rather vague speculation – he evidently believed that the human soul was capable of intellectual discrimination, but that exercising this capability required some effort. Men could rest content with 'bastard knowledge,' the result of the haphazard impact of the world on their

---

[75] See Alexander, also cited in A 117; cf. Arist. *De an.* 409a32; for the distinction between powers of creatures with *psuchē* and those of man, see B 278; in B 164 note *psuchē*, not *logos*.

[76] A 115: note the implication that not all perceptions genuinely identify *things*.

[77] A 116: note the implication that wisdom is associated with perceptual capacity.

[78] I.e. the equivalent of *ep' elatton*.

senses, or they could shape their understanding more 'subtly' and achieve a discriminating distance from crude sensation.[79] After citing Democritus' views on the difference between 'bastard' and 'legitimate' *gnomē* (B 11, above), Sextus records a report that: 'There were three *kriteria* according to Democritus: (1) of the conception of the obscure (*adelon*), the phenomena, (2) of inquiry, thought, (3) of choosing and avoiding one's condition or experiences. We should choose that to which we are associated (related?) and flee that which is alien' (A 111). The meaning of (2) is rather obscure.[80] Whatever its exact import, (2), and (3) as well in a somewhat different realm, indicate that Democritus thought there existed objective, though not impersonal, standards of validity. (1) accords with other evidence that Democritus (like Anaxagoras) believed the 'sight of things unseen' must proceed from what can be seen or sensed directly.[81]

A fragment preserved by Galen, the second-century A.D. physician and philosopher, though interpreted by him[82] as revealing Democritus' awareness of the precariousness of his own theory, affirms the atomist's reliance on the phenomena. According to Galen, Democritus was aware that since he could not 'begin from outside the visible,' his conclusions, premissed on 'the visible,' were unsound. Thus, says Galen, he slandered the phenomena on which he relied, by contrasting conventional qualities (color, sweetness, etc.) with what existed in reality (*eteēi*), namely atoms and the void, and 'made the senses respond to the understanding' thus: 'Wretched mind, having derived from us the evidence, would you overthrow us? The overthrow is a fall for you' (B 125).[83] The point of this riposte is that man's higher faculties cannot begin or end elsewhere than in the realm of the perceptible, the phenomenal. The mind does not (indeed, cannot) show that the senses are mistaken, but on the contrary explains, at a different level, why they perceive as and what they do. The mind must not overreach itself, as perhaps it is tempted to do, by abandoning the senses for the imperceptible world to which the senses themselves have pointed. Here again is a hint of Democritean agnosticism: it is the

---

[79] See Vlastos (1945/6) 392 for the connection between Democritus' view of chance and his theory of knowledge. Cf. DK B 197.

[80] Taylor (1969) 26 'following the hint given by Sextus' reference to *Phaedrus* 237b7–c1' construes it as 'the criterion of the worth of an investigation is one's conception of the nature of its object.'

[81] For a brief discussion of contemporary uses of the principle, with references, see Vlastos (1945/6) 61.

[82] And recently by Barnes (1979) 261; *contra* Sedley (1983) n. 31 and Vlastos (1945/6) 389; cf. Taylor (1967) 19–20.

[83] The language (*dianoia phrēn, pisteis*) is reminiscent of B 11.

mind which must, in the end, retreat, if retreat be necessary. For man is incapable of direct knowledge of the behavior of atoms and void; his knowledge of their existence and general character is derived from phenomenal experience and answerable to it.

The tradition has preserved two Democritean examples of the mind's capacity to supplement and explain experience without rejecting it. The first consists in the merest of hints (a title: *Concerning Differing Judgments* or *Concerning the Touching of a Circle and a Sphere* DK 68 B 11l)[84] that Democritus responded to Protagoras' 'refutation of the geometers.'[85] Protagoras (B 7) had argued that a hoop does *not* touch a straight edge at a point. Democritus' answer is likely to have been that the geometers' definition seems at first sight preposterous, but that the more closely we observe a hoop and a straight edge, the more the area of contact approximates a single point. Of the two kinds of *gnomē* referred to in the title, the 'legitimate' completes the process that 'bastard' judgment began (there is no reason to believe that Democritus argued that an existing hoop – the physical embodiment of a circle – *actually* touches the straight edge at a point, but rather that it closely approximates the mathematical ideal). The second example is more fully preserved. Democritus posed the following puzzle: if one slices a cone parallel to its base, are the two exposed surfaces equal or unequal? If unequal, then the cone is 'stepped,' its surface rough; if equal, then the 'cone' is in fact a cylinder (B 155). Plutarch does not report Democritus' intentions, nor his conclusions. But it seems likely that the paradox was designed to show that we must posit some imperceptibly small but substantial quantity in order to explain why the cone, which *must*, if the perceptible distinction between 'cone' and 'cylinder' is to be preserved, be 'stepped,' looks smooth. Just so would the atomist have sought to show that we must posit atoms and void, which we cannot see or 'grasp' sensorily, in order to render our sensory experience intelligible and coherent.

The 'sight of things unseen' is thus achieved through the phenomena in two related ways. First, the senses 'grasp' the character and behavior of perceptible things and by analogy that of their imperceptible counterparts cum constituents, assuming, as Democritus does, that bodies with similar features will behave similarly, whether they are micro- or macroscopic.[86] So, for example, Democritus appeals to

[84] *peri diaphorēs gnomēs ē peri psausios kuklou kai sphairēs.*

[85] See DK's note *ad loc.*; and Vlastos (1945/6) n. 62.

[86] See Lloyd (1966) 338–9. This assumption has no place in a modern, hierarchical view of order, mentioned in n. 30 above. Democritus, however, had no access (e.g. via a microscope) to a world governed by utterly different principles.

the observation of motes of dust (to illustrate the behavior of atoms) and to the behavior of a crowd (to explain wind – DK 68 A 93a). The second way in which the phenomena point to the non-phenomenal is implicit in the 'tangent' and 'cone' examples just cited and is perhaps more fundamental. Sensory experience, when examined reflectively, often leads to contradictions or incoherence or lacunae which cannot be explained in terms of sensory experience itself. The 'sight of things unseen' to which the resolution of these matters leads is not (or not so much) an account of how things are, exactly, at the atomic level but rather the reasonable inference that there must be such a level and, in a general sort of way, an account of what it is like and how it explains what we perceive.

The tradition reflects the various aspects of Democritean doctrine without revealing them to be one theory. Although it is evident from the testimony of both Theophrastus and Aristotle[87] that Democritus ascribed the character of sensory experience to regular and persistent atomic features as well as to the human sensory apparatus, yet the atomist is lumped together with thinkers who 'thought "that which is" was identical with the sensible world' and that 'there would be nothing if animate things were not; for there would be no faculty of sense.'[88] In one well-known passage of the *Metaphysics* (1009b8–12) Aristotle comments that those thinkers who have 'inferred from observation of the sensible world the truth of appearances' have noted that animals and men experience various different sensations in response to the same thing.[89] Each of these sensations is a physical alteration;[90] it is caused; no sensation can, therefore, be regarded as more *real* than any other. This, says Aristotle, is the reason why Democritus says that either *nothing* is true or what is true is unclear (*adelon*) to us.

Atomism is designed to explain the phenomena.[91] By positing the possibility of innumerable minor alterations in the composition of imperceptible atomic structures, the atomists could explain, as Aristotle says, how 'the same thing' (i.e. a thing with a persistent phenomenal character) can in some respect 'seem different and conflicting to different people' (*GC* 315b11–12). According to Theophrastus,

[87] See, e.g., Theophr. *De sens.* 64; Aristotelian passages cited in n. 27, above.
[88] Arist. *Met.* 1010a2, 1010b30, cf. 1009b1–2; *GC* 315b6–10; *De an.* 404a27–8; Theophr. *De sens.* 63; Taylor (1967) 23–4.
[89] Cf. *Met.* 1009b3–4; *GC* 315b11f.; Theophr. *De sens.* 63.
[90] *Met.* 1009b13.
[91] See Arist. *GC* 325a24–9.

Democritus in some passages 'says that the becoming of anything and its being are real (or true)' (*De sens.* 71). There is, therefore (despite what Theophrastus says in his claim that there is another and contradictory strain in atomist thought) 'objective reality in sensory objects' (*De sens.* 70). But their reality is insensible. For Democritus, either nothing is true – men simply experience what they happen to experience, which tells them nothing about the basic features of reality that account for and explain that experience – or to us what is true is unclear (*adelon*) – we can make inferences about the 'real' substratum on the basis of phenomenal experience, but the substratum itself lacks 'formal' qualities and must remain unseen. The quality that sensory objects cause us to perceive is not a feature of their basic constituents as such, but of the interaction between those constituents and us (cf. Arist. *Met.* 1010b21). Although Theophrastus repeatedly accuses Democritus of a 'glaring inconsistency' because 'he no sooner declares [flavors] to be experiences [i.e. effects] in the perceptive faculty than he distinguishes them by their figures [i.e. shapes]' (*De sens.* 69), elsewhere Theophrastus himself points to the cogency of the Democritean account:

No one of all these figures is present, he holds, pure and without admixture of the others; on the contrary . . . the self-same taste includes figures that are smooth, rough . . . The preponderant figure exerts the most influence upon the perceptive faculty and the effect; and moreover the condition in which it finds <us influences the result>. For it makes a great difference <what our condition is>, inasmuch as the same substance at times causes the opposite experience (*pathos*) and opposite substances cause the same. (*De sens.* 68)[92]

That there is, in Democritus' view, a preponderant figure associated with each of a variety of different tastes suggests that atomism set out to explain not just the contradictory aspects of experience but also, reasonably enough, its stable and persistent features. Men tend to experience certain substances as 'bitter,' and 'bitterness' itself is a definite and identifiable sensation whose sensible properties lead Democritus to inferences, via metaphor, about the 'shape' of the atoms whose preponderance is experienced as bitterness.[93] Such an account can accommodate those few occasions when men taste as

[92] Cf. *De sens.* 72, where Theophrastus seems to accuse Democritus of having neglected precisely this aspect of the account – and perhaps he did, in terms of *specifying* the interaction; and Arist. *Met.* 1009b1–6, though it is unclear what Aristotle is referring to. Note the reference to health, here and in 1009b7.

[93] See Theophr. *De sens.* 70–1; cf. Arist. *Met.* 1010b20.

sweet something which most men experience as bitter. This need not mean (as Theophrastus supposes in criticizing Democritus' account as inconsistent, *De sens.* 69) that the 'bitter' shape fails to have the effect on some men which the account of its features is designed to reflect, but simply that, for reasons of his own condition (*hexis*) or a change in the configuration of the substance, or both, the man is influenced by the other atomic shapes in the mixture, i.e. that the preponderance of hooked shapes is in some way masked. Atomism is capable in principle of explaining *all* phenomena because it locates basic causation, and material continuity, in the realm of the imperceptible.

Yet atomism purports to be a genuinely explanatory theory; the world of atoms and void cannot be jerry-built, haphazardly, to 'explain' individually every observed phenomenon, but must possess a structure which meets and matches the structured world of phenomena. In setting out his theory, the atomist argues that a theory of this shape can best meet the most general claims of phenomenal experience and logic; he then seeks to show, where he can, that experience gives us access to the specific as well as general explanatory power and validity of the theory. Thus Democritus describes in detail the atomic character of those sensible qualities which are not only most amenable to, that is most vividly and directly explained by, such an account, but which also come as close as possible to being perceptions of the imperceptible world as it is said to be: he declared that in the sensation of bitterness, caused by small atoms with 'hooks,' we 'have a portion of understanding' (Theophr. *De sens.* 66, 71). All men recognize 'bitterness'; there is, therefore, reason to posit a definite atomic shape as the cause of the taste, and a shape of a particular sort which interacts in a particular way with the human body (see, e.g., *De sens.* 65ff.). Most men regularly regard certain substances as 'bitter'; there is, therefore, reason to suppose that these substances are stably composed primarily of atoms of a certain shape, and that the human body is (relatively) stably constituted so as to be affected in a certain way by such compounds. Atomism can also explain deviations and exceptions (indeed, as I have suggested, these anomalies are themselves evidence for the truth of a theory such as atomism), but only in terms of the plausibility of the theory as a whole and with reference to those regular features of the atomic realm which constitute ordinary sensory experience and can be inferred from it.

As I have already indicated, Democritean theory entails a certain fundamental agnosticism at the level of the specific and detailed atomic explanation of a particular sensory experience. For example, it is hard to see how one might confirm or prove that bitter atoms are 'hooked' as opposed to some other definite shape. The theory is not, however, riven by 'a fatal inconsistency' in the sense that it relies on empirical confirmation yet undermines the very notion of any judgment based on sensory experience being any truer than any other.[94] For atomism does not require the conclusion that all sensory phenomena are equally 'veridical.' All are *real*; all are genuinely constituted by the interaction of particular configurations of atoms and void. None are 'veridical' in the sense that they are direct *perceptions* of the atomic interaction. But some (indeed, most) register the persistent character of reality at the atomic level, while others are anomalous. It is the function of the 'legitimate' *gnomē* to tell the difference and to make the appropriate inferences, to discriminate when the other senses no longer can, to posit a reality which the five senses themselves cannot apprehend but which they can within limits, and once properly focussed, confirm.

Human nature

Atomism's appeal to a non-phenomenal reality to explain phenomenal experience constitutes a theory that is both objective and centered on man, his experience and autonomy. The world to be explained is the world man sees and experiences, and the theory is constructed via man's imaginative and intellectually rigorous interpretation of his perceptions. Man's ability to know what the world is like both depends upon and confirms his own participation in the atomist structuring of reality, participation which sanctions the autonomy and the order characteristic of human experience. Man's qualities of mind, his imagination and resourcefulness, which enable him to understand how he is constituted, are a function of his physical constitution. And it is the stability of that constitution which makes possible a general understanding of himself, the world and his place in it. Two otherwise rather puzzling fragments (B 165, 124) are intelligible as contributions to this picture of man as having a basic nature, constituted by his atomic make-up, which underlies the possibility of understanding the order, and indeed the existence of such order, in human experience.

Democritus evidently regarded 'man' as a significant and stable category of being with a particular faculty for apprehending the world, namely mind, a property of the soul. According to Sextus, Democritus asserted: 'I say this concerning all things: man is what we all know' (B

[94] Taylor (1967) 24.

165).[95] Like Protagoras, to whom he may here as elsewhere be alluding indirectly, Democritus believed that 'man is the measure.'[96] However, man is the measure for Democritus not because there is nothing that *can* be measured other than phenomena as they are registered by man, but rather because man himself has a nature *qua* man whose shape at the phenomenal level and interaction with the world ('what we all know') is genuinely revealing of the more fundamental, non-phenomenal, structure of reality.[97] This fact is relevant to 'all things' not only because man can extrapolate from his understanding of himself and his experience to the structure of the cosmos, but also because, as I have tried to indicate, man's stable nature itself determines what we experience of the world (a whole range of experience is 'mind-dependent') and (together with the stability of the rest of the cosmos) ensures that experience is sufficiently regular to be wrought into knowledge. Fragment B 165 expresses Democritus' belief that atomism preserves the phenomena, the phenomena confirm atomism, and that all men have access to at least some portion of this understanding through reflection on what it is to be man.

Democritus conceived of human nature as a stable category which transcended the individual and was defined materially, but which accounted for phenomenal experience and to which that experience gives us access. Democritus is said to have believed that the sperm derives and is composed of elements from the whole body (and not, as Plato for one alleged, from the head and spine). The source goes on to quote a Democritean statement: 'Democritus said "men are one and man is all"' (B 124). It has been suggested that perhaps Democritus was here referring to the existence of a unitary human nature.[98] And indeed, a passage in Aristotle's *PA* provides a context for the apparently incongruous elements in the report and confirms this hypothesis. Aristotle argues that it is the form or essence of the creature which is

---

[95] DK speculate that this may have stood at the beginning of the *mikros diakosmos*. This is an unconfirmable hypothesis, but one which would fit the view offered below. As Kapp (1936) 61 notes, Sextus is wrong to think Democritus was offering a (laughable) definition.

[96] See Vlastos (1945/6) 389.

[97] Like Plato, Democritus is said to have deployed the *peritropē* against Protagoras' man–measure doctrine (DK 80 A 15). This suggests that he construed man–measure as, like his own theory, making assertions about truth *simpliciter*, i.e. about the world as it is in itself (e.g. both hot and cold, or flux). Democritus seeks to preserve the earlier theory's capacity to legitimate appearances, while evading what he took to be its unacceptable implications by providing a non-phenomenal basis for the stability of the world and of judgment.

[98] Vlastos (1945/6) 389 with n. 67.

reproduced in every generation: 'A given germ does not give rise to any chance living being' (641b27–9). In this general discussion about formal cause, Aristotle considers and dismisses what he takes to have been a Democritean attempt to provide a definition of natural entities in terms of form, not just in terms of ultimate material constituents: 'Democritus says that it is evident to everyone what form (*morphē*) man is, seeing that he is distinguished by his shape (*schema*) and surface complexion (*chroma*). And yet a dead body has the same form of shape [as a living one], but for all that is not a man' (640b32–6). The reference to *morphē* is probably Aristotelian and the whole passage may well be a synthetic reformulation of various Democritean beliefs,[99] but it is likely to preserve genuine Democritean doctrine. In the *PA* as elsewhere,[100] Aristotle portrays Democritus as the scientific thinker who came closest to grasping the notion of essence, and presents him as a theorist struggling to explain the persistence and integrity of natural types. For Democritus as for Aristotle, the human sperm derives from and reproduces the formal properties of the whole parent, as B 124 indicates: all men share a common structure, or configuration, and each man embodies it. In Aristotle's view, however, Democritus had rested content with locating man's form 'in the realm of perception.'[101] The terms 'shape' and 'color' permit the Aristotelian construal, for they can refer to 'surface' qualities evidently not constitutive of a thing's 'essence.' Yet in the context of Democritean atomism, the juxtaposition of the two terms can be seen to reflect the peculiarities of a theory which, in trying to account for the stability and the fluctuations of the phenomena, constantly moves between two conceptually discrete realms, the phenomenal and the atomic. Thus color is a mind-dependent quality *par excellence*, a quality which does not exist in an object but only in the interaction between the object and a perceiver. Shape, on the other hand, is in atomist terminology a bridge between perception and nature, and a reminder that even color (*chroma*) is caused by certain definite features of the

[99] See Langerbeck (1935) 84–6, who believes that 'seeing that he is distinguished by his *schema* and *chroma*' is an Aristotelian gloss. Whatever the exact words of the original doctrine, however, Aristotle is unlikely to be distorting Democritus' views by citing *schema* and *chroma* as among those phenomenal criteria which enable us to distinguish a man from other species or objects. See Langerbeck p. 86 on Aristotle's use of *schema* to refer to phenomenal shape and to the atomic 'figures.'

[100] See discussion by Langerbeck (1935) 84–5, with references. See especially Arist. *PA* 642a25–8.

[101] Langerbeck (1935) 84–5.

atomic realm. *schema* evokes not just the outer shape of the human form, equally the shape of a dead body, but also the human configuration:[102] the persistent integrity of a material soul in a human body, and the atomic structure which constitutes the character of the whole.

Democritus' conception of a stable human nature could offer man an understanding of himself which both explained and respected the way in which he actually experienced the world, and which enabled him better to appreciate and secure his own interests. Democritus seems to have believed that man's own stability as a configuration, which underlies his ability to grasp a structured pattern in reality, also enables him to perceive the requirements of his long-term well-being, requirements imposed by his material make-up. As Democritus observed in what appears to have been a challenge to Protagoras, 'the good and the true are the same for all men; the pleasant differs for different people' (B 69).[103] This fragment does not say that 'the good is identical with the real,' i.e. that it is (an arrangement of) atoms and void.[104] However, the claim that the good and the true are equally unlike the 'pleasant'[105] in their stability and mind-independence amounts to more than an analogy.[106] The 'true' is not, at any rate in this fragment, interchangeable with the 'real,' i.e. 'atoms and void' *tout court*. The point of *this* fragment, so far as one can tell from the formulation itself, is not so much that pleasure/sensation is conventional, but that it is variable. Sensations are certainly caused and constituted by the interaction of atoms, but they do not reveal the consistent and stable connection that exists between atomic patterns and phenomenal ones.[107] What is the same for all men is this structure. The 'true' is a standard for assessing sensation; individual sensory perceptions contribute to the definition of this standard, but only once amalgamated and interpreted as the perceptions of man *qua* man do they constitute it. While fragment B 69 does not say that the good and

---

[102] Langerbeck (1935) 86.

[103] Cf. A 114; see Vlastos (1945/6) 388–9, Taylor (1967) 14, 25–6 for discussion of the issues raised by this fragment.

[104] Taylor (1967) 10, 14.

[105] The pleasant here involves the idea of 'sensation,' not only because Democritus also says that sensory perceptions may vary, but also because, as Taylor points out (1967) 25 with n. 51, pleasure and pain were associated by contemporary thinkers with *aisthesis*.

[106] Taylor (1967) restricts the significance of the fragment to an epistemological parallel – without asking what underlies the parallelism.

[107] Note this *re* Taylor's comments (1967) 14 and 26 that in Democritus' view every state of atoms and void and thus every perceptual judgment is true.

the true are equivalent, it does imply that they are equally the same for all men for the same reason.[108]

What is the 'good'? If it is defined simply as the condition which men over time find pleasant, then it is odd that B 69 is formulated as a response to Protagoras, who could have accepted such a definition and that the fragment emphasizes the variations in the experience of pleasure. It seems more likely that Democritus is appealing to a concept of human nature and human good which rests on an account of man's material condition *qua* man. Sextus' report on the three *kriteria* adopted by Democritus (A 111) supports this view: just as the phenomena are the criteria for grasping the obscure (*adelon*), the criteria of choosing and avoiding are reactions to experience characteristic of one's condition (*pathos*). So far, this is consistent with the view that Democritus is simply drawing a formal analogy.[109] But he goes on to elaborate the last point: 'One should choose that to which one is associated, and flee that to which one is alien.' That is, pleasure and pain do not of themselves indicate the appropriate choice. Democritus apparently[110] invokes a wider and more stable criterion of judgment, namely what is genuinely appropriate to one's condition. This inference gains further support from the fragments which are often taken as evidence of Democritean 'hedonism.'[111] In his characterization of human experience in terms of the interaction of elements, Empedocles observed that 'pleasures arise from what is appropriate,' that is from completion. Democritus appears to be saying something similar in fragment B 188: 'pleasure and dis-pleasure are the "mark" [or "measure"] of what is appropriate and inappropriate.'[112] Democritus may have echoed Empedocles in order to emphasize his own revision of Empedoclean theory. The pleasure referred to in fragment B 188 is the enjoyment which persists over time, the enjoyment associ-

---

[108] This would be true for Taylor's example (1967) 14 of 'red' and 'green.'

[109] And this is all that Taylor (1967) 26 cites.

[110] This phrase alone is not sufficient evidence, as it may be a gloss added by the source.

[111] See Irwin (1983b) on the difference between complex hedonism and complex anti-hedonism, and the difficulty of telling them apart. I argue that Democritus is a complex anti-hedonist. On this view (in Irwin's words) a person's good 'consists in some condition of which pleasure is a concomitant.'

[112] *horos sumphorōn kai asumphorōn terpsis kai aterpiē.* For a discussion of *horos* in this fragment, see Vlastos (1945/6) 388, Gosling and Taylor (1982) 32. Cf. the bizarre interpretation advanced by Langerbeck (1935) 65–6. He does, however, point out that *sumphoros* probably means 'appropriate' or 'suitable' not 'advantageous,' although the meanings overlap.

ated with overall well-being.[113] Democritus counsels men to 'accept no pleasure [*hedu*: a "particular pleasant thing"] which is not appropriate or beneficial (*sumpherei*)' (B 74).[114] The experience of pleasure is neither identical with nor a sure sign of a shift toward organic well-being.[115] In his claim that 'the pleasant (*hedu*) is different for different men' (B 69), Democritus appears to be correcting Empedocles: not pleasure but rather enjoyment of life is a mark of human flourishing, and enjoyment is not identical to the reconstituting of a healthy state of the organism, as pleasure is for Empedocles, but is the regular concomitant of such a condition. That is, Democritus, like Empedocles, envisions a desirable organic condition, but argues that pleasures must be assessed in terms of their contribution to this condition; and the 'sign' that this condition has been attained, namely calm enjoyment of life, is not itself constitutive of the condition.[116]

Taken together, the relevant fragments (B 4, 69, 74, 188) indicate that Democritus appealed to a standard for well-being or happiness (*euthumia*)[117] independent of both pleasure and enjoyment: a materialist standard, like Empedocles' 'mixture' or the Hippocratic 'equilibrium' interpreted in atomistic terms. The 'good' referred to in B 69 cannot be simply 'a state of untroubled enjoyment of life,'[118] for like pleasure (though far less so), enjoyment may vary from one man to another. Most men who enjoy good health do *enjoy* it;[119] and so, too, virtually all men who attain the serenity of *euthumia* will experience a sense of well-being; in neither case does the optimal condition *consist* in enjoyment. The puzzling fragment B 4 may be speaking to this point: 'Pleasure and displeasure are the mark or [measure] of those

---

[113] See Gosling and Taylor (1982) 31–2. Cf. B 189.

[114] See Gosling and Taylor (1982) 32 on the distinction between *hedu* and *terpsis*, not strictly preserved by Democritus. Barnes (1979) 230 reads 'regard nothing as pleasurable'; this makes reconciliation with B 188 apparently easier by focussing not on the difference between a particular pleasure and overall enjoyment, but on one's attitude toward sensations. If Barnes were right, one would expect a 'truly' or something of the sort.

[115] Gosling and Taylor (1982) 36–7 dissociate Democritus from the 'physiological tradition' represented by Empedocles, because 'there is no direct evidence that he associated pleasure with any particular physical process . . .' But for their argument from the silence of Theophrastus, see p. 22.

[116] A distinction denied to Democritus by Gosling and Taylor (1982) 33. However, reconciliation of the relevant fragments (esp. B 4, 69, 74, 188) requires the assumption that he appealed to an independent standard of well-being.

[117] *euthumia* is Democritus' term of art for flourishing, which in most writers is denoted by *eudaimonia*.

[118] As Gosling and Taylor (1982) 35 allege.

[119] I owe this formulation to T. H. Irwin.

who are fully formed.'[120] Perhaps, in context, Democritus was maintaining that the standard or mark referred to in fragment B 188 is the
enjoyment or distress experienced by those who are in their prime,
those whose experience provides a standard of normality.[121] But however valid this interpretation of B 4, it remains the case that the fragments discussed, taken as a group and as formulated in response to the
theories of Empedocles and Protagoras, point to Democritus' reliance
on an organic definition of well-being. Other fragments emphasize
that control of the desire for pleasure is essential (B 214), that some
pleasures are damaging, others appropriate (B 207, B 189), and that
the moderation crucial to *euthumia* (B 191) enhances and enlarges
pleasure (B 211, B 194, B 232). Enjoyment of life is a sign of living well
and properly (cf. B 200, B 201 with B 202–3), and the evident desir-
ability of enjoyment (B 230, B 200) is adduced as a reason to observe
moderation (B 233). But all men, whatever their cravings, have a real
interest in living temperately: 'Doing the opposite they become betrayers of health by desires (*epithumia*)' (B 234).[122]

It might, however, be objected that this characterization of the self
has nothing to do with atomism *per se* but simply combats the contemporary externalization of what man takes to be good for himself
by appealing to man's experience of the consequences of indulging
ephemeral pleasures or of failing to control his desires.[123] And indeed,
Democritus does appeal to what men experience, to phenomena; this
is the strength of his interpretation of the cosmos and of its human
portion. But, as I have already argued with respect to atomism as a
physical theory, the power of the interpretation rests in its ability to
explain phenomenal experience by appealing to a reality which is not
phenomenal but which is intelligibly and causally connected to the
world as we perceive it. *euthumia* is a physical as well as a psychological condition. Yet the claim that Democritus deployed physics as the
foundation of ethics[124] has recently been challenged on the grounds

[120] *terpsis gar kai aterpiē houros tōn periekmakotōn. peri* as at LSJ I, 'all round' or II,
'exceedingly.' DK try to make this fragment repeat B 188, but this seems to me illicit:
periekmakotōn, as Langerbeck points out (1935) 64, is too colorful a word to have been
inserted by Clements into his otherwise dry report. See Langerbeck's discussion, though I
do not follow him in his interpretation of the fragment.

[121] Cf. Arist. *EN* 1113a31–1113b1.

[122] *Contra* the view of Gosling and Taylor (1982) 33 that Democritus did not distinguish the
desirable, and concomitantly pleasant life, from the life which is desirable because it is
pleasant.

[123] Taylor (1967) adopts the view that Democritean ethics appeals to man solely at this level.

[124] See the classic article by Vlastos (1945/6) to which I am deeply indebted. Cf. Taylor
(1967), who suggests a link between ethics and epistemology; Gosling and Taylor (1982)
37. Barnes (1979) 232 dismisses this possibility a priori.

that we have no evidence that or how Democritus envisioned the physical condition of the *euthumos* and how it might be secured.[125] Before considering this claim, it is important to point out that we should not expect a Democritean account of the physical basis of well-being either to be detailed in its references to atomic structure or to be expressed in terms which cannot also be construed metaphorically. For Democritus did not in general attempt to provide specific descriptions of the atomic make-up (shape, disposition, arrangement) of particular compounds, and he sought to connect the phenomenal and the non-phenomenal by describing atoms in terms appropriate to the world of experience and by invoking similar principles to describe behavior in the two realms.[126] Yet there is an important divide in atomism between the phenomenal and the non-phenomenal, or the perceptible and the imperceptible, even though the latter are characterized in phenomenal or 'sensible' terms.[127] Atoms are both characterized in such a way that their interaction makes sense of macroscopic experience and also regarded as alien to sensory perception.[128] This is essential to the cogency of atomism as a theory of the world: for example, atomic compounds persist precisely because atoms do not exhibit the qualities of elements.

The use of analogies between the behavior of atoms and phenomenal objects to span the perceptually-unbridgeable chasm separating atoms and void from the phenomena they constitute applies to clusters of atoms as well as to particular shapes.[129] The metaphorical refer-

---

[125] Taylor (1967) 15–16.

[126] See von Fritz (1963) 19f., Lloyd (1966) 338–9; cf. Barnes (1979) 68–75.

[127] Barnes (1979) 68f. has suggested that the atomists did not mean to 'distinguish between sensible and non-sensible qualities and to deny their atoms the former,' and that 'real' qualities (as opposed to conventional ones, B 9; Plut. *Adv. Col.* 110e; B 125; B 117) include shape, size, weight and motion, 'sensible' features of atoms. The relevant distinction, according to Barnes (1979) 74 is between intrinsic properties and mind-dependent ones. See the rough distinction in Theophr. *De sens.* 63 between qualities of phenomenal objects directly explicable in terms of the properties of atoms and void (weight, hardness) and 'affections of perception' (color and flavor). Cf. Arist. *Met.* 1010b. However, as Barnes himself observes (pp. 141–3) all atomic conglomerations are equally *nomōi*, so all qualities of phenomenal objects are 'unreal' and 'sensible,' while atoms and void are not. See Theophr. *De sens.* 71.

[128] Democritus has described the interaction which produces sensation as the interaction of men with bodies of particular shapes – as 'touch' (see Arist. *De sensu* 442a = A 119) – and in terms whose appeal to the behavior of phenomenal objects serves to explain why this interaction has the effect it does (see Theophr. *De sens.* 66). But this interaction is only analogically assimilable to the sense perception it explains: men cannot 'touch' or 'see' or 'taste' atoms and the void. We sense them, but not *as* what they are.

[129] See Theophr. *De sens.* 73–5.

ence of Democritus' characterization of the soul and its well-being is not an alternative to a physical reference, but its complement. Both the terms used by Democritus, *euthumia* and *euestō*, refer to man's well-being in the sense of flourishing, enjoying prosperity. However, it is, I think, no accident that Democritus chose these particular terms to express his concept of well-being. *euthumia*, whose root refers to a part of man, his *thumos*, describes the condition of the soul (cf. the dangerous desires, *epithumia*), and *euestō* refers to the atomic structure underlying that organic condition.[130] Whether *estō* is judged to mean 'nature' or simply 'being,'[131] it can be taken in 'an ontological, i.e. physical sense,'[132] and is likely to have had this sense for a theorist responding to the puzzles posed by Parmenides and his followers. For Democritus, 'being' referred to atoms and the void. Diogenes describes *euthumia* as the condition in which the soul persists 'calmly and steadfastly' (A 1). It has been argued that these terms should be read simply as metaphors.[133] There is, however, good evidence for the contention[134] that Democritus was referring to a physical condition as well as a moral or psychological one.

The crucial text is part of fragment B 191, one of the longest extant fragments: 'Men achieve *euthumia* through moderation of enjoyment and harmony of life. Excess and deficiency tend to change drastically and to impart large movements to the soul; and souls moved from large intervals are neither steadfast nor *euthumoi*.'[135] If we regarded Democritus' language as purely metaphorical, then we would interpret *megalas kinesias* as meaning 'movements from one extreme to the other.'[136] But as I have suggested, it is a peculiar virtue of the Democritean approach that it is at once metaphorical, appealing to phenomenal experience, and descriptive, pointing to the substratum of atoms and void. Oscillation between extremes of pleasure and distress[137] is

---

[130] *estō* derives from the Greek verb 'to be.' See von Fritz (1963) 35; Vlastos (1945/6) n. 38.

[131] Vlastos (1945/6) 384: *phusis*, as in Doric philosophical writing; Taylor (1967) 12: Ionic verbal substantive 'being.'

[132] Vlastos (1945/6) 384.

[133] Taylor (1967) 12.

[134] Vlastos (1945/6) 383.

[135] As Procopé (1971) 92 points out, it is not *dia* (over), but *ek* (from, out of) *megalōn diastematōn*.

[136] Taylor (1967) 13; cf. Kirk, Raven, Schofield (1983) 432.

[137] Taylor's language (1967) 13. Note that the idea that extremes are undesirable is pervasive in Greek thought. See, e.g., Plato, *Laws* 732b3–c8, 733e10–734c1. At 728d8–729a2 Plato draws a connection between the condition of the body, a mean between extremes, and the condition of the soul which, when the body is unbalanced, will exhibit excessive boldness or abjectness.

destructive of man's peace of mind and well-being, as Democritus observes in other fragments (e.g. B 235). Emotional upheaval of this kind was regularly and plausibly, if not correctly, according to Aristotle, interpreted as movement in or of the soul (*De an.* 408b). In what sense, for Democritus, does the soul 'move from large intervals' when it indulges in extremes of sensation? It could be taken to mean that 'great movements' occur within the soul, i.e. that the soul atoms are in violent motion.[138] This interpretation is not easily derived from a phrase that refers to the movement of the *soul* as a whole,[139] and leads to the conclusion that 'the unhappy soul is distinguished from the happy one by the fact that its atoms move over greater intervals.'[140] There does not seem to be good reason or evidence to confirm that this was the Democritean view. Yet good sense can be made of a similar view, both as a reading of B 191 and as an implication of Democritean doctrine as reported by Theophrastus and others. First it should be noted that the atomic soul permeates the body. The soul has a persistent character and order, but part of what it is to be a soul in a body is to infiltrate it, so that soul atoms are interspersed among other sorts of bodily atoms. From this perspective it makes more sense than it first seemed to say that the movement of the soul is appropriately described as the movement of its atoms. 'Large movements' or movement 'from large intervals [or distances]' can then be seen to refer to the consequence of greater dispersal of the soul atoms within the body.[141] How is this condition of the soul in the body associated with 'excess and defect' or with the loss of well-being? According to Theophrastus, Democritus 'explains thought by the composition of the body – not an unreasonable view for someone who regards the soul itself as corporeal' (*De sens.* 58; cf. 64). As Theophrastus later observes, in Democritus' theory 'a man's physical state[142] accounts for his inner presentation' (*De sens.* 64). In the *De sensibus*, Theophrastus provides a number of clues to the connection between man's 'composition' and his experience which illuminate the doctrine of fragment B 191. Theophrastus (*De sens.* 58) reports that: 'Concerning thought, Democritus says merely that "it arises, when the soul's composition (*kresis*) is duly proportioned." But if one becomes excessively hot or

---

[138] Vlastos (1945/6) 383f., Taylor (1967) 13.
[139] Taylor (1967) 13.   [140] Taylor (1967) 13.
[141] Cf. the reference to *magnis intervallis* in Lucretius 3.566–75, with Furley (1967) 229–30; Lucretius' 'point is that the work of the *psyche* is a matter of restrained and ordered movement.'
[142] *he diathesis*, his 'arrangement,' an atomic term.

cold, he says, [thinking] is transformed. And it was for some such reason, the ancients well believed, that the mind became "deranged."'[143] The Hippocratic author of *On the Sacred Disease* 'thinks of violent motion in the brain as the physical condition of mental derangement, and concludes: "So long as the brain is quiet so long is man intelligent."'[144] For Democritus the harmonious condition of the soul, which enables thought, is not absolute quiet or rest, but stable orderly motion.[145]

Are we entitled to associate this harmonious condition, conducive to thought, with the avoidance of 'excess or defect' as well as of excessive heat or cold? The 'due proportion' required in the soul is reflected in the description of the *euthumos* in B 191 as enjoying a balanced or proportioned life – but this may be a 'mere' metaphor. The views of other somewhat later thinkers suggest (1) that it was common to regard the experience of pleasure and pain, especially excessive pleasure and pain, as affecting the physical condition of the body – not just its phenomenal condition but, as Theophrastus notes, the elements in the body[146] and (2) that emotions are commonly associated with temperature: Aristotle comments that the scientific thinker would define anger as 'a boiling of the blood or warm substance surrounding the heart' (*De an.* 403a30–1), and Lucretius observes that 'there is more of the hot element in those [like the lion] whose bitter heart and wrathful mind easily explode in anger,' while deer 'cower transfixed by the chilly arrows of fear' (3.294–307).[147] The Hippocratic author of *Visits* describes the physiological effects of 'sudden anger' (*oxuthumiē*), which include warmth, a debilitating condition eased or prevented by *euthumia* (*Visits* 6.5.5).[148] A link between such views and Democritean theory is provided by two obscure fragments: one associates psychic upheaval with raised temperature (B 152a = A 77); the other suggests that the harmonious and beneficial movement of the soul is undermined by strife (B 150). The aim implicit in the Hippocratic and Democritean texts is the maintenance of emotional balance – or a 'dynamic equilibrium'[149]

---

[143] See Vlastos (1967) 385. On the pre-Socratic interpretation of Homer's phrase about Hector, unconscious, 'thinking other thoughts' (*allophronein*), see Arist. *De an.* 404 and *Met.* 1009b. The latter passage cites Empedocles and Parmenides as arguing that 'when men change their condition they change their knowledge.'

[144] Vlastos (1945/6) 384. Cf. Kapp (1936) 167. [145] Vlastos (1945/6) 385.

[146] Stratton (1917) 50, citing *De an. defect.* 7.

[147] Furley (1967) 197. Note that man is somewhere in between.

[148] Cited by Vlastos (1945/6) 385 with n. 38.

[149] Vlastos' term (1945/6) 385.

– which is, like thought, associated with an even temperature, neither too hot nor too cold.

The connection I have sought to establish between emotional indulgence or imbalance and the extreme temperatures which, says Democritus (according to Theophrastus) derange man, making him incapable of thought, is confirmed by fragment B 191 and tied to 'excess and defect' once one views the fragment as both metaphorical and descriptive. 'Excess and defect' refer not to emotion and absence of emotion but to the extremes of emotion experienced by men who are upset by the gifts and blows of fortune. The men Democritus admonishes suffer emotional upheaval; they display envy and jealousy and hostility or ill-will (B 191). The effects of this upheaval on the soul – large movements, movement from great distances – are precisely those which are said by the atomists to accompany heat. Democritus discusses miscarriages caused by hot winds: the heat causes the mother's body to become porous, to expand and to dissipate (A 152).[150] According to Theophrastus, Democritus regarded heat as having an analogous effect at the atomic level. The 'sour' shape 'heats the body since it produces emptiness within; for whatever has most of empty space [void] <amongst its atoms> is most heated' (*De sens.* 65). This account of the effect of heat illuminates a rather obscure passage in Theophrastus' analysis of Democritean doctrine.

[Democritus] holds that none [of the sensory objects] has an objective reality (*phusis*), but that one and all are effects in our sensuous faculty as it undergoes alteration . . . For not even of heat or cold is there for him a *phusis*; but configuration [of the atomic compound] in 'undergoing a change,' effects an alteration in us also; since what is massed together in anything prevails in it and what is widely diffused is imperceptible. (*De sens.* 63)

The change undergone by a configuration (*schema*) in getting warmer or cooler is towards greater atomic dispersal and density respectively. The connection between the final clause and what precedes it is difficult to interpret, but Democritus (as filtered through Theophrastus) seems to be suggesting both (1) that cold objects, which are atomically compact, are more intensely or readily perceived by the soul[151] and (2) that the warmth or coolness of objects effects a change in the configuration of the soul, dispersing or consolidating its atoms, causing man to feel warmth or coolness and perhaps also causing the soul to be less or more acute sensorily (which links up to (1)).

[150] Vlastos (1945/6) 384–5 with n. 35: 'This is Aelian's account and we cannot press any of the words too far, though it is tempting to compare *diistasthai* with *ek megalōn diastematōn* in B 191.'

[151] See Stratton (1917) n. 149.

Heat, these texts suggest, causes diffusion of soul atoms, and thereby affects the soul's capacity to think (*De sens.* 58) or perceive. Heat and the corresponding condition of the soul are also associated with intense and fluctuating emotions.[152] Yet among compounds, the soul is relatively diffusely structured and is composed of small, spherical, very mobile atoms, like fire. It is therefore also relatively 'hot.' The soul possesses both characteristics that, for Democritus, constitute heat: it is rarefied and composed of fine atoms. According to Theophrastus, Democritus argued that 'the fine is hot' (*thermon gar to lepton*) (*De sens.* 75).[153] Elsewhere Democritus implies that it is 'fineness' which makes possible reflective understanding (*epi leptoteron*, B 11).[154] Both Epicurus and Lucretius observe that rarefied bodies or substances (like air) consist of atoms that rebound at long intervals while atoms that rebound at short intervals make up compact, hard objects.[155] Thus the soul is characterized by subtlety and diffusion; but there is (apparently) a level of diffuseness that enables the soul to function properly. Compare Lucretius, who argues that 'no doubt because the soul atoms . . . are contained within the whole body and cannot over great distances freely leap apart, for this reason they move, restrained, with sense-giving movements' (3.566ff.).[156] If, as seems likely, the mind was conceived as a concentration of soul atoms,[157] then the containment of their movements can be regarded as essential to the power of thought. For Democritus, the maintenance of the soul's integrity and order and of its power in the body requires not only that it be contained within the body, but also that its atoms interact over (relatively) moderate distances. The same conditions that are conducive at once to thought and to emotional equilibrium are constitutive of man's organic well-being, the proper functioning of the soul in the body. Thus intelligence and temperance or self-restraint are mutually reinforcing at the organic level, as well as in the more familiar form of prudence.

Democritus' account of *euthumia* is not, therefore, an empirical account of what men happen to desire, although *euthumia* does, he

---

[152] Note, in A 152, the reference to cold bodies not being tossed by waves; and cf. Theophrastus' account of Empedocles, *De sens.* 11, who by contrast links impetuousness to *compactness* of the elements.

[153] See Stratton (1917) n. 181.

[154] Note the fact that this description works at the metaphorical level: a refined, 'subtle' mind.

[155] Epicurus, *Ep.* 43–4, with Englert (1981) 64 with n. 38 (citing the Greek); and Lucretius 2.95–111, with Furley (1967) 171.

[156] Cited by Furley (1967) 229–30.

[157] Kirk, Raven, Schofield (1983) 429.

argues, contribute to pleasure and enjoyment. Democritus' argument
is an attempt to persuade men to control desire in the interests of
health by appealing to an objective criterion of well-being. It is not a
Socratic attempt to show that the wish to achieve *euthumia* is implicit
in everyone's existing wants or aims.[158] The good for man could not be
reduced to pleasure, which every man implicitly wants. The fragments
of Democritus are more reminiscent of the popular portrayal of incontinence than of Socrates' denial that it is possible, after reflection, to
want what is not good. The indulgence of ultimately destructive desires bulks large. B 214 reveals the emphasis Democritus placed upon
the control of desire: 'The brave man is not only he who is stronger
than enemies, but also he who is stronger than pleasures.' Some men
achieve this strength through habituation, rather than understanding
(B 53, 54, 178, 242). However, it is evident from the fragments that
Democritus believed that many of those who succumb to self-
indulgence and moral lassitude lack understanding of their own real
interest (see, e.g., B 237). Such understanding can help men achieve
euthumia: 'It is hard to fight passions. But triumph belongs to the man
who reasons well' (B 236). For Democritus as for Thucydides, reason
both interprets and rules. Understanding can secure noble things with
effort, he remarks; without effort, shameful things flourish (B 182).
Democritus' version of Empedocles' account of the organic appropriateness of pain and pleasure portrays the soul as capable of distinguishing between ephemeral pleasures and the enjoyment which
marks well-being, and as responsible for promoting the latter through
self-control.

   The implication of fragment B 191 is that men are capable, through
manipulation of their attitude to the world, of achieving psychological
and intellectual equilibrium and a correspondingly temperate (in the
literal and metaphoric sense) condition of the soul. Throughout the
fragments recurs the idea that the soul is responsible for ensuring and
is able to promote the well-being of the whole body–soul compound.[159] Not only man's own undirected initiative, but also teaching
and habituation (including, perhaps, the teachings of the atomist) can
shape man and by shaping him, make his nature (B 33). The term used
in both instances for making or shaping, *metarhusmiō*, refers to 'a
change in the ultimate physical *rhusmos* (configuration) of the soul-
atoms,' and *phusiopoiei* 'suggests the force with which Democritus

---

[158] Cf. Gosling and Taylor (1982) 35.
[159] See, e.g., B 187; Taylor (1967) 14 may be right about the interpretation of this fragment,
   contra Vlastos (1945/6) 382 but this does not make much difference to Vlastos' case.

grasped the idea of human nature in the making.'[160] Here again, it is important to keep in mind that Democritus' language attempts to transcend the barrier between the phenomenal and the atomic.[161] Atomic compounds have phenomenal 'shape' – thus the doxographers use *schema* to refer to atoms, atomic structures and phenomenal elements or objects (see A 73, 125, 132, 135). The *rhusmos* at issue in fragment B 33 is not 'the physical shape [i.e. visible shape] of the person taught'[162] but the order of the soul–body compound, an order which man experiences and which depends on maintenance of the proper relationship between soul and body and the proper atomic configuration of the soul. The term *ameipsirhusmiē*, change of configuration, is attributed to Democritus, and defined as 'to alter the compound or to transform' (B 139).[163] This interpretation of fragment B 33 as a claim that teaching can shape man's nature in an atomic as well as an ethical sense is bolstered by Theophrastus' report, mentioned earlier, that 'Democritus believes "men vary in composition" (*kresis*) according to their condition/experience (*pathos*) and age; whence it is evident that a man's physical disposition (*diathesis*) accounts for his inner presentation' (*De sens.* 64).[164] A fragment preserved by Stobaeus, one of a number of Democritean observations on the plight of 'men without understanding,' also illuminates and confirms the doctrine of fragment B 33: 'The *anoemones* are shaped (*rhusmountai*) by the benefits/gains of fortune (*tuchē*), men of understanding by the gains of wisdom (*sophiē*)' (B 197).

Physics and ethics coalesce in the atomist construal of human nature. Atomism could provide man with a new way of seeing himself and his interests: he is a creature whose organic and phenomenal well-being depends upon his own powers. Understanding of the way the world is – atomically and phenomenally – can enable man to appreciate the necessity of and the means to preserving a dynamic equilibrium. Democritus' conception of the good for man is both a particular

---

[160] Vlastos (1945/6) 391. See references in his n. 80. Against Taylor's objection that *rhusmos* 'was used as an atomistic technical term meaning the shape of the individual atoms, while the word for their arrangement was *diathigē*' (Taylor (1967) 14–15), Vlastos (1945/6, n. 79) points out that 'all we know is that *diathigē* was a term for this purpose,' and 'our data by no means preclude [the] use of *rhusmos* in other senses.'

[161] See von Fritz (1963) 36, *re* B 33: *rhusmos* is not only a metaphor, but traces the external aspect of a process to its inner coherence.

[162] Taylor (1967) 15, asserts that this is the only alternative, on Vlastos' account, to the untenable view that teaching changes the shape of the atoms themselves.

[163] *allassein tēn sunkrisin ē metamorphousthai*. Vlastos (1945/6) 39 with nn. 78 and 79. Cf. *ameipsikosmiē* in B 138, *peri ameipsirhusmōn* in B 8a.

[164] Cf. the reference to *pathē* in DK 68 A 111, discussed above, p. 219.

condition of the *psuchē*, a condition undermined by acting immoderately or unjustly or impulsively, and also a particular relationship with the external world, a moderation which is the product of mediation between the soul and internal and external circumstances, 'according to necessity' (see B 285) in the interest of well-being. Like the Thucydidean *polis*, Democritean man has two aspects: internal order and stability, and unified interaction with the external world. These two aspects are, in Democritean theory, mediated by the soul. The atomist account of the power of the soul constitutes a redefinition of the 'self.' The self ruled by the soul is the locus of freedom and control, and is constantly engaged in extending its own power and preserving its own balance in the process of mediating its relations with the external world. The power of the soul is the power to preserve the integrity and health of the self through constant reinterpretation of and adaptation to experience. The powers of self-affirmation and self-elaboration are complementary but differently oriented, the one inward, the other outward. The appeal to atomism linked to phenomenal experience (rather than to phenomenal experience alone) enables Democritus to argue that each man has intrinsic reason and the capacity to restrain his own desires. Not only man's well-being but his freedom, his capacity to pursue and to *secure* his own interest, depend upon the exercise of the powers of the soul.

Self-sufficiency

The internal aspect of psychic power appears in the fragments as the claim that man is free and self-sufficient, subject neither to *tuchē* nor to his own passions. What it is to be autonomous is to pursue one's own real interests, to act as a cause. Man is not the instrument of gods or laws, nor is he the plaything of fortune (the obverse of divine providence) or of pleasure. Democritus' choice of *euthumia* – rather than, e.g., prosperity (*olbos*), good fortune (*eutuchia*) or blessedness (*eudaimonia*) – to describe human well-being reflects his emphasis on the internal source of the condition. This term is the only one which refers to a part of man (*thumos*), and it 'stands out among the older concepts which all view fortune in terms of external circumstances or deduce it from external influences . . . *euthumia* is something which emerges from a man himself and is proper to him.'[165]

It it significant, too, that *euthumia* has the same root as the term which recurs in the fragments to denote the treacherous, greedy de-

[165] Von Fritz (1963) 34–5.

sires (*epithumiai*; B 224, 234, 235). *euthumia* consists in the proper ordering and control of desire. Fools, as the fragment cited earlier (B 197) observes, allow themselves – their thoughts, beliefs, desires – to be determined by whatever may chance to happen,[166] while men of understanding fashion their own interpretations of sensory experience and their responses to events because they interact with the world as creatures shaped by their own intelligence.[167] Those whose 'shape' – character, behavior, configuration – is determined by fortune (in the colloquial sense of the term) abandon themselves to excess (cf. B 191).[168] And, in a reconstrual of the traditional belief that triumph presages disaster, Democritus argued that abandoning oneself to the gusts of ambition and desire is an act of submission to *tuchē*, a refusal to take control of one's own fate. For 'when reckless daring is the beginning of action, *tuchē* is responsible for the end' (B 269).[169] Desires can 'enslave' a man (B 214); *thumos* is portrayed as an enemy to be conquered by thought (B 236). The soul must tame violent desires or be blinded by them (B 72), and it is wisdom which induces this self-control and unwavering perception: 'Just as medicine cures the body of disease, so wisdom removes sufferings from the soul' (B 31; cf. 290).

Thus 'a wisdom which is imperturbable is worth everything' (B 216). Wisdom and self-control (*sophrosunē*) are the marks of man's autonomy, his self-reliant refusal to be guided by the vagaries of 'fortune' rather than by his own powers. '*tuchē* is generous but unreliable. *phusis*, however, is self-sufficient. Therefore it is victorious, by means of its smaller but reliable [power] over the greater [promise] of hope' (B 176). What man can secure for himself through moderation or self-control (B 210) is in fact *secured*; what comes from the outside may seem splendid, but it is ephemeral.

Many of the ethical fragments can be interpreted as injunctions to men to understand that they are causes, that their world is to a very large extent mind-dependent. This liberating knowledge is in part achieved through awareness that the gods are, if not dead, at any rate

---

[166] 'Chance' in the colloquial sense of what seems fortuitous and/or is unanticipated, *not* in the sense of something *uncaused*.

[167] On 'bastard' knowledge, i.e. crude sensation, and its connection with the notion of chance, see Vlastos (1945/6) 392.

[168] See Vlastos (1945/6) 391–2.

[169] The most plausible reading of the fragment misunderstood by Stobaeus. See Edmunds (1972) 356.

insignificant.[170] Men of old, Democritus remarked, regarded all-powerful gods as the cause of all cosmic events, the rulers of the world for good or ill (A 75, 76, B 30). In another fragment, Democritus corrects this primitive view. All things may still be attributed to the gods, but their import for man is up to him (B 175). Men may 'reap ill' from those very things from which they derive benefit, but they can also devise means of countering the bad consequences (B 172, 173).[171] Democritus argues that men must abandon the idea that the gods are responsible for their fate: 'Men petition the gods with prayers for health, yet they do not know that they possess the power (*dunamin*) for this in themselves. Doing the opposite through incontinence (*akrasia*) they themselves become betrayers of health by (their) desires' (B 234). Running through many of the fragments is the theme that man's status as a cause, his freedom, depends upon the soul's (or mind's) assertion of control and responsibility at the expense of the gods and also of the body. The soul can ensure bodily health (B 159, 187, 223)[172] and the psychological well-being (*euthumia*) that accompanies the avoidance of sensual excess (B 189, 235).

Moreover, a soul that exercises its powers of control and of intelligence demonstrates the naïveté of the (potentially enervating) belief in *tuchē* (divine providence or chance). As atomist cosmology sought to demonstrate, *tuchē* is not a *cause*[173] but merely an apparently ordering and influential force external to man and outside his control, in reality consisting of a very few unpredictable (not uncaused) events. Order and necessity were not imposed, but created through the interaction of material constituents. The materialist assertion that everything is caused by material interaction, that there is no Zeus and only a human *nous*, struck a blow at once for the intelligibility of the cosmos, personal autonomy and personal responsibility; all three were compromised not by natural causality, but by the traditional belief in the divine, mysterious workings of *tuchē*. According to Democritus, *tuchē* is in no way relevant to what man himself genuinely is or does. 'Men have fashioned an image of *tuchē* as an excuse for their own lack of thought. On few occasions does *tuchē* conflict with intelligence; and most things in life can be set in order by an intelligent sharp-sightedness' (B 119). This 'image of *tuchē*,' like the belief in the power

[170] For a persuasive account of the function of references to divinity in the fragments, see Vlastos (1945/6) 382–3.
[171] Note that these three fragments are catalogued by Stobaeus under the heading *hoti oudeis hekōn poneros*.
[172] Cf. Antiphon, fr. DK B 2.
[173] See above, ch. 4 and Edmunds (1972) 353f.

of the gods with which it is associated, is destructive because it gives man a reason or excuse not to act as a cause in one of two ways: either by failing to exercise his full powers[174] or by treating as empty the very idea that a man has determinate powers. This last possibility surfaces in Democritus' warning that a man's *euthumia* is threatened by participation in activities 'beyond his power and nature':[175] 'When *tuchē* strikes him and leads him on to excess by means of appearance he must put this aside and not attempt things beyond his powers' (B 3). Understanding of his own powers, his own ability to preserve the proper balance in the soul, enables the agent to dismiss the seductive 'appearance' of *tuchē*.

It is his reconstrual of the self as virtually freed from *tuchē* and liberated from external coercion which constitutes the revisionary aspect of Democritean ethics. The conventional terms in which a man's worth or status was assessed made 'flourishing' a hostage to fortune, the gift of the gods or of mysterious 'chance,' as readily snatched away as bestowed. Democritus' emphasis on the power of the soul is a rejection at once of the traditional, socially-defined and divinely-sanctioned notion of well-being and the sources of order and, it seems, of a purely political understanding of them. For Democritus, order and well-being both depend primarily upon each individual's capacities, whatever his external condition. This is evident in his references to *eudaimonia*, the traditional term for god-given fortune and prosperity. According to Democritus, *eudaimonia* 'doesn't reside in cattle or gold. The dwelling-place of the *daimōn* [the god, the source of fortune] is the *psuchē*' (B 171).[176] The 'god' of fortune, man's fate, dwells in the individual soul. Democritus identifies the relevant features of the *psuchē* in another fragment: 'Men do not flourish (*eudaimonousin*) by means of their bodies or possessions, but by uprightness and understanding' (B 40). Elsewhere Democritus refers to wealth as 'so-called *eudaimoniē*' (B 251). Not only is wealth not equivalent to 'prosperity,' but the desire for it positively undermines the psychic stability necessary for well-being. Democritus repeatedly sounds this theme: the unbounded desire for material possessions is 'much more burdensome than the worst poverty,' for like indulgence in the 'mortal' pleasures or 'pleasures of the belly' (B 189, 235), covetousness is an appetite which 'breeds greater want' (B 219). The idea that personal serenity and a stable sense of well-being are more decis-

---

[174] See Vlastos (1945/6) 392.
[175] Cf. Thucydides' portrayal of the Athenians, discussed above, ch. 5.
[176] Cf. B 170, and Heraclitus frr. 9 and 119, cited by Kirk, Raven, Schofield (1983) 433 n. 1.

ive for man's happiness than his wealth or poverty is itself a radical transvaluation. The insistence that man is the guardian of his own fate leads to similarly revisionary interpretations of nobility, friendship and courage. Good birth (*eugeneia*) for cattle, says Democritus, is 'stoutness of body, while for man it is the good condition [or disposition] (*eutropiē*) of the character' (B 57). The well-ordered disposition (*tropos*) (an atomic term as well as a metaphorical one) ensures a regulated life (B 61), and this order is achieved not by luck or birth, but by understanding and effort (see B 33, 242). Friendship, Democritus asserts, is not a kinship relation [i.e. a matter of *tuchē*], but a bond among men who share a certain outlook, who 'agree concerning what is good or appropriate' (B 107).[177] And even courage, an aristocratic and a civic virtue, is interpreted as an attitude to oneself and one's desires: 'The brave man is not only he who is stronger than enemies, but also he who is stronger than pleasures' (B 214, cf. 213). A man's virtues and his social ties and standing are defined by features of his character.

Only character, the condition of man's self, soul and body, is potentially stable, reliable and under man's control: 'Reputation and wealth without intelligence are not secure possessions' (B 77). More than once Democritus refers to man's capacity to render himself 'safe' (*asphalēs*, B 3)[178] or 'self-sufficient' (*autarkēs*, B 176) by exercising his powers – intellectual and, in general, psychological – to the full. Self-sufficiency, *autarkeia*, is an achievement of the mind – not the capacity to provide for one's own well-being at some fixed level but the capacity to be fortunate whatever one's fortune may be. Democritus seems to hold out the prospect of complete immunity from contingency by making well-being largely mind-dependent. Thus 'courage makes disaster (*atē*) small' (B 213). And 'life abroad teaches *autarkeia*. The sweetest remedy for hunger and fatigue is barley-cake and a straw pallet' (B 246).[179] That is, an austere life awakens the recognition that man is self-sufficient: the mind experiences keen pleasure in the simple satisfaction of the most basic needs (see also B 223, cf. 230, 232). The theme is pursued in a number of fragments about man's capacity to exercise personal strength and achieve *euthumia* even in unfortunate circumstances, through force of mind and soul. 'If you do not desire (*epithumeō*) much,' Democritus declares, 'then a little will seem a great deal. Limited desire makes poverty as powerful as wealth' (B

---

[177] Cf. Creon's *civic* construal of friendship in Sophocles' *Antigone*, noted above, ch. 4.
[178] Cf. Thucydides' concern for *asphaleia*.
[179] Cf. Heraclitus fr. 111, cited by Kirk, Raven, Schofield (1983) 433 n. 1.

284). The point that man makes his own 'fortune' is expressed in two further fragments about wealth, and emerges particularly clearly when the two are juxtaposed:

Fortunate (*eutuchēs*) is the man who is *euthumos* with moderate resources, unfortunate (*dustuchēs*) the one who is miserable (*dusthumos*) with many. (B 286)

Prudent or reasonable is he who isn't distressed about what he doesn't have, but rejoices in what he does have. (B 231)

A prudent man is fortunate whatever his circumstances. Wealth and poverty describe states of mind, not states of affairs: 'Poverty and wealth are names for want and having one's fill. For neither is that man wealthy who is in need nor is he poor who is not in need' (B 283). The claim that poverty is as potent as wealth if it is not *experienced* as deficient indicates that Democritus was engaged in a radical revaluation of social norms.

Democritus' sketch of a self that is capable of creating and preserving its own internally-defined prosperity reflects one aspect of the power of the soul: the capacity to control one's response to circumstance so that, whatever comes, one may remain secure and unperturbed. In the long fragment on *euthumia*, after warning men about the dangers of psychic 'movement over large intervals,' Democritus declares that:

Therefore one must keep one's mind on what is possible and be satisfied[180] with what is the case, and have little regard for envied and admired things, not dwelling on them in one's mind. Rather one must consider the lives of the wretched, reflecting on their intense suffering, in order that one's own resources and condition may seem great and enviable and one may, by ceasing to desire more, cease to suffer in one's soul. (B 191)

Democritus believes that it is genuinely possible not merely to cobble together psychic well-being out of the life one happens to have, but also to shape that life into a life readily accompanied by psychic well-being by, for example, investing in certain pleasures rather than others (B 189, 233, 235). However, Democritus does suggest repeatedly that *euthumia* is a triumph of perspective. Men must accept things as they are but use the power of the soul to alter how they seem. Or rather, the reverse: men must accept things as they seem – that is, the external features of life – and use their power to determine how things really are, namely how the self is.

---

[180] *arkeesthai*, cf. *autarkēs*.

The soul as mediator

The claims of man's atomic nature are the foundation not just of well-being but of social order. The moderation of human experience by the soul (as mediator between the human configuration and the world) is, in Democritus' theory, at once the best possible condition for man *qua* man and the source of virtuous behavior toward others. In fragment B 191 Democritus argues (in the passage cited above) that the insatiable desire for more[181] is incompatible with *euthumia*, and that men must therefore adopt a perspective which will enable them to regard their own lot as enviable, and cease to desire more. For, he continues: 'He who admires those who have and who are called happy by other men, and who dwells on them in his mind all the time is constantly compelled to take some new measure and to desire to do something irreparable among those things which *nomoi* forbid' (B 191).

Men have intrinsic reasons and the inner power to act justly. Like Plato, Democritus sought not to redefine the conventions of just behavior but to reconstrue the self and its interests so as to show that every man has reason to be just. Man's freedom, Democritus maintains, rests in acting justly for his *own* reasons, not because of external sanctions. He observes that 'some men, who do not believe in the dissolution of mortal nature and who are conscious [*suneidesis*, a 'sharing in knowledge'] of the evil deeds they have committed in the course of their lives, suffer through life in disturbance and fear, shaping false notions of the time after death' (B 297). There is no life after death, no divine retribution. Consciousness of wrongdoing should shape one's experience of life, not reduce life to fearful anticipation of death. Man's consciousness imposes its own sanctions for misdeeds. This inner awareness of wrongdoing is – like the sense of serenity about one's own condition which arises from reflection on the lot of the miserable – part of the process of securing well-being by modulating one's approach to the world. According to Democritus, 'repentance for shameful deeds is life's salvation' (B 43). Taken together with fragment B 60 – 'it is better to examine one's own faults than those of others' – this suggests that what men learn from their own mistakes and failings, through repentance and reflection, can make their lives more secure.[182] It can do so in two ways: first, by strengthening man's

---

[181] *pleonexia*, in Aristotle's ethics the motivation that defines injustice. See Williams, 'Justice as a virtue' in (1981b) 30–1.

[182] The political interpretation of B 43 advanced by Procopé (1971) 297 treats the fragment in isolation from, e.g., B 60 and Democritus' pervasive psychological outlook. Note that it was thought desirable by, e.g., Antiphon 5.93, 6.1; Ar. *Knights* 184, to be free of *suneidesis* (Procopé (1971) 257). Plato and Aristotle do not use the term.

powers of self-control, his capacity to triumph over *thumos* (B 236) (Democritus observes that 'obliviousness of one's own wrongdoings generates insolence,' B 196), and secondly, by strengthening man's commitment to behaving honorably and justly for his own reasons.

Democritus' characterization of the autonomous self which can appreciate and secure its own well-being depends on an interpretation of man's *phusis* that transcends the conception of, for example, the sophist Antiphon, discussed in chapter 4, so that social order will depend on motivations more compelling than those founded on agreement, and more stringent than the primitive natural desire, even if 'all mankind fails to notice,' as Antiphon says (B 44a, Col. 2), to escape bodily pain and damage. Like Socrates and Plato, Democritus sought to revise the current conception of the 'good' so as to combat the looseness of fit of a social order freed from a traditional hierarchy, by restoring the notion of personal qualities as the source of well-being and order. These qualities were now to be considered as independent of social position, power or circumstance. In one fragment Democritus asserts that 'one should abstain from wrongful acts not on account of fear, but because it is needful' (B 41). What is needful (*to deon*) is distinguished from and preferred to fear as a motivation because fear is contingent on expectations about the way others will respond to an action, whereas *to deon* rests on the individual's assessment of his own interests. The latter, internal consideration is evidently a more reliable motivation, likely to guide man's behavior whether or not he is observed (see B 181). Fragment 41 implies the existence of an account which would show that it is in fact in every man's interest not to act wrongly. Democritus' emphasis on intention (cf. B 62, 68, 89) is also an attempt to suggest that it is an individual's steady grasp on what is 'good,' and not merely his actions, that reveal his virtue: 'The good is not just to abstain from injustice, but not even to think of it'[183] (B 62, cf. B 68). Democritus' point is not that consequences do not *matter* morally, nor that an unintentional act is not blameworthy. Moreover, Democritus is not arguing that a better state of affairs would result if everyone were to act justly from inclination, as the expression of good character, rather than from fear or some other contingent motivation, although his approach is in part motivated by some such belief; he is asserting that justice and injustice are to be evaluated as states of character (B 68, 89). The corresponding conditions of the soul are, respectively, good and bad *for* the agent.

---

[183] Or 'wish' it – *ethelein*.

Democritus defines man's freedom with respect to social as well as
divine sanctions, and his responsibility to himself to behave in ways
consistent with social order, by shifting 'inside' what was formerly
external. Man is literally *autonomos*: 'One should not respect (*aideisthai*) [cf. *aidōs*] other men more than oneself, nor be more likely to do
wrong if no one will know than if all men will. Rather, one should
respect oneself most of all, and establish this *nomos* for the soul, to do
nothing unsuitable' (B 164). 'Unsuitable' refers to three levels of appropriateness: to what is unfit or harmful from the point of view of
society, and to what is unfit for or harmful to the individual's soul and
his phenomenal sense of well-being. For Democritus, these three standards coincide in the injunction to cultivate wisdom and *sophrosunē*.
Democritus gave new force to this traditional and rather worn ethical
principle by arguing that violations of *sophrosunē* are their own
punishment. *hubris* will lead to downfall not because the gods are offended (there are no such gods) nor even because of civic sanctions
(which a man might well evade or override) but because excessive ambition or self-indulgence is the mark of a disordered soul, and a soul
deranged is unhealthy and vulnerable. Unlike Protagoras, in whose
theory *aidōs* and *dikē* are social virtues for which man has the potential because he is a creature who must live in society, Democritus
regards the same two virtues as features of man as an individual: *aidōs*
is self-respect, *dikē* a condition of the *gnomē*. A just mind (*dikē
gnomē*) garners praise (B 215). This 'glory' does not, however, consist
in peer recognition or material reward, but in confidence and that
imperturbability which Democritus believes is 'worth everything' (B
216). An unjust mind reaps fear of events (B 215). Internal well-being,
Democritus suggests, coincides with the fearless, unconstrained desire
to do those things which social order demands: 'The *euthumos* is
borne onwards toward just and lawful deeds, and rejoices both asleep
and awake, and is strong and free from care.' The man who lacks this
internal security and guidance is liable, rather like Antiphon's calculating citizen, to be anxious and constantly on his guard, as both the
requirements of justice and the sanctions of injustice appear to him to
be external and contingent: 'Whoever is ignorant of *dikē* and does not
do what is required, to him all such things are unpleasant when he is
reminded of them, and he is fearful and reproaches himself' (B 174).

In Democritus' ethical theory, the feeling of respect for the opinion
of others or fear of the reaction of others is turned inward; knowing
oneself, one comes to feel the influence of self-regard (see B 84, 244).
Moreover, the attentiveness to the soul and its equilibrium enjoined

by atomist theory requires that self-consciousness which generates the soul's internal motivation to do what it takes to be right. Man enforces upon himself a law which he alone has enacted. This act of self-legislation is an expression of man's freedom not, as in Kant's ethical system, because it expresses the autonomy of man's rational nature, which obeys the moral law simply because it *is* the moral law and for no other reason, but because it embodies man's own purposes, his pursuit of his own good. In reflecting on his own deeds and experiences, man comes to appreciate that the demands of just behavior are not external; they are demands which man is disposed to make of himself.

So stated, the Democritean theory sounds strikingly Platonic. In order to secure man's reasons *qua* man for behaving in ways consistent with social order, both Democritus and Plato radically reconstrued the notion of what constitutes human happiness and well-being. But Plato's construal required a substantial reorientation of man's understanding of his own experience, by making justice and the good a function of man's internal make-up and the make-up of society, not of man's *actions* or *powers*, so that autonomy and well-being consist in accommodation to an external order whose externality is masked by being cast in psychological terms. Democritus' construal, by contrast, is a radical reinterpretation of what is the case at the non-phenomenal, i.e. the atomic, *not* the psychological level, which leaves intact the teachings of man's phenomenal experience while providing a basic definition of man's nature and thus of his happiness and well-being *qua* man. The soul's power for good or ill is rooted in the capacity to mediate man's interaction with the world. In Democritus' theory, in contrast to Plato's, justice is defined not as a particular condition (a hierarchy) of the soul, but rather as a feature of man's attitudes to other men. Justice is one aspect of the dynamic equilibrium which the soul, in search of happiness and well-being, preserves between the self and the world as it is. The demands of justice are thus grounded in the definite claims of man's atomic nature, yet they are relevant to the condition of the self and to the circumstances it encounters. While the Socratic/Platonic redefinition of the self and its happiness as the exercise of reason insulates ethically-relevant considerations from the influence of circumstances or external constraint, the soul's inner freedom and order, its formal autonomy, is only one side of the Democritean equation, one aspect of the soul's power. Democritus' emphasis on man's capacity to be fortunate whatever his fortune may be is not to be explained away. It is an integral part of a

larger theory which does not, as a whole, represent a Socratic flight
from the influence of fortune and circumstance; but the astringency of
Democritus' vision of self-control remains, signaling an ambivalence
akin to Thucydides' ambivalence about the power of the *polis*. Internal order is essential to the imposition of order upon the world; but
perhaps it is safest simply to absorb life's bumps, and not strive to
shape its course. This ambivalence, evident in the atomist portrayal of
human nature as both an inward-facing condition and an outward-
facing capacity, emerges at a different level in Democritus' comments
on political life. However, the present point is that if Democritus'
theory was ambivalent, it was genuinely *ambi*valent. Man must confront the world as it is.

Democritus' rejection of the primitive theodicy of Aeschylus in
favor of atomistic materialism – his rejection, that is, of traditional,
providential *tuchē* – leads him to conceive of the constraint man
experiences as the consequence of the self's deliberations about its
own capacities and about the nature of the world it confronts. The
practical necessity implicit in the Democritean depiction of the self is
thus a secularized version of Agamemnon's plight, or of Ajax's reflection before he commits suicide: 'Now I am going where my way must
go' (Soph. *Ajax* 690).[184] The sense of constraint experienced by the
tragic hero is at once internal and external. The constricting webs of
circumstance are woven by the (obscure) working of divinities – and
patterned not providentially or in accordance with justice, but mysteriously and (apparently) irrationally.[185] This double causation gives
way, in Democritus' account, to the self's awareness that there is no
transcendent order, nor any ordering force in the world as it is other
than the human mind. Although the sense of constraint experienced
by the heroes of Aeschylean and Sophoclean tragedy may be rendered
in secular terms,[186] it is in fact the shift from the theism of these writers
to the 'a-theism' of the fifth-century thinkers which prompted and
required an ethics expressed explicitly in terms of practical necessity.
The external world, though in some respects still unpredictable and in-
comprehensible, is no longer in the same sense compelling. 'I must' is
the self's conclusion concerning its own capacities and incapacities,
reached through reflection about itself and the world it inhabits.[187]
Democritus not only places the burden and responsibility of deciding

---

[184] Cited in this connection by Williams (1981b) 131, to whom I am indebted for this notion
of 'practical necessity.'

[185] See Williams (forthcoming).

[186] As Williams has suggested, see preceding note.

[187] See Williams (1981b) 130.

how one should act on the self – not on the gods, not even on society or law – but he also insists that the necessity of acting in a particular way emerges from the interaction of the self-conscious soul and the world it experiences.

To say that Democritus sought to characterize man's good without reference to *tuchē* (providence, external determination, luck) is not to suggest that this good rested in a realm impervious to circumstance, but rather that it is the self's interaction with the world, not circumstance itself, which determines what and how he is. Indeed, as I have indicated, atomist theory makes it clear that this interaction, mediated by the soul, is decisive for man's well-being. For example: 'One should know that human life is feeble and short, and confounded by many calamities and difficulties [literally, incapacities] so that one takes charge of moderate possessions and so that suffering (*hē talaiporiē*) [cf. 297] is moderated according to what is necessary' (B 285; cf. 289). Personal moderation is not enough; man must accommodate himself to necessity. Moreover, in Democritus' view, he should secure moderate possessions – presumably because this will in fact, society being as it is, render him less vulnerable to life's calamities.[188] Although *eudaimonia* is not a function of wealth, and a poor but realistic man may be better off than a rich and deluded one, yet it is the case that most men will, in general, be happiest with moderate resources. Democritus' account of what men have good reason to be and do does not conclude that one's worldly condition is irrelevant. On the contrary, it is in part man's capacity to alter his worldly condition which constitutes his character and determines 'what the world permits'[189] – and therefore what he must do. Moreover, it is this capacity which makes man a creature who must constantly assess his needs, interpret the world and adjust his behavior.

Man and society as human creations

Reflecting man

The atomist redefinition of the self as a configuration ordered by the soul and the resulting relocation of the source of freedom and order to within the individual enables Democritus to span the gap epitomized by the contrast between Protagoras and Antiphon, i.e. to reconcile the claims of *nomos* and *phusis*. *nomos* is, for Democritus, an expression

[188] In B 3, Democritus suggests that one may be swept away by 'appearances' and desire more than one is capable of attaining.
[189] Williams (1981b) 130–1.

of what man needs and, over time, creates, yet this expression is itself limited by and grounded in human nature.[190] The atomist definition of human *phusis* serves as a standard distinct from social norms (an *internal* constraint), but it is not a reductionist or primitive account. Just as in its general explanation of phenomena, the atomist theory of human nature succeeds in accounting at once for the variety and mutability and the regularity of human experience by providing a non-phenomenal foundation for reality, Antiphon's characterization of what is 'natural' to man as the preservation of life cannot explain the existence and persistence of a system of social norms which is hostile to this end. The appeal to man's atomic configuration permits Democritus to argue that there is a stable 'good' for man without identifying this good with some fixed phenomenal experience, like longevity or pleasure. Indeed Democritus explicitly asserts that the mere desire to live, as opposed to the desire to be well, is characteristic of the foolish (B 199–206, cf. B 160). And pleasure is a necessary but not a sufficient condition of physical-cum-mental health (see B 74, 188, 194, 267). Well-being may take a variety of different forms; defined as it is in terms of the interaction of a material soul (with the capacity for rational thought) with the body and with the external world, well-being is relative to persons and circumstances, and it can be achieved at different levels. Man's unique strength as well as his vulnerability[191] rests in his capacity to elaborate and revise his aims, beliefs and attachments.

Democritus' interpretation of human nature permits him to explain the evolution and elaboration of the forms of human life – including *nomos* and the *polis* – while retaining an objective standard of well-being applicable to man *qua* man. Democritus' interpretation of the *polis* and its relation to human interests is an exercise in reconstruction and extrapolation, not analysis. While Protagoras had interpreted society in order to reveal the lineaments of human nature, Democritus characterized society as the context created over time by creatures of a certain sort. Protagoras unearthed man's social nature; Democritus investigated man's cosmic *phusis* and projected a society composed of and by human natures. The remaining scraps of Democritean comment on social practices combine references to contempor-

---

[190] The atomist's valuation of *nomos* and *ta nomisdomena* (what men believe), also has an epistemological component: there is an objective reality, but access to it proceeds by way of what men actually experience; and indeed much of what man experiences is not present *in* reality, but is the phenomenal product of interaction between man and other configurations.

[191] See Nussbaum (1986).

ary political interaction with general observations about customary behavior and allusions to apparently more primitive social conventions.[192] The character of the fragments does indicate that unlike Protagoras, who made analytical use of contemporary 'anthropology,'[193] Democritus preserved the historical approach of anthropological theorizing. 'Historical' here does not suggest the existence of proof, but merely that the project, not unlike Thucydides' Archaeology, was to fashion a plausible reconstruction of human development based on the criterion of 'likelihood' or 'probability' which depended for its validity on the assumption of the persistence of certain general features of human nature and action.[194] Although these features emerge through time as man elaborates and seeks to fulfill his own needs, they are grounded not in a historically revealed reality but in an atomic one. These fragments depict the phenomenal or outward aspect of the soul's power. The soul's function as mediator of relations between the internal self and the external world involved not just self-control and constant interpretation and adjustment, but also active alteration of man's life and his environment to meet developing human needs. Man is by nature a *nomos*-creating animal. Democritus' observations of man in society also suggest how a being of this sort might best elaborate *nomos* and pursue his interests in the world as it presently is.

Like Thucydides, who traced the course and exhibited the character of human nature, including the balance between judgment and passion, in the contexts constructed over time by the operation of this 'nature,' Democritus used a (naturalistic) historical approach to human development to reveal man's (phenomenal) nature and his needs. Democritus both reveals man to be a creator and interpreter who assesses and reassesses his own needs in the light of (collective) experience, and himself offers an interpretation of experience, an as-

[192] It is impossible to say, on the basis of the surviving fragments, whether or not Democritus himself formulated a connected historical account of man's cultural evolution, or whether he simply exploited an existing 'naturalistic and anti-teleological' description of human development. Cole (1967) *passim* and 47, with reviews by Solmsen (1969) and Furley (1970). Cole argues that Democritus was the source of all the later remnants of *Kulturgeschichte*. But I share Solmsen's and Furley's skepticism. Cf. DK *ad* B 5; Kirk, Raven, Schofield (1983) 405 n. 1, Vlastos (1946).

[193] See above, ch. 2, and Cole (1967) 51.

[194] Democritus' adoption of the 'historical' approach does not mean that he must have provided a connected history, a 'continuum' which 'thoroughly motivated' all 'stages in the development of culture,' as Cole (1967) 47 argues. As they stand, many of the relevant Democritean fragments are aetiological. (Cole (1967) 128–9 suggests they were digressions in a connected narrative.) Democritus used the naturalistic, historical approach to illustrate and interpret man's inventiveness.

sessment of man's needs. Unlike Protagoras, therefore, Democritus
makes room within a conception of social order for man's evolving
reflectiveness about his own interests within society, since for Democritus social practices are simply reflections of man's interests as he
perceives them, and must adapt to changes in man's understanding of
himself and the world. Despite the ability of atomist theory to provide
a stable foundation for complex and mutable phenomenal experience,
or rather because it provides this foundation at a non-phenomenal
level, Democritean ethical and political theory relies on an individual,
personal basis for the elaboration and attainment of human interests.
The social order constitutes a context and an external reality of which
man must take account, but the fundamental source of human well-
being is – and here Democritus differs significantly from Thucydides –
primitively personal. Man shapes himself; Democritus' own interpretation, therefore, appeals to individuals as such and not, as does Thucydides, via a particular form of political interaction to a political
construal of human interests in the world as it is.

For Democritus, man's uniqueness rests in his possession of reason,
of an intelligent soul.[195] Man 'thinks new thoughts every day' (B 158).
Man, like the rest of the universe, is composed of atoms and void. And,
like other stable atomic configurations, man is a cosmos, an ordered
thing (see B 34),[196] whose orderliness is the product of interaction.
Democritus uses the term cosmos to refer to human society (B 258–9;
cf. B 266). This reflects the general analogy between the behavior of
atoms and man which follows from the absence of divine design in all
realms and not, as has been suggested,[197] an 'atomistic' account of
social genesis which treats aggregations of men as aggregations of
atoms that must either constantly absorb new matter from other
cosmoi or collide with other cosmoi and be destroyed.[198] The fragment

---

[195] Democritus reportedly believed that animals and men were generated from mud (and not,
it seems, in the original 'whirl'): they emerged from the interaction of matter, without the
benefit of divine design (A 140). There is, however, no indication that man developed
from a non-human creature, that he evolved in his *phusis* in ways which were then transmitted biologically to his descendants. No glint of evolutionary theory appears in any of
the fragments of pre-Socratic 'anthropology' (including Empedocles). Even Anaxagoras
(DK 59 A 101, 102) does not adopt an evolutionary perspective on man's nature *qua*
man. (*Contra* Havelock (1957) 109f.) DK 59 A 102 should not be interpreted as a primitive version of the modern theory of 'gene–culture evolution.' (See Gould (1983) 5–6.)
Man is regarded by these thinkers as possessing a determinate *phusis*.

[196] Cf. Segal (1961) 83ff.; Cole (1967) 109f.

[197] By Cole (1967) 107f.; cf. Furley (1970).

[198] Even as an account of Democritus' understanding of the behavior of the cosmos, this
reading is suspect. See Furley (1970) on the interpretation of A 40.

cited as evidence that Democritus did formulate such an account is his comparison of the behavior of animals and inanimate objects to the behavior of atoms on the principle of 'like to like':

> Animals associate with similar animals, as pigeons with pigeons and cranes with cranes, and so with all other creatures without reason. And so also with the soul-less things, as it is possible to see with sieved seeds and pebbles on the beach . . . through the movement of the waves, oblong stones are thrust in the same place with other oblongs, circular with circular, as if similarity has some unifying force over things. (B 164)

The fragment does not imply that the behavior of men is also governed by this principle.[199] On the contrary: it 'illustrates sorting processes which do not involve conscious choice.'[200] The ordering processes characteristic of human interaction are marked precisely by the exercise of conscious choice. Man's *phusis*, defined both in terms of atomic configuration and phenomenal character, establishes his biological potentiality.[201] His actual condition is the consequence of the conscious choices of which he is capable, of his fruitful interaction with the world. Man differs from other animals in his ability to shape his own life, to make the world useful and more secure, to exploit what exists and create his own future.

One fragment indicates that Democritus observed that language developed haphazardly, that it expands and evolves.[202] Similarly, man develops technical skills gradually, by learning from his observations of the world around him. According to Plutarch, Democritus showed that 'we are pupils of the animals in important matters: of spiders, in the art of weaving and repairing, of the swallow in building homes, and of the clear-voiced swan and nightingale, in the art of song by means of imitation' (B 154). Some arts are so essential to human survival that they are promptly mastered; others are more recent developments, perhaps inspired by human desires rather than by urgent needs: '[Music is a young art.] It was not created[203] by necessity, but arose from the existing superfluity' (B 144). Democritus seems to be making a distinction between techniques of use, developed to satisfy needs, and the arts of leisure, which are cultivated for pleasure once

---

[199] As Cole (1967) 110 argues that *alogos* implies.
[200] Furley (1970).
[201] See Gould (1983b) on the distinction between biological potentiality and biological determinism.
[202] B 26, perhaps an indication that Democritus was interested in the issue of whether language is natural or conventional. See Cole (1967) 67–9; Havelock (1957) 118.
[203] Literally 'separated out' (*apokrinai*).

pressing needs have been met.[204] Still other practices are the consequence not of imitation of regular features of animal behavior, but of
the observation and exploitation of unusual occurrences. Aelian
reports Democritus' opinion that the mule is not the work of nature
but a human contrivance: '"And I suspect," said Democritus, "that a
mare became pregnant after she happened to be raped by an ass, and
that men were students of this violence and proceeded to [establish]
the practice of breeding [mules]"' (A 151). Man's achievements are
the product of cumulative responses to need and opportunity, shaped
by experience. An Arabic translation of Galen offers a glimpse of this
aspect of Democritean theory:

We find that of the bulk of mankind each individual by making use of his frequent
observations gains knowledge not attained by another; for as Democritus says,
experience and vicissitudes have taught men this, and it is from their wealth of experience that men have learned to perform the things they do. (DK 68 A 171 Nach-
trag)[205]

Man's creative powers are manifested not just in his technical
achievements and the development of useful customs, but also in his
constant efforts to understand and interpret his experience. Sextus
reports that according to Democritus 'Men in early times observed the
occurrences in the heavens, thunder, lightning, conjunctions of stars
and eclipses of sun and moon and were afraid, thinking that gods were
the cause of these' (A 75). Another fragment reveals that these early
men referred to the heavens as 'Zeus,' and interpreted the cosmos in
political terms, as ruled by a divine king:[206] 'A few among the ones
skilled in speech[207] extended their arms to what we Greeks now call
"air" [and said,] "All things Zeus declares and gives and takes away,
and he is king of all"' (B 30). Man is an interpretative animal who
analyzes and classifies experience and regularly criticizes and
improves on his understanding of himself and the world. In doing so,
he not only finds new ways of meeting his needs, but also reconstrues
those needs. It is the nature of man, unlike other animals, to elaborate
and revise his own way of life, inspired by considerations of utility.

Democritus' reflections on child-bearing include both an account
and an instance of this feature of human nature. He observes that:

Humans think it necessary that they should have children, [and they think this] as
a result of *phusis* and a practice instituted long ago. This is evident by comparison

204 See Havelock (1957) 119–20, Cole (1967) 43.
205 See Cole (1967) 58.
206 For this interpretation, see Cole (1967) 203–4.
207 Cole (1967) 57–8, Havelock (1957) 412.

with the other animals. They all have offspring naturally and not because of any benefit [to them from doing so]. When an offspring is produced, [the animal] suffers hardship on its behalf and nourishes it as far as possible and fears for it while it is small, and – should anything happen to it – grieves. Such is the *phusis* of all ensouled creatures. Among men, however, there has come into being an established usage (*nomizon*) that there is also some benefit from offspring. (B 278)

The example of animal behavior serves to isolate those aspects of human life which are attributable to *phusis*.[208] However, man's belief that he needs to have children arises not just from natural urges but also from the customary expectation, long since established, that children, in return for the care lavished upon them, will be useful to their parents.[209] In child-bearing as in his exploitation of the rape of a mare by an ass (A 151), his adaptation of animal practices (B 154) and his interpretation of celestial phenomena as the work of a king-like divinity (A 75, B 30), man organizes and elaborates nature for his own use. Moreover, as a further group of fragments about child-bearing (B 275–7) makes clear, man may even, through reflection on his own needs, decide to abandon certain forms of human behavior which are 'natural' as well as those which are customary.[210] In these comments Democritus himself exhibits the quality described in other fragments, namely man's capacity to reinterpret and transform his way of life. While in fragment B 278 he observes that men think it necessary to have children, Democritus asserts in fragment B 276 that *he* believes it is *not* necessary: 'For I observe in the possession of children many great dangers, many cares, and few blessings (and these slight and insubstantial).' Democritus here challenges both the natural urge to beget and care for offspring and the expectation that rearing children will prove beneficial in the end (see also B 275). However, for those who do believe they must have children, Democritus advises complete abandonment of the natural urge to do so and adoption of a calculating approach in the interests of one's own well-being and benefit:

For whomever it seems a necessity to have children, I think it better for them to take children from their friends . . . And this differs from the other, inasmuch as in this case it is possible to select a child according to one's disposition, out of many,

---

208 See Cole (1967) 110.

209 Havelock (1957) 117 and 122, anachronistically and illegitimately interprets *katastasios tinos archaiēs* as a reference to 'the establishment of sexual reproduction in place of spontaneous generation.' The development of *mores* of this kind is elsewhere (see A 75, B 70) associated with 'men of old.' See also Cole (1967) 112–15.

210 Cf. Cole (1967), who asserts that according to Democritus, begetting children is 'natural and unavoidable,' and 'follows inevitably from man's nature.' Cole does not consider frr. B 275–7. See also Havelock (1957) 122–3.

such as one requires. On the other hand, should one have one's own, there are many dangers. For it is necessary then to make what use one can of whoever happens to be born. (B 277)

The criterion of use has virtually supplanted 'nature.' Also implicit in these fragments is the suggestion, characteristic of the Democritean outlook, that men can and should exploit *tuchē*, not allow themselves to be governed by it.

The personal in the political

If, as Democritus' observations on child-bearing suggest, all established usages must continually be reassessed to ascertain if they do indeed still serve human purposes, this is particularly true of the social order as a whole. In the climate of opinion fostered by, for example, Antiphon in response to the questions raised by democracy, it must have seemed that civic institutions could survive only if they could be shown to express and secure man's genuine interests. Democritus, as I have suggested, tackled this difficulty by construing the individual's intrinsic interests as dictating behavior consonant with social order. In a remarkable series of fragments (B 257–62), he shows that the continual reflectiveness about one's interests enjoined by the atomist doctrine of well-being, which one might expect to promote cynicism and alienation, was itself essential to the ability of the social order genuinely to reflect human interests. Certain basic features of man's condition, as one man among others, remain constant. Reaffirming the existence of these features and their importance constitutes a contribution to man's constant effort to make the world he inhabits more useful and beneficial. The relevant fragments are the following:[211]

With respect to animate creatures [the rule concerning] killing and not killing in given cases is as follows: he who kills either a wrongdoer or one who intends wrong is exempt from punishment and to do this contributes to well-being rather than not [i.e. 'rather than to the reverse'? or 'rather than not doing this'?]. B 257

It is necessary to kill those things which do harm contrary to right (*para dikēn*), all of them in every way. And the one who does this will have a larger portion of *dikē* and security ['grounds of confidence' *tharsos*, cf. B 215] in every social order (*kosmos*). B 258

Just as has been written about enemies among beasts and creeping things, so also with respect to man it seems to me to be necessary to do: to kill an enemy in accordance with ancestral customs in every social order (*kosmos*) in which custom–law (*nomos*) does not forbid it. It may be prohibited by local religious

[211] My translations draw upon those of Cole (1967) and Havelock (1957).

sanctions, or treaty or oaths. B 259

Anyone who kills a highway robber or pirate is to be exempt from punishment whether he kills him by his own hand or by giving an order or by vote. B 260

It is necessary to avenge those who have suffered wrong, to the extent of one's power, and not to neglect this. To do this is just and good; not to do it is unjust and bad. B 261

Those who do something worthy of exile or imprisonment, or who deserve punishment, must be condemned by vote and not acquitted. Anyone who would acquit in violation of custom-law, deciding on the basis of gain or pleasure, does wrong, and this will of necessity be on his heart. B 262

These fragments have been construed as part of an account of man's gradual organization into social groupings for the purpose of protecting himself against wild beasts.[212] If one compares these observations with other ancient accounts of man's social development, it is argued, one can see that Democritus regarded political skill as compounded of justice and the skills of war: in order to defend themselves against other species, men had to preserve their own unity by enforcing peaceful relations among members of the group.[213] Certainly Protagoras establishes this connection: man's ability to protect himself by making war on his enemies, the beasts, is a social virtue dependent upon co-operation (*Prot.* 322b). Social unity and co-operation in turn depend on man's willingness to refrain from harming his fellow man. Presumably respect (*aidōs*) and justice (*dikē*) both prevent men from killing others who have done no wrong and require them to punish anyone who defies such constraints and commits an unprovoked murder. A late Epicurean source (Hermarchus) explicitly states that prohibitions against homicide within the social group and the absence of prohibitions against killing animals were both motivated by the desire to ensure security.[214] Hermarchus is offering an aetiology of present-day practices which draws a sharp line between social relations within the group and the treatment of hostile outsiders (other men, as well as animals). Protagoras, by contrast, is analyzing the nature of man as a species: he must co-operate if he is to survive. Interpretation of the Democritean fragments in terms of a homogenized mixture of Protagoras and Hermarchus and other 'anthropological' theories yields the conclusion that 'Democritus saw the origin of society's attitude toward criminals in man's early struggle for survival against other

---

[212] See Havelock (1957) 129ff., Cole (1967) 123ff.

[213] Cole (1967) 123–5.

[214] Reported by Porphyry, *De abstinentia* 1.10–11, cited and discussed by Cole (1967) 71ff. and 123–5.

species.'[215] Yet despite the fact that the Democritean fragments refer to
the killing of animals and the need to kill beings who themselves kill in
violation of justice, Democritus' point is not that justice within the
polis is an essential element of the capacity to wage war directed
against those outside, and his aim is neither aetiology nor an analysis
of man's nature *qua* member of the species 'man.'

There is no indication that Democritus is here concerned with
man's survival as a species. He says (B 259) that men should kill
human enemies as well as non-human ones; man's security – not as a
species, but simply as a *being* – depends upon protecting himself
against deadly animals, human and otherwise. Moreover, it is only
possible, not certain, that Democritus regarded hostile relations between man and beast as more primitive and more evidently necessi-
tating violent retaliation than, and thus serving as a standard for,
comparable relations among men.[216] And there is no sign of the connection, established by both Protagoras and Hermarchus, between the
promotion of justice necessary for social co-operation and the ability
to cope with external threats.[217] The constant refrain in these fragments is that any creature, man or beast,[218] that does wrong or intends
to do wrong may and should be killed. Thus *dikē* is not uniquely
characteristic of relations within the *polis*, but governs relations between individual man and all other creatures: it is necessary to kill any
being that injures, in violation of justice (B 258). To injure in violation
of justice is to harm a creature which has neither done any harm nor
intends any. Although the stress in these fragments is on the need to
kill to prevent such injury (any creature that 'intends' wrong is to be
punished) and to avenge wrongdoing, this is precisely because it is assumed to be wrong or 'bad,' and risky, to kill other creatures.[219] Consider the emphasis of Democritus' dicta: a man who kills a wrongdoer
is not to be punished; his action promotes well-being rather than its
opposite (B 257); the man who does this will improve his position
within the community (B 258); the need to do so must not be ignored
(B 261). And, in a fragment not yet cited, Democritus declares that

---

[215] Cole (1967) 124, with Havelock (1957) 129–30.

[216] As Havelock assumes (1957) 129. 'As has been written' in B 259 may well refer to what
Democritus himself has written.

[217] Elsewhere (B 250), Democritus remarks that *homonoia* is essential to success in wars
against other *poleis*, but no primitive version of this principle informs the fragments
under discussion.

[218] Note *zōa* in B 257.

[219] See Segal (1961) 116–17. Cf. the scruple governing Spartan treatment of helots, discussed
in de Ste Croix (1972) 92.

'justice is to do what is necessary, injustice to fail to do what is necessary, but to turn aside' (B 256). Throughout it is implicit that men dread performing such an act, perhaps because of fear of pollution, divine retribution or vengeance.[220] It may at first seem peculiar to speak of the killing of animals in these terms, but there were ancient prohibitions against such killing, and debates about the merits of such prohibitions.[221]

If this interpretation is correct, then Democritus is arguing that one must overcome personal qualms and kill threatening animals and men even when, as often in political society, one's own safety is not directly threatened. The fragments do not focus on the issue of self-defense *per se* (though B 257 and B 259 may be referring to it and B 257 to the killer's freedom from taint), but rather on the implications and necessity of acting to ensure that unprovoked harm to the members of a social order (from within or without) is prevented or avenged. Any man who kills a wrongdoer is assured not just that he will escape punishment for the deed (and Democritus may also be denying that he need fear the taint of pollution or divine displeasure) but that he will benefit personally and be honored by the community (B 257, 258).[222] In some social orders – perhaps the more advanced – the obligation to kill enemies 'in accordance with ancestral custom' is mitigated by other provisions laid down by the community (B 259). Moreover, to protect its members the social order contrives means of institutionalized, communal punishment, instead of relying on the strength and initiative of individual men (B 260, 262).

The force of Democritus' account becomes clearer by comparison with Antiphon's critique of the rule of law, discussed in chapter 4. According to Antiphon, the administration of justice fails to protect every member of society because (1) it cannot prevent the lawbreakers from victimizing those who obey the law or ensure that the former are punished, and because (2) it requires men to harm each other without direct provocation, thus causing them to violate a fundamental principle of justice and put themselves at risk for causes not their own. Fragment B 260 suggests that Democritus is concerned about issues similar to those addressed by Antiphon's second point. Highway robbers and pirates evidently qualify as men who do wrong or intend it to the community as a whole, although only some persons are directly threatened. Men who kill such persons can plausibly be

---

[220] Note *anekeston* in B 191, with Segal (1961) 116–17.
[221] See Cole (1967) 124 with n. 42.
[222] See Segal (1961) 116–17.

said to be acting in self-defense in the extended sense which informs all requirements on men to help enforce the ban on unprovoked violence. This is a vivid illustration of Democritus' more general argument (implicit in B 257, 258, 261, 262) that all wrongdoers and potential wrongdoers pose a threat to the community at large. Antiphon's point is that such an extended sense is in fact a violation of the principle of self-defense – that it is only just (conventionally) to harm someone if he has harmed you – and that the demand that men adopt the wider viewpoint exposes them to the risk of revenge, a risk they must take if the system is to function but which is unnecessary and dangerous with respect to personal well-being. Democritus argued, it seems, for the necessity and the justice (in this basic sense) of adopting the community-wide perspective. Fragment B 260 suggests that he maintained that even those relatively remote from the crime, whose action in condemning the wrongdoer to death is a violation of the principle of self-defense (narrowly construed), are to go unpunished. In fragment B 260, Democritus repeats his assertion that the killer of wrongdoers is to be exempt from punishment, but elaborates the point by distinguishing the man who kills the pirate or robber himself, presumably in the course of trying to prevent the crime, from those who are comparatively removed both from direct threat and from the act of retaliation. The latter respond and act impersonally, and they do not thereby risk hatred or revenge (by friends and relatives of the wrongdoer?) or any other sanction: they are to be exempt from punishment.

But how is society to ensure that those who act justly are not victimized and that those who do wrong are in fact punished? The issues raised by Antiphon's first criticism of the administration of justice are also addressed by Democritus. What ensures that the fit of the laws is *not* loose is precisely the same personal motivation that prompts the establishment of civic sanctions in the first place, namely the desire to prevent or punish wrongdoing (i.e. the harming of creatures who themselves mean no harm). Justice, for Democritus, does not – as Antiphon's account would suggest[223] – consist simply in acquiescence to the laws of the land. Justice is an active virtue: as he notes in one fragment (cited above): 'Justice is to do what is necessary, injustice to fail to do what is necessary, but to turn aside' (B 256). Fragments B 261 and 262 explicitly assert that those who have suffered wrong must be avenged: to do so is just and good (B 261). In fragment B 262, Democritus affirms that this principle applies to individuals in societies

---

[223] Antiphon's formula suggests a *passive* obedience, but note his discussion of the necessity of testifying against others.

which mete out punishment by law, individuals who may be tempted to regard their own good as resting elsewhere than in ensuring that the wrongdoer will in fact suffer. Anyone who, moved by the desire for gain or pleasure, votes to acquit a man who has done something worthy of punishment, does wrong, Democritus insists, 'and this will of necessity be on his heart.' The citizen who chooses to flout what is *nomos*, which is his own true safeguard, will feel burdened. This weight is both a sanction and a motivation: it is the reflective sense of having done wrong, a sign that one has undermined one's own well-being, and it is a reason not to do so again. Here as in his construal of self-consciousness, Democritus assumes that men will, and argues that they should, internalize the norms of society. 'The man who does wrong,' he claims, 'is more unfortunate than the man who is wronged.' Despite appearances to the contrary, Democritus is not, in Socratic fashion, disavowing the *lex talionis*, the principle of retaliation. On the contrary: what it is to do wrong is either to harm someone who means no harm, *or* to fail to avenge such harm. Democritus appeals to man's sense of security, confidence, and well-being in society, as well as to the sources of organic stability, to ground his argument that every man has an intrinsic interest in acting justly in both the passive and the active sense. If every man in society reaffirms the principle which, Democritus suggests, is a primitively personal principle of justice, namely that all harm to those who mean no harm must be prevented or punished, then the civic administration of this principle will in fact ensure that it is universally and consistently enforced, thus contributing to each man's security and well-being.

As the fragments on the killing of wrongdoers indicate, it is in Democritus' view self-consciousness that secures virtue, and the virtue of the citizens that secures the force of law and social norms, not vice versa. Yet Democritus also believed that the *polis* benefits man. Man's capacity for and intrinsic interest in self-legislation, his (literal) *autonomia*, means that the *nomoi* created by men as a group can readily be interpreted as doing for man what he has good reason to do for himself. *nomoi*, Democritus observes, 'would not prevent each of us from living according to the capacities/resources proper to him if we did not injure one another. Malicious envy is the origin of factional strife' (B 245). This does not mean that *nomoi* serve only to prevent men from harming each other, but that they interfere with man's *self-development* only because he tends to indulge in envy. The *stasis* fomented by personal envy is harmful to all concerned (B 249).[224]

---

[224] See B 237 on the danger to oneself of indulging in *philonikiē*.

Democritus evidently regarded both *nomos* and the *polis* as contributing to man's well-being: '*nomos* wishes to benefit the life of men. And it is able to do so when they themselves wish to fare well. To those who obey, it (*nomos*) reveals its [or their?] own *aretē*.' If men are disposed to seek their own well-being, they will benefit from the law. Other fragments suggest that social interaction may serve to foster psychic order and promote the internalization of social norms. Education 'shapes' man, and in so doing 'makes his nature' (B 33). Children must be made to engage in activities which will nurture 'that which most of all encompasses excellence (*aretē*): the practice of respect (*to aideisthai*) [cf. *aidōs*]' (B 179). Undisciplined rearing of the very young, Democritus observes, is 'the worst of all evils,' for 'it is this which gives birth to those pleasures from which badness arises' (B 178). Children must be trained to have those virtues of character – reverence, including self-respect and the desire for noble pleasures – which are essential to their well-being. Moreover, society should be constituted in such a way as to promote discipline and self-control throughout life, not just in childhood. If Democritus' views on education have an Aristotelian ring, some of his observations on social order verge on the Platonic: 'Well-ordered (*kosmion*) behavior consists in obedience to the law, the ruler, and the man wiser [sc. than oneself]' (B 47). All three encourage order – restraint, moderation – in the soul. When Democritus states (as he is said to have done) that 'rule belongs by nature to the better/stronger' (B 267), he is not advocating a Calliclean doctrine of natural right. In the context of his general theory, this maxim must mean that rule is most suitable for those who are better in their *phusis*, that is, whose souls are (through their own efforts) well-ordered (see B 61).[225] Democritus proclaims the obverse of this sentiment in another fragment: it is burdensome to be ruled by someone inferior[226] (B 49). If this is anything more than an expression of annoyance at the prospect of being ordered about by someone more stupid than oneself, then it probably means that it is grievous to be ruled by an inferior for the same reason that it contributes to order (i.e. is *kosmion*) to obey a wiser man: government by others should buttress, not undermine, the capacity to rule oneself. Some individuals are better able than others to maintain self-control under conditions of stress, temptation and responsibility: 'When the bad enter upon

[225] Cole (1967) 111–12 suggests that this fragment refers to primitive society and man's political development. This seems implausible in view of the fact that the same sentiment is expressed as a straightforward observation about political life in B 49.
[226] *chalepon archesthai hupo chereionos.*

office, the more unworthy they are, the more neglectful they become, and they are filled with folly and recklessness' (B 254). Not only is it bad to be ruled by such men, but it is also bad *for them* to rule. A number of fragments speak of the importance of the proper – that is, the appropriate – apportionment of honors, praise and blame within society, presumably to ensure that good, wise men and actions flourish (B 63, 95, 192, 263); one such fragment (B 113) asserts that 'those who praise the unintelligent do them great injury.'

These fragments on education and social order are consistent with and should be interpreted in the light of Democritus' repeated insistence that it is the understanding and self-control achieved by the individual which is decisive for his well-being, and for social order. *nomos* (as B 248, cited earlier, indicates) cannot forcibly improve the condition of man; it can only persuade him to develop his own virtue and seek his own true benefit. The man most effective in inculcating excellence is the one who

uses exhortation and the persuasion of words rather than [the force of] law and constraint. The man who abstains from unjust acts because of *nomos* is likely to do wrong in secret; the man guided toward what is needful by persuasion is not likely to do anything faulty either openly or secretly. The man who acts rightly through intelligence and understanding is [or becomes?] at the same time brave or manly [cf. B 214] and [a person] of good judgment. (B 181)

For Democritus, persuasion is not a form of coercion, but rather a means of making social standards truly one's own. A passage in Aristotle's *Nicomachean Ethics* has been construed[227] as a retort to the Democritean vision of social order as the product of rational self-control fostered by persuasion. Whether or not it was conceived in response to Democritus, the passage takes issue with a position that closely resembles the one I have attributed to the atomist, and indicates the difference between such a position and that of Plato and Aristotle. At the end of the *Ethics, en route* to the investigation of political questions, Aristotle observes that while arguments seem able to

make a character which is gently-born, and a true lover of what is noble, ready to be possessed by virtue, they are not able to encourage the *many* to nobility and goodness. For these do not by nature obey the sense of shame, but only fear, and do not abstain from bad acts because of their baseness but through fear of punishment;[228] living by passion they pursue their own pleasures and the means to them, and avoid the opposite pains, and have not even a conception of what is noble and

---

227 By Luria (1964) 16. The use of *metaruthmisai* is suggestive. But the passage could be making a general point, or challenging Socratic methods and assumptions.
228 Cf. Democritus B 41.

truly pleasant, since they have never tasted it. What argument would remold[229] such people? (*EN* 1179b3–16)

Although Democritus recommends the early shaping of character by education and, throughout life, by law and persuasion, and the entrusting of power to those who are intelligent and self-controlled, these measures are intended to fortify – not replace – autonomous internal control.[230]

Political atomism

As Aristotle's observation suggests, a theory of the Democritean kind cannot account for its own ethical force except in rationalistic, egoistic terms. The atomist's injunctions to man to exercise prudence and self-control and to achieve self-sufficiency are grounded in an understanding of man's atomic nature, his nature *qua* man, not his social identity. The constraints imposed by atomism are not social constraints, and the capacity for judgment demanded by it is not fundamentally shaped by social interaction; the theory itself does not depend for its efficacy on the operation of society: it appeals directly to the individual's understanding of the sources of his own well-being. Democritus' approach to the characterization of social order marks a significant though intelligible departure from the essentially political understanding of human nature and interests manifested by Protagoras and Thucydides. In its attempt to preserve their commitment to autonomy while at the same time giving ethical constraints greater force for each individual whatever his circumstances or resources, Democritus' theory sought to maintain a precarious equilibrium. The scales were tipped by Plato, who shifted all the weight on to the second consideration: he abandoned the claims of autonomy and fused man's social and his ethical identity. The Democritean equilibrium, despite its distinctively ancient features, can usefully be construed, in the terms outlined in chapter 3 above, as situated at some distance from a Protagorean understanding of human nature as constituted in and by a political order of a certain kind, and rather closer to an instrumental conception of society as constructed to fulfill individual ends, a con-

[229] *metaruthmisai*, cf. B 33.
[230] Contrast Plato, who expects the guardians to manipulate and control the desires of the masses, and Aristotle, who argues that most people must be controlled by the laws, for they obey 'punishments rather than the sense of what is noble,' *EN* 1180a4. However, since Aristotle believes that men may become good by acting as a good man does, his view of law could be construed as a way of forcing man to *become* good, i.e. to develop his own capacity for virtue. See, e.g., *EN* 1180b25–8.

ception characteristic of seventeenth-century social contract theory and its modern descendant, atomism, the radical individualism which assumes that man's ends are specified in advance of his participation in society.

If it is illuminating to compare ancient to modern (political) atomism, to make visible the individualism in Democritean theory, it is also important to identify those aspects of the theory which the glare of a modern perspective casts into shadow. Unlike modern atomist or contractarian political theorists, Democritus is not offering a theory centered on the notion of rights. Although the rights-theorist can be shown to be making implicit assumptions about those qualities in human beings that render them worthy of respect,[231] he typically represents the theory as founded on the attribution of rights to all human beings simply *qua* biological humans. This claim is conceptually linked to a view of man's freedom as resting in the bare (critics would say empty) capacity to choose.[232] Democritus, by contrast, explicitly articulates a conception of a properly human life and the qualities and character required for the fulfillment of human potential. Moreover, although in a sense Democritus, too, lays stress on man's distinctive capacity to choose how to live, this is for him a demanding criterion of freedom which requires of men that they actively promote their own autonomy through understanding and criticism of themselves and their condition. Every man, therefore, has reason to develop certain qualities which might otherwise lie dormant. But – and here the resemblance to modern atomism grows stronger – Democritus is not concerned to claim that these qualities can be developed only within a particular kind of society, that the capacity for autonomy is itself an artefact of political decision-making and responsibility, or that we ought to promote the development of the characteristically human qualities in others as well as in ourselves.[233] It may be desirable that we should do so and organize society accordingly, but in the end the claims on us as social beings are conditional and must be assessed in terms of our unconditional responsibility to promote our own well-being.

According to Democritus, although man's well-being is fortified by the existence of an ordered society, it is not constituted by it; man's reason for abiding by the laws of the society constructed by man is not, as a modern theorist might argue, that he has agreed to do so, or

[231] Taylor (1985) 192–6.
[232] See Taylor (1985) 196–7.
[233] See Taylor (1985) 188, 194.

that he is coerced into doing so, or even that he has an instrumental reason for doing so, but that man's physical-cum-psychological well-being *qua* individual man who lives among men rests on just those features of behavior which promote political order. If for Protagoras it is the existence of society that makes society possible, for Democritus it is the power of the soul. Intended as a response to the apparent looseness of laws and social conventions and their consequent inability to give each man, whatever his social status or resources, reason to behave in ways consonant with the common good, this approach itself leads to an external portrayal of those social institutions and practices which are not (unlike the administration of justice) a direct expression of intrinsic personal interests. Men have intrinsic reason, namely psychic stability, not to be too contentious or ambitious (elsewhere, Democritus observes that the desire to triumph is foolish, for it distracts man's attention from his own good, B 237). Democritus seeks to extend this argument to the claim that every citizen has an interest in seeing that the *polis* is well-managed:

One must give the highest importance to the affairs of the *polis*, that it may be well-administered; one must not pursue quarrels contrary to what is reasonable nor acquire a power contrary to the common good. The well-run *polis* is the greatest basis of security and contains all in itself; when this is safe, all is safe; when this is destroyed, all is destroyed. (B 252)

The fragments suggest that Democritus tried to tie the demand for and the assessment of effort in behalf of the common good to the most basic criteria of harm and benefit. The point of holding office, according to Democritus, is to manage the affairs of the city competently, not to gain an illustrious reputation. Men, he observes, 'remember one's mistakes rather than one's achievements. This is just; for as those who return a deposit do not deserve praise, whereas those who do not do so deserve blame and punishment, so with the official: he was chosen not to do things badly, but well' (B 265). But how can one ensure that magistrates and the people to whom they are responsible will in fact adopt this attitude? The fragments indicate that, in Democritus' view, officials are often treated unfairly. He remarks that:

There exists no mechanism in the presently-established [political] structure (*rhuthmos*) to ensure that magistrates are not wronged, even if they are altogether good. <It does not seem fitting for them to be subject to others, to anyone other than to themselves.>[234] In some way this as well should be ordered (*kosmethenai*)

---

[234] Freeman (1948) 115–16 takes *tous archontas* as the subject of *adikein* and translates as follows: 'There is no means under the present constitution by which magistrates can be prevented from wrong-doing, however good they may be. For it is not likely for anyone

so that the man who does no wrong, but examines wrongdoers strictly, will not be subject to these, but some ordinance or something else will protect the man who does just deeds. (B 266)

This fragment echoes the concern expressed in the series of observations on the punishment of wrongdoers: those who act justly and impose sanctions on the unjust must be protected. Men who recognize the problem should seek to remedy it; but other fragments reflect Democritus' belief that the laws fit too loosely to do the trick. The only true solution is awareness on the part of all citizens that they have a personal interest in preventing and punishing wrongdoing.

Democritus' appeal to individual well-being characterized in atomic terms results in an essentially negative and limited portrayal of the benefits of participation in political society and of man's freedom within it. Even with respect to the punishment of wrongdoers, Democritus' emphasis indicates that men must be given very good reason, and assurances of safety, before they will be willing to take actions which may involve some risk to themselves. In the case of public service, the difficulty is the greater because the benefit is less evident. According to Democritus,

To good men it is not advantageous that they should neglect their own affairs to do other things; for their private affairs suffer. But if a man should neglect public matters [i.e. not participate in political life] he develops a bad reputation, even if he has not stolen anything or done anything unjust. And if he is not neglectful [i.e. does participate][235] and does wrong, he is in danger not only of being ill-spoken of, but also of suffering some harm. To make mistakes is inevitable, but it is not easy for men to forgive. (B 253)

This fragment appears to be a protest against the prevailing tendency to judge men by peculiarly public criteria: however personally upright a man may be, if he does not serve the community he is reviled; and a man who does attempt to serve the community and chances to trip up is deemed to have done something unforgivable. Why, then, should a worthy man wish to hold office? Attention to public matters interferes with the pursuit of private concerns, and even to enter public life, without any intention of doing wrong, indeed even exhibiting great

else [any more] than for oneself, that he will show himself the same man in different circumstances.' Freeman's solution to the difficulty of interpreting the second sentence assumes that the constitutional device mentioned as lacking in the first sentence concerns a different issue entirely than the device mentioned as desirable in the last sentence. I venture a different rendering, assuming that the second sentence is complete but difficult, and reading *huph'* instead of *eph'*, with Jacobs (see DK apparatus, *ad loc.*).

[235] Ignoring Diels–Kranz's inserted *mē*, which renders the last line incongruous.

virtue and talent (B 266), is a risky business. In Democritus' theory, a standard of intrinsic self-interest provided a powerful reason for every individual to develop the qualities compatible with the negative virtues of citizenship, but it also tended to neutralize any particular person's incentive to participate actively in the administration of the *polis*, to see for himself that it is well-managed. To ensure that the *polis* is well-run, it is necessary for individual men to take a wider, more impersonal view of their own interests. In one fragment, Democritus declares that the creations of political skill and effort are the greatest and most glorious of human goods (B 157). But given his strenuous warnings about the risks of over-extending oneself and losing one's psychological balance, risks associated in the fragments with the desire for personal wealth, glory and power, and the dangers to one's reputation or well-being involved in public service, Democritus was not in a position to argue convincingly that excellence (*aretē*), which for him consisted in respect (*aidōs*) for oneself, or self-control, included political *aretē* in the sense of political leadership, or that personal well-being depended on political interaction.

If for Democritus social goods are not defined by political criteria but by the individual's conception of his own interests, it is also true that goods which depend on personal initiative are not limited to those that can be secured politically. True social harmony, Democritus suggests, is a function of personal generosity and the greater economic, not just political, equality that such generosity would promote: 'When the [rich and] powerful dare to lend to those who have nothing, and help them and care for them, then in this lies sympathy and an end to desolation and the beginning of companionship, and mutual aid and civic harmony and innumerable other good things' (B 255).[236] The kind of freedom and voluntarism envisioned by Democritus could bind men more closely than political ties because they are united as *men*, not as citizens, and on their own terms. Thus even the natural but in a sense arbitrary bond between parent and child should be replaced with a relationship based on sympathy and temperamental compatibility. And membership in the circle of one's intimates should not be based on kinship nor, as Creon suggests in Sophocles' *Antigone*, on civic fraternity, but on shared values and beliefs. Democritus values the freedom offered by democracy for its negative virtues: it makes possible the unhampered exercise of the power of one's soul, in pursuit of the good. 'Poverty in a democracy,' Democritus declares, 'is as

---

[236] Cf. Archytas, DK 47 B 83.

much to be preferred over so-called prosperity (*eudaimonië*) in an oligarchy (*dunasteia*) as freedom is to slavery' (B 251). Well-being is not a function of social status or material resources; the freedom characteristic of democracy makes possible the pursuit and attainment of genuine prosperity.

Democritus' account of human interests and social order is not essentially political: it is directly tied to personal motivation and aspires to universality. It is therefore also inward and in the modern sense atomistic, and has to strain to connect human interests in more than a negative sense with the claims of political interaction. The Democritean vision of man as constituted of a material body and a material soul does not lend itself to a radical bifurcation of the spiritual and the corporeal, and hence to the abrogation of personal and political autonomy in the interests of reason envisioned in the philosophy of Plato. For Democritus, the personal autonomy of the individual is central. It is the soul's utilization of its powers that is decisive for the well-being and autonomy of the whole, yet these can only be secured through the soul's interaction with the body, which has its own claims and competence. According to Plutarch, Democritus blamed the soul for all unhappiness or misfortune and used a political metaphor to illustrate his point:

If the body brought a suit against the soul with respect to the pain and ill-treatment it had suffered throughout life, and he himself, Democritus, should be the judge of the charge, he would gladly condemn the soul on the grounds that it destroyed the body through neglect and . . . spoiled and tore it asunder through love of pleasure. (B 159)

Democritus' use of a political metaphor to analyze the relationship between body, soul and human well-being reveals at once both his commitment to a political system which respects human autonomy and is accountable for the fulfillment of human interests, and his fundamentally apolitical approach to the understanding of these ends. For Democritus as for Thucydides, man's freedom, his power, his capacity to reflect on the good, are both the source of the problems in social relations and the basis of a solution to those problems. For Democritus it is not democratic interaction, which expresses and guides these qualities, that is the answer, but rather the soul's own power and its own intrinsic motivation to guide itself.

Extrapolation of the Democritean vision of the self to political relations would suggest that it is rule by an unscrupulous elite, men with ill-formed minds, which constitutes enslavement, while the interaction of the body of the people with those men who through effort,[237] not the gifts of fortune, are well-ordered, constitutes freedom and order. The body, he claims, has simple requirements, easily met without distress or hardship (B 223).[238] It is not the body but the ill-formed mind which desires unceasingly and imprudently, making life difficult and eventually ruining the health of the whole configuration, the self. Democritus frequently assails those who seek wealth, their desires unconstrained by educated understanding (B 185); they are enslaved by these desires, which lead them into injustice (B 5) and which, he says, are far more burdensome than the worst poverty. Perhaps we have here a glimpse of a critique of the greedy exploitation and oppression of poor by rich. Democracy does not provide a remedy for these disorders. Such a remedy must, in his view, come from within and be founded not on an understanding of the sources of social well-being but of the constituents of personal well-being as laid down by atomism. Yet this solution, which appeals to the soul as the source of order as well as freedom, is no solution. Pity and concern for others may be motivated by the attempt to achieve and preserve *euthumia* through reflection on the suffering of others (B 191); but such reflection may as readily lead to complacency and self-satisfaction. The injunction constantly to assess and modulate the relationship of external events to internal well-being is a recipe for alienation and withdrawal as much as for active efforts to order the world.

This ambivalence, which bedeviled the atomist conception of man's nature and his good, also troubled Thucydides: should man seek to order the world or simply to ensure his own inner security? For both Democritus and Thucydides the choice was only apparently a choice, and the tension it revealed was genuine and deep. Man's security depends upon his ability to mediate his response to the world, and although both thinkers toyed with the idea that perhaps stupidity, forged into moderation (*sophrosunē*) by the buffetings of circumstance (see B 54, 76) could secure well-being, yet both understood that the only human qualities that can *genuinely* secure well-being are precisely those which prompt and enable man actively to order the world, thereby increasing the risks to well-being, and to reflect on his own condition and situation, thus destabilizing and fragmenting the social

---

[237] This emphasis on toil, *ponos* (see, e.g., B 157, 179, 240, 241, 243 with Vlastos (1945/6) n. 84) is another indication of Democritus' rejection of aristocratic values as the criteria of virtues.

[238] Cf. B 198: 'That which needs knows how much it needs, but he who needs does not know' with Segal (1961) 108, who suggests that the subject of the first 'know' is the body, of the second, the man with an ill-ordered *gnomē* (B 223).

order on whose integrity his well-being depends. In a world with no transcendent order the determinants of man's condition, for good or ill, lay within man. Man's characteristic qualities, his imagination, his personal resources, his capacity to reflect, constituted the danger and the remedy. Thus, for Thucydides, it is the imagination, energy and intelligence of the citizens of Athens which underlie her capacity to exploit and adapt to experience, and make possible her greatness under the guidance of judgment (*gnomē*). It is these same qualities which prompt her, under the influence of men without *gnomē*, to overreach herself, ignoring the realities of her situation. Thucydides reveals that the exercise over time of man's ability (associated with the Athenian *polis*) to order the world creates a situation in which the author of this extraordinary achievement must maintain constant inner self-control and self-restraint in her external relations in order to preserve what she has wrought. This civic self-control is rendered more difficult, more necessary and, with proper guidance, possible by the tendency of the Athenian citizen constantly to reflect on his situation and to assess the contribution of civic order and civic policy to his own well-being.

Democritus represents man's capacity to elaborate his needs and desires and shape the world so as to fulfill them as his characteristic excellence, a constitutive feature of the power of the soul. Yet the world that man creates, and which makes possible both glory and safety (see B 252 and 157) also increases man's exposure to fortune (*tuchē*) and his related vulnerability to passion (*orgē*). Thus the power of the soul must be directed to the maintenance of strict self-control internally and restraint in relations with other members of the *polis* to preserve the self's well-being and the integrity of the world it has created. Both Democritus and Thucydides offer reasons why men should exercise self-control, reasons which appeal to each man's own understanding of his own good and rely on man's capacity to reflect, to imagine and to deploy his resources, while also constraining or shaping that understanding and those capacities. For Thucydides, however, this shaping process is not simply a matter of invoking a particular vision of human nature and thus of individual good. Rather, the Thucydidean argument occurs within society, as part of the political transformation of man's self-understanding. If this appeal to the political interpretation of man's phenomenal experience is less tightly bound to the individual's own good than the exigencies of atomistic materialism and is a less stable and secure standard, it is also less alienating, more plausibly a way of connecting man's good to his relationship to other men and to the world, and more likely actually to succeed in shaping man's understanding and behavior. Democritus' appeal to a stable objective standard outside society but compatible with (indeed a confirmation of) individual autonomy, is an attempt to tie social order to a criterion of human good applicable to each individual *qua* man, whatever his circumstances: being a good man, i.e. realizing one's own real interests and fulfilling one's potential, is sufficient for good citizenship. And being a good man is motivated simply by coming to understand the nature of the cosmos and one's place in it. But how is this to be achieved? And even if one does attain this understanding, how *does* politics fit on to the human good so construed? I have suggested that Democritus' theory could not in the end cope with such queries.

Plato, who also invoked a criterion of reality and human good independent of society, but one removed from phenomenal experience and accessible only to a few, provided an apparently more cogent account by abandoning the principles of personal independence and autonomy. Not only do those who are incapable of exercising self-control submit to the control of the guardians, but the guardians themselves must abandon the highest self-realization of which they are capable, contemplation of the forms, in order to return to the cave, to serve as political rulers. Plato appeals to what is best and highest in man, and seeks to connect this vision of human good, designed as a stable criterion applicable to all men (either directly or via society), to the good of society. He does not succeed in doing so; neither does Aristotle, who tries to formulate a criterion of human good that operates within society as men experience it but is drawn away, by consideration of what is genuinely best in and for man, to a vision of the solitary contemplator. The best men are moved by ends outside and beyond society. They do not realize themselves politically; they are tied by more binding forces than those that are deemed to animate men within political society. The question Protagoras, Thucydides and Democritus addressed, the question posed by democracy, has been side-stepped: if men do constitute themselves politically, via their own understanding of their good, a good attainable within society, what is to prevent politics from dissolving into a cynical or ruthless or alienated pursuit of individual self-interest?

7   Living democracy?

To secure order, Plato and Aristotle turned away from the politics of democracy. The alienation, conflict and narrow self-concern charted by Thucydides and confronted by Democritus prompted Plato to bind the pursuit of the good to the existence of a stable, unified, hierarchical society, the earthly embodiment of a cosmic order. For Plato as for Democritus, the disintegration of community provoked a heightened concern with matters of justice. Justice is remedial;[1] it comes to the fore when the connection between the demands of society and the good of individuals is called into question. Democritus invoked justice in the course of arguing that men did in fact have good reason to regard the demands of civic life as binding. For Plato, it was not enough to appeal to men to see themselves as creatures of society; society itself had to be restructured so as to embody justice. To bind the individual to social order, Plato rejected the very basis of politics, namely autonomy.

Aristotle, responding both to Plato and to the diminished unity and homogeneity of the fourth-century *polis* and a widening gap between rich and poor, sought to preserve the bond between individual and society from the other direction: instead of violating man's autonomy by extending the grip of the *polis*, he fortified the ordering power of autonomous political interaction by restricting the range of the *polis* itself. In restructuring society so as to provide a firm foundation for order, Plato and Aristotle abandoned the aims of democratic politics and democratic thinkers. Despite their commitment to integrate the individual with society, or rather because of their determination to weld rather than integrate them, both Plato and Aristotle sapped politics of its power to perform this task, the one by extending, the other by constricting the range of politics so far as to render it meaningless. The individual's autonomous capacity for order was reduced to nothing or elevated to everything. This retreat from politics has its counterpart in modern thought and experience. To see the power and the

---

[1] See Sandel (1982) 32–3.

weaknesses of the Platonic and Aristotelian rejections of the Athenian model is to appreciate whether that model, or the critique of it, or both, have force for us: is it possible to live democracy?

Plato and Aristotle: the retreat from politics

As the structure of the argument in Plato's *Republic* makes clear, Plato's theory is radically revisionary – it proposes an unconventional picture of what it is to flourish as a human being – yet it remains tied to the question of what men need and want. The challenge posed in the *Republic*, which the elaborate account of the just city seeks to answer, is whether justice is essential to human well-being. In Book One, the sophist Thrasymachus declares that justice is what is in the interest of another, not oneself, and that it is foolish for anyone, and particularly for any powerful person, to act justly. In Book Two, Glaucon and Adeimantus offer a 'contractarian' analysis of the foundation and motivation for justice, which presents what man has good reason to do as a function of his circumstances: all men are, as it happens, relatively equal, so they have an interest in agreeing to refrain from harming one another. Such an account cannot explain why even the most invulnerable of men, Gyges, possessor of a ring that makes him invisible, should be just. The *Republic* provides a revisionary account of both justice and well-being which reveals that even for Gyges, justice is not folly. The bonds of justice had to close firmly around each man, regardless of his powers or ambitions.

Plato argues that justice is constitutive of the good for man, for *all* men. It is a condition of society and of the individual. Justice consists in each man getting his due, not *qua* human being but *qua* member of a harmonious social order with particular qualities to contribute to that order; and it consists in each part of man (appetite, spirit, reason) getting its due on the same principle.[2] The rule of reason over appetite is the essence of order in the cosmos, the *polis* and the individual, and each level of the hierarchy buttresses the others. Justice is a condition of the soul that prevents the indulgence of the individual's desire for more (*pleonexia*) which is for Plato (as for Aristotle) the source of unjust behavior toward other members of society.[3] The unity of the society and the universal and compelling grip of the claims of justice depend upon a hierarchy not, as in traditional aristocratic societies, of persons, but of person-parts: intellect and appetite. The individual's

---

[2] See Vlastos (1977) and (1981).
[3] See Vlastos (1977) and (1981) and Williams (1981b) 83–93.

ethical status, and his freedom and well-being, is not for Plato dependent on his own possession of wisdom. Rather, the talents of men capable of abstract reasoning, deployed in mobilizing cosmic principles for the good of the entire *polis*, ensure the universal subjection of passion to reason, of the contingent to the absolute, and thereby secure the well-being of all. Plato, anxious to construct (or discover) a metaphysical basis for the good of all men in society, utterly abolished integrity and autonomy, dissolving the boundaries of the self.

Plato's radical reconstrual of the self whose freedom and good the ideal city is designed to secure undermines the very foundations of democracy, politics and indeed of worldly agency. Plato, like Kant, disempowers men in the process of 'liberating' them. Men who must rely on their own humble wits are, according to Plato, enslaved. Man has to flee this world, make his way up out of the cave or be ruled by someone who has done so, in order to escape being mired in the flux of his own bodily desires, material causality and the contingencies of circumstance. For Plato, genuine freedom depended on attaining this higher ground. Prudence, the informed assessment of circumstance, is rejected as subject to contingency: it is inadequate to the task of identifying and adhering to the good for man, because it is too implicated in the mutability of events and desires. Plato thus rejects the whole notion of autonomous participation in the creation of order and unity under the tutelage of reason which, in the theories of Protagoras, Thucydides and Democritus, reflected the experience of a democracy guided by an elite in the interests of the whole. The individual soul's capacity to mediate the equilibrium between inner and outer, and between passion and judgment, the leader's capacity to persuade the citizens to pursue a vision of the common interests, the competence of men in society to determine what their interests are, the cosmic order created through the interaction of matter – all, conceived as visions of ordered freedom, as the antithesis of slavery, are for Plato equally slavish.[4]

The Platonic redescription of freedom flies in the face of conventional belief. Both democratic man and the tyrant, each in his own way apparently the epitome of freedom, are in fact slaves. They are enslaved by appetite. And men controlled by others, slaves in the ordinary understanding of that term, are truly free. In order that appetitive man 'may be ruled by a principle similar to that which rules the best man, we say he must be a slave to the best man, who has a divine ruler

[4] See Vlastos (1941) 158; Plato, *Laws* 888e3–890b1.
[5] *Rep.* 561d–e, 574e, 576–579d10. See Nussbaum (1980) 405–7 and *passim*.

in himself' (*Rep.* 590c). To be free is not to rule oneself but to be ruled by reason from outside, to be a slave. The *logos* that had expressed the citizen's own purposes and freedom has been fully externalized. It still addresses man's interests, but these are no longer interests he can be brought to appreciate, nor can they be realized in society as it is, nor indeed can he participate in their realization. Plato has sapped the *polis* of its political structure by extending the claims of the *polis* to all inhabitants, whatever their status in the community,[6] however disparate their resources and capacities and experience. The Platonic city does not rest on relative equality, nor does it aspire to instill competence and independence in its members; autonomy is not, in Plato's view, possible for the vast majority of individuals, and it is not necessary. In the process of, as he thought, liberating men who were enslaved internally, Plato dismissed not just democracy, but politics. For politics depends upon the capacity for autonomy. For this very reason, a world organized politically would necessarily, in Plato's view, be disordered and unstable.

Aristotle decried the excessive unity of Plato's republic. His theory sought to rehabilitate politics, the relationship between autonomous individuals and social order. As he says in the *Politics*, 'Even if we could suppose the citizen body to be virtuous, without each of them being so, yet the latter would be better' (*Pol.* 1332a36).[7] In rejecting Plato's argument for communal ownership and relationships,[8] Aristotle asserts that men will not care for the community as a whole unless they care for some portion of it which has to do with them personally. Thus Aristotle apparently rehabilitates man's capacity to assess and pursue his own interests in a society which is his own construction. Aristotle attempts to give worldly force to Platonic teleology by restoring to man his basic integrity.[9] Aristotelian teleology is founded not on a transcendent form of the good but on a (biological and metaphysical) account of the ends proper to man as a certain kind of creature. This creature cannot be reduced (or elevated) to its incor-

---

[6] See Vlastos (1968) 145–6. Slaves are not mentioned in Plato's functional analysis of the *polis* into three parts, but he may have assimilated them to the free part of the economic sector. Since they participate in *dikaiosunē*, they should presumably be included in a division which purports to be an exhaustive analysis of justice in the city. However, it is possible that Plato is operating with a narrow (political) and a broader (social) conception of the *polis*. See Vlastos (1968) 140–1, with notes.

[7] See Nussbaum (1980) 417–18.

[8] In the *Republic*, the guardians share property, mates and children, and are to 'feel pleasure and pain together,' *Rep.* 464c–d; cf. *Laws* 739c–d.

[9] Cf. Rawls (1971) who seeks to give worldly content to Kantian autonomy by restoring to men some basic aims and interests.

poreal soul.[10] Not (or not merely) the philosopher's understanding, but practical wisdom tied to habituation of the sentiments, to character, is essential to man's realization of his true nature. The well-being of the individual requires the exercise of the virtues, including the virtues of citizenship, and it includes earthly attachments that render him vulnerable to fortune.[11] According to Aristotle, 'Man is by nature a *polis* animal' (*Pol.* 1253a1). For Aristotle as for earlier Greek thinkers, including Plato, politics is an extension of ethics (and *Politics* of *Ethics*), but Aristotle rejects Plato's conflation of the two at the expense of human integrity and autonomy.

Yet because Aristotle seeks to effect a reconciliation between a strong theory of the good and the dispositions of particular men and to preserve a political ordering of the world founded on human autonomy which is, however, stable and just, he relies on a restructuring of politics which, though different from Plato's, is only somewhat less revisionary. Although Aristotle's teleological account of human nature (based on a notion of well-being and of man's proper activity or work) would seem to imply that the end, or *telos*, is something characteristically attainable by most members of the biological species (on the analogy of other natural substances), yet it appears that many men, perhaps most, are capable only of a much-diminished form of life. Man can realize both his personal and his political nature only in a *polis* radically different from the one he inhabits and accessible only to a minority of men. Aristotle adopts the model embodied by the *polis* he knew best, democratic Athens, that all citizens are relatively equal and that all are capable of both ruling and being ruled. Aristotle insists, against Plato, that the rule of a master and political rule are not the same: 'Political order is a government of free men and equals' (*Pol.* 1.7). But Aristotle, like Plato, is committed to a strong distinction between what men in general take to be their interests and the human excellence based, in this case, on practical reason, which man *qua* man is capable of realizing. Both believe that the *polis* exists not just for the sake of life, but for the sake of the good life. Whereas Plato's belief that civic order required the abrogation of autonomy led him to absorb all individuals into the *polis* and into the realization of the good, Aristotle's view that order must accommodate autonomy, that it will not embody man's freedom or nature unless it is the product of

---

[10] But note *EN* 1177a11–1179a31, where Aristotle suggests that happiness consists in realizing one's divinity, not one's humanity. See the discussions of this notorious difficulty in interpreting the *EN* in Cooper (1975), Nussbaum (1986) 373–7 and Nagel (1980). Cf. the account of the *summum bonum* at *Pol.* 1325a17–b32.

[11] See Nussbaum (1980) and (1986) ch. 12.

politics, leads him to narrow the realm in which such order is possible, to restrict the boundaries of the *polis*. If autonomy, the pursuit of good by each man, is to result in political order and the good life via what men themselves can come to appreciate, then the realm of the political must be circumscribed, and all men incapable of practical reason and virtue must be excluded.

While Plato preserved the transforming power of the *polis*, the foundation of the Athenian democratic ideal, by a hierarchical restructuring of society which dissolved autonomy, Aristotle pre-served the Athenian commitment to self-rule at the expense of the power of political interaction to shape ordinary men into responsible citizens. According to Aristotle, the good life is not available to all men, because the good is not simply an order embodied in a society as a whole, but a way of living, of contributing to an order rather than simply constituting a fragment of it. It is not merely slaves who are barred from civic life. If the despotic rule of a master does not count as political order, if such order cannot be stretched, as in Plato's *Repub-lic*, to encompass both the philosopher-king and the slave, it is also true, for Aristotle, that it cannot, as the democracy assumed, accom-modate those men preoccupied with their own needs as well as men attuned to a broader vision. The *polis* cannot free men enslaved to their passions by subjecting them to the rule of the enlightened, nor can it transform and broaden men's understanding of their own sur-vival or advantage by involving them in civic life. All men who are en-gaged in 'servile' activities, free laborers and mechanics as well as slaves, are excluded from citizenship of the ideal state and from true well-being: they live in society for the sake of mere life, but do not par-ticipate in the good life attainable in the political community.[12]

Aristotle's analysis rests on an implicit distinction between society and the *polis*: survival and the fulfillment of human needs, which serve in the theories of Protagoras, Thucydides, Democritus and Plato, in different ways,[13] as the foundations for arguments about the good and political order, are for Aristotle the ends of society, not of the *polis*. All men need society: men wish to live together, Aristotle says, and they are brought together by their common interests (*Pol.* 1278b, cf. 1160a10). The *polis* embodies a distinct and higher good.[14] The distinction between what is merely useful or advantageous and what is

---

[12] See *Pol.* 1277b34–1278a14.

[13] In Plato's *Republic*, the city meets the requirements of life and the good life; and it is by reasoning from the structure of civic needs that Plato arrives at the structure of justice in the city and individual.

[14] See Segal (1961) 577 on the shift from *to sdēn* to *to eu sdēn* ('living' to 'living well').

good or virtuous runs like a seam through Aristotle's ethical and political philosophy.For example, it is the desire for 'gain' which characterizes injustice; friendships based on pleasure and utility are both inferior to friendships based on ethical excellence (*aretē*) but at least the former are relatively free-spirited (*eleutherion*) while useful friends are for the commercially-minded (*agoraion*; *EN* 1158a20); and Aristotle reviles as mere money-grubbing the form of wealth-getting associated with commerce (*Pol.* 1257b–1258a15). In the best form of *polis*, a share in civic administration is allotted 'according to virtue and merit' and 'no man can practice *aretē* who is living the life of a craftsman or laborer' (*Pol.* 1278a19).[15] Aristotle declares: 'It must be admitted that we cannot consider all those to be citizens who are necessary to the existence of the *polis* ... The necessary people are either slaves who minister to the wants of individuals, or craftsmen and laborers who are the servants of the community' (*Pol.* 1277b35, 1278a12).

The exclusion of the 'necessary and the useful' from the life of the best *polis* or the best man is both a reflection of fourth-century developments in the condition of the city state and a rejection of the implications of those developments. It was becoming increasingly obvious that some of the men now indispensable to the *polis* – not just slaves, but wealthy metics and, of course, mercenaries – were not part of it politically.[16] It is, I think, no accident that Aristotle was the first political theorist, so far as we know, explicitly to defend the institution of slavery, and in terms that justify the exclusion of slaves from political life. It is significant that these same criteria, namely the ability to act according to virtue and practical reason, associated with leisure and liberal pursuits, are invoked to exclude men whose services to the state – military[17] and other – would traditionally have entitled them to a civic function. Aristotle was also the first to identify peace as the end appropriate to the *polis*, indeed as analogous in relations with other nations to the good of the contemplative man (*Pol.* 1324a–1325b30). These features of Aristotelian theory suggest that political categories were blurring and that Aristotle was responding to what he took to be a breakdown in the integrity of the political community by seeking to

---

[15] Compare Thucydides' Pericles, who asserts in the Funeral Oration that the democracy honors men according to merit, but that no man is excluded by his occupation from playing a leading role in shaping the public good, whether as a leader or simply a magistrate or assemblyman, for each citizen is expected to participate after his own fashion.

[16] See Pečírka (1976).

[17] Note that according to Aristotle, even men of the hoplite class, capable of paying for their own armor, are likely to possess only military virtue (*Pol.* 1288a12–13; 1279b1–3).

specify and to shore up the concept of the *polis*.*Aristotle argues, against some of his contemporaries, that if the *polis* were viewed simply as a grouping designed to ensure 'security from injustice' or 'for the sake of exchange and mutual intercourse,' then 'all who have commercial treaties with one another would be the citizens of one state' (*Pol.* 1280a35). In the absence of a strong sense of community and of communal power to transform man's understanding of his good, the criteria of survival and material need seem degenerate, and are associated in Aristotle's mind not with man's political nature or good but with the distasteful mentality of the wage-earner or the participant in commerce.

Aristotle's attempt to rescue the political from the effects of the disintegration of community and social change, and from Plato's drastic solution, is itself a retreat from politics. Aristotle does not rely on politics to create community or transcend narrow self-interest. In his theory politics does no work; it simply serves as the context for the exercise of practical excellence by men autonomously capable of such excellence. The *polis* no longer expresses, reconciles and transforms the beliefs and desires of ordinary men, promoting the well-being of all by enabling each to exercise the political virtues. What appears to be a formulation of the contemporary view of citizenship at Athens – citizens rule and are ruled – is in fact a rejection of Athenian practice. In all but the ideal state, there is a division of function between rulers and subjects.[18] Citizens of the ideal state are able to rule and be ruled because they are not merely relatively equal but identical, and equally capable, *qua* men, of practical wisdom. Aristotle's teleological conception of the good centers on the good man, not the good citizen; the two are not equivalent, nor even concomitant. Only in the ideal state, composed of men endowed with practical wisdom, is the good citizen also a good man: 'The *aretē* of the good man is necessarily the same as the *aretē* of the citizen of the perfect state' (*Pol.* 1288a38; cf. 1277a13, 1277b25).*Good men in imperfect societies will not be good citizens, nor will good citizens of imperfect societies qualify as good men. *

Unlike Plato, Aristotle recognizes two sets of standards, or two levels of order, one of which is relative to circumstances: it is coherent to speak of being a good citizen of a democratic or oligarchic state, and to establish corresponding guidelines. Thus in Aristotle's theory the concepts of 'good man' and 'good citizen' have come apart, and it

---

[18] See, e.g., *Pol.* 1288a39–b2.

is the concept of the good man that is basic, stable and compelling. This concept is defined in terms of character and intellect, which together constitute the capacity for self-realization (i.e. realization of the good for man, not some purely subjective aspiration). Neither the highest nor the lowest condition of human existence is characterized politically, but rather in terms of intrinsic qualities. Slavery is not a conventional or institutional category, but a natural condition, the state proper to those who 'participate in the rational principle enough to apprehend but not to have such a principle' (*Pol.* 1254b20). And the summit of self-realization is the condition in which man is free of what is merely necessary and useful for life, and practices the highest virtue of which man as a species is capable, namely the activity of contemplation (*EN* 1177a10–1179a30). Man's *telos* is to be in the best *polis* but not of it, to engage in the exercise of abstract reason, not civic virtue.

Both Plato and Aristotle sought to bind individual and society together, to demonstrate that civic order was a constitutive, not an instrumental, feature of human well-being. Plato serves to remind modern political thinkers of, among other things, the importance of taking seriously the differences as well as the similarities among individuals when constructing a vision of the social order.[19] Justice must be tied to desert as well as equality,[20] that is to the idea of contributing to a shared, mutually beneficial order. Aristotle reveals the virtue of placing practical judgment, character and self-realization, founded on a conception of man as having a nature, a fundamentally social nature, at the center of ethical and political thought. Both theorists attempted to reconcile internal and external, freedom and order, via a reconstrual of what it is to lead a fully human life and what is good for man. The task of providing a stable, objective basis for such an account seemed imperative in the face of an apparent disintegration of communal life. In the search for stability, Plato and Aristotle both, from different directions, violated the fragile equilibrium of autonomy and order at the heart of a community that risks disintegration but is also, for that very reason, capable of achieving genuine reflective stability. At bottom, Plato and Aristotle base their conceptions of order on society and on man, respectively; they are unwilling to rely on the interaction of the two. Thus theories designed to bind man to society in fact split the individual from the community, by cleaving the

[19] See Dunn (1979).
[20] See MacIntyre (1984) 38.

individual and destroying his autonomy, or by cleaving society and abandoning the attempt to create order from diversity which is essential to the very concept, and the point, of politics.

Living history, living democracy

It is no accident that we have tended to look right past the fifth-century thinkers and to treat Plato and Aristotle as the first political theorists. For like Plato and Aristotle, we have lost confidence in democracy and its corollary, the integration of the reflective and the concrete. That is, we have lost confidence in politics, in the possibility of reconciling the autonomy of particular individuals with a social order that can withstand reflective scrutiny. We think of ourselves as private individuals with concrete sentiments and desires, imbedded in our personal lives; we think of the political order either instrumentally, as the arena for the fulfillment of antecedently-established desires, or as a formal system for realizing abstract principles of equality and fairness. Unlike Plato and Aristotle, however, we do not seek to bridge the divide by binding man and society in one universal order. We do not attempt to unite ethics and politics by reconstruing man or society in terms of the cosmic foundations of the good. Modern thinkers turn neither to a meaningful universe nor, as the ancient democratic theorists did, to political order, to integrate man's understanding of himself in society. We rest discontent with a schism between the realms of the 'private' and the 'public' citizen. The self of private existence is isolated and hemmed in; its values find no anchor, no supporting structure outside their own sphere of operation, and when challenged can seem arbitrary, pointless, without connection to any larger order of nature or society, merely self-indulgent.[21] If the way we structure the world comes to seem an expression of self-indulgence or narrow self-interest and the formal, procedural order intended to buttress our sense that this is not all there is to human interaction comes to seem unrelated to our sense of self and our purposes, then we are apparently left without any basis for attributing worth or objective force to our values. The choice appears to be between a formal, abstract order and pure self-interested struggle.[22]

It is democracy, as conceived and lived by Athenians in the fifth century B.C., that offers at least the possibility of healing this spiritual and social fragmentation. The political order as portrayed by Prota-

[21] See Bellah et al. (1985) *passim*. Bellah points out the oddity of the term 'private citizen.'
[22] See Williams (1985) 194–6.

goras, Thucydides and Democritus did not aspire to transcend self-interest but to shape (not coerce) it, to provide men with a social identity and a civic understanding of their own good. All citizens were thought to be capable of appreciating and feeling the connection between their interests and those of the community because they were constantly, as active political participants, asked to assess and interpret that connection. As later theorists such as Aristotle recognized, this general access to political efficacy and the resulting integration of all citizens in a civic sensibility was due to the relative equality of the citizens of Attica as well as to institutional measures deliberately designed to make political participation possible for even the poor citizens. In part because of the assumption that men are self-interested individuals with given desires, remote from the claims of political order, modern theorists, like Plato and Aristotle, regard politics as dangerous. They fear the force of unregenerate human desire and emotion, and man's vulnerability to manipulation. The political shaping of need, desire and understanding is seen to be dangerous, a threat both to personal integrity and to the stability of the state. Apathy and ignorance on the part of the mass of the population is regarded as a normal, predictable state of affairs, and indeed as desirable. The founders of the American republic saw their task as the embodiment of the civic virtue and educated leadership characteristic of aristocratic republics in a democratic form appropriate to a large, commercial society.[23] They recognized the need to inculcate the public virtues, but these were construed not as the qualities required to rule, but rather to choose public-spirited and capable rulers. Madison and others may well have taken for granted the formative influence of tightly-knit local communities. Their explicit strategy for securing the public good did not depend on the diffusion of experience in local self-government or other forms of political participation,[24] but on constitutional mechanisms designed to counteract the operation of self-interest and to channel popular feeling into the selection of virtuous leaders.[25] Because of their belief in the importance of cultivating civic virtue and their lack of confidence in the transforming power of democratic political interaction, all of these theorists, like Aristotle, defined and analyzed politics in such a way as to exclude the mass of ordinary people from full democratic participation.

[23] See Bellah et al. (1985) 254–5.
[24] But Thomas Jefferson and Thomas Paine recognized this need, and this strand in American political life was powerfully articulated in the 19th century in Tocqueville's study of American democracy. See Bellah et al. (1985) 36–9, 167–8, 212, 253.
[25] See Bellah et al. (1985) 255.

*The challenge is to turn toward the example of a living democracy, ancient Athens, and away from the temptation to which Aristotle succumbed, the temptation to reject it for an apparently more manageable alternative. Fifth and fourth-century Athens serves as a case-study of the possibility of combining social integration with active popular participation and sharp political controversy.[26] It also exhibits the intimate relationship between such successful integration and reflective stability. Athenian politics shaped man's self-understanding along civic lines. Athenian political theory addressed reflective questioning of the connection between politics and the human good by making explicit the force and the point of this shaping process, of which political theory was itself part. Reflective questioning, and the need for a more reflective understanding of political order, were prompted by the challenge of incorporating the masses, the poor, into the world of civic virtue and civic responsibility, and of explaining how a polity composed of such men could be ordered.

Our need for such an approach to political order is comparable but even more acute. Both politically and reflectively, we must span a greater and less mediated distance. Unlike the ancients, we now claim to respect the dignity and the moral worth of every human being. Partly because of the inclusion in the modern polity of the functional equivalents of the slaves and aliens of the ancient world, who were denied political and ethical status, modern democracies are marked by a far greater disparity of condition among citizens. To treat all human beings as equally worthy of basic moral respect, we must see ourselves from one angle as stripped of differentiating characteristics, and as standing in an abstract relationship to the structures of political power, the state. Our moral respect is generally expressed in purely procedural terms, which facilitate the construction of an extremely thin consensus based on the formal resolution of conflict. Our determination to treat all men as morally and politically worthy is a genuine ethical advance, and procedural safeguards are essential. But the real challenge facing a democratic culture that purports to encompass all the human beings within its reach is to show them substantive respect, to accord them genuine dignity. This would mean letting, or rather making, citizenship and politics matter, and thereby risking the expression of intense substantive disagreement.[27] Yet the alternative of simply excluding the poor and the ignorant from politics except in

[26] See Finley (1973) 33.
[27] See Taylor (1985) 231–3; Lukas (1985a) and (1985b) on the clash between community and equality in the Boston desegregation dispute; Bellah et al. (1985) 202–7. Bellah et al. (1985) note the paradox that in this highly individualistic culture that values pluralism 'it

the most abstract sense and leaving them without even local or personal structures of meaning in a consumer society is in the long run likely to be more destructive of political stability.

The challenge is to create a political culture that is both democratic and republican, i.e. that functions not merely to accommodate competing interests, but also to shape every citizen's understanding of and ability to achieve well-being. The aims of the political must be deepened and extended, and tied to man's self-understanding. Greater democracy does not, therefore, mean the deployment of such mechanisms as a computerized voting procedure,[28] but rather the creation of forms of political participation, education and integration suited to modern society.[29]

Like our political identity, our historical self-understanding must span a greater distance than that of the Athenians, or include an additional level. Historically, as well as politically, we interpret ourselves in part in terms of abstract impersonal considerations remote from our subjective experience, such as economic, cultural and ideological transformations. These requirements have their analogues, as I have indicated, in the world of Thucydides. But our sense of who we are is less bound up with a political structure, open to greater change and more reflective. The challenge of combining autonomy with order, of achieving social integration and genuine democracy is correspondingly greater. Yet even those modern thinkers who point to the need for social integration, and seem to recognize that a historical self-understanding can contribute to this,[30] do not see history itself as a political task in the Thucydidean sense. Their histories are not histories of events, of political action and interaction, but of ideas and institutions and cultural transformation. Their historians are not politicians and citizens, but intellectuals or academics, who contribute to public discourse only obliquely.[31] Such a perspective is itself part of

is consensus that is appreciated and the conflict of interests that is suspect. There is something baffling and upsetting in the actual differences that divide us' (203). This may in part be due to the fear that differences are in principle irreconcilable, that they are founded on pure arbitrary subjectivity and can be resolved only through force. Cf. MacIntyre (1981) on the character of modern ethical conflict.

[28] See Walzer (1983) 310.

[29] See Finley (1973) 36, Pateman (1970) chs. 3, 4, 5, Bellah et al. (1985) 286–96, Cohen and Rogers (1983) 147f., Walzer (1983) ch. 12, Barber (1984) and Dahl's revision of his earlier and influential procedural account of contemporary democracy to address what he now sees as the damaging implications for civic consciousness of interest-group pluralism, in Dahl (1982).

[30] E.g. MacIntyre (1981), Taylor (1985).

[31] Bellah et al. (1985) 296, 303–7 seek to spark and engage in a public debate among citizens. But the public philosopher is, in their view, the social scientist, not the politician.

the modern identity which histories and historians of this kind reveal. Although Thucydides' own work stood at one remove from the realm of public discourse dominated by Pericles, it can be seen as a broader, deeper version of Periclean civic history. Just as the institutional and social mediation of the distance between our personal and political identities is part of today's Periclean task, so, too, relatively abstract arguments for the importance of reconstituting concreteness are part of the Thucydidean task, part of what it is to show (as this book, itself a history of ideas, has sought at least to indicate) that we need both Thucydides and Pericles, both reflective, political history and reflective, historical leadership.

As readers of Thucydides' *History*, we are certainly outside not merely the community whose experience he interprets, but also outside any such context for a common life. However, we are in need of such a context and the approach to self-understanding characteristic of it, and we are increasingly aware of our need. Thucydides' narrative, analytical exploration of human interests cannot restore us, even imaginatively, to the *polis*. It nonetheless has force for us; it is genuinely, as Thucydides declared, a 'possession for all time.' His history can suggest to us, as to his contemporaries, that there is a way of reflecting on our good which ties us to the world of experience instead of removing us from it, and gives us reason to fashion communities which we can inhabit reflectively. Because we are reflective, and because understanding transforms us, we need a structure of thought and life which can accommodate as well as guide these transformations. History as practiced by Pericles and Thucydides is a form of self-examination which does not divorce past from present and future, the external from the internal perspective, spectator from agent, or privilege one at the expense of the other. The historical approach to self-understanding, an exploration of judgment that also cultivates it, is not just a way of thinking but also, as the assimilation of Thucydides and Pericles suggests, a way of living: a way of living democracy.

Bibliography

I. Ancient authors and texts cited

Thucydides
  Historiae. 2 vols., ed. Jones, H. S., 2nd edn, Oxford 1970
  History of the Peloponnesian War, 4 vols., transl. Smith, C. F., Loeb Classical
      Library, London and Cambridge, Mass. 1965
  The Complete Writings of Thucydides, transl. Crawley, R., New York 1943
  History of the Peloponnesian War, transl. Warner, R., Harmondsworth 1972
Herodotus
  Herodotus, 4 vols., transl. Godley, A. D., Loeb Classical Library, London 1920
      (rev. and repr. 1975)
  Herodotus, The Histories, transl. de Sélincourt, A., rev. by Burn, A. R.,
      Harmondsworth 1954 (rev. and repr. 1972)
Pre-Socratics
  Die Fragmente der Vorsokratiker, Diels, H., 6th edn by Kranz, W., Berlin 1951
      (cited as DK)
Aeschylus
  Septem quae supersunt tragoediae, ed. Page, D., Oxford 1972
Sophocles
  Fabulae, ed. Pearson, A. C., Oxford 1923
  Sophocles, transl. Storr, K., Loeb Classical Library, London 1912–13 (repr.
      1978)
Euripides
  Euripides, transl. Way, A. S., Loeb Classical Library, London 1912
Plato
  Opera, ed. Burnet, J., Oxford 1902 (repr. 1968)
Aristotle
  Ethica Nicomachea, ed. Bywater, I., Oxford 1901
  Politica, ed. Ross, W. D., Oxford 1957
  The Basic Works of Aristotle, ed. McKeon, R., New York 1941
Inscriptions
  A Selection of Greek Historical Inscriptions to the end of the fifth century B.C.,
      eds. Meiggs, R., Lewis, D., Oxford 1969
  Supplementum epigraphicum Graecum, Leiden 1923–79 (cited as SEG)
  A Selection of Greek Historical Inscriptions to the end of the fifth century B.C.,
      ed. Tod, M. N., 2nd edn, Oxford 1951–62 (cited as Tod)

II. Modern works

(Journal titles have been abbreviated according to the initials used by *L'Année philologique* or in a self-explanatory fashion. Where a reprint is mentioned, pagination in the notes refers to the reprinted version.)

Adkins, A. W. H. (1960) *Merit and Responsibility*, Oxford
    (1973) 'Aretē, Technē, democracy and sophists: *Protagoras* 316b–328d,' *JHS* 43: 3–12
Aiken, H. D. (1948) *Hume's Moral and Political Philosophy* (an edition of Hume's writings), New York
Allan, D. J. (1965) 'Causality ancient and modern,' *The Aristotelian Society* Suppl. Vol. 39: 1–18
Altham, J. E. J. (1979) 'Reflections on the state of nature,' in Harrison, R., ed., *Rational Action*, 133–45, Cambridge
Andrewes, A. (1960) 'The Melian dialogue and Pericles' last speech,' *PCPS* n.s. 6: 1–10
    (1962) 'The Mytilene debate,' *Phoenix* 16: 64–85
    (1966) 'The government of classical Sparta,' in Badian, E., ed., *Ancient Society and Institutions*, Oxford
Annas, J. (1981) *An Introduction to Plato's Republic*, Oxford
Arendt, H. (1958) *The Human Condition*, Chicago
Aron, R. (1965) *Main Currents in Sociological Thought*, I, transl. Howard, R. and Weaver, H., Harmondsworth
    (1967) *Main Currents in Sociological Thought*, II, transl. Howard, R. and Weaver, H., Harmondsworth
Austin, M. M., Vidal-Naquet, P. (1977) *Economic and Social History of Ancient Greece*, London
Aymard, A. (1948) 'L'idée de travail dans la Grèce archaique,' *Journal de Psychologie* 41: 29–45
Bailey, C. (1928) *The Greek Atomists and Epicurus*, Oxford
Balme, D. M. (1939) 'Greek science and mechanism. I. Aristotle on Nature and Chance,' *CQ* 33: 129–38
    (1941) 'Greek science and mechanism. II. The Atomists,' *CQ* 35: 23–8
Barnes, J. (1979) *The Presocratic Philosophers*, London
Beiner, R. (1983) *Political Judgment*, London
Bellah, R. N., Madsen, R., Sullivan, W. M., Swidler, A., Tipton, S. M. (1985) *Habits of the Heart: Individualism and Commitment in American Life*, Berkeley
Binder, G., Liesenborghs, L. (1976) 'Eine Zuweisung der Sentenz *ouk estin antilegein* an Prodikos von Keos,' in Classen, C. J., ed., *Sophistik*, 452–64, Darmstadt
Bodin, L. (1940) 'Diodote contre Cléon,' *REA* 42: 36–52
Bonner, R. J., Smith, G. (1930) *The Administration of Justice from Homer to Aristotle*, Chicago
Bordes, J. (1982) *Politeia dans la pensée grecque jusqu'à Aristote*, Paris
Bowersock, G. (1967) 'Pseudo-Xenophon,' *HSCP* 71: 33–56

Braudel, F. (1972) *The Mediterranean and the Mediterranean World in the Age of Philip II*, transl. Reynolds, S., London and New York

Brunschwig, J. (1984) 'Démocrite et Xeniade,' *Proceedings of the 1st International Congress on Democritus*, Xanthi 6–9 October 1983

Brunt, P. A. (1952) 'Thucydides and Alcibiades,' *REG* 65: 59–96
  (1967) 'Thucydides and human irrationality,' review of Stahl (1966), *CR* n.s. 17: 278–80

Burkert, W. (1966) 'Greek tragedy and sacrificial ritual', *GRBS* 7: 87–121

Burnyeat, M. F. (1975) 'Protagoras and self-refutation in later Greek philosophy,' *Philosophical Review* 84: 44–5
  (1976) 'Protagoras and self-refutation in Plato's *Theaetetus*,' *Philosophical Review* 85: 172–95

Buxton, R. (1982) *Persuasion in Greek Tragedy: a Study of Peitho*, Cambridge

Calogero, G. (1957) 'Gorgias and the Socratic principle *nemo sua sponte peccat*,' *JHS* 77: 12–17

Canfora, L. (1977) 'La préface de Thucydide et la critique de la raison historique,' *REG* 430–1: 455–61

Cherniss, H. (1964) *Aristotle's Criticism of Presocratic Philosophy* (repr. of 1935 edn), New York

Cochrane, C. N. (1929) *Thucydides and the Science of History*, London

Cogan, M. (1981) *The Human Thing*, Chicago

Cohen, J., Rogers, J. (1983) *On Democracy: Toward a Transformation of American Society*, Harmondsworth and New York

Cole, A. T. (1966) 'The apology of Protagoras,' *YClS* 19: 103–18
  (1967) *Democritus and the Sources of Greek Anthropology*, Cleveland
  (1972) 'The relativism of Protagoras,' *YClS* 22: 19–45

Collingwood, R. G. (1946) *The Idea of History*, Oxford

Connor, W. R. (1971) *The New Politicians of Fifth-Century Athens*, Princeton
  (1977a) 'A post-modernist Thucydides?' *CJ* 72: 289–98
  (1977b) '*Tyrannis Polis*,' in D'Arms, J. H., Eadie, J. W., eds., *Ancient and Modern. Essays in Honor of Gerald F. Else*, 95–109, Ann Arbor
  (1984) *Thucydides*, Princeton

Cooper, J. (1975) *Reason and Human Good in Aristotle*, Cambridge, Mass.
  (1980) 'Aristotle on friendship,' in Rorty, A. O., ed., *Essays on Aristotle's Ethics*, Berkeley

Cornford, F. M. (1907) *Thucydides Mythistoricus*, London

Davies, J. K. (1971) *Athenian Propertied Families 600–300 B.C.*, Oxford
  (1977/8) 'Athenian citizenship: the descent group and the alternatives,' *CJ* 73: 105–21
  (1978) *Democracy and Classical Greece*, London
  (1981) *Wealth and the Power of Wealth in Classical Athens*, New York

Davison, J. A. (1949) 'The date of the *Prometheia*,' *TAPA* 80: 66–93
  (1953) 'Protagoras, Democritus, and Anaxagoras,' *CQ* n.s. 3: 33–45

Dawe, R. D. (1978) 'The end of *Seven Against Thebes* yet again,' in *Dionysiaca*, Dawe, R. D., Diggle, J., Easterling, P. E., eds., Cambridge

Denyer, N. (1983) 'The Origins of Justice,' in Macchiavoli, G., ed., *Susdētēsis:*

Studi sull' Epicureismo Greco e Romano Offerti a Marcello Gigante, Naples

Derenne, F. (1930) *Les procès d'impiété intentés aux philosophes à Athènes au Vme et au IVme siècles avant J.-C.*, Liège (repr. New York, 1946)

Dihle, A. (1981) 'Die Verschiedenheit der Sitten als Argument ethischer Theorie,' in Kerferd, G., ed., *The Sophists and their Legacy*, 54–63, Wiesbaden

Dodds, E. R. (1951) *The Greeks and the Irrational*, cited from 1973 edn, Berkeley
    (1960) 'Morals and politics in the *Oresteia*,' *PCPS* n.s. 6: 19–31

Dover, K. J. (1974) *Greek Popular Morality in the Time of Plato and Aristotle*, Oxford
    (1976) 'The freedom of the intellectual in Greek society,' *Talanta* 7: 24–5
    (1981) 'Strata of Composition,' in *A Historical Commentary on Thucydides* v, Andrewes, A., Dover, K. J., eds., Oxford

Dreher, M. (1983) *Sophistik und Polisentwicklung*, Frankfurt a.M.

Dunn, J. (1967) 'Consent in the political theory of John Locke,' *The Historical Journal* 10: 153–82
    (1969) *The Political Thought of John Locke*, Cambridge
    (1979) *Western Political Theory in the Face of the Future*, Cambridge
    (1980) *Political Obligation in its Historical Context*, Cambridge
    (1981) 'Grounds for despair,' *London Review of Books* for 17–30 September

Dworkin, R. (1978a) *Taking Rights Seriously*, London
    (1978b) 'Liberalism' in Hampshire (1978)

Edmunds, L. (1972) 'Necessity, chance, and freedom in the early atomists,' *Phoenix* 26: 342–57
    (1975a) 'Thucydides' ethics as reflected in the description of *stasis*,' *HSCP* 79: 73–92
    (1975b) *Chance and Intelligence in Thucydides*, Cambridge, Mass.

Edmunds, L., Martin, R. (1977) 'Thucydides 2.65.8: *eleutherōs*,' *HSCP* 81: 187–94

Englert, W. G. (1981) *Aristotle and Epicurus on Voluntary Action*, diss. Stanford

Ferguson, J. (1965) 'On the date of Democritus,' *Symbolae Osloenses* 40: 17–26

Finley, J. H. (1942) *Thucydides*, Cambridge, Mass.

Finley, M. I. (1954) *The World of Odysseus*, New York
    (1962) 'Athenian demagogues,' *Past and Present* 21: 3–24, repr. in and cited from *Studies in Ancient Society*, Finley, M. I., ed., 1–25, London and Boston 1974
    (1965) 'Technical innovation and economic progress in the ancient world,' *Economic History Review* 2: 18: 29–45, repr. in and cited from Shaw, B. D., Saller, R. P., eds., *Economy and Society in Ancient Greece*, 176–95, London and New York
    (1968) *Aspects of Antiquity: Discoveries and Controversies*, London
    (1971) 'The ancestral constitution,' Inaugural Lecture, Cambridge, repr. in *The Use and Abuse of History*, London 1975
    (1973) *Democracy Ancient and Modern*, New Brunswick, N.J. and London
    (1982) 'Authority and legitimacy in the classical city-state,' a J. C. Jacobson Memorial Lecture, *Historisk–filosofiske Meddelelser* 50: 3
    (1983) *Politics in the Ancient World*, Cambridge

Fishkin, J. (1984) *Beyond Subjective Morality: Ethical Reasoning & Political Philosophy*, New Haven

Fornara, C. (1983) *The Nature of History in Ancient Greece and Rome*, Berkeley

Forrest, W. G. (1960) 'The tribal organization of Chios,' *Annual of the British School at Athens* 55: 172–89

(1970) 'The date of the pseudo-Xenophontic *Ath. Pol.*,' *Klio* 52: 107–16

Fränkel, H. (1974) 'Xenophanes' empiricism and his critique of knowledge,' in Mourelatos (1974) 118–35

Freeman, K. (1948) *Ancilla to the Presocratic Philosophers*, Oxford

Frere, J. (1981) *Les Grecs et le desire de l'être, des pré-Platoniciens à Aristote*, Paris

Fritz, K. von (1945–6) '*Nous, noein* and their derivatives in pre-Socratic philosophy,' *CPh* 40: 223–42, 41: 12–34, repr. in and cited from Mourelatos (1974) 23–85

(1957) 'Protagoras,' in *Paulys Real-Encyclopädie der classischen Altertumswissenschaft* XXIII, Halbb. 908–23, Stuttgart

(1963) *Philosophie und sprachlicher Ausdruck bei Demokrit, Plato und Aristoteles* (repr. of 1938 edn), Darmstadt

Furley, D. J. (1967) *Two Studies in the Greek Atomists*, Princeton. Part One: 'The Atomists' reply to the Eleatics,' repr. in and cited from Mourelatos (1974) 504–26

(1970) Review of Cole (1967) *JHS*: 239–40

(1981) 'Antiphon's case against justice,' in Kerferd, G. B., ed. *The Sophists and their Legacy*, 81–91, Wiesbaden

Glaston, W. (1980) *Justice and the Human Good*, Chicago

Garvie, A. F. (1969) *Aeschylus' Supplices: Play and Trilogy*, Cambridge

Geertz, C. (1973) *The Interpretation of Cultures: Selected Essays*, New York

Gellner, E. (1983) *Nations and Nationalism*, Oxford

Gernet, L. (1917) *Recherches sur le développement de la pensée juridique et morale en Grèce*, Paris

(1938) 'Les nobles dans la Grèce antique,' *Annales d'histoire économique et sociale*, 36–43, repr. in and cited from *Droit et Prédroit en Grèce Antique*, 215–28, Paris 1982

(1965) 'Thucydide et l'histoire,' *Annales* ESC 20: 570–5

Geuss, R. (1981) *The Idea of a Critical Theory*, Cambridge

Gilligan, C. (1982) *In A Different Voice*, Cambridge, Mass.

Gomme, A. W. (1937) *Essays in Greek History and Literature*, Oxford

(1945) *A Historical Commentary on Thucydides* I, Oxford

(1954) *The Greek Attitude to Poetry and History*, Sather Classical Lectures, Berkeley

(1956a) *A Historical Commentary on Thucydides* II, Oxford

(1956b) *A Historical Commentary on Thucydides* III, Oxford

Gomme, A. W., Andrewes, A., Dover, K. J. (1970) *A Historical Commentary on Thucydides* IV, Oxford

(1981) *A Historical Commentary on Thucydides* V, Oxford

Gosling, J. C. B., Taylor, C. C. W. (1982) *The Greeks on Pleasure*, Oxford

Gould, S. J. (1983a) Review of F. Capra, *The Turning Point, The New York Review of Books,* 3 March

(1983b) 'Genes on the brain,' review of Lumsden and Wilson, *Promethean Fire: Reflections on the Origin of Mind, New York Review of Books,* 30 June

Grene, D. (1950) *Man in his Pride,* Chicago (later publ. as *Greek Political Theory*)

Griffith, G. T. (1966) 'Isegoria in the assembly at Athens,' in *Ancient Society and Institutions: Studies Presented to Victor Ehrenberg,* Oxford

Gronewald, M. (1968) 'Ein neues Protagoras-Fragment,' *ZPE* 2: 1–2

Guthrie, W. K. C. (1965) *A History of Greek Philosophy* II, Cambridge

(1969) *A History of Greek Philosophy* III, Cambridge

Habermas, J. (1971) *Knowledge and Human Interests,* transl. Shapiro, J., London

Hampshire, S. (1962) *Spinoza,* Harmondsworth and New York

ed. (1978) *Public and Private Morality,* Cambridge

Hampton, J. (1986) *Social Convention Theories,* diss. Harvard (publication in revised form forthcoming)

Harrison, A. R. W. (1937) 'Thucydides 1, 22,' *CR* 51; 6–7

Hart, H. L. A. (1961) *The Concept of Law,* Oxford

(1979) 'Between utility and rights,' in Ryan., H., ed., *The Idea of Freedom,* Oxford

Havelock, E. A. (1957) *The Liberal Temper in Greek Politics,* New Haven

(1978) *The Greek Concept of Justice from its shadow in Homer to its substance in Plato,* Cambridge, Mass.

Hegel, G. W. F. (1956) *The Philosophy of History,* transl. Sibree, J., New York

(1967) *The Philosophy of Right,* transl. Knox, T. M., Oxford (translation first published in 1942)

Heinimann, F. (1945) *Nomos und Physis,* Basel (repr. Darmstadt 1965)

Hignett, C. (1952) *A History of the Athenian Constitution to the end of the Fifth Century B.C.,* Oxford

Holaday, A. J., Poole, J. C. F. (1979) 'Thucydides and the plague of Athens,' *CQ* n.s. 29: 282–300

How, W. W., Wells, J. (1912) *A Commentary on Herodotus,* Oxford

Huart, P. (1968) *Le vocabulaire de l'analyse psychologique dans l'oeuvre de Thucydide,* Paris

(1973) *Gnōmē chez Thucydide et ses Contemporains,* Paris

Humphreys, S. C. (1974) 'The social structure of the ancient city,' *ASNP* 3: 329–67, repr. in *Anthropology and the Greeks,* London, 1978

(1977/8) 'Public and private interests in classical Athens,' *CJ* 73: 97–104

Hunter, V. J. (1973) *Thucydides, The Artful Reporter,* Toronto

(1982) *Past and Process in Herodotus and Thucydides,* Princeton

Hussey, E. (1972) *The Presocratics,* London

(1986) 'Thucydidean history and Democritean theory,' in Harvey, F. D., Cartledge, P. A., eds., *Crux: Essays Presented to G.E.M. de Ste Croix on his 75th Birthday,* 118–38, London

Immerwahr, H. R. (1960) 'Ergon: history as a monument in Herodotus and Thucydides,' *AJP* 81: 261–90

(1973) 'Pathology of power and the speeches in Thucydides,' in Stadter (1973)

Irwin, T. H. (1977) *Plato's Moral Theory: the Early and Middle Dialogues*, Oxford

(1979) Plato's *Gorgias*, transl. and commentary, Oxford

(1980) 'Reason and responsibility in Aristotle,' in Rorty, A. O., ed., *Essays on Aristotle's Ethics*, Berkeley

(1983a) 'Euripides and Socrates,' *CPh* 78: 183–97

(1983b) 'The pleasant and the good,' a review of Gosling and Taylor (1982), *TLS*, 16 September: 1003

(1986) 'Socratic inquiry and politics,' review of Kraut (1984) *Ethics* 96: 400–15

Jaeger, W. (1947) *Paideia* I, 2nd English edn, Oxford

James, S. (1984) *The Content of Social Explanation*, Cambridge

Jones, A. H. M. (1953) 'The Athenian democracy and its critics,' *Cambridge Historical Journal* 9: 1–26; repr. in and cited from Jones, *Athenian Democracy*, 41–72, Oxford 1957, paperback 1977

Jones, J. W. (1956) *Law and Legal Theory of the Greeks*, Oxford

Kagan, D. (1974) *The Archidamian War*, Ithaca, N.Y.

(1975) 'The speeches in Thucydides and the Mytilene debate,' *YClS* 24: 71–94

Kahn, C. H. (1979) *The Art and Thought of Heraclitus*, Cambridge

(1981) 'The origins of social contract theory in the fifth century B.C.', in Kerferd, G., ed., *The Sophists and their Legacy*, 92–108, Wiesbaden

Kapp, E. (1936) 'Langerbeck, *Doxis Epirusmiē*,' *Gnomon* 12: 158–69

Karavites, P. (1979) 'Morality and the Mytilenean revolt,' *ASNP* 9: 895–917

Kerferd, G. B. (1953) 'Protagoras' doctrine of justice and virtue in the *Protagoras* of Plato,' *JHS* 73: 42–5

(1957) 'The moral and political doctrines of Antiphon the Sophist: a reconsideration,' in *PCPS*, 26–32

(1981) *The Sophistic Movement*, Cambridge

Kirk, G. S., Raven, J. E., Schofield, M. (1983) *The Presocratic Philosophers*, 2nd edn, Cambridge

Kraut, R. (1984) *Socrates and the State*, Princeton

Langerbeck, H. (1935) *Doxis Epirusmiē*, Berlin

Laslett, P. (1956) 'The face-to-face society,' in Laslett, P., ed., *Philosophy, Politics and Society*, Oxford

Lear, J. (1982) 'Leaving the world alone,' *Journal of Philosophy*, July

(1984) 'Moral objectivity,' in Brown, S. C., ed., *Objectivity and Cultural Divergence*, Cambridge

Lee, E. N. (1973) 'Hoist with his own petard: ironic and comic elements in Plato's critique of Protagoras (*Tht.* 161–171),' in Lee, E. N., Mourelatos, A. P. D., Rorty, R. M., eds., *Exegesis and Argument*, 225–61, Assen

Levi, A. (1940) 'The ethical and social thought of Protagoras,' *Mind* n.s. 44: 284–302

Levy, E. (1976) *Athènes devant la défaite de 404; histoire d'une crise idéologique*, Paris

de Ley, H. (1969) '*Doxis Epirusmiē*, a critical note on Democritus Fr. 7,' *Hermes*
    97: 496–7
Lloyd, G. E. R. (1966) *Polarity and Analogy*, Cambridge
    (1979) *Magic, Reason and Experience*, Cambridge
Loenen, D. (1941) *Protagoras and the Greek Community*, Amsterdam
Loraux, N. (1981) *L'invention d'Athènes: Histoire de l'oraison funèbre dans la
    cité classique*, Paris
Lukas, J. A. (1985a) 'Community and equality in conflict,' *NYT*, 8 Sept., E25
    (1985b) *Common Ground: A Turbulent Decade in the Lives of Three
    American Families*, New York
Luria, S. (1964) *Zur Frage der materialistischen Begründung der Ethik bei
    Demokrit*, Berlin
MacIntyre, A. (1967) *A Short History of Ethics*, London
    (1971) *Against the Self-images of the Age*, London
    (1981) *After Virtue, a Study in Moral Theory*, South Bend, Indiana
    (1984) 'The relationship of philosophy to its past,' in Rorty, R. M., Skinner, Q.,
    Schneewind, J., eds., *Philosophy in History*, Cambridge
Mackenzie, M. M. (1981) *Plato on Punishment*, Berkeley
Mackie, J. L. (1977) *Ethics: Inventing Right and Wrong*, Harmondsworth
Macleod, C. W. (1974) 'Form and meaning in the Melian dialogue,' *Historia* 23:
    385–400
    (1977) 'Thucydides' Plataean debate,' *GRBS* 18: 227–46
    (1978) 'Reason and necessity: Thucydides iii 9–14, 37–48,' *JHS* 98: 64–78
    (1979) 'Thucydides on faction,' *PCPS* n.s. 25: 52–68
    (1982) 'Politics and the *Oresteia*,' *JHS* 102: 124–44
Maguire, J. P. (1973) 'Protagoras – or Plato?,' *Phronesis* 18: 115–38
    (1977) 'Protagoras – or Plato? II. The *Protagoras*,' *Phronesis* 22: 103–22
Maier, H. (1913) *Sokrates: sein Werk und seine geschichtliche Stellung*, Tübingen
Mansfield, J. (1981) 'Protagoras on epistemological obstacles and persons,' in
    Kerferd, G. B., ed., *The Sophists and their Legacy*, 38–53, Wiesbaden
McDowell, J. (1973) Plato's *Theaetetus*, transl. and commentary, Oxford
Méautis, G. (1935) 'Le dialogue des Athéniens et des Méliens,' *REG* 48: 250–78
Meier, C. (1970), *Die Entstehung des Begriffs 'Demokratie': Vier Prolegomena
    zu einer historischen Theorie*, Frankfurt
    (1980) *Die Entstehung des Politischen bei den Griechen*, Frankfurt
Mejer, J. (1972) 'The alleged new fragment of Protagoras,' *Hermes* 100: 175–8,
    repr. in and cited from Classen, C. J., ed., *Sophistik*, 306–11, Darmstadt 1976
Mittelstadt, M. C. (1977) 'Thucydidean psychology and moral value judgement
    in the *History*: some observations,' *RSC* 25: 30–55
Momigliano, A. (1966) 'Time in ancient historiography,' *H & T* 6: 1–23, repr. in
    Quatro Contributo, Rome 1969
    (1972) 'Tradition and the classical historian,' *H & T* 11: 3, 274–93, repr. in
    Quinto Contributo, Rome 1975
Moore, J. M. (1975) *Aristotle and Xenophon on Democracy and Oligarchy*,
    Berkeley
Morrison, J. S. (1941) 'The place of Protagoras in Athenian public life,' *CQ* 35:
    1–16

(1961) 'Antiphon,' *PCPS* n.s. 7: 49–58

(1972) 'Introduction' to a translation of the works of Antiphon, in Sprague, R. K., ed., *The Older Sophists*, 108–11, Columbia, S.C.

Morrow, G. R. (1941) 'Plato and the rule of law,' *Philosophical Review* 50: 105–26

Mossé, C. (1969) *The Ancient World at Work*, transl. Lloyd, J., London

(1978) 'Le thème de la *patrios politeia* dans la pensée grecque du IV siècle,' *Eirene* 16: 81–9

Mourelatos, A. P. D. (1974) *The Presocratics: a collection of critical essays*, New York

Moxon, I. (1978) 'Thucydides' account of Spartan strategy and foreign policy in the Archidamian War,' *RSA* 8: 7–26

Muir, J. V. (1982) 'Protagoras and education at Thourioi,' *G & R* 29: 17–23

Murray, O. (1983) 'By coercion and by consent,' *TLS*, 26 August

Nagel, T. (1980) 'Aristotle on Eudaimonia,' in *Essays on Aristotle's Ethics*, ed. Rorty, A. O., 7–14, Berkeley

Neumann, H. (1969) 'The philosophy of individualism: an interpretation of Thucydides,' *JHPh* 3: 234–46

Nicholson, P. P. (1980/1) 'Protagoras and the justification of Athenian democracy,' *Polis* 3: 14–24

North, H. (1966) *Sophrosunē: self-knowledge and self-restraint in Greek literature*, New York

Nozick, R. (1974) *Anarchy, State and Utopia*, Oxford

Nussbaum, M. C. (1980) 'Shame, separateness and political unity: Aristotle's criticism of Plato,' in Rorty, A. O., ed., *Essays on Aristotle's Ethics*, 395–435, Berkeley

(1986) *The Fragility of Goodness: Luck and Ethics in Greek Tragedy and Philosophy*, Cambridge

O'Brien, M. J. (1967) *The Socratic Paradoxes and the Greek Mind*, Chapel Hill

Ostwald, M. (1969) *Nomos and the Beginnings of the Athenian Democracy*, Oxford

(1982) *Autonomia: its genesis and early history*, New York

Parfit, D. (1984) *Reasons and Persons*, Oxford

Parker, R. (1983) *Miasma: Pollution and Purification in Early Greek Religion*, Oxford

Parry, A. M. (1957) *Logos and ergon in Thucydides*, diss. Harvard, repr. as a monograph in Classical Studies, New York 1981

(1972) 'Thucydides' historical perspective,' *YClS* 22: 47–61

Pateman, C. (1970) *Participation and Democratic Theory*, Cambridge

Patterson, C. (1981) *Pericles' Citizenship Law of 451/0 B.C.*, New York

Pečírka, J. (1976) 'The crisis of the Athenian *polis* in the fourth century B.C.,' *Eirene* 9: 5–29

Perry, B. E. (1952) *Aesopica*, Urbana, Illinois

Phillipson, R. (1924) 'Demokrits Sittensprüche,' *Hermes* 59: 369–419

Pouilloux, J., Salviat, F. (1983) 'Lichas, Lacédémonien, Archonte à Thasos et le livre VIII de Thucydide,' *CRAI* avril–juin

Pouncey, P. R. (1980) *The Necessities of War; A Study of Thucydides' Pessimism*, New York

Procopé, J. (1971) *Democritus the Moralist and his Contemporaries*, diss. Cambridge

Putnam, H. (1981) *Reason, Truth and History*, Cambridge

Quinn, T. J. (1969) 'Political groups at Chios,' *Historia* 18: 22–30

Raaflaub, K. A. (1983) 'Democracy, oligarchy and the concept of the free citizen in late fifth-century Athens,' *Pol. Theory* 2: 517–44

Rankin, H. D. (1981) 'Ouk Estin Antilegein,' in Kerferd, G. B., ed., *The Sophists and their Legacy*, 25–37, Wiesbaden

Rawlings, H. R. (1981) *The Structure of Thucydides' History*, Princeton

Rawls, J. (1971) *A Theory of Justice*, Cambridge, Mass.

Regenbogen, O. (1933) 'Thucydides als politischer Denker,' *HG* 44: 2–25, repr. in Herter, H., ed., *Wege der Forschung: Thukydides*, Darmstadt 1968

Reich, R. B. (1983) *The Next American Frontier*, New York

Rhodes, P. J. (1972) *The Athenian Boule*, Oxford

　(1981) *A Commentary on the Aristotelian Athenaion Politeia*, Oxford

Riedel, M. (1984) *Between Tradition and Revolution: the Hegelian Transformation of Political Philosophy*, transl. Wright, W., Cambridge

Rist, J. M. (1982) *Human Value: A Study in Ancient Philosophical Ethics*, Leiden

Romilly, J. de (1956a) *Histoire et Raison chez Thucydide*, Paris

　(1956b) 'L'utilité de l'histoire selon Thucydide,' *Entretiens Hardt* IV, 41–81, Geneva

　(1963) *Thucydides and Athenian imperialism*, transl. Thody, P., Oxford (1st edn, Paris 1947)

　(1965) 'L'optimisme de Thucydide et le jugement de l'historien sur Périclès,' *REG* 78: 557–75

　(1966) 'Thucydides and the cities of the Athenian empire,' *BICS* 13: 1–12

　(1968) Review of Stahl (1966), *Gnomon* 40: 232–6

　(1978) Review of Schneider (1974), *Phoenix* 32: 84–6

Ste Croix, G. E. M. de (1972) *The Origins of the Peloponnesian War*, London

Sandel, M. J. (1982) *Liberalism and the Limits of Justice*, Cambridge

Scheffler, S. (1982) *The Rejection of Consequentialism*, Oxford

Schneider, C. (1974) *Information und Absicht bei Thukydides*, Göttingen

Seager, R. (1973) 'Elitism and democracy in classical Athens,' in Jakes, F., ed., *The Rich, the Well Born, and the Powerful: elites and upper classes in history*, 7–25, Urbana, Illinois

Sedley, D. (1982) 'Two conceptions of vacuum,' *Phronesis* 27: 175–93

　(1983) 'Epicurus' refutation of determinism,' in Macchiavoli, G., ed., *Susdētēsis: Studi sull' Epicureismo Greco e Romano Offerti a Marcello Gigante*, 11–51, Naples

Segal, C. P. (1961) *Reason, Emotion and Society in the Sophists and Democritus*, diss. Harvard

　(1962) 'Gorgias and the psychology of the *logos*,' *HSCP* 66: 99–155

Shorey, P. (1983) 'On the implicit ethics and psychology of Thucydides,' *TAPA* 24: 66–88

Simon, B. (1978) *Mind and Madness in Ancient Greece: the Classical Roots of Modern Psychiatry*, Ithaca, N.Y.

Sinclair, T. A. (1961) *A History of Greek Political Thought*, 2nd edn, London

Skinner, Q. (1964) 'Hobbes's Leviathan,' *Historical Journal* 7: 21: 321–33

 (1984) 'The idea of negative liberty: philosophical and historical perspectives,' in *Philosophy in History*, Rorty, R., Skinner, Q., Schneewind, J., eds., 193–221, Cambridge

Smart, J., Williams, B. (1973) *Utilitarianism: For and Against*, Cambridge

Snell, B. (1960) *The Discovery of the Mind*, transl. Rosenmeyer, T. G., New York (Oxford 1953)

Solmsen, F. (1969) Review of Cole (1967), *Phoenix* 23: 399–402

 (1975) *Intellectual Experiments of the Greek Enlightenment*, Princeton

Sorabji, R. (1980) *Necessity, Cause, and Blame: Perspectives on Aristotle's Theory*, London

Sprague, R. K., ed. (1972) *The Older Sophists*, Columbia, S.C.

Stadter, P. A. (1973) *The Speeches in Thucydides*, Chapel Hill

Stahl, H.-P. (1966) *Thukydides, Die Stellung des Menschen im geschichtlichen Prozess*, Zetemata 40, Munich

Starr, C. G. (1978) 'Thucydides on sea power,' *Mnemosyne* 31: 343–50

Stewart, Z. (1958) 'Democritus and the Cynics,' *HSCP* 63: 179–91

Strasburger, H. (1954) 'Der Einzelne und die Gemeinschaft im Denken der Griechen,' *Historische Zeitschrift* 177: 227–48, repr. in Gschnitzer, F., ed., *Wege der Forschung: Zur Griechischen Staatskunde*, Darmstadt 1969

 (1958) 'Thukydides und die politische Selbstdarstellung der Athener,' *Hermes* 86: 17–40, repr. in Herter, H., ed., *Wege der Forschung: Thukydides*, Darmstadt 1968

Stratton, G. M. (1917) *Theophrastus and the Greek Physiological Psychology before Aristotle*, London

Taylor, C. C. W. (1967) 'Pleasure, knowledge and sensation in Democritus,' *Phronesis* 12: 6–27

 (1976) Plato's *Protagoras*, transl. and commentary, Oxford

 (1983) 'Political Theory and Practice,' in Lloyd, C., ed., *Social Theory and Political Practice*, 61–85, Oxford

 (1985) *Philosophy and Human Sciences: Philosophical Papers* 11, Cambridge

Tompkins, D. P. (1972) 'Stylistic characterization in Thucydides: Nicias and Alcibiades,' *YClS* 22: 181–214

Tuck, R. (1979) *Natural Rights Theories: their origin and development*, Cambridge

Vernant, J. P. (1981) 'Intimations of the will in Greek Tragedy,' in Vidal-Naquet, P., *Tragedy and Myth in Ancient Greece*, transl. Lloyd, J., Brighton

 (1983) *Myth and Thought Among the Greeks*, London

Versényi, L. (1962) 'Protagoras' man–measure fragment', *AJPh* 83: 178–84, repr. in and cited from Classen, C. J., ed., *Sophistik*, 190–297, Darmstadt 1976

Vlastos, G. (1941) 'Slavery in Plato's thought,' *Philosophical Review*, 289ff., repr. in and cited from Vlastos (1981) 147–63

 (1945/6) 'Ethics and physics in Democritus,' *Philosophical Review*, 1945: 578–92 and 1946: 53–64, repr. in Allen, R. E. and Furley, D. J., eds., *Studies in Presocratic Philosophy* 11, 381–408, London 1975

(1946) 'On the prehistory in Diodorus,' *AJP* 67: 51–9

(1956) 'Introduction' in *Plato, Protagoras. Jowett's translation revised by Martin Ostwald*, Indianapolis and New York

(1968) 'Does slavery exist in Plato's *Republic?*' *CP* 63: 291–5, repr. in Vlastos (1981)

(1969) 'Justice and psychic harmony in the *Republic*,' *Journal of Philosophy* 66: 505–21, repr. in revised form in Vlastos (1981)

(1970) 'Equality and justice in early Greek cosmologies,' in Allen, R. E. and Furley, D. J., eds., *Studies in Presocratic Philosophy* 1, 56–91, London

(1973) 'Justice and happiness in the *Republic*,' in Vlastos, G., ed., *Platonic Studies*, Princeton (2nd edn 1981)

(1975) *Plato's Universe*, Seattle

(1977) 'The theory of social justice in Plato's *Republic*,' in North, H., ed., *Interpretation of Plato, Mnemosyne*, Suppl. Vol. 1–40

(1981) *Platonic Studies*, 2nd edn, Princeton

(1983a) 'The Socratic elenchus,' *Oxford Studies in Ancient Philosophy* 1, 27–58, Oxford

(1983b) 'The historical Socrates and Athenian democracy,' *Pol. Theory* 11, 495–516

(1984) Review of Kraut (1984), *TLS*, 24 Aug.: 931–2

(1985) 'Socrates' disavowal of knowledge,' *Philos. Quarterly* 35: 1–31

Walzer, M. (1983) *Spheres of Justice*, New York

Wassermann, F. M. (1947) 'The Melian dialogue,' *TAPA* 78: 18–36

(1954) 'Thucydides and the disintegration of the *polis*,' *TAPA* 85: 46–54

(1956) 'Post-Periclean democracy in action: the Mytilenean debate (Thuc. 3, 37–48),' *TAPA* 87: 27–41

(1964) 'The voice of Sparta in Thucydides,' *CJ* 54: 289–97

Waterlow, S. (1982) *Nature, Change and Agency in Aristotle's Physics: A Philosophical Study*, Oxford

Wieland, W. (1975) 'The problem of teleology,' from Wieland, *Die Aristotelische Physik* (Göttingen 1962) transl. in Barnes, J., Schofield, M., Sorabji, R., eds., *Articles on Aristotle* 1, 141–69, London

Will, E. (1972) *Le Monde Grec et l'Orient* 1, Paris

Williams, B. A. O. (1978) 'Introduction,' in Isaiah Berlin, *Concepts and Categories: Philosophical Essays*, ed. Hardy, H., xi–xviii, London

(1981a), 'Philosophy,' in Finley, M. I., ed., *The Legacy of Greece*, 202–55, Oxford

(1981b) *Moral Luck: Philosophical Papers 1973–1980*, Cambridge

(1984) 'Personal identity,' a review of Parfit (1984) *The London Review of Books*, 7–20 June: 14–17

(1985) *Ethics and the Limits of Philosophy*, London

(forthcoming) The Sather Classical Lectures 1989

Winnington-Ingram, R. P. (1965) '*Ta deonta eipein*, Cleon and Diodotus', *BICS* 12: 70–82

(1980) *Sophocles – An Interpretation*, Cambridge

Winton, R. I. (1974) *The Political Thought of Protagoras*, diss. Cambridge

Wolin, S. (1960) *Politics and Vision*, Boston

Wollheim, R. (1984) *The Thread of Life*, Cambridge

Woodhead, A. G. (1967) 'Isegoria and the Council of 500,' *Historia* 16: 129–40

　(1970) *Thucydides on the Nature of Power*, Martin Classical Lectures XXIV, Cambridge, Mass.

Zahn, R. (1934) *Die erste Periklesrede (Thukydides I, 140–44). Interpretation und Versuch einer Einordnung in dem Zusammenhang des Werkes*, Leipzig

Ziolkowski, J. E. (1963) *Thucydides and the Tradition of Funeral Speeches at Athens*, diss. Univ. of North Carolina, repr. as monograph in Classical Studies, New York 1981

Indexes

SUBJECT INDEX

INDEX OF PASSAGES